USING FILEMAKER PRO

Using FileMaker® Pro

Barrie Sosinsky

Revised by Barrie Sosinsky and Beth Houghton

QUE®

Using FileMaker® Pro

Library of Congress Catalog No.: 91-67189

ISBN: 0-88022-841-5

94 93 92 91 4 3 2 1

Interpretation of the printing code: the rightmost double-digit number is the year of the book's printing; the rightmost single-digit number, the number of the book's printing. For example, a printing code of 91-1 shows that the first printing of the book occurred in 1991.

Using FileMaker Pro is based on FileMaker Pro and the earlier version, FileMaker II.

Publisher: Lloyd J. Short

Acquisitions Manager: Rick Ranucci

Managing Editor: Paul Boger

Product Development Manager: Thomas H. Bennett

Book Designer: Scott Cook

Production Team: Claudia Bell, Brad Chinn, Michelle Cleary, Brook Farling, Sandy Grieshop, Audra Hershman, Phil Kitchel, Bob LaRoche, Laurie Lee, Anne Owen, Juli Pavey, Tad Ringo, Linda Seifert, Kevin Spear, Bruce Steed, Susan VandeWalle, and Phil Worthington

Product Director

Shelley O'Hara

Production Editors

Kelly D. Dobbs

Gregory R. Robertson

Editors

H. Leigh Davis

Lori A. Lyons

Cindy Morrow

Daniel Schnake

Susan M. Shaw

Technical Editors

Bill Dodson

Daniel Zoller

Composed in ITC Garamond and MCP Digital by Que Corporation

Dedication

To Karen Bluestein, Lloyd Short, and all the other hard-working editors and staff at Que. They have created a library of books that has empowered all computer users.

About the Author

Barrie Sosinsky

Barrie Sosinsky is a regular reviewer for *MacWorld* and *MacUser England* magazines and is an active member of the Boston Computer Society. He is a contributing author of *BCS Update*, the Boston Computer Society's primary magazine. Barrie was the revision author for *Using Microsoft Works: Macintosh Version*, 2nd Edition, published by Que Corporation.

Barrie owns a small manufacturing company in Newton, Massachusetts, and is a microcomputer consultant. He has a doctorate in chemistry, and his interests include all aspects of personal computer use, for fun and profit.

Trademark Acknowledgments

Que Corporation has made every effort to supply trademark information about company names, products, and services mentioned in this book. Trademarks indicated below were derived from various sources. Que Corporation cannot attest to the accuracy of this information.

4th Dimension is a trademark of ACIUS.

Apple, HyperCard, LaserWriter, ImageWriter, AppleTalk, Macintosh, MacPaint, MacDraw, and MacWrite are registered trademarks and AppleShare, Finder, and MultiFinder are trademarks of Apple Computer, Inc.

Canon is a registered trademark of Canon, Inc.

CompuServe is a registered trademark of CompuServe, Inc., and H&R Block, Inc.

dBASE is a registered trademark and Ashton-Tate, FullWrite Professional, and Full Impact are trademarks of Ashton-Tate Corporation.

Encapsulated PostScript is a registered trademark and Illustrator is a trademark of Adobe Systems, Inc.

FileMaker is a registered trademark and Claris is a trademark of Claris Corporation.

FoxBase is a trademark of Fox Software, Inc.

HP is a registered trademark and DeskJet is a trademark of Hewlett-Packard Company.

IBM is a registered trademark of International Business Machines Corporation.

Managing Your Money is a registered trademark of MECA.

Microsoft, Multiplan, and PowerPoint are registered trademarks of Microsoft Corporation.

PageMaker is a registered trademark and Freehand is a trademark of Aldus Corporation.

Acknowledgments

This book exists because Karen Bluestein likes the Macintosh and FileMaker Pro; she served as the project champion throughout the process. Someone had to sign off on the project and assume the risk, and Lloyd Short was that person. They have been great through everything, even when I missed my deadline and blew my page count.

Other people at Que worked hard to bring this book up to Que's standard. Shelley O'Hara was the product director for the book, making it more coherent, less redundant, and more focused to the audience likely to read it (beginners, too, I remember!). I also want to thank Greg Robertson, the production editor for the first printing of the book. They never get the recognition they deserve, and that's why this book is dedicated to them.

Bill Dodson served as a technical editor for this book. Bill has been involved with FileMaker as a developer and trainer for quite some time and is well known to the members of the Boston Computer Society Macintosh User's Group, and to the BCS community (world's best user's group!) in general. He took valuable time away from his business in FileMaker at Gradient Resources to add his insight to the book, time he could have spent working on new products. I am grateful.

Other people also were most kind in sharing their expertise in FileMaker with me. Keith Kiel at MacAcademy lent me MacAcademy's video tapes; Personal Training Systems lent me the company's cassette-guided course; and Dennis Marshall, the Product Manager for FileMaker at Claris, lent me the Claris training course. Dennis Marshall, in particular, spent time answering my technical questions and pointing me in the right direction. These people are real FileMaker experts, and I learned from them. Thanks also go to Packer Software for the use of a figure from The Small Business Retailer.

On a personal level, I must say that this book never could have been written if not for the love and friendship of Carol Westheimer. She is the creator of MacDining Room, a shareware platform of which only one copy exists. Special thanks also go to my sister, Gina Sosinsky, for service above and beyond. This book is as much theirs as it is mine.

Any book this size invariably contains errors or misstatements, and they are mine alone. I welcome your comments, suggestions, and criticism so that we can improve future versions of this book. Write to me in care of Que Corporation.

Conventions Used in This Book

The conventions used in this book have been established to help you learn to use the program quickly and easily.

- Material the user types is in *italic* type or on a line by itself.
- Command names and field names are written with initial capital letters, such as the Delete Multiple command and the Picture field.
- Screen messages appear in a `special typeface`.
- Dialog boxes are named by the command used to call them up, such as the Create a New File dialog box.
- Icons are used in the margins to indicate various points. One icon indicates Speed Keys, which are keyboard shortcuts you can use to issue commands. Warning icons indicate operations that can be dangerous to your data. In addition, tips and notes give information to help you get the most out of FileMaker.

Contents at a Glance

Table of Contents

II Working with Layouts

III Printing

Introduction

Few tools are more singularly useful to you than a database. A database is a record holder and organizing system. The capability to store, organize, and retrieve large amounts of information is at the heart of the invention of computers. FileMaker Pro is one such database; it is the engine of your business, and the information it's capable of managing is the lifeblood. *Using FileMaker Pro* teaches you this program and shows you how to apply it to your business and everyday life.

If you stop and think about it, you will realize how much easier and empowering working with a database is, compared to working with a paper-based system. Cart away that file cabinet, pack those file folders, and stop buying all those erasers. Tasks that took hours or days are now accomplished with a single mouse click. Tasks that were once impossible are now just a command away.

When, for example, The Lonely Hearts Dating Service puts the name of its new client, Joe Cool, into its database of nearly 9,500 people, it only takes one search to find all 17 women between the ages of 27 and 32, 5' 2" to 5' 10", who ski, listen to Motown music, have a great sense of humor, and like sushi. If you forgot that Joe doesn't like to drive his mint-condition, 1966 fire-engine red GTO too far on a date, one more sort of each match by ZIP code brings up the right candidates. All the operations described take about a minute to set up and about 10 seconds for FileMaker to accomplish.

Setting up a database may be enough justification to buy a computer, and the power of FileMaker coupled with the ease of use of the Macintosh is a potent combination. Perhaps you're looking at this book in a bookstore and wondering, "Should I learn FileMaker Pro?" With such a large selection of Macintosh databases to choose from, what makes FileMaker Pro special enough to warrant the effort?

FileMaker Pro is one of the most award-winning Macintosh programs ever produced. Right from its introduction, FileMaker has won best in its category (database) awards from nearly every magazine that reviews software. These magazines include the following:

MacWorld Reader Class Award—Best Database (record third time)

InfoWorld 1988 Product of the Year

MacGuide Golden Gavel Award for best Macintosh product, 1989

MacUser US Best Database, 1989

MacUser Australia Best Database, 1989

FileMaker Pro also is the best-selling Macintosh database, with nearly 40 percent of the market. Outgrowing this product is difficult because FileMaker Pro is enormously flexible and powerful. This package rewards you time and time again with its capability to manipulate data, create graphical output, and control reports to accomplish your goals.

If you are an average user or the person responsible for running a database that is shared by several computers, FileMaker Pro is an excellent choice. Unlike many complex, high-end databases that require you to learn a programming language, with FileMaker, everything you need is found right on your screen. FileMaker Pro is menu-driven; all other selections are found as a set of choices in dialog boxes. Database developers often advise their clients to use FileMaker in business operations because it's a program that the average user can understand.

When the Macintosh was being developed by Apple, its developers courted a number of software companies, requesting that they write databases for the machine. FileMaker 1.0 was the 4th database to appear, and it was the 28th commercial product ever shipped for the original 128K Macintosh. The program was written by a small company called Nashoba Systems in Concord, Massachusetts, and was introduced in the spring of 1985, retailing for $195. FileMaker Plus, an updated and enhanced version, appeared in September 1987, selling for $295.

FileMaker Plus was published originally by Forethought, until that company was acquired by Microsoft in July 1988. When Nashoba Systems decided to publish the program on its own, after declining a publishing offer from Microsoft, Microsoft destroyed the 200 copies of the program in existence, despite an offer by Nashoba to buy back the product.

After being unavailable for nearly two months, FileMaker Plus reappeared in November 1988. FileMaker Plus instantly became the best-selling database product for the Macintosh, a position it has held ever since. FileMaker 4 shipped on June 21, 1988, and was a substantial upgrade that added new graphics, multiuser capabilities, and more than 50 other features.

On July 5, 1988, Claris acquired Nashoba Systems and renamed the product FileMaker II. Claris has shipped FileMaker II in fully translated localized versions of English (that is, for Great Britain), as well as French, Swedish, Japanese, German, Dutch, Danish, Spanish, Icelandic, Finnish, Greek, and Italian versions. FileMaker II Version 1.1, which added network support, was shipped in August 1989.

This book is based on FileMaker Pro Version 1.0, which is a substantial upgrade over FileMaker II, although users of FileMaker II and FileMaker Plus will find the book useful. This book was written on a Macintosh II, using Macintosh system software (System 6.0.4 and Finder 6.2).

What Is a Database Used For?

Anything you can organize into a data set can be a database. This category includes the telephone book, ZIP codes, and all the applications you will find in this section. As you read, remember that you can use FileMaker Pro to accomplish many of these tasks.

You use databases everyday of your life in different forms that you may not recognize. Your bank account or checkbook is a database. You may own a personal accounting program, such as MacMoney, Managing Your Money, or Quicken, each of which has the structure and features of a database. You could, in fact, create a FileMaker Pro database that would emulate your checkbook.

When you go to the bank or use an automated teller machine that allows you to draw out cash, deposit a check, or check your account balance, you are logging onto a database system that is kept on a large computer. Banks and financial institutions are heavy users of databases and database programmers. In fact, most accounting packages are nothing more than databases that have been specially written for that purpose.

Databases are showing up in more and more places. Consider the computer that sits in your local library, replacing the card catalog, or the one in the airport or bus station that contains information about the city you're in. And maybe you have seen a computer sitting in an art museum that shows a picture of each piece of art and describes its importance. Perhaps the next time you consider buying or renting real estate, your realtor will put you in front of a computer and show you pictures of homes and apartments to find all the relevant information as you ask for it.

When you log onto an electronic on-line information service, you are accessing a database. Information services like CompuServe or Prodigy are databases. That may not be entirely clear to you as the user, because it appears that you are communicating with the service. Most of the information resides in data structures that the user navigates to (finds) and selects from.

The capabilities to organize and select data and to output that data in a form or report structure combine to make databases one of the most common business tools in use today. Your favorite direct marketer with his or her friendly 800 number probably has someone sitting at a computer terminal and using a database (maybe even FileMaker) to enter and process your order. Any invoice, packing slip, or statement you receive has been generated by some sort of database application.

Some database programs have had an impact in your daily life, and some have been applied to problems. Computers were developed to calculate numerically intensive problems and to access and organize large quantities of information. Computers are needed to track moving targets and to calculate artillery trajectories, and they are needed to collect information about a population so that plans can be made for the well-being of those people (and to collect taxes). Both problems historically led to government investment of the large sums of money needed to develop computers in times of war and peace.

Consider that the IRS uses supercomputers for data processing—and that a database application was specifically written for the IRS at considerable taxpayer expense. When a database grows to the size the IRS uses, it is processed by a network of supercomputers that can do calculations at the needed rate. The government is a heavy user of this type of database system, both for the public sector and military work. Another example of databases is the order/reservation system used by your travel agent.

Although the IRS's use of a database may not excite you, you can get excited when FileMaker Pro automates your business, speeds up data entry, does paperwork, and saves you enough time so that you can get out of the office on a sunny day. Throughout this book, you will find potential uses for your FileMaker Pro program, and this introduction tries to be particularly helpful in that regard.

For more information about the historical nature of databases and the various uses to which they have been applied, you might want to consult Time-Life Library's *Understanding Computers*. Although this is a ponderous series of books, it contains many useful historical and conceptual examples for beginners. Unfortunately, this book doesn't have enough space for a more complete exposition of this interesting topic.

What Can You Do with FileMaker Pro?

FileMaker Pro is a database with a strong graphical layout and reporting structure. With this program, you can organize data both in a data-entry sense and in a display-format sense. Stored data can be selected by criteria you supply in a find operation, organized in a sort operation, and output as a report, either in hard copy (print) or as a disk file. You control exactly what pieces of information you want to work with or display.

Built into FileMaker are calculation and logical functions that enter values for you, check the accuracy of a result, or check to see that your new data fall into some range of values that you define. Using functions you create, your data can be analyzed in various ways that are important in all those operations.

To summarize, with FileMaker Pro, you can do the following:

- Display data in a number of ways
- Search for and find, or select, a set of information
- Organize your information in new ways
- Print reports and forms with the data you specify
- Perform calculations and summaries
- Automatically enter data and check its validity

Most database applications can be addressed with FileMaker Pro. These applications include projects ranging from organizing your home record collection, creating a bibliography for your dissertation, and putting your town's library books into an electronic card file, to running your business's accounting and order-entry system.

If you can think of a reason to use a database, someone out there probably is using FileMaker Pro for exactly that purpose. There are documented cases of FileMaker Pro files with more than half a million records in them. The program imposes a maximum 32 megabyte (32M) file size limit, so its full potential is hard to reach. Some very large businesses use FileMaker Pro.

What's in This Book?

U*sing FileMaker Pro* contains four parts, divided into 17 chapters (four of which are quick starts, described in the following paragraphs). The chapters are best read sequentially, but some chapters may be of limited interest to you and may be skimmed or skipped. Use your own judgment regarding the material you feel you need and consult the index if you need assistance.

This book has four ways of helping you locate information quickly:

> **Quick Starts**. Spread throughout the book are four quick start chapters. Unlike the other chapters, the quick starts are designed to be worked as self-contained exercises at any time. For a hands-on tutorial of FileMaker Pro features, read the quick starts. If you have a basic need, or if you are in a hurry, you may find all the necessary instructions in the appropriate quick start. In addition, each quick start operation refers you to the section in the book where detailed information about that operation may be found.
>
> **Index.** At the back of the book is a complete subject index.
>
> **In Review.** At the end of each chapter is a summary of all the important concepts covered in the chapter.
>
> **Icons.** You will find two icons—Speed Key and Warning—throughout each of the 17 chapters in the book. Speed Keys are shortcuts for commands or options that will speed up your work. Warning icons indicate an operation that can be dangerous to your data.

Tips and notes, set in the margins, are important techniques that will help you better organize or refine your working style. All readers can benefit from careful study of these important techniques.

The following paragraphs describe the parts and chapters in detail:

Part I, "FileMaker Basics," contains introductory material. This part includes Chapters 1 through 5. If you are a beginner with just a passing need for FileMaker Pro skills, Part I may be all you need to start performing your tasks.

Chapter 1, "Understanding Database Concepts," introduces you generally to database terms and to terms pertaining specifically to FileMaker Pro.

Chapter 2, "Quick Start: Creating a Database," instructs you in creating a file. You define how your data will be organized, select and organize some information, create a simple display, and print a report.

Chapter 3, "Creating a File," offers specific details on Macintosh basics, including using the mouse, menus, windows, and various boxes that are specific to FileMaker. This chapter also explains how to establish and define a new file and describes some of the important basic information you need to know to work with a file.

Chapter 4, "Editing, Finding, and Sorting Records," describes record selection and organization.

Chapter 5, "Automating Data Entry," shows you how to create and work with special FileMaker fields. You learn how to use automated entry from other files, perform calculations, and check data accuracy.

Part II, "Working with Layouts," describes in detail various techniques for enhancing the appearance of your output. FileMaker is a graphical database, and you can create and modify the manner in which your data is displayed or printed. Part II includes Chapters 6 through 8.

Chapter 6, "Creating a Layout," introduces you to the mechanics of layouts, the style of layouts, and the creation of new layouts.

Chapter 7, "Enhancing Layout Appearance," describes advanced features of FileMaker that enable you to create more precise layouts.

Chapter 8, "Quick Start: Creating and Using Forms," shows you how to work with forms, both the kind you create and the kind that already exist. More advanced features of working with displays are found here, and simple data entry and printing are addressed.

In Part III, "Printing," you learn how to create a report, set up a page, and print to various output devices. Part III includes Chapters 9 through 11.

Chapter 9, "Preparing To Print," shows you how to set up a page to create the report you want. A page part is a FileMaker device that enables you to position objects on a page, and page parts are used to set up a database display. Page parts give you enormous flexibility in the style of printed output you can create.

Chapter 10, "Printing Basics," gives specific instructions on how to use your printer with the options that are available.

Chapter 11, "Quick Start: Creating Mailing Labels," teaches you how to create and print various kinds of mailing labels.

In Part IV, "Advanced FileMaker Features," you find special topics, such as scripts and templates. The chapters in this part also discuss file management. Part IV consists of Chapters 12 through 17.

Chapter 12, "Creating Scripts and Buttons," shows you how to speed up your work by going to a layout automatically and placing it in a condition you defined previously. The use of buttons makes this process even easier.

Chapter 13, "Using Templates and Other Resources," lists already-written FileMaker databases that you can buy and sources that sell them. Also included in this chapter are other available resources that may prove useful to you.

Chapter 14, "Quick Start: Creating a Summary Report," trains you in some advanced concepts needed to create a report. You learn how to work with page parts, use summary fields, and automate your report.

Chapter 15, "Importing and Exporting Data," describes in detail how to import and export data between FileMaker files and between FileMaker and other programs.

Chapter 16, "Managing Files," describes some advanced ways in which FileMaker operates within the Macintosh file system. Instructions on how to protect and back up your data and recover from disasters also are contained in this chapter.

Chapter 17, "Using FileMaker Pro on a Network," describes sharing FileMaker Pro files on a network. Setting up passwords and groups also is explained.

The appendixes cover special details. Both the Macintosh system requirements and the various operation limits of FileMaker are found in Appendix A. Instructions on installing FileMaker Pro on either a floppy disk or a hard drive are in Appendix B. Appendix C is a menu summary, and Appendix D is a product index that tells where you can find products mentioned in this book.

Who Should Use This Book?

This book is written for new and experienced users alike. If you are new to the Macintosh, you will find in this book references to all the resources needed to become proficient with FileMaker. Basic techniques specific to FileMaker Pro are covered, primarily in Chapter 3. By necessity, *Using FileMaker Pro* overlaps some with the program's documentation. What makes this book different is its coverage of the program's features. You will learn helpful techniques and receive advice on problems to avoid.

For experienced FileMaker Pro users, power user tips have been added and are enclosed in shaded areas. FileMaker Pro is an established product with a large number of users, and many add-on products now exist that power users will want to know about. The text refers to these products, and a product guide is contained in Appendix D. In addition to tips, this book contains some techniques developed by experts, techniques that may be worth the cost of the book. *Using FileMaker Pro* will find a place as a reference on your bookshelf, alongside your FileMaker program.

How To Use This Book

When possible, *Using FileMaker Pro* tries to follow terms and descriptions developed for the Macintosh and recommended by Apple in its guidebook, *The Human Interface Guidelines: The Apple Desktop Interface*. Terms used by Claris in its documentation also are followed in this book. FileMaker generally follows the Macintosh interface guidelines; deviations are noted.

Material that you should type on your keyboard (in a Quick Start, for example) is in *italic* type or on a line by itself. Sometimes important information is in **bold** or *italic* type for emphasis. Commands, menu names, and dialog boxes are written with an initial capital letter, such as the Open command, the Edit menu, and the Print dialog box. Messages that appear on your computer monitor are written in a `special typeface`.

Other Resources

No one approach to learning FileMaker Pro can be complete, nor is any single approach always right for every user. Several other training aids are available that may be worth your attention.

Two courses, one a set of two videotapes and the other a course consisting of floppy disks and four self-paced audio cassettes, are available. MacAcademy sells the videotapes, and Personal Training Systems sells the cassette course. Both are highly recommended. Claris also sells a course for classroom training in FileMaker in which a teacher leads small classes through disk-based exercises. Also, large user groups frequently offer a FileMaker class. The Boston Computer Society Macintosh User's Group does, as do many others. Consult your local group for information. Many dealers and computer institutes also offer such courses.

You can find references to products in the product index, Appendix D, at the end of this book.

PART I

FileMaker Basics

Includes

USING FILEMAKER PRO

CHAPTER 1

Understanding Database Concepts

Consider the office of yesteryear. Before the Children of the Sixties Holistic Natural Health Food Emporium bought a Macintosh and FileMaker to organize their catalog sales, their office had a roomful of customer, inventory, vendor, and other records. The office was more organized than most, so each of the file cabinets was logically organized around a general category. Open a file drawer, and you found all the purchase orders. Another drawer had sales slips, a third drawer had packing slips, and so on. After the owners looked at their sales slips, each slip was put into a section of file folders, according to month, and each was further subdivided into individual file folders by ZIP codes. Many businesses still work this way.

Businesses always have used databases, but not necessarily the computerized kind. A Rolodex is a kind of database. This chapter begins by defining computer database terminology. After a review of important database terms, you learn about the different types of databases. By surveying where FileMaker fits into the overall scheme of data-management programs, you can better appreciate the power of this program and understand what FileMaker offers.

The last section of this chapter contains important information on some guidelines you should consider when constructing a database. Most people construct a database from scratch without thinking much about how they will work with their data. Their files evolve and grow more complicated over time, until even some basic operations become difficult. Good planning can eliminate some frustrations.

USING FILEMAKER PRO

You may find that you want to know about databases on a deeper level. Fundamental database theory is beyond the scope of this book. The topic is covered in books ranging from general introductions through college textbooks, both the descriptive and the highly mathematical. You can find a listing of some of these in Appendix D, "Product Index," under "Database Theory."

Defining Database Terms

In the sections that follow, you find terms that FileMaker and other databases use to organize data. These terms are basic to understanding the program, and you should feel comfortable with them before you proceed to new material.

Files

Information that you can connect in a logical, organized fashion can be stored in a database. This data set can be a reference for a bibliography, a customer history, an inventory, or any of the other uses mentioned in the Introduction. If you can recognize that connection, a database is the appropriate application to use. The overall data set is stored in a database *file*, and those files can grow large over time.

A phone book is an example of a database file. Your phone company actually keeps an electronic version of your phone book available when you call for information. You could certainly have a phone book that listed all the telephone numbers in the universe, but that would be unwieldy. Your phone company splits up phone books into logical data sets, one of which is your hometown. In comparison, when your file becomes too large, you should split the file into smaller files so that your Macintosh can operate more efficiently.

Records

Files are organized into data *records*, and a record holds the items for a single entry. One person's name, address, and phone number make up one record in a phone book database. When you define a database, you specify what each record can contain. A record is the smallest whole part of a file that you can logically define—the basic connection from which a file is built. A record defines the relation, which is the purpose of your database.

Fields

You create a further data structure, a category within a record, called a *field*. A field holds a single data item within the data record. For example, in the phone book database, the address is one entry in each person's record. When you create fields, you assign names and attributes. Attributes include the type of data entered in the field (Text, Number, Date, Picture, or time, for example) and the formatting (how the data appears). A key point to remember is that you can control not only the data type of a field, but also how the data is displayed or formatted.

All databases create an index of values. A database uses each index to do finds and sorts. In FileMaker, that index is each individual delimited entry (see Chapter 3, "Creating a File"). In a Text field, the text string "United States of America" would be indexed under four separate words, because a space is a delimiter. A spelling checker is just a database of acceptable, indexed text strings; if you have seen a particularly good spelling checker like WorksPlus Spell, then you know how fast FileMaker is. FileMaker indexes Text, Number, and Date fields. Unlike these fields, the calculation and summary fields are all lowercase because they are derived fields. You don't enter data into a derived field. FileMaker calculates the data for you by relationships that you define to other fields.

In figure 1.1, you can see how an index is constructed. Each invoice number is listed as a separate entry in the index with a single value. If any of the numbers had a space character, that number would be indexed as two separate numbers because a space is a delimiter. In the index for the item field, you may expect the index to look the way it does in figure 1.1. Each individual word in the item index, however, is a separate referenced value. To get an index for the item field as shown, you press Option-space character, which is not a delimiter.

The relationship of files to records to fields can be summarized with the following three common examples:

- Your bank account or checkbook is a database file. In a checkbook, each check is a record, each line you fill in is a field, and each item (check, deposit, or withdrawal) on a line is an entry.
- Your phone book is a file. Each person's account (name, address, and phone number) is a record, each item (name, address, or phone number) is a field, and each piece of data is an entry.

- Most database books use the analogy of paper filing systems to explain database terms: the room full of records is a database, each file cabinet is a file, each folder is an organized or selected set of records, each piece of paper is a record, each kind of data type is a field, and each filled-in piece of information is an entry.

Fig. 1.1
Elements of a flat-file database, with five records and two field indexes showing.

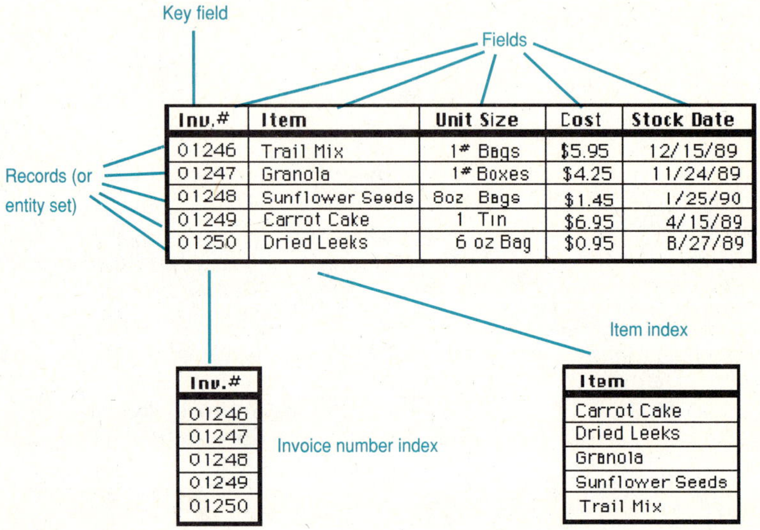

When you create a record in FileMaker, the record receives a record number one higher than the number of the preceding created record. The *record number* is the key by which the data set is organized. You can change the data set by finding some individual records and sorting them. Doing that changes the key field to whatever you sorted them by; only the found records are left to be operated on. The omitted records are still in the database file; they are just hidden from view.

Layouts

Although you define data structures and create data entries, not all data is useful for each particular application. You have the power in a database to display only information you want to see. You can show only the fields that are appropriate. A *layout* is an arrangement of data with graphical elements that can be displayed and printed. FileMaker has a Layout window with which you can design the elements you want to have in your display.

The form of the display you see on your screen is controlled by the layout. You can have many layouts and switch between them; the one you see on-screen is the current layout. FileMaker separates seeing your data from actually entering or working with the data itself; you can enter data but not change the data's appearance at the same time.

You can have a display, often called a list, where all fields and entries for all browsed records can be viewed up to the limit of the size of your monitor. In a display called a form, a single record's data shows. All databases enable you to display and output only that set of data useful for a particular purpose. A list might be useful for evaluating data against a large data set or for creating a report of some kind. A form is useful for individualized output, such as a single invoice (see fig. 1.2).

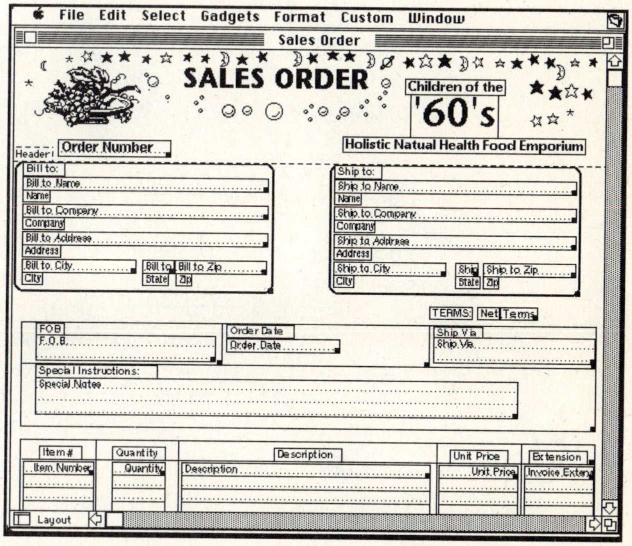

Fig. 1.2
A form layout of a sales invoice shown in FileMaker.

Some databases, such as the one included with Microsoft Works, provide only a list or form view for each file. To create more output formats, you must create another database file or create some kind of output or mail-merge mechanism. FileMaker enables you to create any number of layouts or reporting structures without having to leave the program. All the chapters in Part II, "Working with Layouts," explore aspects of FileMaker's layout features.

Understanding Database Types

You are probably familiar with the tree structure of folders that is used as a file directory by your Macintosh. Files appear to occur once in only one folder. This system, although logical, could be replaced by equally logical structures. A simple example would be having all folders at the same level (this was the scheme for the original Macintosh File System). A more complex example would be to have your files belong to more than one folder at a time. That is, imagine that each folder contains the address of a number of files. Your files could be anywhere, and the folder metaphor would no longer be that it contained that file, but that it contains an address that enables you to access the file. Each icon would be an alias for the file; that organizational scheme is called *aliasing*.

Similarly, databases can be organized in several different ways. In the sections that follow, the four major classifications of databases—flat file, hierarchical, relational, and networked—are defined.

Flat-File Databases

FileMaker is a flat-file database. In a flat-file database, each file can be conceptualized as a two-dimensional array or matrix of records and fields. Each intersection has a unique address where a data entry can be shown (see fig. 1.1 again). Flat-file databases have some distinct advantages. Because of their structure, they're fast, easy to understand, and simple to operate. Novices tend to make fewer errors in this kind of database because the data structures are easier to visualize.

A flat-file database is the simplest database structure; it's organized like a spreadsheet. In a spreadsheet, fields correspond to columns, rows correspond to records, and cells contain entries. Excel, Wingz, and Full Impact are examples of powerful spreadsheets sold for the Macintosh; Microsoft Works also comes with a more basic spreadsheet module.

Databases are different from spreadsheets in some ways that are not all that obvious. In Microsoft Excel, for example, you can select a range of cells, and with a menu command, designate that range to be a database. An Excel database restricts the range of functions that are available for data manipulation without giving you the report generation or formatting muscle of a true database like FileMaker.

When you have a computer project that entails managing related pieces of information, organizing them, and outputting them in different ways, you need to work with a database program. On the other hand, when you have a project that requires sophisticated mathematical and logical manipulation of each piece of data on an individual basis, you need to work with a spreadsheet.

In a database, each related group of data is separated into a record. Databases have functions built into them to manage those data sets. By comparison, spreadsheets contain data in separate compartments called *cells*. Although cells in a spreadsheet may be related mathematically or logically to other cells, there is no concept of a group of values, similar to records in a database. The existence of records in a database restricts the range of functions available to the user, making it mathematically more structured.

Hierarchical Databases

A hierarchical database-management system is another simple kind of organizational scheme and is often referred to as a tree structure. Records at each level are related by "owning" or "belonging" to each other. The nodes, or intersections, of the branches might represent an entity set, such as a record that is associated with other records. Very large databases are often organized in this manner.

Consider a telephone company database composed of records of each subscriber's address. Each individual's record intersects by phone number with the database composed of all of the incoming and outgoing calls and charges. The phone number can serve as the key field. For a hierarchical database, the relationship consists of a parent data set, with associated children, who are associated with grandchildren, and so on.

Relational Databases

Relational databases create records with data entries from different sources. The user can create links or join data in a relationship that is part of the definition of the database. Information can come from more than one disk file and from more than one record of different types. This sort of structure makes it much easier to structure your database files to eliminate redundant or repetitive information. You can, for example, compare data in an invoice file with data in an inventory file for cross-referencing. You also can define criteria that act as filters to further define the synthesized data set. Figure 1.3 shows the elements of a relational database.

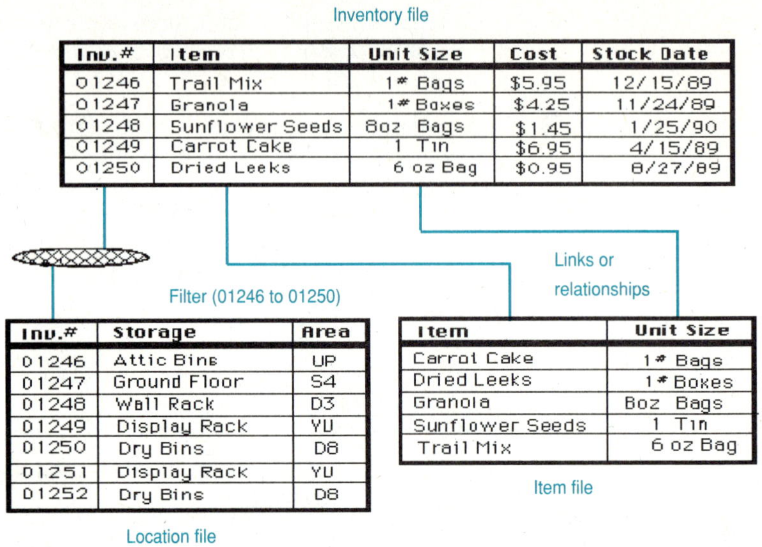

Fig. 1.3 Elements of a relational database.

In figure 1.3, you can see how a relational database constructs files from other files. You define a relation or a link to one or more files, and those links define a new file, called the item file in figure 1.3.

Although creating a file from a single file isn't all that useful, when you use the same process on many files to create the item file, you have a powerful method for constructing databases. Another construct, called a filter, enables you to select which pieces of information are allowed in the newly constructed file. Usually, high-end relational databases (dBASE, 4th Dimension, Double Helix, Omnis 5) use a scripting or programming language to achieve these features.

Computer trade publications often praise relational databases. Relational databases certainly can do more sophisticated operations than a flat-file database, and they almost always come with a built-in programming language. You pay for this added power, however, with a much steeper learning curve and more complicated operation. A relational database often requires the assistance of a developer for its design and a systems operator to run it effectively. It has been estimated that for more than 95 percent of database projects, flat-file systems are sufficient. With good design, you often can create a solution to a relational database problem by using a flat-file system.

FileMaker is not a simple flat-file database. FileMaker incorporates a lookup feature (see Chapter 5) that creates links you define as part of a field definition. With a lookup, if the values match in two fields that you specify, FileMaker puts a value from another field into your lookup field. Although a true relational database enables you to create multiple links with a single command, you can at least create links with FileMaker for each field, from one file to another. Bear in mind that this FileMaker link is one-way only.

Networked Databases

A network is a system of wires or electrical connections and associated software that is used to connect two or more computers. In a sense, FileMaker is a networked database because it enables many users to share data at the same time. Any database, however, can be written to operate on a network. A true networked database is a structure in which data resides at several locations on a network, and a user can synthesize a file with a customized structure.

If you work for a company or are in a work group, you can imagine the benefits of being able to share the work involved in entering and manipulating all of the data in a database file. Sharing data requires rules so that you can access and work with data without bothering other people or going into places you don't belong. On a network, a database file can be accessed by any user. What that user is able to do with the database is defined by the set of privileges assigned. For more information on using FileMaker on a network, see Chapter 17.

Organizing Databases

The single best thing you can do when you first organize a database is to spend some time thinking about all the functions you want to accomplish with the database. Make a list of every conceivable operation that you might want to do. Sketch out each field, try to organize them compactly, and create a logical structure. Use the guidelines in the following sections to aid you in your thinking.

Consider these factors when you are planning a database:

1. **Be consistent.** When you create (define) a field, you name that field. FileMaker uses that name to locate and work with your data. Use the same field names in all your data and for all your databases. If you create a field called "First Name," always call it that

instead of changing to "F Name" or "1st Name" later on. This consistency allows for easier data recognition and import or export of data.

2. **Think through the implications of your data.** If you use a First Name field and enter names like Barrie A., you may have a problem. Imagine doing a mail-merge letter and having it read `Dear Barrie A.`

3. **Test your database.** It's a lot easier to change your database when you first create it than to change it later on. Create it, define your operations, and enter 10 to 20 sample records. Perform all the operations you think you will want to do. It's likely that if your database performs properly with 10 to 20 records, it will perform properly when it is larger.

4. **Eliminate redundancy.** With proper planning, you can consolidate data into fewer places. Try to enter data only once into all of your database files or consider creating a master lookup file. FileMaker can look up or automatically enter data for you, which ensures better accuracy, faster operation, and less duplication. Whenever possible, use FileMaker to eliminate duplication.

5. **Automate your database.** FileMaker gives you powerful tools to auto-enter data, look up data, perform calculations, and use logic. You can create pop-up fields from which to choose possible entries and have FileMaker validate the data you enter. Accuracy is the key. Create operations that reduce the chance of making errors. You also can create a defined tabbing order to aid you in accurately entering data.

6. **Choose the right data type.** Most of the time, which data type you should use is obvious—it's difficult to confuse a picture with a number. Sometimes, though, it's not so obvious. With ZIP codes, for instance, it's better to have a Text field than a Number field, to allow for more efficient searches and sorts.

7. **Create the smallest piece of data that you are likely to use.** If you break ZIP codes into five- and four-number fields, they will be easier to sort. An address is a more trivial example. If you use

   Dr. Frederick Hawthorne
   Humongous Corporation
   12 Carborane Way
   Los Angeles, CA 90024
   USA

as a single field entry, finding and sorting this information as a unit will slow down FileMaker to a crawl and limit the useful operations that you can do with the information later on.

To help you in creating files and entering data when you are planning your database, consider the following suggestions:

1. **Reduce your data entry to the simplest form and never calculate anything.** Let FileMaker do the calculating.

2. **Be careful about data deletions or other operations that FileMaker cannot undo.** FileMaker has an excellent set of alert boxes. Stop and read them before you go on.

3. **Create a layout with all of the data contained in your file.** One complete layout enables the user to get a good overall view of the structure of the file. This layout will be available to a user with full file access.

4. **Use a layout for each output form.** Consider your data in a file to be central; do not create individual files for each form of output.

5. **Create or use templates.** Maybe you can save yourself the effort of creating a database by using one that someone else has created. "Canned" databases, called *templates*, contain empty fields already set up for your use. Using templates can speed up your work (see Chapter 13). Consider creating or purchasing a template.

6. **Learn about and use scripts.** A script is a macro that automates a set of tasks (see Chapter 12). If you do a task once and record it as a script, then FileMaker remembers it for you. Scripts and menu commands can be captured as a button. Defining and using buttons on your layouts can speed up your work.

Here are four more tips to help you maintain your data safely:

1. **Protect your data.** Double-protect your data. Triple-protect your data. Your database will have incredible value to you over time, probably more than your computer itself. Create backups and store a copy off-site. Consider rotating backups over time, and think about the maximum amount of information that you are willing to lose. A little paranoia is good for you.

2. **Never work on original data.** If the power goes out, your file can be damaged, or you can accidentally delete information. Working on a copy enables you to recover gracefully. Because FileMaker performs autosaves, some manipulations cannot be undone (see Chapter 3).

3. **Control access to your data.** FileMaker has password protection and file locking, or what FileMaker calls making a *file exclusive*. Password protection gives access to a file only to users who can provide the password, and it limits the user to specified access rights. File locking permits only one user at a time to change data in a record.

4. **Archive your data.** When you no longer need data, consider creating a file to which you can output that data. For example, if you have a file with invoices and a customer pays a bill, move the invoice to a separate file. Removing data to a secure location, called archiving, simplifies your database, speeds up performance, and makes information easier to find.

In Review

Databases are filing systems for information that is related in some logical way. The basic unit for a database is a record, and a set of records forms a file. Records are made up of fields in which you enter appropriate values.

A layout is a display of data in your database in a format that is appropriate for some kind of output task, such as a report, a form, a label, and so on. Most databases create lists and form windows to display data.

Databases can be classified as flat file, hierarchical, relational, or networked. A flat-file database creates a two-dimensional array of records and fields for a file. Hierarchical databases are organized in a tree structure, with records at each level related by owning or belonging to each other. Relational databases enable the creation of synthesized files by using links and filters. A networked database permits multiuser access of data across the network. FileMaker is a flat-file database with some relational features. It has multiuser capabilities, can run on a network, and contains strong graphical reporting features.

Spend time planning your database right from the start by deciding what you want the database to do. Create the database, enter some records, and test your creation.

CHAPTER 2

Quick Start: Creating a Database

Most of what you need to learn to begin using FileMaker is in this quick start. This unit is intended to get you up and running with some of the basic operations that you learn in Part I.

In this first quick start, you learn how to do the following:

- Create a file
- Define fields and set field types
- Work with fields and records
- Enter data
- Create a simple layout or form
- Select and organize some records
- Print your data

Creating a Client Database

Your company, Children of the Sixties Holistic Natural Health Food Emporium, is organizing a direct-mail campaign in time for the holidays to promote its new catalog of organically grown produce.

To begin, you want to create a file of previous customers so that you can ship the catalog to them and track the resulting orders. This quick start leads you through the steps to set up the database needed for the task.

Starting the Program

To begin this quick start, you already should have installed FileMaker Pro, and you should be ready to begin creating a database. (If you need help installing the program, see Appendix B.)

Start the program by following these steps:

1. Either on a hard drive or a floppy drive, open the folder containing the FileMaker program by double-clicking on its icon (the picture representing the FileMaker program).
2. In Finder or MultiFinder, create a folder by selecting the New Folder command on the File menu or by pressing ⌘-N. Change the name of the folder from Empty Folder by typing *60's Nat. Food Emp.* Your screen will look like figure 2.1.

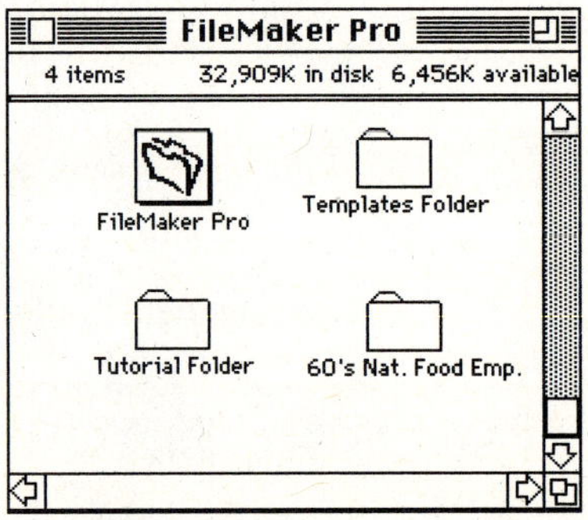

Fig. 2.1
FileMaker's folder on the Desktop.

3. Double-click the application icon (the picture with the file folders on it) shown in the upper left corner of the window, click once to highlight the icon and give the Open command on the Edit menu, or press ⌘-O. The Open File dialog box appears. If this is the first time you have launched FileMaker, the program prompts you to personalize your copy (see Appendix B).

You should be familiar with using the Macintosh and know how to operate the file system to open folders, use menus, launch a program, or use dialog boxes and buttons. If any of the preceding steps are unfamiliar to you, you might want to stop here and review these topics in the first half of Chapter 3.

Creating the File

After you have started the program, you are ready to create the database file. In the Open File dialog box that appears when you start FileMaker, you can either create a file or open previously defined files. For this example, follow these steps:

1. Place the file you want to create inside the 60's Nat. Food Emp. folder by double-clicking on the name

   or

   click once on the name to highlight it (see fig. 2.2) and then click the Open button.

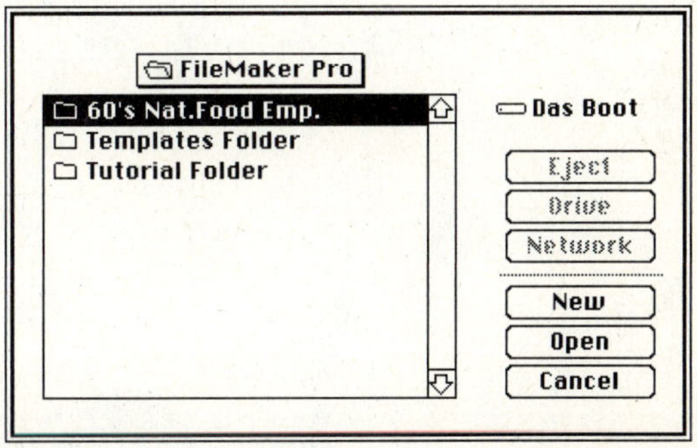

Fig. 2.2
The Open File dialog box.

2. Click the New button.

   A second standard file dialog box appears, which enables you to create and name your file. The Create a New File dialog box prompts you for a new file name.

3. Type *Catalog Mailing* in the text box (see fig. 2.3).

4. Click the New button in the Create a New File box to create your file. Note that you have clicked two New buttons, but they are in different dialog boxes.

The program automatically displays a Browse window with the Define Fields dialog box shown (see fig. 2.4).

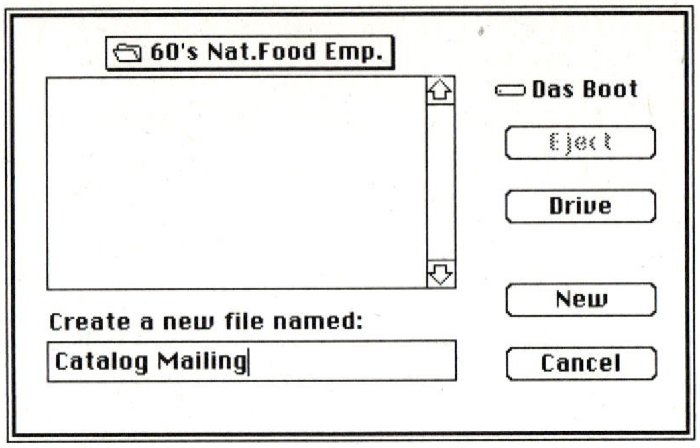

Fig. 2.3
The Create a New File dialog box.

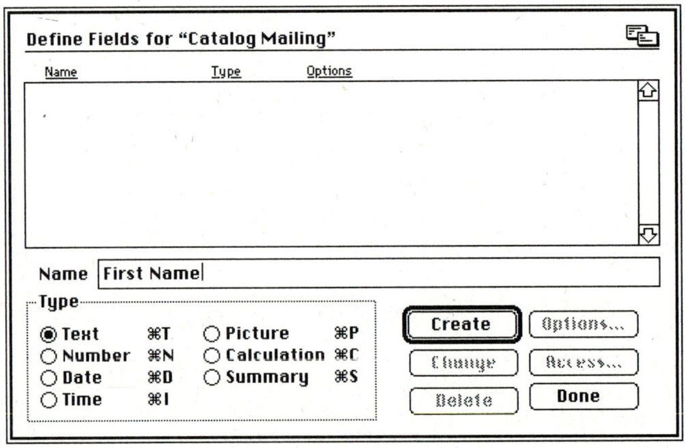

Fig. 2.4
The Define Fields dialog box.

Defining Fields

When you first create a FileMaker file, no defined fields exist to receive your data. *Fields* are places or boxes that will hold your data. FileMaker requires that you name the boxes and tell it the purpose of the boxes. This process is called *define mode*, and when you click the New button in the Create a New File box, you are placing the program into this mode. The Define Fields dialog box appears in define mode.

The Define Fields dialog box is the key to creating fields, naming them, setting field types (also called *attributes*), creating calculations or summaries, and setting other entry options such as auto-entering data. If you are in any other FileMaker window, you can return to the define mode (and the Define Fields dialog box) by selecting the Define command or pressing the ⌘-Shift-D keystroke. What you do with fields is so important that its discussion forms the basis for much of the first part of this book. For more information about fields, consult Chapters 3, 4, and 5.

You want your database to contain fields for the first and last names, company name, address, city, state, and ZIP Code of your customers.

To create fields, follow these steps:

1. In the Field Name text box, a flashing insertion point prompts you to type a name. Type the name *First Name* for the first field.

   This first field is a Text field, and text is the default (note that the radio button for this option is darkened). A default is the setting that your computer chooses automatically. If you accidentally click another radio button, click on the Text radio button or press ⌘-T. Text fields treat all entries as character strings without further evaluation, and they permit you to enter any character.

2. Click the OK button to create the field.

3. Continue creating text fields for Last Name, Company, Address, City, and State, as you did in steps 1 and 2.

   If you make a mistake or want to change the name of a field, click on the name of the field to select it and edit the name in the Field Name text box.

4. Create a field named Zip Code to contain five-digit ZIP codes. Make Zip Code a text field, not a number field. You are now at the stage shown in figure 2.5.

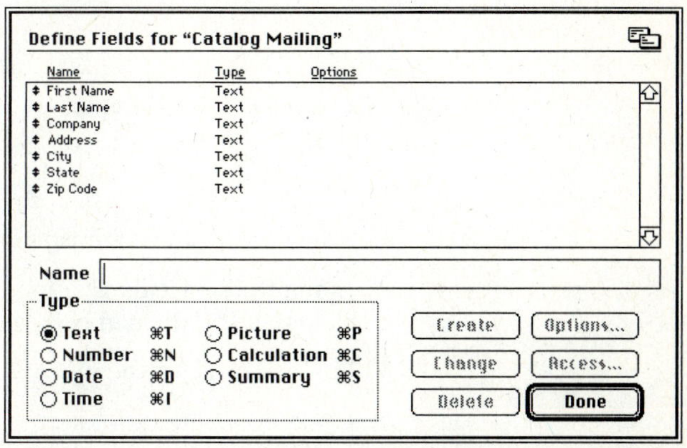

Fig. 2.5
The first seven fields in the Catalog Mailing address.

You should make the Zip Code a text field because Text fields enable you to search for pieces of a ZIP code instead of the whole number. A Number field recognizes only numbers in its search, and it requires that you enter the entire number string. It is particularly annoying to have to enter 10 digits to find a telephone number or 16 digits for a credit card; you must enter the entire string if that field is a Number field. See "Organizing Records," later in this chapter, for more information on creating fields.

You now have created all the fields for a complete mailing address.

5. Click the Exit button or press the Return or Enter key to go to the Browse window.

A Browse window that is identical to fig. 2.6 appears. If, for some reason, you do not see the field boxes on the screen, press the Enter key.

Fig. 2.6
The first blank record in a standard layout in the Browse window.

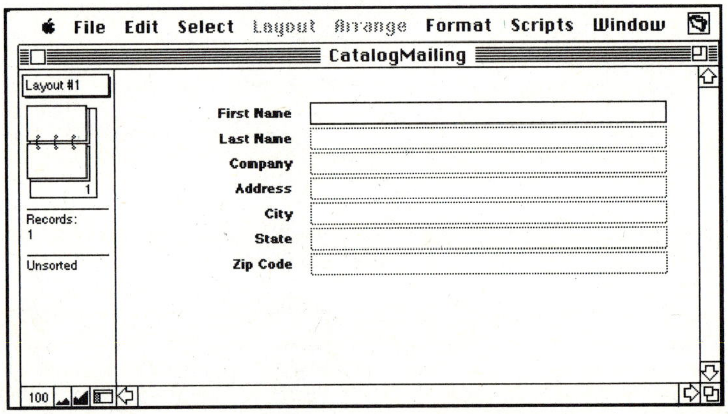

If you made a mistake in a field name, you can return to the define mode by choosing the Define command on the Select menu. The Define Fields box appears.

To correct a field name, follow these steps:

1. Select the Define command from the Select menu.
2. In the Define Fields dialog box, click on the field name to be changed, and the name appears in the Field Name text box.
3. Enter the correct (new) name.
4. Click the Exit button to return to the Browse screen.

FileMaker has three different types of windows: a Browse window, a Layout window, and a Find window. The following elements of a FileMaker window are common to all Macintosh windows: the scroll bars; the close, grow, and resize boxes; and the title bar. If these elements are unfamiliar to you, you might want to stop and look at Chapter 3.

FileMaker windows have some additional elements that you need to know about. The status area on the left side of the window contains some tools you use for your work. Currently, only the Book and the Slide Control Mechanism, along with the pop-up layout title box, are shown. The Book and Slide Control Mechanism are used to move about from one set of data structures to another, and the following section, "Entering Data," explains their use. The Layout title box enables you to switch quickly between layouts. The status area tells you that there is currently only one record, the one in which you are about to place data.

Entering Data

In this section, you learn how to do the following:

- Enter data for the first record
- Create records
- Move from record to record

When creating a file, the Browse window usually is displayed. You can return to the Browse window (and mode) from another window by choosing the Browse command on the Select menu. Just as fields are boxes, a set of fields comprises a *record*, and a record is the fundamental related unit of a database. Browsing means looking at, or working with, a set of records.

When you open a Browse window, what you see depends on how you lay out your data—your *current layout*. When you create a file, FileMaker organizes all your data into what is called a standard layout (see fig. 2.6 again).

The Browse window is the only place where you can enter data into FileMaker. In a Browse window, you can enter data, but you cannot change the way data is displayed on the screen; you must be in a Layout window to change the data display. You also cannot control the type of data in a field directly from a Browse window; you must return to the Define Fields dialog box by selecting the Define command on the Select menu to redefine the type of data in a field.

Note

Screens shown are in MultiFinder; the FileMaker icon is in the upper right corner of the screen. In System 6, in Finder, the FileMaker icon is missing. The FileMaker procedures described in this book apply to Finder and MultiFinder.

To enter data, follow these steps:

1. Place an insertion point in the field by clicking in the desired field. To enter data for your first customer, activate the First Name field.

   If the screen shows only the field names and no entry boxes, click to the right of the field name to activate its entry box; all the field boxes appear. By clicking outside a field box, all boxes disappear. With all field boxes missing, press the Tab key to activate the first field (First Name). An activated field contains a flashing insertion point.

   To move from field to field, press the Tab key. Press Shift-Tab or Option-Tab to move to a previous field. FileMaker's *tabbing order* usually goes from left to right and then from top to bottom.

2. Type *Frost* in the First Name field entry box and press the Tab key.
3. Type *Heaves* for the Last Name field entry and press the Tab key.
4. Type *Hard Disk Cafe* for the Company field entry and press the Tab key.
5. Type *82 Main Street* for the Address field entry and press the Tab key.
6. Type *North Conway* for the City field entry and press the Tab key.
7. Type *NH* for the State field entry and press the Tab key.
8. Type *03860* for the Zip Code field entry, which completes the entry of the first record (see fig. 2.7).

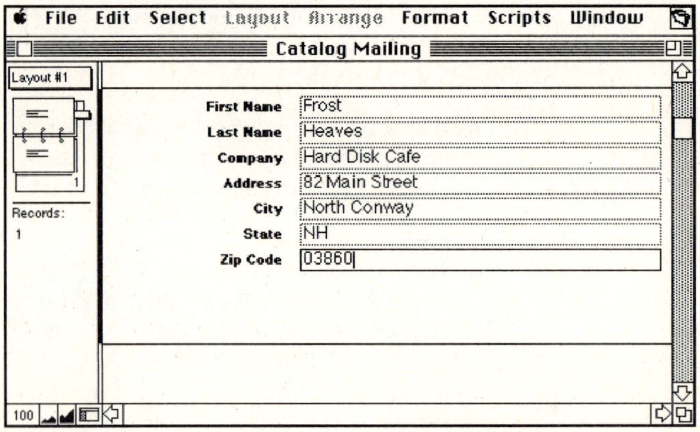

Fig. 2.7
The first completed record for Frost Heaves.

To create records, follow these steps:

1. Select the New Record command on the Edit menu or press the ⌘-N keystroke equivalent.

   A blank record like the one in figure 2.6 appears. Notice that every time you create a record, the number of records in your browsed set increases. This increase is indicated by the counter beneath the Book icon in the status area. You can create a record, fill in the desired data entries, and then create another record. Or, you can create blank records and then fill them in. In this case, create four blank records.

2. Select the New Record command three more times so that you have five records.

   In figure 2.8, five records have been created, and the Book icon shows the resulting changes. A handle for the Slide Control Mechanism and the record counter have been added. Notice also that the bottom page of the book icon tells you that the current record is 5—the fifth record (in order) of the browsed set.

Fig. 2.8
The Book icon.

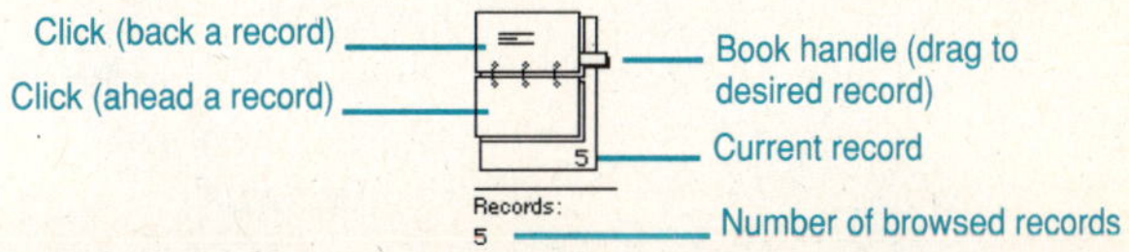

Next, you want to move to the second record. To move from record to record, use one of the following procedures:

- Click in the bottom page of the Book icon to move ahead one record (higher record number) or press the ⌘-Tab keystroke.
- Click in the top Book page to move back one record (lower record number) or press the ⌘-Shift-Tab or ⌘-Option-Tab keystroke.
- Drag the handle of the Slide Control Mechanism to move forward or backward any number of records until the desired record number shows in the middle of the Book. This record number is the *current record*.
- If you know the exact record number desired, drag over the record number in the center of the Book (or double-click on it) to highlight it, type the desired record number, and press the Return or Enter key.

3. Start at the second record and add the following data entries:

   Record 2:

   Dusty
   Rhodes
   Trail End Saloon
   1 Santa Fe Trail
   Santa Fe
   NM
   87501

   Record 3:

   Nippin
   Tair
   Log Cabin Builders
   5000 Many Mooses Drive
   Bangor
   ME
   04401

   Record 4:

   Sonny
   Breaks
   Nevada Ocean Realty
   42 Quake Road
   Santa Cruz
   CA
   95060

   Record 5:

   Fred
   Hawthorne
   Humongous Corporation
   12 Carborane Way
   Los Angeles
   CA
   90024

At this point, you have a database in the standard layout with five records, but you can view only one record at a time. Viewing only one record is appropriate for printing a form or a record card like the ones you keep in a Rolodex, but inappropriate for an overall view of your data. You can create a display—called a *layout*—to give you a good overview of all your data.

Creating a Layout

You change the way your data is displayed by altering the current layout. In this section, you do the following:

- Create a simple columnar report layout
- Place fields on the layout
- Align fields vertically and horizontally
- Create layout text and simple layout graphics
- Make formatting choices to enhance your report
- Move from layout to layout

Layouts affect your data's appearance. You create and work with layouts in the layout mode in a Layout window. FileMaker offers six types of layouts: standard, columnar report, single-page form, label, envelope, and blank layouts. You have just seen a standard layout. Layouts are so important that you will use them again and again in this book. In Quick Start: Creating and Using Forms, you will work from a blank layout; Quick Start: Creating Mailing Labels uses a label layout; and Quick Start: Creating a Summary Report uses a columnar report layout. In fact, all of Part II is devoted to "Working with Layouts."

You are currently in the Browse window with five selected (browsed) records. To go to the layout mode and view the current layout, choose the Layout command from the Select menu or press ⌘-L. The Layout window appears (see fig. 2.9).

Fig. 2.9
The Layout window of the database in standard layout form.

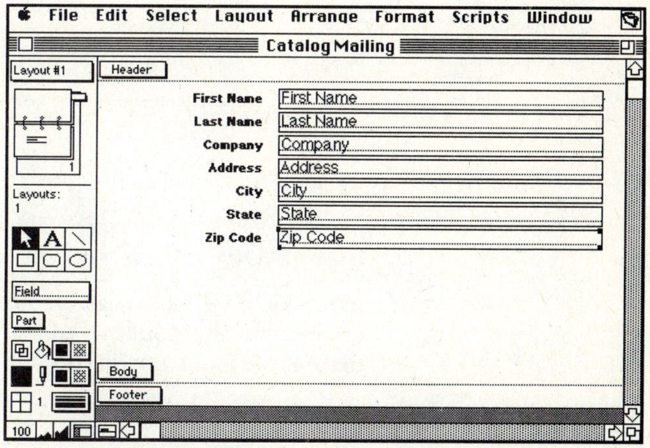

The Layout window looks similar to a Browse window. The window contains a Book and Slide Control Mechanism and a status area. A Tools palette and Field and Part icons have been added to the status area of the window. The window also contains line width controls and fill patterns. These new tools enable you to add graphic elements, fields, and parts to your layout, respectively. Other features include the zoom controls, status panel control, and part label control, which can change how the window looks on your screen.

Note that field data-entry boxes have been replaced with a new type of field box that you can alter in size and shape. These field boxes demonstrate the limit of how much data will show when you return to the Browse window and browse that field. Notice the selected Zip Code field in figure 2.9.

Other areas of the standard layout—called *parts*—are marked by dotted lines and labeled Header, Body, and Footer. Header controls the top margin of the page; footer controls the bottom margin. The body part controls each record's display and output. Chapter 9 includes a broader discussion of parts.

To create a layout, follow these steps:

1. Select the New Layout command from the Edit menu, or press the ⌘-N keystroke. The New Layout dialog box appears (see fig. 2.10).

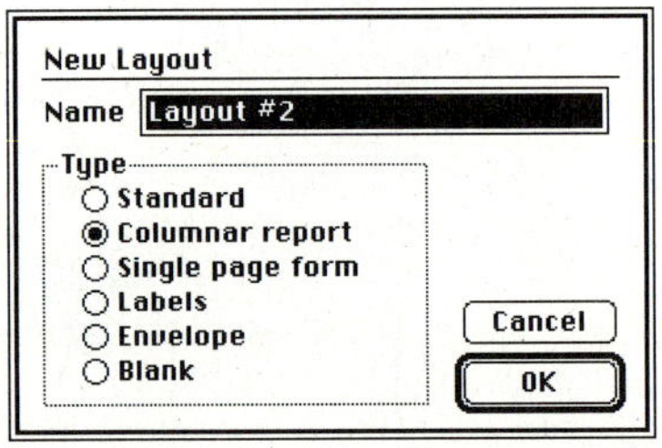

Fig. 2.10
The New Layout dialog box.

2. Click on the Columnar Report radio button.
3. Click the OK button or press the Return or Enter key. You see a Set Field Order dialog box.
4. In the Field List box, click on the field name First Name (which enables the Move button) and then click on the Move button to make it the first name in the Set Field Order box

   or

   double-click on the field name to move it.

5. Repeat the procedure in step 4 for the following fields, in this order: Last Name, Company, and Zip Code (see fig. 2.11).

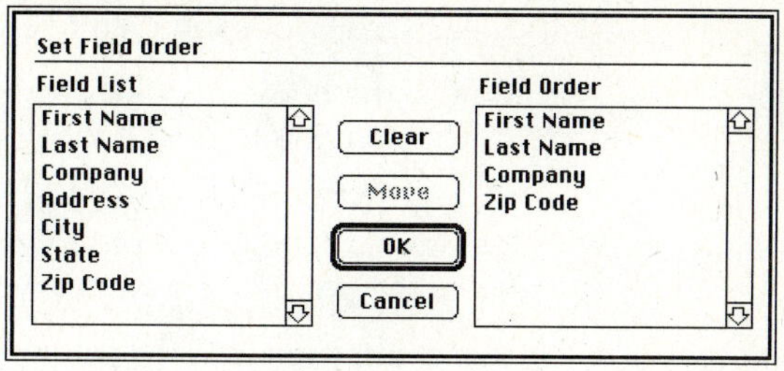

Fig. 2.11
The Set Field Order dialog box.

6. Click the OK button or press the Return or Enter key to go to the new columnar report layout (see fig. 2.12).

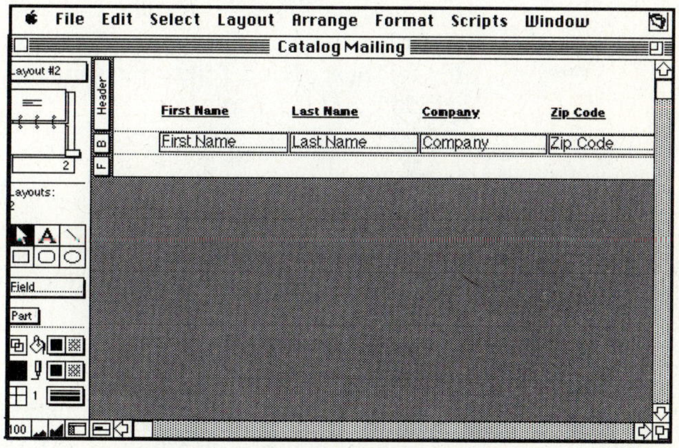

Fig. 2.12
A columnar report layout.

On a layout, FileMaker permits you to use any number of fields you choose, up to the number of fields in your file. When you eventually return to the Browse screen, you will see data for only those fields that you placed on the current layout. All your data in all the fields is still in the file, but it is not displayed by the current layout. You now have two layouts in your file. The current layout is indicated by the number in the lower right corner of the Book and in the Layout title bar directly above the book.

To move from layout to layout, you can do one of the following:

- While in any mode, click on the Layout title box, and a pop-up menu bar appears. Drag through the choices to highlight the desired layout and then release the mouse button.
- Use the Book and Slide Control Mechanism in exactly the same manner you learned previously for moving from record to record.
- Use ⌘-Tab to go forward to the next layout (higher number), and use the ⌘-Shift-Tab or ⌘-Option-Tab keystrokes to go backward to the preceding layout (lower number).

At this point, you are at the columnar report layout shown in figure 2.12. Layout text (First Name, Last Name, Company, Zip Code) that describes each field is placed in the header so that it will print once at the top of each page. Note that although you can see all the fields by scrolling the window horizontally, some fields are larger than they need to be, and there is no delineation between records. You will make three changes so that your data is easier to view and understand: enlarge layout text that describes the field, draw a line between records, and resize and move fields. These changes illustrate some basic operations of the Layout window and the Toolbox.

To create layout text, follow these steps:

1. Click on the letter A in the Toolbox to select the Text tool.
2. Click an insertion point in the center of the header section, just under the file name in the title bar.
3. Pull down the Format menu and select Geneva for Font, 18 Point for Size, Shadow for Style, and Center Align for Align Text.
4. Type *Catalog*. Each line of text is a single text object. Pressing the Return key creates another text object.
5. Click on the Arrow tool in the Toolbox to deselect your title.

Suppose that you made a mistake in the layout text. You wanted to type *Catalog Mailing*. You can modify the text you have just created.

To modify text, follow these steps:

1. Select the Text tool in the Toolbox.
2. Place an insertion point to the right of the word `Catalog`.
3. Type a space and then type *Mailing*.

The titles in the header above each field are too small. To change these titles, you first select them.

To select an object, follow these steps:

1. Click on the Selection tool (the arrow in the Toolbox).
2. Select each field name by clicking on one and then shift-clicking on the rest in turn

   or

   click your mouse and drag a selection marquee (it looks like marching ants). Any object the selection marquee touches is selected.
3. Choose 12 Point from the Size submenu on the Format menu.

You have reached the stage shown in figure 2.13.

Notice that the fields are a little too large. Because ZIP codes have only five numbers, you can resize its field box and make it smaller. When selected, each field box has a small black reshape box at each corner. The reshape box operates in the same fashion as the resize box for a Macintosh window.

To resize a field, follow these steps:

1. Click on any one of the reshape boxes and drag the field to the desired size.

   When you drag a field in the Layout window, FileMaker draws a guideline, called the *baseline*, below where your text will appear. An invisible "magnetic" grid also aids placement of text. You can activate the grid by selecting Align To Grid from the Layout menu.

   The command is check marked when it's on, unchecked when it's off. You also can hold down the ⌘ key while dragging to turn off the magnetic pull of the grid temporarily.
2. Resize the fields so that each has just enough space to accommodate its data. To resize perfectly horizontally or vertically, press the Option key before resizing and hold it down. (If you resize the fields, you also need to move the fields so that they are next to each other.) You can check placement by returning to the Browse window momentarily. Select the Browse command on the Select menu or press ⌘-B to see your new layout. Then return to the Layout window by selecting the Layout command on the Select menu or by pressing ⌘-L.

With these changes, your field names do not line up properly with the field boxes. You need to move them.

To move an object, follow these steps:

1. In the Layout window, make sure that the Selection tool is highlighted. Click it on if it is off.
2. Select each field name in the header section by clicking on it. Drag the field name so that it aligns properly with the left margin of its field box.

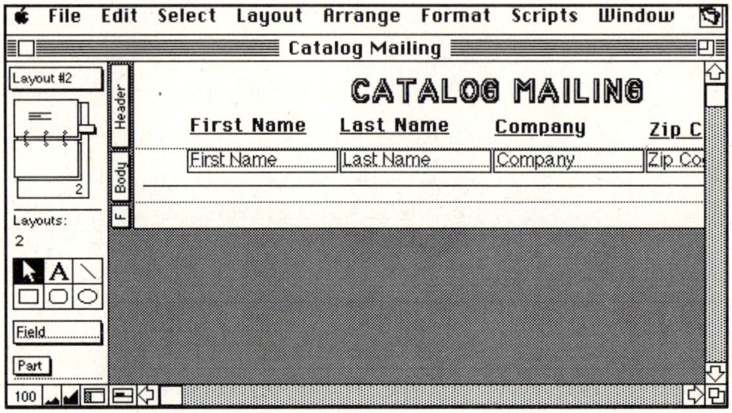

Fig. 2.13
The layout with a title and some formatting changes.

Notice that when you drag a text object, FileMaker draws a baseline, and you can use this baseline to align field names. If you make a mistake, select the Undo Move command on the Edit menu. FileMaker supports the Undo command for nearly all your actions in the Layout window. To complete your formatting, draw a line between each record.

To draw a line, follow these steps:

1. Make room for the line in the body section by clicking the Selection tool, then clicking on the body section boundary (dotted line), and dragging down about 0.25 inch.
2. Click on the Line icon in the Toolbox in the upper right corner.
3. Check the setting of the Line Width control on the status panel. You want a line that is one point thick, which is the default. Click on the Line Width control to access the pop-up menu. See if the line just below the word `Hairline` is checked.
4. Press the Option key to constrain the line to be perfectly horizontal and draw a line underneath all the field reshape boxes, releasing the Option key when you are finished.

Holding down the Option key or the Shift key constrains the line to be perfectly straight. The Shift key allows only 90-degree increments, however; whereas the Option key allows 45-degree increments.

Now your new customer file layout is just the way you want it (see fig. 2.14). Your next step is to work with your records.

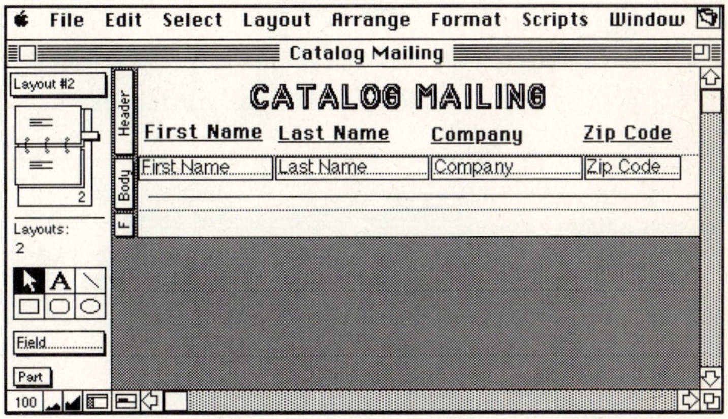

Fig. 2.14
The new columnar report layout with all desired formatting changes.

Organizing Records

When you switch back to the Browse window by selecting the Browse command or by pressing ⌘-B, you see your columnar report (see fig. 2.15). Now multiple records appear on-screen, enabling you to see all your browsed records. In this format, which FileMaker calls a *list*, the selected or *current record* has a black vertical bar next to it. You can tell you are in a list by pulling down the Select menu; the View as List command is checked and active. The program goes to this form automatically when you select the columnar report layout. To select another record in a list, use any of the techniques you learned previously, or just click on a record's data to make that record current.

With your selected records, you can choose to print your database immediately. You can, however, work further with your data set to demonstrate some basic organizational skills.

In this section, you do the following:

- Select a set of records by performing a Find operation
- Add records
- Organize your records by using the Sort command
- Duplicate a record
- Delete a record
- Browse all your records by using the Find All command
- Repeat a previous search by executing a Refind command

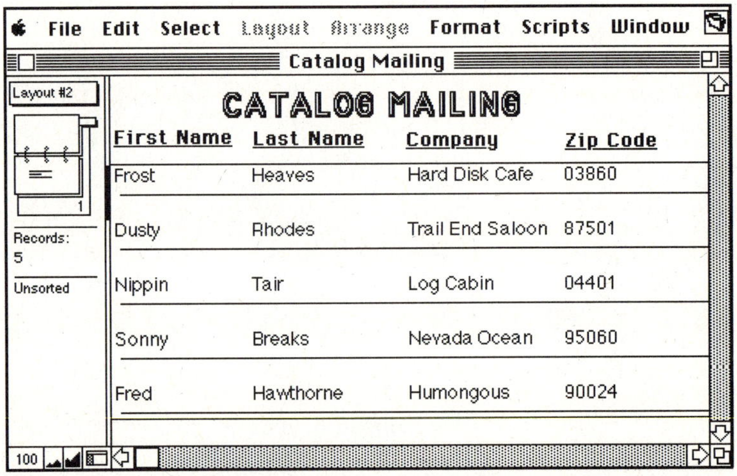

Fig. 2.15 The Browse window corresponding to the layout in figure 2.14.

After you enter data, the data is useless unless you can find it when you need it. Suppose, for instance, that you want to search for a certain range of ZIP codes. With FileMaker, searching for and finding records is easy. When you choose the Find command, FileMaker displays a Find window like the one in figure 2.16. You type the criteria to select records to create a *request*, and then FileMaker chooses a set of records. *Criteria* are what a field must contain (a value or a range of values, logical validating, and so on). *Requests* form a set of criteria that define a search.

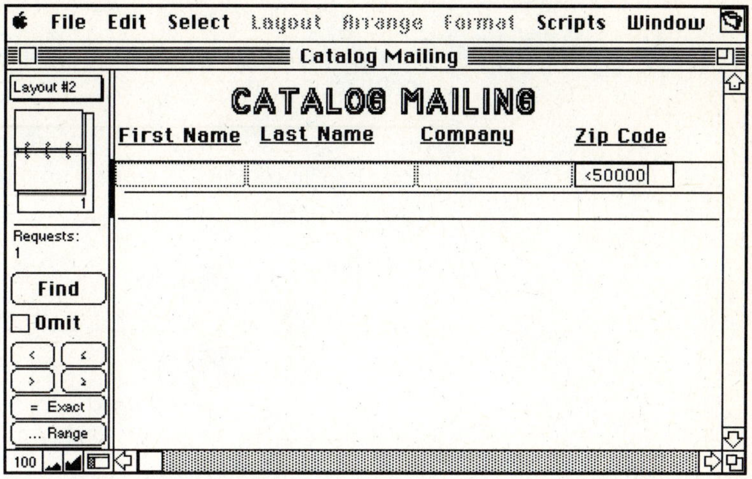

Fig. 2.16
The Find window.

To perform a find, follow these steps:

1. Select the Find command on the Edit menu or press ⌘-F from either the Browse or Layout window.
2. Click in the Zip Code field and enter *<50000*.

   In the Find window, you select fields and move between them by using the Tab key.
3. Click on the Find button in the status area or press the Return or Enter key. FileMaker performs the search and returns the Browse window with all the records selected that met your criteria.

Only two records were found—those for Frost Heaves and Nippin Tair. FileMaker displays the following in the status area:

```
Records:<

5

Found:

2
```

This message indicates that you are now browsing the two records that met the search criteria.

In addition to searching for particular records, you can add records. You first need to switch back to the standard layout to enter your data, because the standard layout contains all the needed fields.

To add three more records, follow these steps:

1. Click on the Layout title box above the Book icon to access the popup menu. Select Layout 1.
2. Select the Browse command on the Select menu or press ⌘-B.
3. Select the New Record command on the Edit menu or press ⌘-N.
4. Enter the following data for record 6:

    Record 6:

    Wye
    Knott
    Fruit and Nuts
    400 Park Avenue South
    New York
    NY
    10103

5. Repeat step 4 and enter data for records 7 and 8:

    Record 7:

    Elysian
    Fields III
    Alter Ego Press
    45 Lexington St. #2
    Newton
    MA
    02165

    Record 8:

    Santa
    Claus
    Way Cool Stores
    1 Northern Boulevard
    North Pole
    NY
    12946

6. Click on the Layout title bar and, using the pop-up menu, switch back to Layout 2.

You have just entered complete records, but the layout shows only four fields. Notice that as you add records 6 through 8, their displayed numbers are 3 through 5 in the browsed set and only the field placed on a layout appears. These records have been added to the found browsed set. Your file has all eight records in it.

Mailing out catalogs randomly is inefficient, because the post office discounts your postage if you sort the mailing by ZIP codes. To sort records, follow these steps:

1. Choose the Sort command in the Select menu or press ⌘-S. The Sort Records dialog box appears (see fig. 2.17).
2. Click on the field name Zip Code to highlight it (which enables the Move button) and click on the Move button. You also can double-click on the Zip Code name to move it into the sort order.

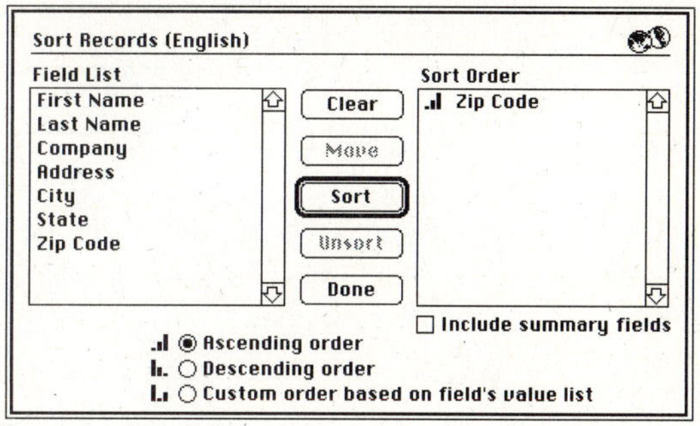

Fig. 2.17
The Sort Records dialog box.

You can sort your fields by ascending or descending order, either alphabetically or numerically (see Chapter 4 for further details). A third choice is a custom order based on a field's value list (see Chapter 5 for details). Ascending order is the default choice and is what you should use.

3. Click on the Sort button or press the Return or Enter key to go to the Browse window shown in figure 2.18.

Your records now are sorted by ZIP code.

Now, send Santa Claus two separate catalog mailings (one is for Ms. Claus). You can do this quickly by duplicating his record.

To duplicate a record, follow these steps:

1. Select Santa Claus's record to make it the current record. Click on any piece of its data.
2. Select the Duplicate Record command from the Edit menu or press ⌘-D.

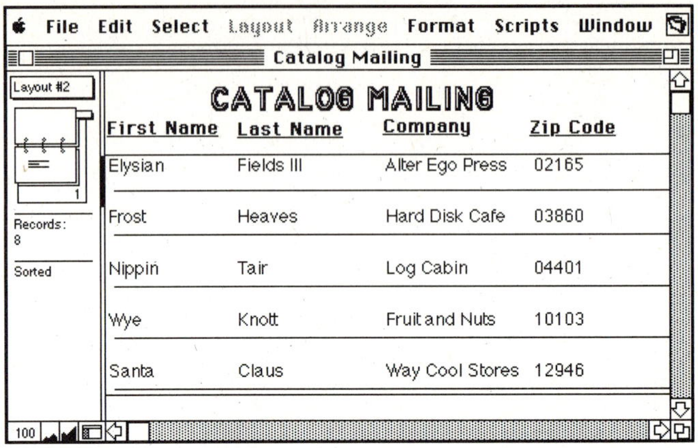

Fig. 2.18
The Browse window with five found records selected and sorted by ZIP code.

Santa's probably out delivering presents, so the Clauses really need only one copy of your catalog after all. You can delete one of the duplicate records.

To delete a record, follow these steps:

1. Click on either of the Santa Claus records to make it the current record or practice selecting records by using one of the other techniques you have learned.
2. Select the Delete Record command on the Edit menu or press ⌘-E.

   An alert box appears, asking `Permanently delete this record?`
3. Click the Delete button.

It's a good idea to keep a printed copy of your mailing list around the office. You can browse all your records by choosing the Find All command on the Select menu (⌘-J). A screen appears that is similar to the one shown in figure 2.19. In the next section, "Printing Your Database," you view what your printed copy will look like.

Printing Your Database

You can print only selected or browsed records. (For more information on printing, see Chapters 9 and 10.) For now, you can use the default settings to print your database.

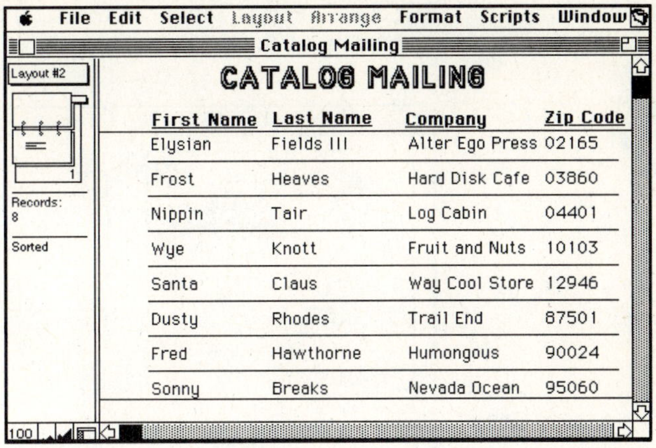

Fig. 2.19
The complete set of eight records in the Browse window of Layout 2.

To preview your printed output, follow these steps (skip to step 4 if you know the correct printer already is selected):

1. Pull down the Apple menu and select the Chooser DA. Click on the icon for an ImageWriter (see fig. 2.20). If you have a LaserWriter, click on that icon and select its name in the scrolling window. For some types of LaserWriters, AppleTalk must be active.

2. Close the Chooser window by clicking in the close box in the upper left corner of the title bar.

3. Choose Page Setup from the File menu. Click OK to accept the default page setup setting, which is US Letter size (8 1/2 inches by 11 inches).

4. Select the Preview command on the Select menu or press ⌘-U.

   In a Preview window, you are shown the exact way your file will print. Figure 2.21 shows the result.

5. Choose Browse on the Select menu or press ⌘-B to return to your field.

If you have trouble with step 2, the default letter-size output may have been changed in the Paper Sizes and Page Setup dialog boxes. If you think this has happened, do one of the following:

- Select the Paper Sizes command and click on the US Letter radio button. Click the OK button or press the Return key. (This option is not available for LaserWriter users.)

- Select the Page Setup command and click on the US Letter radio button. Click the OK button or press the Return key.

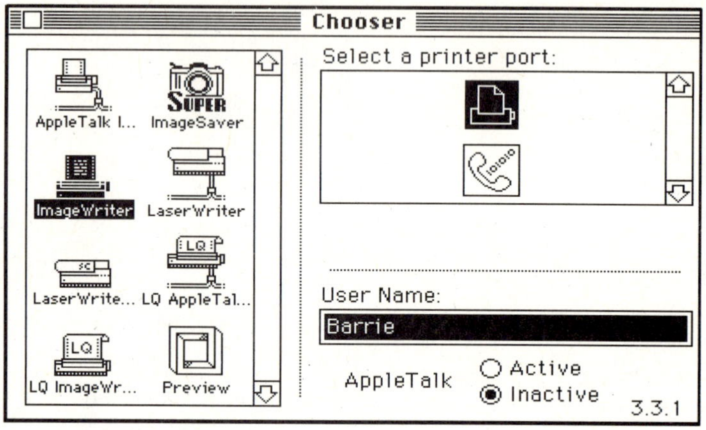

Fig. 2.20
Selecting an ImageWriter in the Chooser desk accessory.

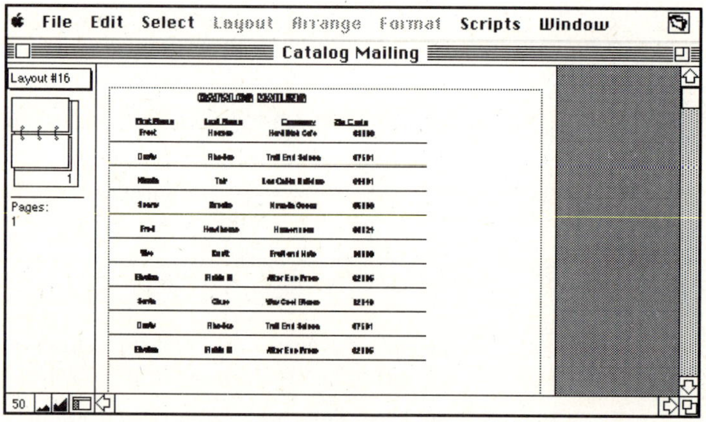

Fig. 2.21
The Preview window for your database file.

If you have an ImageWriter or LaserWriter, you may want to print your records. If not, skip ahead to the paragraphs at the end of this quick start that explains how to save a copy of a file.

To print to an ImageWriter or LaserWriter, follow these steps:

1. Select the Print command or press ⌘-P. The Print dialog box results.
2. Click on the OK button or press Return or Enter.

Perhaps you noticed that you have not saved your work throughout this work session. FileMaker deviates from standard Macintosh practice because it does not have a Save or Save As command on the File menu. Database files are quite large and change quite frequently, so FileMaker has an autosave feature. At regular periods, around 45 seconds of inactivity, FileMaker saves your changes automatically.

Often you may want to save a subset of a data file that you have created and selected in some manner because it is of special value to you. Also, working on a copy is an excellent way to protect your data. FileMaker offers a set of options through its Save a Copy As command on the File menu. You can save a copy of the selected records, save a compressed copy, or save a clone (copy with no records) of the copy under a new name. Chapter 3 describes these options in detail.

To save a copy of a file, follow these steps:

1. Select the Save a Copy As command on the File menu.
2. A standard file Save box appears, suggesting the name "Copy of Catalog Mailing" (see fig. 2.22).
3. Click the Save button or press Return to make the copy.

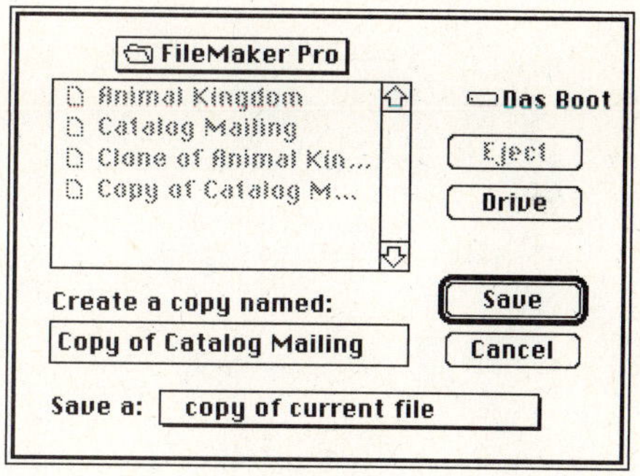

Fig. 2.22
The Save a Copy As dialog box.

Quitting FileMaker

In this quick start, you have used most of the important commands to perform basic data entry and file manipulation. FileMaker has many more shortcuts and power features that you can learn by reading the following chapters. If you want to continue using hands-on tutorials, do so. The next quick start (Chapter 8) teaches you how to work with forms.

Because you now have a copy of your file, feel free to continue practicing techniques you have learned in this quick start, experiment with new layouts, or try out the Toolbox options. Be sure, however, to save a copy of your file for the future quick starts.

To quit FileMaker, select the Quit command on the File menu or press ⌘-Q.

CHAPTER 3

Creating a File

This chapter provides some basic information on using your Macintosh. You will find a brief explanation of how to use the Finder and file system; how to use the mouse to select items, give commands, and make choices in a dialog box; and how to use windows. This chapter emphasizes commands you need to operate FileMaker. If you are a beginner, you will find enough information in the section, "Reviewing Macintosh Basics," to make you feel comfortable with using FileMaker. If you are an advanced user of the Macintosh, you may want to skip to the section, "Launching the Program."

In this chapter, you learn how FileMaker implements the general database concepts you learned in Chapter 2. The full range of data types or field attributes that the Macintosh allows can be organized in a FileMaker file. If you have worked with other Macintosh applications, such as Microsoft Excel or Microsoft Works, you will recognize some of the data types, such as Text, Number, and Date. FileMaker also recognizes graphics of all types, such as draw or paint, which enable you to construct "picture-book" databases.

Information related to creating a file, defining fields, setting field types, creating records, getting help, saving files, and quitting FileMaker is discussed in this chapter. You also will find an amplification of many of the steps covered in the preceding chapter, "Quick Start: Creating a Database." When you have finished reading this chapter, you will know many of the basic details of handling data in a FileMaker file.

Reviewing Macintosh Basics

Many of the features that make the Macintosh special reside in a set of computer instructions called the Toolbox, which has been encoded in the Macintosh memory chips. To create a Macintosh program, a programmer must adhere to the design principles dictated by Apple in the construction of the Macintosh. The basic idea is that when you learn how to work with one Macintosh program, you learn skills that will help you to learn any other Macintosh program.

The Macintosh was one of the first computers to use what is called a *graphical user interface*. A graphical user interface (GUI) is a screen that contains pictures, each of which is associated with an action and is meant to look like the function it performs. An icon is the common graphical element. Icons are small pictures that represent such things as a disk or hard drive, a file, an organized collection of files called a *folder*, a program file, and so on. Icons have actions associated with them. You place the *cursor* on the icon, double-click, and the appropriate function is performed. For example, if you double-click on a disk icon, a window opens and shows you the disk's contents. After a program has started, some icons perform an action if you click on them once.

When you turn on a Macintosh equipped with a hard drive or insert a disk that contains the necessary system files, a screen similar to the one shown in figure 3.1 appears. You can see several elements of the Macintosh: icons, a menu bar, and windows. These elements are used by all Macintosh programs to perform actions, and they are discussed in detail in the sections that follow.

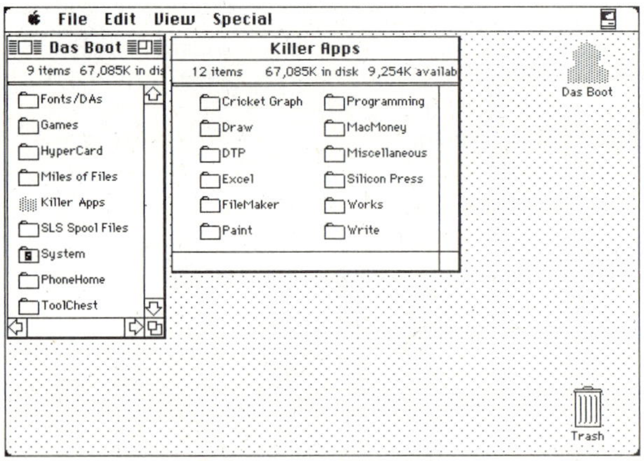

Fig. 3.1
The Macintosh desktop in MultiFinder.

Your Macintosh contains what is called an *operating system*, which is a program that tells your computer what to do, in what order, and by whom. The operating system allocates memory—a complex and dynamic process—monitors for conditions that will cause problems, and does many basic housekeeping chores in order to keep your computer running smoothly. Few users want to be bothered with these details, so the Macintosh shields you from this unnecessary complexity by using a program called the Finder. The Finder is responsible for all the graphical elements you see on your screen. When you start your Macintosh or quit FileMaker to return to the desktop, you are working with the Finder.

Different versions of the Finder exist. System Software 6.0.5 was used for this book. Starting with System version 5, Apple introduced a more powerful version of the Finder, called MultiFinder. In Finder, only one program can run at a time. You must quit one program to work with a different program. MultiFinder offers the option of reserving a place in memory for several programs. The number of programs you can use depends on the amount of memory you have in your computer. The advantage to MultiFinder is that you can switch back and forth rapidly between programs. You always can tell when you are in MultiFinder because the small Macintosh icon in the right section of the menu bar is missing when you are in the Finder.

Using the Mouse and Keyboard

The one-button mouse that comes with your Macintosh is a distinctive input device that enables you to select and manipulate objects on your screen. A pointer or cursor appears on your screen, and you can manipulate it by moving your mouse. The cursor's shape tells you what operations are available to you at the moment. The *arrow cursor* is associated with selection, and an *I-beam cursor* is associated with insertion. You make a selection or insert the cursor by *clicking* the mouse. Some actions require two clicks in rapid succession, which is called *double-clicking*. *Dragging* is another action that you perform with the mouse by holding down the mouse button and "dragging" the mouse across the desk. This action is often used to define an area you want to modify. Dragging is complete when you release the mouse button.

The mouse usually is used to select objects. When you click on an object, that object is selected. By clicking on an object and dragging it, you can move the object to the new position indicated by the outline. You also can move a group of selected objects in the same manner.

To select a set of objects, follow these steps:

1. Click on the first object in the selection.
2. Hold down the Shift key and click on the next object to add it to your selection.

You can select a set of objects by dragging the mouse to create a rectangle on-screen. This rectangle is called a *marquee*. When you release the mouse button, all the objects the marquee touches or encompasses are selected.

To remove an object from a selected range of objects, hold down the Shift key and click on the object. To deselect all objects, click anywhere outside the selection.

You use the keyboard to enter text, and you also can issue commands with certain combinations of keys pressed together, which are called *keystrokes*. If you know how to type, a Macintosh keyboard should be familiar to you. *Modifier keys* are the extra keys on the keyboard that you also need to know about.

The four modifier keys are as follows:

- The Shift key
- The Command key (⌘)
- The Option key
- The Control key

When you press modifier keys, they change the action of other keys. Using the Shift key places uppercase letters and symbols on your screen. The Command key performs commands; these commands often are called *keystroke equivalents*, because they are equivalent to another mouse action. The Option key can modify other keystrokes, or it can modify a cursor action. The Option key also gives Mac users easy access to an extended alphanumeric key set. The Control key, missing from some keyboards, is not used in the FileMaker program, but it is used for some telecommunication programs. Modifier keys greatly enhance the functionality of your keyboard.

In addition to the keyboard character set, some other special keys deserve explanation. The Enter key tells your application program to enter data, to format, and to perform calculations. Often, but not always, the Enter key is equivalent to the Return key. The Return key also serves as a carriage return when you are typing text. Most FileMaker actions use Enter or Return for the same action. The Tab key is a movement key.

When you enter data, pressing the Tab key moves you to the next space in which data can be placed. The Backspace key, called the Delete key on some keyboards, removes a character at the left of the insertion point. The Clear key removes a selection. Clear and Enter keys often are placed on the numeric keypad.

Using Windows

A window is a frame used to view and manipulate objects, which can be files or folders. A folder is a conventional means of organizing your files and other folders. Double-click on your drive or disk icon, and a window opens. Select a folder and double-click on it, and the folder opens. Just as Finder uses windows, FileMaker uses several windows to manipulate files. Now look at some of the common elements of a Macintosh window. The special elements of FileMaker windows will be discussed at the appropriate time.

Macintosh windows are part of the Toolbox. Actually, they are programmed into the operating system and have some common elements (see fig. 3.2). Several windows can be open at the same time on your desktop (FileMaker allows 16 in Finder and 14 in MultiFinder), but only one window—the active window—can be manipulated at a time. You activate a window by clicking on it, and the active window is indicated by a six-line striped title bar along the top border. You can move and resize the windows, and *scroll bars* are used to move around inside a window.

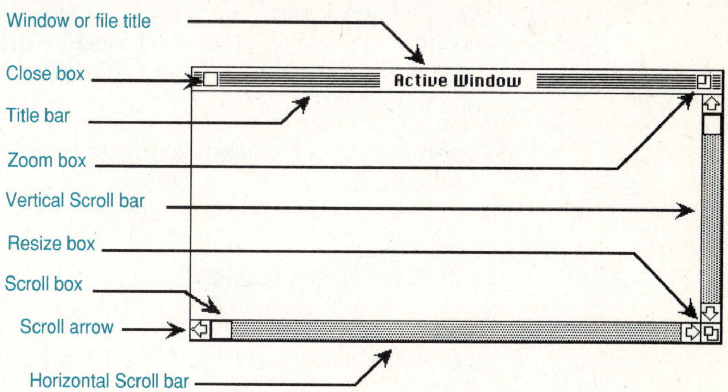

Fig. 3.2
A standard Macintosh window.

Up to 16 files may be opened in FileMaker II and Filemaker Pro, instead of 8 in FileMaker Plus.

The following list summarizes the parts of a standard Macintosh window and the actions you can perform with them:

Close box. Click this box to close the window. In FileMaker, clicking this box closes the file.

Horizontal scroll bar. This scroll bar works in the same manner as the vertical scroll bar, but it moves in the horizontal direction.

Resize box. The resize box is sometimes called a grow box; you drag it to resize a window.

Scroll arrow. A single click on a scroll arrow moves the window contents one increment in that direction. An increment may be one line in a word processing program, for example. Each application program defines the increment. Hold down your mouse button on the scroll arrow, and your window contents continue to scroll.

Scroll box. The scroll box indicates relative position in the window. Additionally, you can drag the scroll box any distance to view a window's contents.

Title bar. The Title bar gives the file name and indicates whether the window is active. Drag this bar to move a window on the screen. Hold down the Command key and drag to move a window without making it the active window.

Vertical scroll bar. The vertical scroll bar indicates your vertical position inside a window. Click once in the bar above the box to move up one full window; click once in the bar below the box to move down one full window.

Zoom box. Click this box to toggle between a window size you set and a full-screen size.

Resizing or Moving Windows

When you open a window, Macintosh remembers both the cursor location and the size of the window the last time you closed it.

To resize a window, do one of the following:

- Drag the resize box until the window is the desired size and then release the mouse button.

- Click on the zoom box to toggle between the window size you set and one full-screen size; or, when in FileMaker, press the ⌘-Shift-Z keystroke equivalent.

⌘-Shift-Z toggles the window size between the size you set and a full-screen size, which simulates the action of clicking on the zoom box.

To move a window, drag the window's title bar to the desired location and then release the button. To move a window without activating it, hold down the Command key and then drag the title bar to the desired location before releasing the button.

To scroll the window, use one of the following methods:

- Use the horizontal scroll bar to move horizontally; use the vertical scroll bar to move vertically.
- Click on the arrow to move one line at a time.
- Click and hold to continue scrolling (or moving) a window.
- Click on the scroll bar once to move one full window in the desired direction.
- Drag the scroll box to move any amount in the window.

The scroll box indicates the relative position of your view of the contents window. If you are in the middle of a file, the scroll box is in the middle of the scroll bar, regardless of the file size. If the file contains less than one full window of material, the scroll bars are disabled (they appear white instead of gray).

Switching Windows

You can activate a window by clicking on it anywhere. Some programs, including FileMaker, offer you a Window menu that enables you to choose the active window. Because FileMaker displays only one window per file, you can have 16 files open on your desktop and 16 windows showing on your Window menu. When a window is active in FileMaker, the file is active. This file is referred to as the *current file*. A sample FileMaker Window menu is shown in figure 3.3.

FileMaker indicates which file is the current file by check marking it on the Window menu, in addition to showing it as an active window that is above all other windows. Other windows are listed in the order in which they overlap, from the top of your desktop to the bottom—just like the desktop in your office.

Fig. 3.3
The FileMaker Window menu.

To switch files, do one of the following:

- Click on the desired file to activate it.
- Drag down the Window menu until the desired window name (or, for FileMaker, the file name) is highlighted; then release the mouse button to activate the window.

Hiding Windows

FileMaker offers an additional option that does not follow standard Macintosh window practice. Usually, when you have an open file that is stored or retained in memory, that file window is open on your screen. By using FileMaker's Hide Window command, however, you can remove that window from your screen to cut down on window clutter while keeping the window in memory for quicker retrieval. Another reason for hiding a window is to keep it available for other users on a network when you don't want to work with that file yourself.

To hide a FileMaker window, follow these steps:

1. Make that window active (the current file).
2. Select the Hide Window command on the Window menu.

FileMaker removes that window from your screen and encloses the file name in parentheses in the Window menu to indicate that it is hidden.

When you open a FileMaker file that contains lookup fields, the files that were used to import the data into your current file are opened, but the windows remain hidden. This feature is useful when you want to be certain that the lookup was what you wanted to enter or if you want to change your lookup reference. See Chapter 5, "Automating Data Entry," for more information.

To make a file visible, select that file on the Window menu.

Opening and Closing Windows

In the Finder, you double-click on a folder icon or file icon to open its window. Because FileMaker windows are specific to their related files, opening a FileMaker window is equivalent to opening a file. You use the Open command with the file selected. Closing a window can be done using the same method in either Finder or FileMaker.

In FileMaker, you open a file to make it the current file by selecting it from the Window menu. If the file is closed, select the Open command. Move to the folder where the file is located, and select the file name by clicking on it. Click the Open button in the Open dialog box. For more information on opening a file and working with the Macintosh file system, see Chapter 4, "Editing, Finding, and Sorting Records."

SPEED KEY

⌘-O, the Open command, initiates the open file sequence.

To close a window in Finder, use one of these methods:

- Click on the window close box. In Finder, holding down the Option key while clicking on the close box closes all windows on your desktop.
- Select the Close command on the File menu or press ⌘-W to close a window or file.

SPEED KEY

⌘-W, the Close command, closes a file window.

⌘-Q, the Quit command, exits the FileMaker Pro program.

Accessing the Menus

You issue commands to your Macintosh by using the menu or command equivalents. Each word in the menu bar is a pull-down menu of commands that you may issue. From left to right, you always find the Apple, File, and Edit menus. Different applications create different menus. Depending on the current condition, menu items (commands) and entire menus can be enabled or disabled (they are dimmed when disabled). You cannot issue or select a disabled command.

FileMaker has several menus of its own: Select, Format, Layout, Arrange, Scripts, and Window. The Select menu enables you to switch your current mode of operation in the program. The Format, Layout, and Arrange menus offer choices that help you work with the way your data is displayed and handled internally. The Window menu enables you to switch between open files on your desktop. The Scripts menu is where automatic actions you create are placed and accessed. You can find detailed information about these menus in Appendix C, "Menu Summary."

When you click on a menu name and drag down with the arrow cursor, the commands on the menu are highlighted in turn. You can select a command by releasing the mouse button when the desired command is highlighted (see fig. 3.4). In figure 3.4, choosing the Show option brings up a submenu, from which you make another choice. If you decide that you do not want to make a menu selection, drag the selection arrow cursor off the menu.

Fig. 3.4
Selecting commands from a submenu.

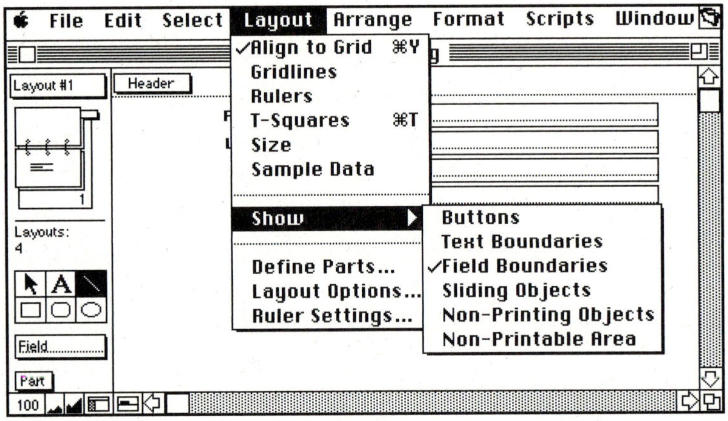

Notice that the menu offers additional pieces of information, such as whether there is a command key equivalent. When a command has an associated dialog box, the command name is followed by an ellipsis (...). Also, menu items sometimes show an arrow, indicating that there is a submenu. When you drag in that direction, the submenu choices are displayed.

Using Dialog and Alert Boxes

Whenever you need to make choices associated with commands or provide settings or choose among options, Macintosh and FileMaker present a dialog box (see fig. 3.5). The purpose of a dialog box is to elicit a response from you. That response can be a simple yes, proceed with the operation; or cancel, do not proceed and return to the current condition. Usually, a dialog box has some standard choices called *defaults*, which you can change.

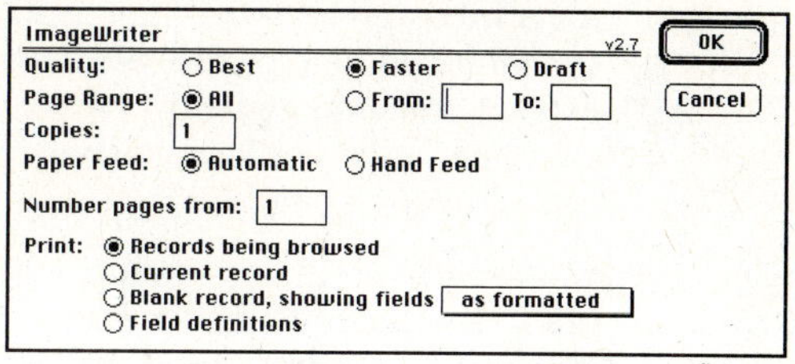

Fig. 3.5
A typical dialog box.

Following is a summary of the elements of a standard Macintosh dialog box:

Buttons. Click on a button to carry out the action indicated. Usually, an OK button executes the command with the settings shown. A Cancel button returns you to the previous screen without executing the command. Usually, the Macintosh enables you to select any button with a double outline—OK, for example—by pressing the Return or Enter key. Usually, but not always, you can execute Cancel by pressing ⌘-. (⌘-period).

Radio buttons. Radio buttons are sets of circles. Usually, only one of the circles has a dot in it. Click on one of the other circles, and the dot disappears from the circle it was in and reappears in the circle you have just clicked. The black dot indicates that the button is turned on.

Check boxes. Check boxes are squares that can display an X. The X indicates that the associated option is active. Click on the X, and the X disappears; the associated option is disabled. Unlike radio buttons, you can click on as many check boxes as options you want to enable or disable.

Disabled selections. Any option not available is dimmed. Some options do not make sense for a particular situation, and your Macintosh makes them unavailable. For example, if you have a Macintosh that isn't on a network, it doesn't make sense to have the network button enabled. Your Macintosh dims this button in the Open File dialog box. Text boxes, radio buttons, and so on also may be disabled and dimmed when not available.

Text boxes. These boxes allow the entry of text characters. Usually, you can edit text boxes, and you can go from text box to text box by pressing the Tab key. Many FileMaker text boxes support the use of the Clipboard; see the following section, "Using Desk Accessories and the Clipboard."

Alert boxes. Whenever you are about to perform an operation that cannot be undone or recovered from, your Macintosh posts an alert box to warn you. You generally can proceed by clicking an OK button (or pressing the Return key) or abort the operation by clicking the Cancel button (or pressing ⌘-.).

Whenever you perform an unusual operation or one potentially dangerous to data, particularly one that cannot be undone, your Macintosh displays an alert box. An alert box is easily recognizable because of the triangle with an exclamation point in it. FileMaker provides one of the best sets of alert boxes found in any Macintosh application. When FileMaker posts an alert box, you should stop, read it once or twice, and then proceed. Usually, an alert box has as a default the action that provides for recovery. Figure 3.6 shows a FileMaker alert box.

Fig. 3.6
A FileMaker alert box.

Using Desk Accessories and the Clipboard

A *desk accessory*, or DA, is a small application or program that may be chosen from the Apple menu (see fig. 3.7). DAs can be calculators, note pads, full-feature draw or paint programs, scrapbooks for graphics, and file managers (substitute Finders). The list of DAs and their uses is nearly endless. DAs run above an application. When opened, some DAs add an extra menu to your program, always to the right on the menu bar. When you are in Finder, using DAs is like having another window open in a program. Click on the DA, and the DA is active. In MultiFinder, a DA is run in its own program layer but is still activated by clicking in its window. To close a DA, click in the close box of its window, or choose a Quit command from the DA menu.

By choosing the About FileMaker command from the Apple menu, you can discover the version of FileMaker that you are using. The introductory graphic shown in figure 3.8 also displays how much memory is available on the current drive. Click on the window to remove it.

Fig. 3.7
The Apple menu for FileMaker, in Finder (l) and in MultiFinder (r).

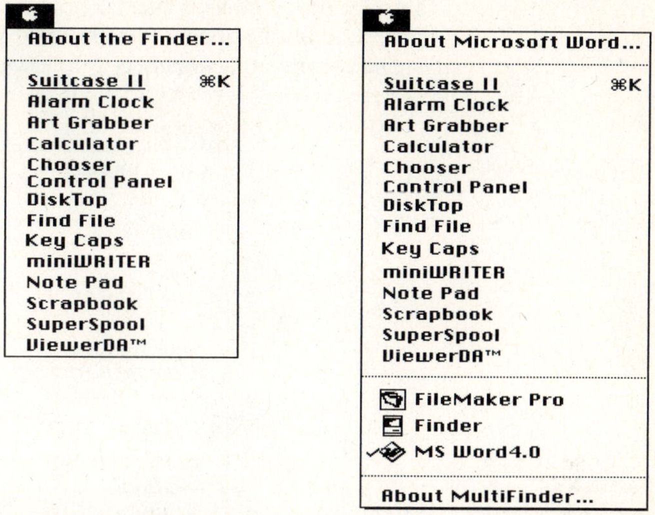

Fig. 3.8
The About FileMaker box.

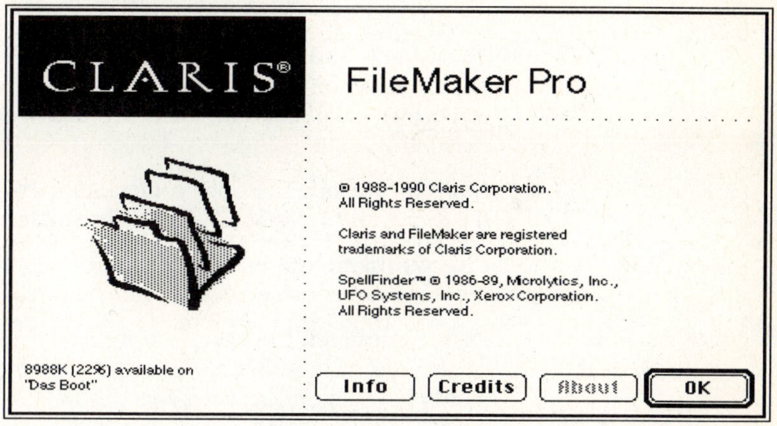

The Clipboard is an important part of the Macintosh operating system. The Clipboard allows for the importing and exporting of information between applications. The Clipboard is actually a section of memory that can hold whatever is cut or copied from a document. The Clipboard's contents remain intact until new information is cut or copied to it. Information can include both text and graphics in a number of different formats.

Consider the actions on FileMaker's Edit menu (see fig. 3.9). A summary of the available Clipboard options and the options that are basic to the Macintosh operating system is as follows:

Fig. 3.9
FileMaker's Edit menu.

Clear command. Clear removes a selection and bypasses the Clipboard. The Clear key on your numeric keypad is the equivalent of this menu command. (Sometimes the Delete or Backspace key performs this function.)

Copy command. The Copy command places a copy of a selection onto the Clipboard. Press ⌘-C as an equivalent keystroke.

Cut command. Cut places a selection onto the Clipboard and removes it from your document. ⌘-X is the equivalent keystroke.

Paste command. Use Paste to place a copy of the contents of the Clipboard onto your screen. There are some restrictions on the placement of certain information. The ⌘-V keystroke can initiate this command.

Paste Special command. This option opens a submenu containing commands used to paste information into layouts, records, or requests. Paste Special is an easy way to enter time, date, and number information.

Undo command. Undo reverses the preceding action, but is not always available in FileMaker. You can select this command with the ⌘-Z keystroke.

Other commands on the Edit menu are discussed in the appropriate sections and chapters that follow in this book.

SPEED KEY

⌘-Z, the Undo command, reverses the preceding action.

⌘-X, the Cut command, places a selection onto the Clipboard and removes it from your screen.

⌘-C, the Copy command, places a copy of your selection onto the Clipboard.

⌘-V, the Paste command, places a copy of your Clipboard contents onto your screen.

Clear on the numeric keypad, the Clear command, removes a selection and bypasses the Clipboard. Clear is sometimes the equivalent to the Delete or Backspace key.

Many programs allow you to view the Clipboard. In Finder or MultiFinder, you can view the contents of the Clipboard in a scrollable window that opens when you select the Show Clipboard command on the Edit menu. FileMaker supports the use of the Clipboard, but it does not offer a specific command to enable Clipboard viewing. Third-party DAs, like SmartScrap and the Clipper, will enhance the actions of the Clipboard while in FileMaker.

Launching the Program

FileMaker will run properly in either Finder or MultiFinder with only a few operational differences. In System 7, only MultiFinder is available to you. MultiFinder offers some definite advantages for running FileMaker. Its major advantage is that it enables you to switch quickly from one application to another. Click in a FileMaker window, and FileMaker is active; click in a word processor window, and the word processor is active, and so on. This capability enables you to use the Clipboard to cut, copy, and paste information between FileMaker and other applications without having to open and quit each application—a great timesaver. Finder requires you to quit each program in turn to use the Clipboard between applications or to switch applications. See Chapter 16 for more information.

Certain other operations, such as background printing (which also requires certain hardware and software), lengthy sorts, and finds also are enabled in MultiFinder, which allows you to continue working in

MultiFinder or in another application while the operations go on. Be aware that background processing significantly slows down the operation of your Macintosh.

To launch FileMaker from Finder or MultiFinder, open the folder containing the FileMaker program and double-click on the icon. Alternatively, click on the icon to select it and then select the Open command on the File menu or press ⌘-O.

If you have FileMaker open but not active in MultiFinder, you can activate the program by selecting its name from the Apple menu or by clicking on the small icon at the extreme right of the menu bar until FileMaker appears.

If you are running FileMaker for the first time, you are asked to personalize your copy (see Appendix B for details). If you already have run the program, you see a screen similar to the one in figure 3.8; it appears on your screen while FileMaker loads and is replaced by the Open File dialog box shown in figure 3.10.

Fig. 3.10
The Open File dialog box.

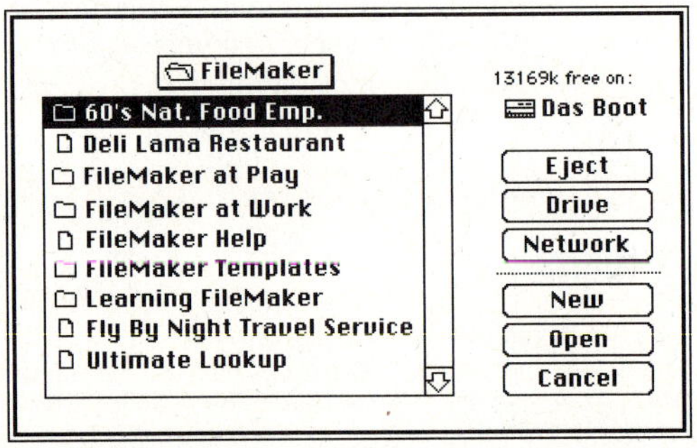

Following is a summary of the Open File dialog box options:

Cancel button. Selecting Cancel removes the dialog box and leaves you with only the FileMaker menu bar open on the screen. If you have previously opened files, they also are open. Pressing ⌘-. (period) also initiates this action.

Das Boot. Das Boot is the name of the current drive or volume in this example. (It's not the name of an ill-fated German submarine.) Your drive name will differ. A drive is a floppy or hard disk drive that can store your files. The drive that contains your system file is commonly called the boot drive.

Drive button. With more than one drive or volume mounted, this button is active; otherwise, it is dimmed. Click this button to switch drives.

Eject button. If you have an ejectable disk (a floppy), this button is enabled; otherwise, it is dimmed. Click to eject the disk. Note that the icon for the disk remains on the desktop.

Network button. If your computer is connected to a network, this button is enabled; otherwise, it is dimmed. Click to go to the network Open File dialog box and navigate to the desired file.

New button. Click New to create a file. See the next section, "Creating a Data File," for details.

Open button. Click Open to open the highlighted folder or file. Pressing the Return or Enter key also initiates this action.

Finding and opening files by navigating the Macintosh file system is covered in Chapter 4. See Chapter 17 or refer to your network documentation if you need additional help in opening a file on your network.

Creating a Data File

You create a file by clicking the New button in the Open File dialog box or by giving the New command on the Edit menu. FileMaker then puts a Create a New File dialog box on-screen (see fig. 3.11). Although you can have only 16 files open in FileMaker, you can create any number of files you want, within the limit of your disk storage space.

Fig. 3.11
The Create a New File dialog box.

To create a file, follow these steps:

1. Launch FileMaker and click the New Button in the Open File dialog box.

   or

   If you already are in FileMaker, select the New command on the File menu.

   The Create a New File dialog box prompts you to enter a file name in the text box (see fig. 3.11).

2. Enter a name for the file.

3. Open the folder in which you want to store your new file and click the New button or press the Return or Enter key. The Define Fields dialog box appears (see the next section, "Defining Fields").

The meanings of the Eject, Drive, and New buttons, and the Current Disk icon of the Create a New File dialog box are identical to those in the Open File dialog box. The New button has a somewhat different action; in the Create a New File dialog box, the New button actually creates the file.

Defining Fields

When you are creating a file, you start by defining the fields. This process is called the define mode, and you can return to the define mode at any time by selecting the Define Fields command on the Select menu. You always know that you are in the define mode because the Define Fields dialog box is open on your screen.

Defining fields has been expanded in FileMaker Pro. Time has been added as a new field type. The order in which fields appear can now be changed by pressing the field order icon in the upper right corner, or fields can be dragged manually to any order desired.

SPEED KEY

⌘-Shift-D, a Define Fields speed key, has been added to FileMaker Pro.

The define mode is where you create fields, assign attributes, set entry options (like auto-enter, validation, and lookups), and create logical, mathematical, and summary fields. In this section of the chapter, you are introduced to most of the mechanics of working with the Define Fields dialog box. Refer to Chapter 5 for a discussion of the entry options and calculation and summary fields. Whenever you want to change the manner in which data is handled by FileMaker, return to the Define Fields dialog box by using the Define command or its ⌘-Shift-D keystroke equivalent. The Define command is a central feature of FileMaker, and you are well advised to understand all of its options and its power.

To define a field, follow these steps:

1. Select the Define Fields command from the Select menu.
2. Enter a name in the Field Name text box and click the desired field type radio button or press its command key equivalent. You can enter a name that starts with an alphabetic character, and the name can have as many as 63 characters. See the next section, "Specifying Field Attributes," for information on field types.
3. Click the OK button or press the Return or Enter key.

In figure 3.12, you see a Define Fields dialog box for a file, with some field names already defined. Their definition includes the field types and any entry options you defined. When you first open this dialog box, the field name text boxes are blank, and the Text radio button is the default.

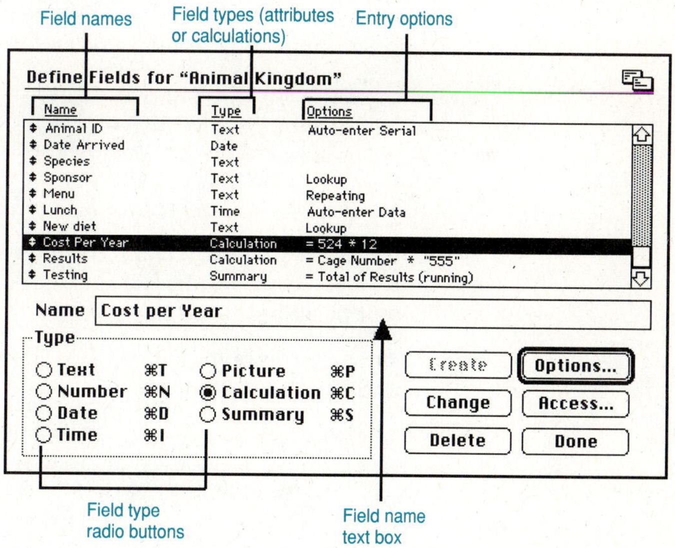

Fig. 3.12
The Define Fields dialog box for an established file.

The field name is limited to 63 characters. This limit increases the speed of any operation for which FileMaker requires a field name.

When you enter field names, do not use a name that starts with a number or a period if you plan to use that field in a calculation. Also, do not use the following operator symbols or words:

* / + – & ^ = < > ( ) " and, or, not, today

FileMaker has difficulty with names that contain these characters when you use them in calculation or summary fields because they are operators.

A summary of the Define Fields dialog box actions follows:

Access button. This button lets you set Access Privileges that can limit a group's access to particular fields or layouts; see Chapter 17 for further discussion.

Change button. The Change button is enabled whenever you select an existing field and edit it. Clicking the Change button makes the edits take effect.

Create button. The Create button allows you to continue creating, modifying, or deleting fields. Clicking this button does not return you to your file. It is only active when you have selected a field name or entered some characters in the Field Name text box. Use the Return or Enter key to initiate this action.

Delete button. Choosing Delete deletes a selected field. Delete is only enabled when a field is selected. When clicked, FileMaker posts an alert box asking whether you want to remove the field and all the information it contains. ***This action cannot be undone.***

Double-arrows control. Double arrows appear to the left of each field name. By selecting any double arrow, you are able to drag the fields to different positions.

Exit button. This button closes the Define Fields dialog box and returns you to your file.

Field Type radio buttons. Use these buttons to select a field type or attribute. You can choose a radio button by clicking it or by pressing the ⌘-T, ⌘-N, ⌘-D, ⌘-I, ⌘-P, ⌘-C, or ⌘-S keystrokes for the Text, Number, Date, Time, Picture, Calculation, and Summary radio buttons, respectively. These shortcuts operate only when the Define Fields dialog box is open.

Field View icon. This icon appears in the upper right corner of the Define Fields dialog box and enables you to view the field order in different ways. A pop-up menu appears when you press the icon. The following options are available: View by Creation Order, View by Field Name, View by Field Type, View by Custom Order.

Name text box. This box is a standard Macintosh text box into which you can enter a name that starts with an alphabetic character and is up to 63 characters long. FileMaker allows blanks between characters here.

Options button. This button is enabled whenever a field is selected. The resulting options' dialog boxes allow for a variety of options; see Chapter 5 for further discussion.

SPEED KEY

⌘-T sets a Text field type in the Define Fields dialog box.

⌘-N sets a Number field type in the Define Fields dialog box.

⌘-D sets a Date field type in the Define Fields dialog box.

⌘-I sets a Time field type in the Define Fields dialog box.

⌘-P sets a Picture field type in the Define Fields dialog box.

⌘-C sets a Calculation field type in the Define Fields dialog box.

⌘-S sets a Summary field type in the Define Fields dialog box.

⌘-Shift-D brings up the Define Fields dialog box.

Specifying Field Attributes

FileMaker stores your data in fields and requires you to define the data that can go into those fields. By specifying the appropriate data, you tell FileMaker how to manipulate the data you enter, and you also optimize the speed at which operations can be accomplished. Think of field types—field attributes—as boxes for your data. When you define a box as a certain type, only that kind of data can be entered into it. Round pegs go into round holes, and square pegs go into square holes. Dates go into Date fields, and numbers go into Number fields.

Your data can be in the form of text, numbers, dates, times, or pictures. These are the five basic *field attributes*, or data types, that FileMaker offers you. Two other field attributes, calculation and summary fields, are derived—or logical—fields. You don't enter data into calculation or summary fields; FileMaker does that automatically. Also, when you export data to another application, FileMaker does not export calculation or summary fields. These field types are discussed in Chapter 5.

Defining field attributes limits the allowed operations to only those that are appropriate to the data type. For instance, you can enter only a date in a Date field. Numbers and dates can be subtracted to give logical results (1/16/90 – 1/1/90 = 15 days), but you wouldn't want to try to subtract two pictures, generally speaking.

Text Fields

Text is any character that you can type from your keyboard: any letter, number, or punctuation mark that you can enter. Choose Text when mixing numbers, letters, and other characters together, or when you're unsure of what to use. You always can change field attributes later on. Your Macintosh adheres to a standard called the American Standard Code for Information Interchange, commonly called the ASCII code. This code is a table of allowed characters that your computer recognizes. Even keyboard operations such as end-of-line symbols (carriage return or Return), spaces, and tabs are accounted for in the ASCII table. Not all fonts, however, can display the entire ASCII code. The ASCII code has an order to it that allows all symbols and characters to be sorted.

Special fonts, such as Cairo, Zapf Dingbats, or Adobe Carta, create additional symbols or pictures that aren't found in the code on your screen. These fonts have a translation table to relate each symbol to an ASCII equivalent, so if you use them they will appear in your Browse screen. FileMaker is unable to enter special fonts in the field index; instead, it enters the keystroke that created the symbol. For example, in the font called Symbol, the letter "b" is displayed as β. Use a beta, and FileMaker puts the letter "b" in the index. Field indexes are described in the section, "Using the Index," later in this chapter.

> **Tip**
>
> Use picture fonts in Text fields instead of using Picture fields or layout graphics. Picture fonts speed up screen display and search operations, but they place meaningless single letters in your index.

A Text field can be very large: any set of characters up to 32,000. This limit is set by the internal Macintosh system software; each 32K chunk is the size of a block of data that can be swapped in and out of RAM (random-access memory) at a time. If you type 32,000 characters and format the text at 9 points, the result is about 16 pages of text. The maximum size of a layout is 36 inches by 36 inches (a square yard), and it's impossible to output a Text field this large.

A Text field provides the fewest restrictions on what characters can be entered in a field, but it also limits the operations that can be performed on those characters. Although you can sort text in ascending or descending order by ASCII code, and you can do certain calculations and summations with text, the range of mathematical and logical functions you can use is limited. You can, for example, use the COUNT( ) function to provide the number of data entries, or you can use Boolean operators (equal to, NOT, OR, and so on), but you cannot use multiplication on text; it doesn't make sense. For information on functions and operators, see Chapter 5.

Number Fields

You can place any character you want in a Number field, as you can in a Text field. FileMaker handles numbers differently from text, and you should pay particular attention to these differences. The two most important differences are that Number fields only recognize numbers when they are being indexed, and you are required to enter an exact string in a find.

Date Fields

Built into your Macintosh is a clock system based on *serial dates*. All Macintosh applications, including FileMaker, use this system to do date and time calculations and conversions. A serial date is assigned an integer starting with 1; each day is incremented by 1; and each hour is incremented by its decimal equivalent. Because serial dates are numeric, you can use dates in calculations: add, subtract, choose a minimum or maximum, and so on. The Macintosh clock starts on Sunday, January 1, 1904 (DAY 1.0), which is the first day of the first year of this century that started on a Sunday. The last Macintosh serial date is December 31, 2039.

To change dates and time, use the Control Panel desk accessory or the Alarm Clock desk accessory. Consult your Macintosh manual for details.

Time Fields

When a time field is selected, the time is displayed as you typed it. However, when you leave the field, the appearance of the time reflects any formatting specified in layout mode.

The Define Fields box can be used to specify automatic time entry, yet you can still edit the value in the field. To prohibit modification of automatically entered time, select this option under the Options button.

The Time field attribute is new to FileMaker Pro.

Picture Fields

If you define a field as a Picture field, FileMaker allows you to place anything you can get to the Clipboard into that field. This includes paint (bit-mapped) or draw (object-oriented) art, Encapsulated Postscript (EPS), PICT, PICT II, or scanned images in the standard TIFF format (including text in this format). After you paste the picture, you cannot edit separate details in any way. You can, however, change its overall size and shape. You also can paste layout text into a Picture field. Also, FileMaker supports color, so if you have a color Macintosh, you can paste in color pictures as entries.

Note that from the Browse window you can have Picture fields that you paste into, and you also can have picture layout objects that you paste into the layout window. A picture that appears in a field appears only in that record; a picture that appears on a layout appears in all records.

Not all databases allow Picture fields, but FileMaker does, and this capability increases the range of the program's uses. You can use a picture of an employee of The Fly-By-Night Travel Service, or the scanned image of the Humongous Corporation president's signature on checks you print in FileMaker. Pictures are particularly useful for the placement of logos on stationery or forms you create. This is a great place to use one of those hand-held scanners, such as Lightning Scan or ScanMan, for graphics.

Now you can directly import graphics of a large size, such as scanned images, and in a variety of formats, including TIFF and EPS.

You also can bring images into FileMaker Pro from other applications, such as MacPaint or MacDraw II, by using Import on the File menu. FileMaker Pro has a set of filters that enable it to recognize picture files from the standard file boxes.

Formatting Fields

To FileMaker, *field attributes are not the same as formatting*. Consider that you can *define* a field as a Date field, which is an attribute. You can, however, *format* that Date field (specify how it appears on-screen) when you are in the layout mode by using the Format Date command on the Format menu. For example, you can format a date as long, "Wednesday, August 27, 1952," or as short, "8/27/52."

When you format a field, FileMaker uses that format to display the field. This sometimes makes what you enter different from what displays on your screen. For example, if you format a date as long, return to the browse mode, and enter the date as 8/27/52, FileMaker still calculates and displays the long date: Wednesday, August 27, 1952. You also can format text while you are in the browse mode (as well as in the layout mode) and make the text the Size, Font, Style, or Alignment you want, but again, this also is a format and not an attribute. Formatting options are described in Chapter 7, "Enhancing Layout Appearance."

Creating a Record

After you define your fields, you enter data into the fields. You create records in the Browse window. New records have all defined fields available for use, but what you see on the screen depends on which layout you are using as the current layout. A layout is how you display the data in a file; that is, although your new records have all fields attached, you may see only the set of fields that you placed on the layout when you formatted that layout. FileMaker uses as a default the standard layout, which shows all fields.

Each new record is placed in your database after the last record that was created and is assigned the next available record number. When you delete records, the record numbers of all the records that came after the deleted records are renumbered in sequence to fill in for the deleted records. Keep in mind that the record numbers you see on your screen after a find or sort operation are not the record numbers assigned by FileMaker to the record and retained in the file; they refer only to the sequence of that selected set.

Although a record's order may change when you work with a file, and its location may be *displayed* in a new location in a browsed (selected) set, you easily can restore the true record order. Just choose the Find All command on the Select menu (or press ⌘-J). See Chapter 4 for more details. You also see your records' true assigned record numbers when you first open a file, so closing and opening a file is another method of finding out the true record order.

To create a record, follow these steps:

1. Go to the Browse screen by selecting the Browse command on the Select menu or by pressing ⌘-B.

2. Select the New Record command on the Edit menu or press ⌘-N.

   Your new record appears on the Browse screen with the next record number, and it is in the current layout. All auto-enter options are entered by FileMaker, and an insertion point is placed in the first field in the tab order.

3. Select the field in which you want to enter data and type the data. Press Tab to move the cursor to the next field.

4. Move to the next field and continue adding data. (See the following sections for more information on what you can enter in each field type.)

You also can create a record that is the duplicate of your current browsed record by using the Duplicate command. See the section, "Using the Duplicate Feature," later in this chapter, for details.

⌘-B, the Browse command, opens the Browse window for data entry.

⌘-N, the New Record command, creates a record when the Browse window is open.

Entering Data

You can enter data only into the *current* or *selected* field while you are in the browse mode. When you create a record in an opened file, the first field in the *tab order* is selected for data entry. This field is surrounded by a solid outline and has a flashing bar or insertion point in it. When you select a data item in the current field, the item is highlighted. If you select the entire field's contents, the field itself is highlighted.

When you first open a previously created file, you see the last record that you worked with in the Browse window. It is in the same condition as when you closed the file, contains all of its entries, but none of the fields are outlined or selected. To enter data, you need to select one of the fields. You always can tell where all the fields are located by holding down the mouse button; all of the fields are then outlined and show the size and shape of the field. This configuration is identical to the position, shape, and size of the field outline you created for that field in the layout mode.

To select a field to make it the current field, do one of the following:

- Click in the desired field to select it; all field boxes are then outlined (see fig. 3.13).

- Press the Tab key to select the first field in the tab order. FileMaker places the insertion point to the right of all previously entered characters.

- Press the Option-Tab key to select the preceding field in the tab order.

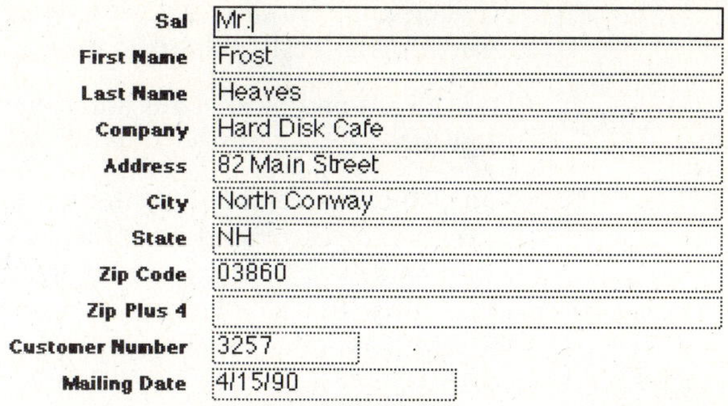

Fig. 3.13
A record with the first field selected.

Creating a record automatically selects the first field in the tab order.

Press the Enter key on the numeric keypad or click the mouse cursor in a blank space outside any field in the window to deselect all fields, enter data, and update all formatting and calculation.

SPEED KEY

Tab selects the first field in the Browse window when no fields are selected.

Whenever you deselect a field, FileMaker saves any data you have entered into it. You have several ways to deselect a field, including moving to a new field, deselecting all fields, or leaving the browse mode. When you do one of those things, you may hear your disk drive whirring away, saving your changes. For more details, see "The Autosave Feature," later in this chapter.

SPEED KEY

⌘-A selects the entire contents of the current field.

To save your entered data, do any of the following:

- Press the Enter key to save your data, format your fields, update your calculation or summary fields, and deselect all fields.
- Click in a blank space outside a field boundary but not in the status area of the window (the left-hand portion containing the Book icon).
- Use the mouse or appropriate keystrokes to move to another field or record.
- Leave the Browse window you are currently in for another operation: layout, find, sort, or define.

SPEED KEY

Pressing Enter on the numeric keypad deselects all fields and updates all formatting and calculations in the Browse window.

You can cut and paste dates and times from the Alarm Clock DA via the Clipboard.

Tip

When possible, choose object-oriented (MacDraw style) graphics in place of bit-mapped (MacPaint style) graphics.

You also can permanently enter the current date into a field by using the Current Date command from the Paste Special command submenu (found on the Edit menu) or by pressing the ⌘- – (minus) keystroke. Do not confuse the ⌘- – keystroke with the Today( ) function. Today( ) puts today's date in the field when you are viewing it. The Paste Special command submenu also enables you to enter the current time, or you use the ⌘-; keystroke.

SPEED KEY

⌘- – (minus) is a date stamp; it puts the current date of entry into the current field.

⌘-; (semicolon) is a time stamp; it puts the current time of entry into the current field.

Entering Data into Text Fields

To enter data into a Text field follow these steps:

1. Select the Text field and type the desired entry.

   Text entry that extends past the end of the field boundary will word wrap down to accept another line (see fig. 3.14). Press Return to force a line ending and to begin the next one.

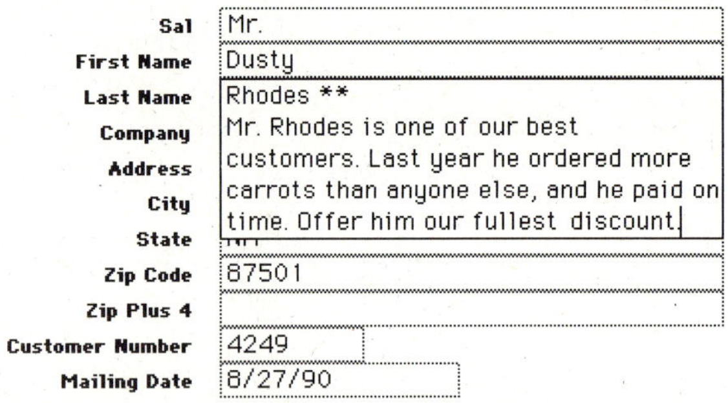

Fig. 3.14
A Text field with word wrap currently selected.

2. Press the right- or left-arrow key to move the insertion point. With more than one line of text, you can use the up- and down-arrow keys to change lines.

3. Use the Format menu to make any changes to the formatting in a Text field. Formatting is discussed in Chapter 7.

4. Deselect the field. FileMaker resizes the field to the size it appears on the current layout (see fig. 3.15).

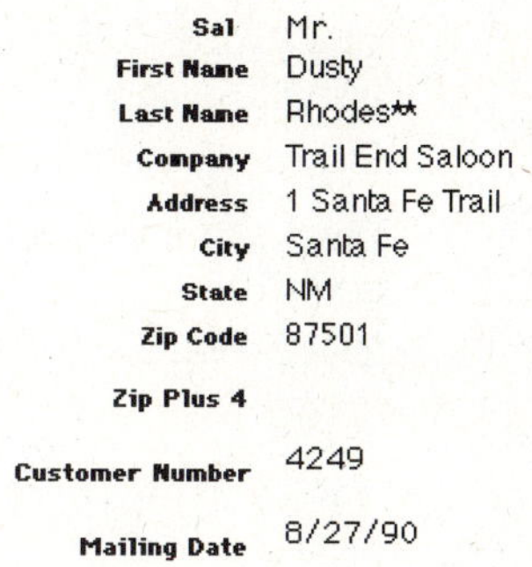

Fig. 3.15
The same field deselected with a flag (two asterisks) to mark the text of importance in the Last Name field.

Note

Because FileMaker can store a larger entry in a field than it can display, you can attach notes. Fields with such notes are indicated by asterisks (see fig. 3.15).

When working with Text fields, you have individual control over the format of each character. Changes you make to a character on one record do not affect entries on other records. Multiple fonts in a record can slow down performance as your Macintosh searches for screen font description, so use this feature as sparingly as you can.

Entering Data into Number Fields

You can enter numbers, up to 255 characters long, on only one line. If you try to press Return to type a new line, Macintosh beeps.

To enter data into a Number field, follow these steps:

1. Select the Number field and enter all desired text and numbers.

2. Deselect the field to enter your data. The number format you choose alters the display of the entry. (See Chapter 7 for information on formatting.)

The recommended practice is to put only numbers in Number fields.

Entering Data into Date Fields

Only one complete date can be typed into a date field. You cannot include other kinds of information in the same field, nor can you use more than one line for the date.

You must enter a date in this order: month, day, and year, separated by any non-numeric character (for example, 5-3-1996). Years can be two, three, or four digits long. Two-digit years are placed in the 20th century.

To enter data into a Date field, follow these steps:

1. Select the Date field, and enter a date on one line. Remember that the shortcut ⌘- – (minus) enters the current day and that the Clipboard also is supported.

2. Deselect the field to enter your data. The date format you chose alters the display of the entry; however, the display can be customized. Chapter 7 covers formatting.

Entering Data into Time Fields

1. Select the Time field and enter the time as hours and minutes separated by colons (HH:MM) or as hours, minutes, and seconds separated by colons (HH:MM:SS). Use either 12- or 24-hour format. If the number is less than 12 without a suffix, such as AM or PM, FileMaker assumes AM.

2. Deselect the field to enter your data. The time format you chose alters the display of the entry. Chapter 7 covers formatting.

Time fields and all the time options are new to FileMaker Pro.

Entering Data into Picture Fields

FileMaker Pro now has an Import feature that allows you to bring in images from other applications, such as MacPaint or MacDraw II.

To import images, do the following:

1. Select the Picture field.

2. Choose Import from the File menu. The dialog box shown in figure 3.16 appears.

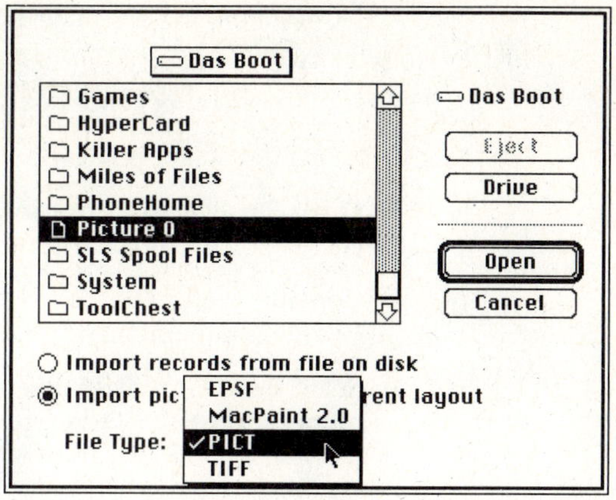

Fig. 3.16
The Import Picture dialog box.

3. Click the Import Picture File into Current Field radio button (if not already selected). The default mode is to import records. Clicking on Import Picture changes the file types listed on the pop-up menu to picture formats.
4. Choose the file format type from the pop-up menu.
5. Select the file you want to import. If necessary, scroll through the list to find the file you want.
6. Click Open. The picture appears in the field, and it may be cropped or scaled as specified in the Picture Format dialog box. (See "Formatting Field Values" in Chapter 7.)

Picture fields with all of the options are new to FileMaker Pro.

To enter data into a Picture field by using the Clipboard, follow these steps:

1. Open an application, desk accessory, or file with the picture you want to enter.
2. Use the Cut (⌘-X) or Copy (⌘-C) command on the Edit menu to put the picture onto the Clipboard.
3. Return to the Browse window of FileMaker and select the Picture field into which you want to place the picture. When the field is selected, it is highlighted. There is no insertion point.
4. Select the Paste command on the Edit menu or press ⌘-V.

5. Deselect the field to enter your data.

FileMaker Pro or FileMaker II users may choose to enter data into a Picture field using the Scrapbook. To do so, follow these steps:

1. Select the Scrapbook DA on the Apple Menu.
2. Open the page that contains the picture you desire to copy by clicking on the dog ear (the folded corner).
3. Copy the picture to the Clipboard by choosing the Copy command on the Edit menu or by pressing ⌘-C.
4. Select the Picture field and use the Paste command on the Edit menu or press ⌘-V to paste your picture from the Clipboard.

Moving from Field to Field

You always can move to a field and make that field the current field by clicking in it with your mouse cursor. If you choose to use the keyboard to move from field to field, FileMaker constrains your movement to the tab order. The tab order is the order in which you can use the Tab key to go from field to field, or the order in which you advance as you enter data into fields. Fields are in order first from left to right and then top to bottom, one level at a time (see Chapter 5).

To move from field to field, use one of these methods:

- Press the Tab key to select the next field (move forward) in the tab order.
- Press the Option-Tab or Shift-Tab keystrokes to select the preceding field (move backward) in the tab order.
- Click with the mouse cursor in any field to select it. If all the fields are not outlined, you may need to scroll the screen to bring a field into view or click the mouse button to see the field's location.

If the next field in the tab order is off your screen, FileMaker automatically scrolls the window to bring it into view.

SPEED KEY

Tab moves from one selected field to the next field on the Browse screen. Option-Tab or Shift-Tab moves from one selected field to the preceding field on the Browse screen.

When you are entering data and you reach the bottom of your screen, FileMaker scrolls one *field* at a time, even if that field is one line high. This can be very disconcerting; often what you would really like is to have the program scroll one screen at a time.

You can define Picture fields so that they act as scroll guides. In the layout mode, define a Picture field that is the height of a screen. Then duplicate that field and move one on top of another. When you tab into a Picture field, the bottom of that field is always shown; therefore, if that field is one screen high, an entire screen comes into view. Also, because you cannot enter characters into a Picture field, you can not inadvertently type something into that field. This method is illustrated on a form that is two Macintosh SE (or Plus) screens high (see fig. 3.17), in which two scroll guides have been created.

Fig. 3.17
Using Picture fields to scroll a window one full screen at a time.

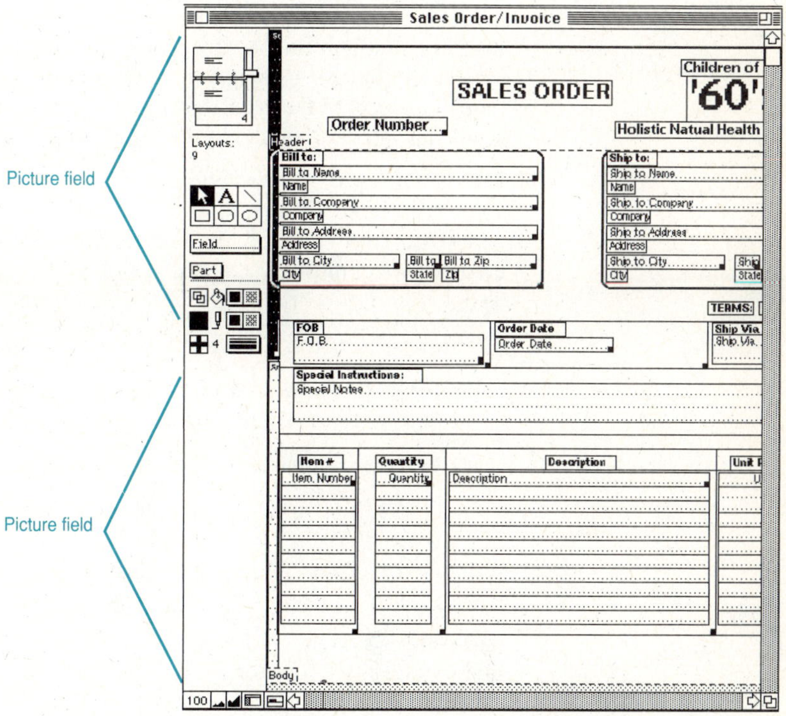

Using Data-Entry Shortcuts

Whenever possible, sacrifice some speed in data entry for accuracy. In the long run, this actually turns out to be the fastest technique, because fewer mistakes make up for the loss in time.

FileMaker offers some data-entry shortcuts, which are described in the following sections. The Duplicate Record command creates a copy of an entire record. You also can enter data by using a field's index and by using the Paste Special submenu from the Index command on the Edit menu; or you can use the ⌘-I keystroke equivalent.

Using the Duplicate Feature

At times you will need to create a record or a number of records that are nearly identical to ones you have already entered. By using the Duplicate Record command on the Edit menu, you can create an exact copy of the record you were browsing when you gave that command. Keep in mind that all aspects of the record, not just the fields and data entries you can see in the current layout, are duplicated.

Use the Duplicate Record command whenever it is less work to change some data on the screen than it is to enter from scratch all the data into a new record. In general, because auto-entering data is less prone to error, this technique has added power. The Duplicate Record feature also is useful in reordering your file (see Chapter 4).

To duplicate a record, follow these steps:

1. Go to the Browse screen. Select the Browse command on the Select menu or press ⌘-B.
2. Go to the record you want to duplicate.
3. Select the Duplicate Record command on the Edit menu or press ⌘-D.

Your new record appears on the Browse screen. The new record has the next available record number and is in the current layout. All fields and data entries have been duplicated, and an insertion point is placed in the first field in the tab order.

⌘-N, the New Record command (on the Browse screen), creates a record with the next record number.

SPEED KEY

⌘-D, the Duplicate Record command (on the Browse screen), creates a record that is the duplicate of whatever record was on your screen when the command was issued.

The Duplicate command has been changed from ⌘-M in FileMaker Plus to ⌘-D in FileMaker II and Filemaker Pro, consistent with the Duplicate command in the Finder.

Using the Index

In Chapter 1, you learned that Text, Number, Time, and Date fields are indexed by FileMaker. An index is the list of all the values entered into a field for every record in a file. A value is any character string between two separator characters, such as spaces. The speed with which FileMaker searches and sorts data is due to the manner in which the program indexes entries.

The index works like a spell checker or a dictionary. FileMaker uses a search algorithm to match character strings character-by-character until it finds a string in the index considered a match for a find (or search) operation. Sorting uses the ASCII code to order strings by the first character, then the second, and so on, in a sort order.

Tip

To speed up the operation of your index, use the Option-Space keystroke to search for a complete compound word. Find operations rely on the index and run faster when you have fewer entries.

FileMaker builds its index of text values by cataloging every text string separated by certain non-alphabetic characters. The characters ', &, - , and / are indexed with text strings and are not considered by FileMaker to be separators. When the words "West Newton" are indexed, they appear as two words: "West" and "Newton." You can force FileMaker to index them together by inserting a hard space between them (press Option-Space). A separate text string is considered a word and can be searched for individually.

Only numeric entries in a Number field are indexed. If you type the address *101 State Street* into a Number field, you will only be able to view the number 101 in your index. FileMaker ignores all non-numeric characters. Notice that each word is indexed separately, and when pasted, each word includes an extra space to the right of the word. A phone number with hyphens is indexed as a single entry, and a period inside a number (1.000, or even 2.13) indexes as a single word. When a period is inside an alphabetic character string (File.lu), each part indexes separately.

Dates you enter in the Browse screen are indexed and can be sorted. They are entered in the index in the short format. FileMaker allows dates to be entered from 1/1/0001 to 12/31/3000. Times entered in the Browse screen also are indexed. They appear in the following format: 7:15:00.

Indexing offers some powerful options for examining your entries and finding errors (see Chapter 5), and it can be used to enter information on a Find window (see Chapter 4). In this chapter, you will see how you can use indexes to aid you in entering data quickly and accurately.

You can use the index of a field to enter data. To do this, you first make that field active (only Text, Number, Time, and Date fields with those results are indexed) and then open its index. Double-click on the data you want to enter. This method of entering data has the advantage of being quick and error-free.

Before you view a field index and enter a value, you must make the selection in the Browse or Find windows by using one of these methods:

- Make your selection by placing the insertion point in the desired field at the desired place.
- To replace a selection in a field, highlight it.
- To replace the entire contents of a field, use the Select All command on the Edit menu or press ⌘-A to highlight the entire field.

To view the index, select Paste Special from the Edit Menu and then select From Index or press ⌘-I. A scroll box appears to the right of the window (see fig. 3.18). You can view the index for a Text, Number, Time, or Date field.

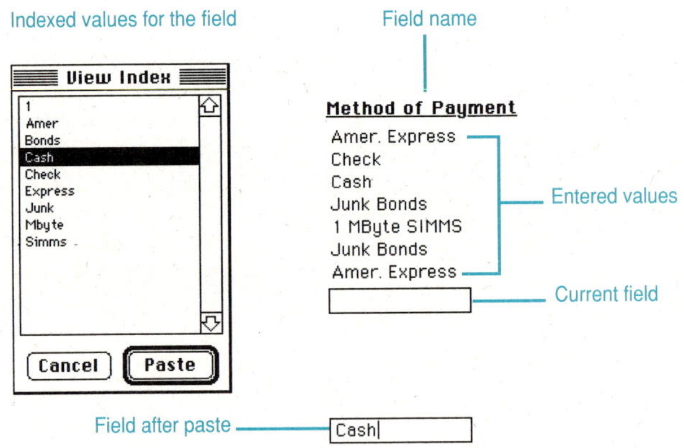

Fig. 3.18
An index for a Text field, before and after a value is pasted from it.

To enter an index value, highlight the value you want to enter by clicking on it, and then press the Paste button. Alternatively, double-click on the desired name to paste the value automatically. Clicking the Cancel button dismisses the Index and returns the Browse window to its condition when you previously viewed it.

SPEED KEY

⌘-I opens the index of the current field in the browse or find mode.

Getting Help

The developers of FileMaker created an on-line help system using a FileMaker file called FileMaker Help. This file usually is stored in the System folder or the same folder as the application or program file. It is included on the disk called FileMaker Pro Help Disk. Any operation you can perform on a FileMaker file can be done when the Help file is open, including find, edit, and print.

The introduction page of the Help file is shown in figure 3.19. Help now operates like a HyperCard-based program and is available under the Apple menu. Information is included about the commands and dialog box choices. On-screen instructions are provided for the most common operations. The contents of Finding Records is shown in figure 3.20.

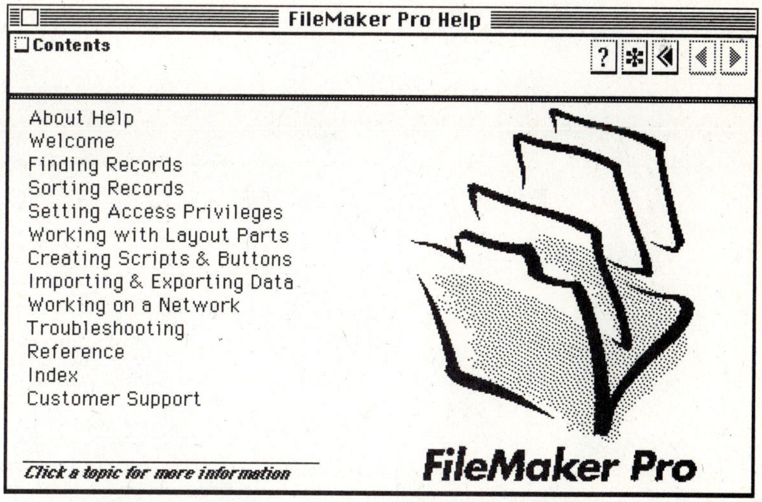

Fig. 3.19
The Help introduction page.

To open and close the on-line Help file, follow these steps:

1. Choose the Help command under the Apple menu or press either of these shortcuts: ⌘-? or ⌘- /. On an extended keyboard, press the Help key.

The dialog box appears, with some brief information (see fig. 3.19). Click a phrase to go to its page description.

2. Click the question mark in the upper right portion of the screen to bring up the Help navigator overview. Click the icons illustrated in figure 3.21.

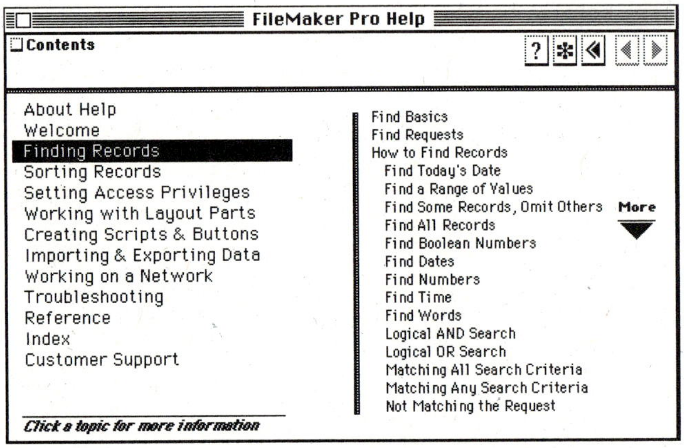

Fig. 3.20
The Finding Records contents page.

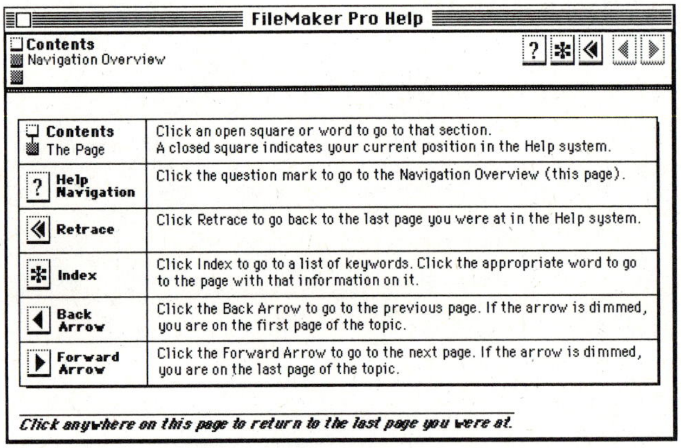

Fig. 3.21
Help navigation overview.

The following buttons in the upper portion of the screen help you navigate throughout the Help program:

Contents button. Click an open square or word to go to that section.

Help Navigation button. This choice takes you to the Navigation Overview page.

Retrace button. This button takes you back to the last page you were at in the Help system.

Index button. This button brings up a list of keywords. By clicking on any word, Help takes you to the information page.

Back Arrow button. This choice takes you to the preceding page. If the arrow is dimmed, you are on the first page of the topic.

Forward Arrow button. Clicking this button advances you to the next page. You are on the last page if the arrow is dimmed.

3. Browse the records of interest.

The following is an example of moving around the Help system.

1. At the introduction page (see fig. 3.19), select Creating Scripts & Buttons.
2. Several topics appear on the right of the window. Select Script Basics. The Contents displays an information page about Scripts, as shown in figure 3.22.
3. Close the Help file by clicking the close box in the window, by choosing the Close command on the File menu or by pressing ⌘-W.

You may want to leave the Help file open as you work with additional files. Figure 3.23 shows an example of leaving the Help window open. Click on the corner of either your file or the Help window. One window moves forward, and the other goes to the background. Click again to reverse.

Choose ⌘-? or ⌘- / for the Help command, which displays the Help file.

⌘-. (period) clicks the Cancel button in a dialog box to dismiss it without changes.

Saving a File

FileMaker does not include a save command. Instead, the program saves your file automatically. Many Macintosh applications, however, have a set of options similar to the Save As command that allow you to create a file from a selected set of records or even to save the shell of a file. The sections that follow detail these features.

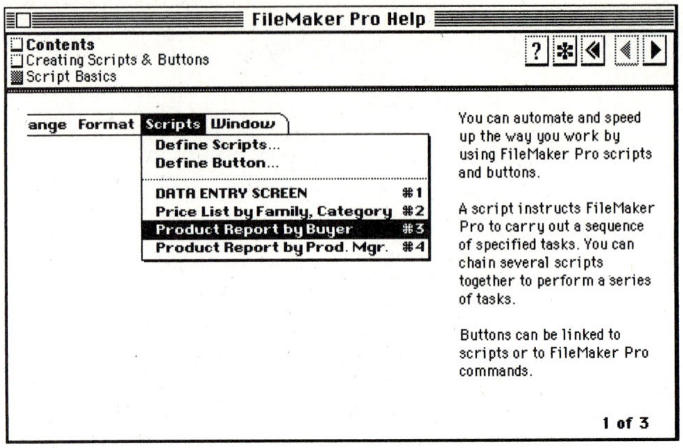

Fig. 3.22 Script Basics sample of moving through the Help contents.

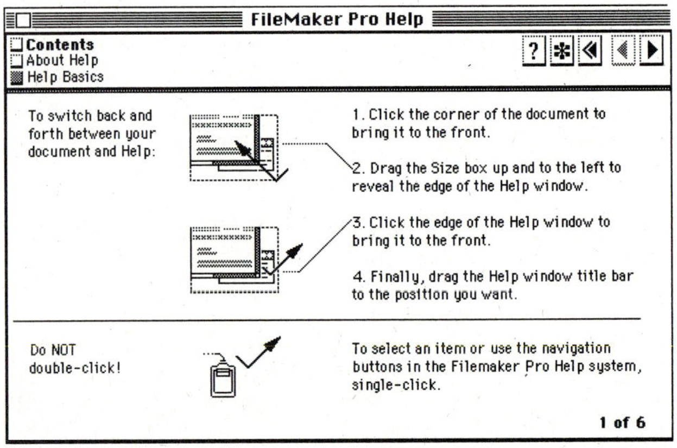

Fig. 3.23 Switching between Help and your database file.

Understanding the Autosave Feature

If you are familiar with Macintosh programs, you may be surprised to find that FileMaker has no save command on its File menu. You don't save your changes because the program does that for you automatically. The original version of FileMaker and FileMaker Plus worked this way, and it's true for FileMaker II and Filemaker Pro, as well.

Three things trigger an autosave:

- No input events for a brief period

- Closing a file
- Running out of allocated memory in RAM

Autosave is intended to provide you with a level of protection, because as you constantly add data to a file, your changes are quickly incorporated onto disk. Additionally, because your file is updated constantly in case your Macintosh has a system crash or you experience a power outage, your file is much less likely to be damaged (see Chapter 15, "Importing and Exporting Data").

The autosave feature also is a device that keeps you from tying up precious random-access memory (RAM) with a large database file. If you have a database file that is several hundred kilobytes or even a few megabytes in size, you easily can use up the available RAM in your Macintosh and make it impossible to run any of your applications. Because it isn't practical to work entirely in memory with a database file as a unit, FileMaker breaks each file into chunks of data called *blocks*.

Usually, you need to work only with a selected set of blocks at one time, which greatly speeds up the operation of the program. Reading from and writing to memory is considerably faster than reading from or writing to disk.

FileMaker solves this problem by using a process called *caching*. A cache is a reserved set of blocks in memory in which data is stored. Your Macintosh has a similar *RAM cache* feature, which you set in the Control Panel (although it isn't particularly well implemented in the system software and doesn't seem to speed up the operation of your computer much). FileMaker uses the disk blocks on which a file's data is stored, and, as needed, reads them into memory as cache blocks. When FileMaker requests additional data, unused blocks are swapped back to disk along with any changes that were made, thus performing a save (the newly required blocks are swapped in). When you close a file, either by issuing the Close command (⌘-W) on the Edit menu or clicking the close box in a window, FileMaker releases all the file's associated cache blocks and writes them to disk.

Reach for a cup of coffee, think briefly about what phase the moon is in, and you will hear your disk drive whirring away, saving your entries and changes. The FileMaker II program documentation says autosave occurs whenever there are "short lulls in your work activity." This undefined time period seems to be around 45 seconds, as measured by the Event Manager, a set of routines in the system software. Events are keyboard entries. Pressing the mouse button, disk insertion or ejection, or cursor movement on the screen also are events.

As you add new data, records, and layouts, you use up more memory. When FileMaker detects that you are out of allocated room in memory, it automatically begins to update the disk file. Block swapping occurs until all the changes have been recorded to disk. Sometimes FileMaker displays a message that says there is not enough memory to do the requested operation. In Chapter 16, "Managing Files," you learn how to avoid this problem.

Because all the preceding events occur without your intervention, you are probably unaware that save operations are constantly occurring. When a program has a save command (unlike FileMaker), you can always go back to the condition the file was in at the time of the last save. Some programs copy a file when you open it and have a revert command that enables you to use that duplicate copy. The problem with autosave is that removing your ability to control when you save data has some serious implications for making mistakes.

Many of the operations you perform, for example, have the Undo command associated with them, which lets you return your data to its previous state. After you have completed the next defined operation, however, the Undo command applies only to the preceding operation. How, then, do you return the file to its condition before the first operation? What's even worse is that FileMaker has a set of actions—field deletions, replace, and so on—that are permanent; they do not have an enabled Undo command. (*Using FileMaker* has attempted to flag these operations for you with warnings in the text.) These complications are consequences of having the autosave feature.

Not everyone likes autosaving, although the reasons for its implementation are obvious. The only satisfactory way to deal with a program that forces an autosave is to pay particular attention to making backups. Think about just how big a period of time you are willing to lose if something happens to your file, and back up after each period. Then, if you make a mistake, at least you have a previous version to work with. For more information, see Chapter 16.

Alternatively, if you have the extra disk space, work on a copy of the file by using the Save a Copy command to create a duplicate (see the next section). Your original copy takes the place of a revert command. When you are sure that you no longer need the original, you can delete it from disk in one of two ways: by dragging it to the Trash in the Finder or by using a file utility program such as DiskTools II or DiskTop.

Using Save a Copy As

Only a browsed set of records can be saved to disk as a unit. You can use a find operation for selection or omission; a sort operation for organization; and you can create, omit, or eliminate new records as desired until you get the set you want to save. You periodically will save the data sets of interest to you, using the Save a Copy As command. This command leads to the Save a Copy As dialog box, which has three options: Copy of Current File, Compressed Copy, or Clone of the File. Each option allows you to create a file with different properties. Consider creating a copy of a file when you have a specific purpose for a data set. You may, for instance, want to take a set of customer names and addresses and separate your best customers to make a set for special mailings. Or maybe you are consolidating files but you want to retain all of your original files in their current condition. Create a copy of the biggest set and input the data into the new file (see Chapter 15).

Anytime you plan to make an important change in a file, especially one that has no enabled Undo command, use a copy of this file to back up your original file. Important changes include deleting a group of records, deleting fields, replacing a set of field values, or inputting information from another file.

To create a copy of a file, follow these steps:

1. With the original file open, browse all of the records you want to include in your new file.
2. Issue the Save a Copy As command on the File menu. Select Save A:, and the Save a Copy As dialog box shown in figure 3.24 results.

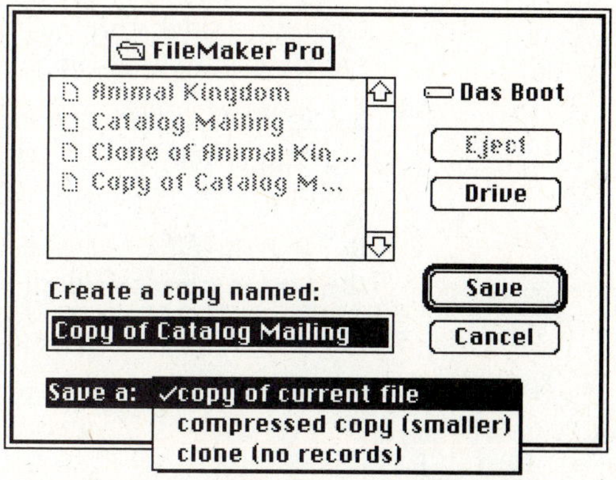

Fig. 3.24
The Save a Copy As dialog box.

3. Drag through the choices to highlight the type of copy you desire.
4. In the Create a Copy file box, enter a file name.
5. Open the folder you want to store the file in and click the New button to save the file, or press Return or Enter. Again, clicking the Cancel button (⌘-.) returns the original file of browsed records.
6. Click the Save button or press Return or Enter, and the copy is saved.

   or

   Click the Cancel button (⌘-.) to return the file to its previous condition.

   Depending on what option you choose when you save your file, for both the Copy of Current File or Compressed Copy (Smaller) options you see the following message:

   ```
   Create a copy named:
   ```

   If you choose Clone (a copy with no records), you see

   ```
   Create a copy named:
   ```

   above the text box in figure 3.24. The text box has the default name `Copy of "File Name"` or `Clone of "File Name"`. For more information about creating a clone or a compressed copy, see the following sections.

To make a copy of a file in the Finder, follow these steps:

1. Quit FileMaker by choosing the Quit command on the File menu or by pressing ⌘-Q.
2. Open the folder with the file you want to copy and click once on the file icon to highlight it.
3. Select the Duplicate command on the File menu or press ⌘-D. A file named `Copy of "File Name"` appears inside the Finder window.
4. Rename the file by clicking on the file name to highlight it, drag the I-beam cursor over the name, and then type the new file name.
5. Move the file to the desired folder.

You may want to make a copy using MultiFinder. If so, follow these steps:

1. Assuming that you are running MultiFinder, choose the Finder program under the Apple menu.
2. Open the folder that has the file you want to copy and click once on the file icon to highlight it.
3. Select the Duplicate command on the File menu or press ⌘-D. A file named `Copy of "File Name"` appears inside thc MultiFinder window.
4. Rename the file and move it to the desired folder.
5. If you want to return to the FileMaker program to continue your work, choose the file's name again under the Apple menu.

You also can duplicate a file in Finder or MultiFinder by dragging its icon to another disk or drive.

The option Copy of Current File is the exact equivalent of a Save As command for the set of browsed records on your screen. A file is created with all the features of the database file intact (layouts, field definitions, find requests, scripts, and so on), but it contains only the browsed set of records. Using this option is different from going to the Finder to duplicate a file. In the Finder, you have no control over which records are copied; all of them are copied. Usually, the Copy of Current File option is as fast as the Duplicate operation in the Finder.

The Save a Copy As command now incorporates the Clone command found in the FileMaker and FileMaker Plus menus. In addition, two new options are available: Copy of Current File and Compressed Copy.

Saving in Compressed Format

As you work with your file and add records and features (fields, graphic objects, layouts, and so on), your database file grows. When you delete records and eliminate features (such as fields, graphic objects, and so forth), you don't necessarily recover the space on your disk that the deleted information occupied. Your files can grow substantially larger than necessary, often 50 to 100 percent larger than the size of the information contained, and that consumes disk space and slows down the operation of your file. The solution to this problem is to operate on the file with a compression algorithm to remove the surplus information. This operation is what the Compressed Copy option does.

You create a compressed copy of a file in the same manner that you create other kinds of copies. Drag through the choices next to Save A:, highlight Compressed Copy (see fig. 3.24), and then name the file in the

Create a Copy standard file dialog box (see fig. 3.24). Creating a compressed copy can take a considerable amount of time, so make sure that you leave yourself a block of time in which to do it.

File compression requires a great deal of time—many minutes to hours for some very large files—so you should consider using this option over a lunch hour or at the end of a day. To cancel a compressed copy operation in progress, press ⌘-. (period). File compression operates under MultiFinder, but your foreground application operates more slowly than usual. Create your compressed file while in FileMaker, operating in the Finder only.

SPEED KEY

⌘-. (period) cancels any operation in progress when the cursor appears on the screen.

Tip

Because compressing a file saves disk space and speeds up many operations, create a compressed file after modifications to that file have been made.

Originally, FileMaker Plus included a compression algorithm in the Recover command, but FileMaker Pro has moved this function to the Save a Copy As command compressed file option. You can achieve dramatic results with compression of files that are heavily modified over time—anywhere from 35 to 50 percent. This difference can speed up many of your FileMaker operations. (Lightly modified files, however, such as lookup files, do not benefit much from compression.) When you compress a file, you need to have as much free space on the target disk as the size of the file being compressed.

Using Clone a Copy

A *clone* is a copy of a file with no records or data copied. All the field definitons (including their attributes and entry options), layouts, find requests, page setups, scripts, and other settings are duplicated. Cloning is particularly useful when you want to create a template for use by others (see Chapter 10, "Printing Basics") or when you need to create an empty file into which you can input data (see Chapter 14, "Quick Start: Creating a Summary Report").

You clone a file by using the same steps detailed in the section, "Using Save a Copy As." You cannot, however, cancel a clone operation in progress by using the ⌘-. (period) keystroke. After you create a clone, you see a blank Browse screen. To enter data, you must create a record. To create a record, issue the New Record command (⌘-N) on the Edit menu or import records by using the Input From command on the File menu.

Quitting the Program

To quit FileMaker, select the Quit command on the File menu or press ⌘-Q, as in any other Macintosh application. You return to the desktop without an alert to save changes; FileMaker automatically saves your changes.

WARNING

If you turn off the power to your Macintosh, you can damage your file, and recovery may be difficult. To turn off your computer properly, close your files and quit the program before you choose the Shut Down command from the Special menu. If possible, work on a copy and keep current backups. If you damage your file, refer to Chapter 16, "Managing Files."

In Review

In this chapter, you learned how to select commands with your mouse and keyboard, use the menus, and work with windows. Other important basics, such as using dialog boxes, alert boxes, desk accessories, and the Clipboard, also were covered.

A file is opened as a single window; you can have 16 FileMaker windows open in the Finder and 14 in MultiFinder. You can hide windows and access them through the Window menu. FileMaker has three kinds of windows: Browse, Layout, and Find.

When you create a file, FileMaker prompts you to name and define fields, set field attributes, and set entry options. Field attributes control how data is handled; entry options offer some powerful devices for automating data entry and checking data validity.

Fields can have seven types of attributes: Text, Number, Date, Time, Picture, calculation, and summary. Only the first five attributes are basic; FileMaker calculates data for the last two. Field attributes are distinct from formatting; attributes control what can be entered into a field and what operations can be performed. Formatting is applied in the layout mode, and it controls how the data is displayed.

Fields are indexed; every entry is placed into a listing similar to a spelling checker. This index is the key to the speed of the database when it performs searches and sorts, and it is useful for checking the accuracy of your entries.

Data is entered only in the browse mode and only into a selected field, using common Macintosh editing techniques. In this chapter, you learned the methods for selecting, entering, editing, and formatting data entries of various kinds.

To move from field to field, use Tab to go forward and Shift-Tab or Option-Tab to go backward in the tab order. When you are in the browse mode, use ⌘-Tab to go to the next record, and use ⌘-Option-Tab or ⌘-Shift-Tab to go to the preceding record. These keystrokes also move you from layout to layout in the Layout window.

New records are created in the browse mode, and each record contains all defined fields, even if some or all of the fields are not showing on the current layout. You can duplicate a record and place a copy at the end of your file.

Each Text, Number, Time, and Date field is indexed. The index can be used for entering data, checking the data's validity during entry, and checking the data for accuracy.

FileMaker Help is an on-line documentation system built from a Hyper-Card-based system and is accessed under the Apple menu.

FileMaker automatically saves your changes when there is a brief period of inactivity, when you close a file, or when all available allocated memory has been used. A set of browsed records can be saved as a copy, either as an exact duplicate, a compressed copy, or a copy that contains no records. Use the Save a Copy As command's Compressed Copy option to reclaim disk space and speed up many FileMaker operations. Creating a clone of a file is a convenient way to create a template file for use by others or to serve as a skeleton into which you can import data.

CHAPTER 4

Editing, Finding, and Sorting Records

In Chapter 3, "Creating a File," you learned some of the Macintosh basics. You learned how to create a FileMaker file, define fields, and save your file. This chapter expands on more of the basics—in particular, the Browse and Find windows—so that you can become proficient with FileMaker. Here, the focus is on records: how to enter them, how to move from record to record, and how to work with groups of records.

The capability to change your data as necessary is important. Perhaps you made a mistake when you entered the data, or perhaps the phone number of your favorite pizza place has changed. Editing information is easy with FileMaker, and this chapter tells you how to replace data found in the same field of many records and how to omit records from a browsed set.

Storing information in a file is useful only if you can organize the data into logical groups and find specific pieces of information when you need them. When you open a file and browse through the records, the entire data set is at your disposal to display, manipulate, and print. Usually, you will want to work with just one record or perhaps a set of records that have been organized in some way. This chapter gives you the details on how to find, select, and organize data.

Opening a File

After you launch FileMaker in a work session, you see a standard file box that allows you to create a file or open an existing file. By using the Open command, you can bring up a similar dialog box that enables you to open any FileMaker file at any time.

To open a file, follow these steps:

1. Select the Open command on the File menu or press the ⌘-Shift-O keystroke equivalent.
2. In the Open File dialog box (see fig. 4.1), double-click on the name of the file you want to open; or click on the name to highlight it and then click on the Open button or press the Return or Enter key.

SPEED KEY

⌘-O, the Open command, opens a file.

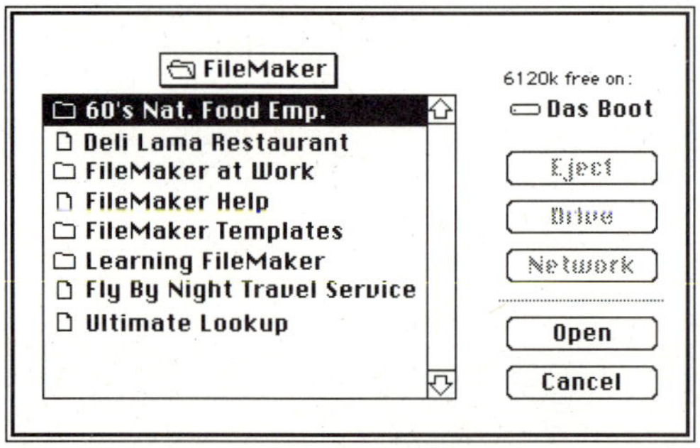

Fig. 4.1
The Open File dialog box.

Sometimes, the file you want to open (or save) is not in the folder you are viewing, so you have to find that folder. The Macintosh has a file system called the *Hierarchical File System* (HFS). This term differentiates this file system from an older one called the *Macintosh File System* (MFS). Few people use the MFS file system, so you need to concern yourself only with the HFS file system. In this book, the file system or the Macintosh file system means the HFS.

In Version 6.0x of the operating system, the Macintosh file system is organized around a directory file in your top folder, called the *root directory*. The Desktop file is usually invisible, but in some utilities you can find it under the file name DESKTOP. Think of the file system as the table of contents for your disk. Folders are organized in a tree shape, one folder inside another. The root directory is at your disk level; any folder inside another folder generally is referred to as *down*.

To go to another folder, follow these steps:

1. Click on the folder name in the file box and hold the mouse button down to display a listing of all folders above the one you're viewing.

2. Drag down until the name of the folder you want to open is highlighted and then release. That folder opens.

   or

   Use ⌘-Up arrow and ⌘-Down arrow to move through the tree of folders.

If the folder you need is on another disk, click on the Drive button to switch disks. If the disk you need is not mounted, click the eject button and insert the floppy or mount the hard drive.

If your file is in a folder on another drive on your network (AppleShare or TOPS), FileMaker enables the Network button. Click on the Network button and then click on the Drive button until the file name appears. Follow preceding steps 1 and 2 until you find your folder.

Many utilities can help you navigate the Macintosh file system. Some utilities, such as DiskTools II and DiskTop, are Finder replacements. The Find File DA comes with the Apple System Software package. Two more utilities, OnCue and QuicKeys 2, add menus, which is another valuable option.

Other utilities, including OnCue, which you may want to investigate, actually load into your standard file boxes, just where you need them. The best utilities include Shortcut and Boomerang. Both are fine additions to your file system and will save you much time.

When you start FileMaker, a folder called FileMaker Temp is created in the Claris folder in your System folder; FileMaker Temp contains information that the program needs to track when a file is opened. When you open a file, FileMaker creates a *temporary file* with the name FILENAME-. After you close a FileMaker file, the program removes the temporary file from the folder. If you experience a power outage, a system crash, or if the file does not close properly, the temporary files are retained in the FileMaker Temp folder. If you attempt to open a file whose temporary counterpart has been left in the FileMaker Temp folder, you see an alert box that tells you FileMaker could not open the file because it could not create the temp file. You can remove these files and the folder itself by dragging them in the Finder to the Trash Can and selecting the Empty Trash command on the Special menu. FileMaker will create a folder and write new files as it needs them.

Editing Data

In browse mode, you work with the information content of your data, as opposed to its display (the layout mode). Browse is the only mode that allows data entry; browse also is the only mode in which you can edit your data. In browse, you cannot change the display format or field attributes, although the Format menu enables you to control the formatting of each character you enter.

Usually, you edit or change your data one record at a time. Therefore, you need to know how to move from record to record and how to make a specific record the *current record*. You usually enter or edit data one field at a time, so you need to know how to select a field and make it the *current field.* Chapter 3 explained how to select fields and enter data. Chapter 4 focuses on editing existing data. Some manipulations allow you to select a field and perform the same operation on that field in all of the records in your browsed set. The replace operation is an example of this kind of editing technique, which you learn about later in the chapter.

In the sections that follow, you will learn more about browsing records. The Browse window is the first of the three FileMaker environments that you will examine; the other environments are the Layout and Find windows. In the "Understanding the Browse Window" section, the unique elements of a FileMaker window are explained. You learn how to move from record to record and how to edit and work with your data.

Browsing through Records

A browsed set of records can include all records in a file or any subset of those records—even a single record, if that's all you want to view. You browse all your records when you open your file, but you may browse any part of your records after you have selected records with a find operation. After selection, you can add or create records, omit certain records, and delete others, and your browsed set grows or shrinks accordingly. You can return to viewing the entire set of records at any time by using the Find All command. (See "Finding Records" later in this chapter.)

What you see on the Browse window is controlled by the current layout. The current layout does not control what records are available: all records are available. Some layouts, however, do not show all of your defined fields. Therefore, it may be necessary to change layouts to view data or to edit or sort the information in which you are interested.

The type of layout determines your options when you move between records, select data, and manipulate data. You will learn much more about layouts in Chapter 6, "Creating a Layout." For now, you need to know that layouts show one record, commonly called a form, or many records together, called a list. In the first Quick Start, Chapter 2, "Creating a Database," you worked with both kinds.

When you want to save a copy of a file, FileMaker saves what is currently selected as a browsed set of records. What you are browsing is the key to what you can do with the records in your file. You can change only information or data that is available in the Browse window.

Understanding the Browse Window

After you first open a file, the Browse window appears. If you are in the Layout or Find window and you want to view the Browse window, select the Browse command on the Select menu or press ⌘-B. A window similar to that shown in figure 4.2 results. Here, you are looking at the Browse window in the standard layout. You are examining the fourth record in a file with five records and eleven fields. You can determine this by examining the Book icon for the current record and the status area for the number of records.

Following is a summary of the actions of the labeled elements in the Browse window shown in figure 4.2:

Book. The Book is a device for finding your current record position and for changing records. Click in the top page to go back a record; click in the bottom page to go forward one record. Double-click in the bottom right corner on the record number to highlight the record number; type the record number you desire to go to; and press the Return or Enter key.

Close box. You click in this window device to close the window and the file. It is equivalent to the Close command or ⌘-W keystroke.

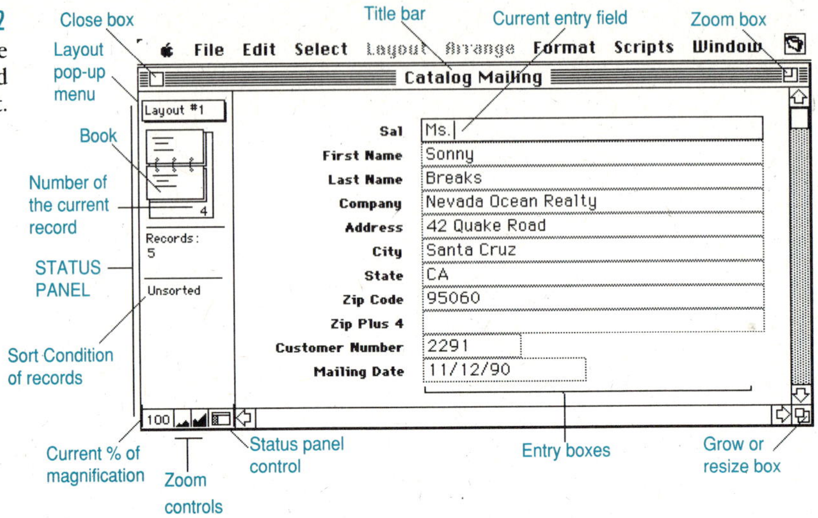

Fig. 4.2 Elements of the Browse window in the standard layout.

Current entry field. This is the active field box for data entry. Use Macintosh text-editing techniques (cut, copy, paste, and clear) to enter data.

Entry boxes. These field boxes are for data entry.

Grow or Resize box. The resize box is a Macintosh window device that you click in and then drag to resize the window.

Field names. Field names are layout text objects; FileMaker adds them automatically in the standard layout. Initially, they match the names you gave the field in the Define Fields dialog box, but because a text object can be edited, you can modify them as you want.

Note

Using the zoom box at the top right corner of a Macintosh window is not the same as using Magnification. Clicking on the zoom box toggles the window's size, not your view.

Magnification. Magnification enables you to display the current view as a percentage of normal size as shown in the bottom left corner. You can toggle between your current view and 100% by clicking on this icon. Another way to change the size is by clicking in the percentage box.

Screen width icon. This icon is a toggle switch. Click on this icon to remove the status area; click again to bring the status area back. You also can use the ⌘-Option-S keystroke equivalent. Use this feature when you need to view more of the window's contents.

Slide control mechanism. This device is used for moving quickly between records. Drag the handle until the desired record number appears in the book and then release the mouse button.

Status indicator. The status indicator tells you how many records you are browsing and whether you have found or sorted them.

Status area. The status area displays the current status of browsed records.

Title bar. The title bar gives you the file name and status (active or inactive). You move the window by dragging the title bar. Hold down the ⌘ key while dragging an inactive file to keep it inactive.

Zoom controls. You click on the zoom controls to change the size of your screen. The left hand icon with the smaller graph in it is the zoom out icon. Click on it to reduce the size of your window by 50% for each mouse click down to 25%. The icon on the right is the zoom in icon. Click on it to expand features in your window; your view is doubled (up to 400%) for each mouse click.

⌘-Option-S is a toggle switch that alternately hides or displays the status area of a window.

⌘-Shift-Z is a toggle that zooms a window in and out.

You can have a Browse window with no records showing when you create a clone of a file (see Chapter 3). You also can delete all the records in your file (see "Deleting Records," later in this chapter).

Moving from Record to Record

When you open a file for the first time in a session, you see the Browse screen of the first record in the last layout that you used before you closed the file in your previous session. The bottom right corner of the Book tells you the number of the record you are currently browsing: the *current record*. You can work with this record when you edit, delete, and omit.

To change records when a single record is displayed, use one of these methods.

To go forward or backward one record at a time:

- Click in the bottom page of the book (if it shows page lines) to go forward one record or press the ⌘-Tab keystroke equivalent.
- Click in the top page of the book (if it shows page lines) to go back one record or press the ⌘-Shift-Tab or ⌘-Option-Tab keystrokes.

To go to a specific numbered record, do the following:

1. Click on the page number in the bottom right corner of the book to highlight it.

2. Type the desired page number and press the Enter or Return key.

   or

   Drag on the handle of the Slide Control Mechanism to change records. Drag to the top of the slide control for the first record, the bottom for the last record, or to the desired record number, as shown in the bottom right corner of the book.

SPEED KEY

⌘-Tab selects the next record in the Browse window.

⌘-Shift-Tab selects the previous record in the Browse window.

⌘-Option-Tab also selects the previous record in the Browse window.

When you view several records at a time in a list layout, you see a display similar to that shown in figure 4.3. This Browse window shows a columnar report layout, which usually is displayed as a list. A list has some additional features, a vertical bar to the left of the records, for example. The current record is marked by a black bar inside the vertical bar. You can use the Book, Slide Control Mechanism, or preceding speed keys to switch records, or you can click on any field of a record in a list to make it the current record.

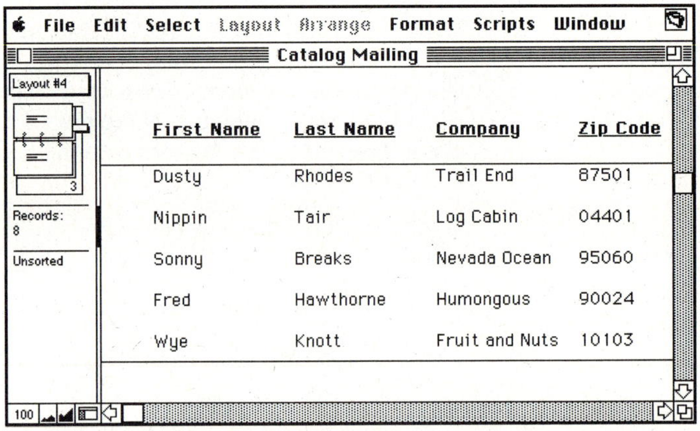

Fig. 4.3
The Browse window of a columnar report layout.

To change records in a list of records, use any of the techniques you have learned so far or click on any field of the record you want. If the record is not showing on the screen, scroll the screen until the record appears and then click on it.

In figure 4.3, record number 3 is selected. None of the fields' boundaries are showing, but you can locate the position of all the fields by pressing the mouse button. After you are finished entering data and you press the Enter key, or when you first open the file to this layout, the condition of your Browse window is displayed. To select the first field, press the Tab key.

By now you may be used to seeing a columnar report layout as a list. In fact, any layout can be set up so that it is displayed on the Browse screen as a list. To do this, you choose the View as a List command on the Select menu while you are in the layout mode (see Chapter 6). If you use this command on a standard layout, you will get the result shown in figure 4.4; one record fills your screen, and only the selected record shows. Don't be confused by this display of the Browse window; anytime you see the vertical bar you are dealing with a list window.

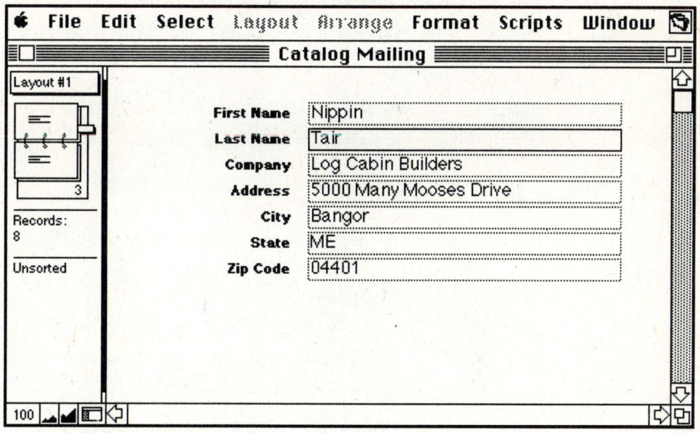

Fig. 4.4 The Browse window of a standard layout displayed as a list.

Editing Information

To edit a field, you need to select the record you want and then the field you want. (Selecting fields was covered in Chapter 3.) After you select a field, use the standard text-editing techniques to enter data. Remember what you learned in Chapter 3: a selected field is outlined in a solid box. When the field is a Text, Number, Time, or Date field, it also will have an insertion point in it, indicating that you can type into it. Picture fields are entirely selected; you can paste, cut, or delete graphics. You cannot select calculated or summary fields, however, because FileMaker automatically enters data into them.

Text, Number, Time, and Date fields also support standard Macintosh text-editing techniques. You can cut, copy, and paste from the Clipboard, and you can drag to highlight a selection. When you highlight a selection, anything you type replaces your selection.

To enter a piece of data, follow these steps:

1. Select the field, and if needed, position the insertion point at the desired place.

   To reposition the insertion point, either click where you want to enter data or use the left- or right-arrow keys to move in the desired direction.

2. Type your entry or paste the entry from the Clipboard. If your selected field is a Picture field, paste your graphic from the Clipboard.

3. To enter your data, deselect all fields by pressing the Enter key or clicking anywhere in the window except the status area or scroll bars.

   Remember that you also can use the Paste Special commands to automatically enter data.

To clear a field, follow these steps:

1. Select the field and highlight the entry.

   or

   Choose the Select All command on the Edit menu or press the ⌘-A keystroke to highlight everything in a field. A Picture field is always entirely selected.

2. Choose the Clear command on the Edit menu or press the Clear key (on the numeric keypad) or the Delete key.

   To remove the entry and place it on the Clipboard, select the Cut command on the Edit menu or press ⌘-X. Pressing Shift-Clear clears an entire field and automatically returns the insertion point to the beginning of the field.

3. Deselect the field, entering the blank entry by pressing the Enter key or clicking outside the field.

The Clear key (on the numeric keypad), the equivalent of the Clear command that clears selected objects or text, was introduced in FileMaker II. On some keyboards, the Escape key operates similarly. In FileMaker Plus, using the Clear key selects an entire field and then clears it while advancing the insertion point. To perform the same operation in FileMaker II and Pro, use the Shift-Clear keystroke. The insertion pointer will appear at the beginning of the cleared field.

SPEED KEY

The Clear key (the Clear command) deletes selected objects or text.

Shift-Clear, the Clear All command, selects an entire field and then clears it.

Replacing Values

Sometimes you will want to make the same change in the same field in a number of records all at once. Maybe an account number has changed, you have detected a misspelled word that appears throughout your file, or a product classification needs to be updated. (FileMaker now contains a spelling checker; see "Using the Spelling Checker" later in this chapter.) You can handle these and any number of other situations by using the Replace command.

You can replace the entire contents of a field by using the Replace command on the Edit menu. You place an insertion point into a field that contains the value you want to use as the replacement value, and then select the Replace command. FileMaker automatically substitutes all other values in the field with that value. You can replace values in the records you are browsing. Browsed records can be all records in a database, any number of records that you have selected through a Find operation (see "Finding Records," later in this chapter), subsequently created, or both. Replace operations can take a while for a large database with many calculated fields, so for a large number of records, make sure to reserve a block of time.

WARNING

The Replace command should be used with caution. All of the browsed records will be replaced with the same data. This command cannot be undone.

To replace the contents of a field with a single value, follow these steps:

1. Browse the records you want to change.

If you need to select a set of records, use the Find command (refer to "Finding Records," later in this chapter). Use the Omit command on the Edit menu to remove from a browsed set any records that you want to remain unchanged. If you want to replace the value in all records in a file, choose the Find All command from the Select menu.

2. Place the insertion point anywhere in a record's field that has the desired value. Or, enter that value into a field in one of the records and keep the insertion point in that field.

3. Choose the Replace command on the Edit menu or press the ⌘-= (equal) keystroke.

   FileMaker displays an alert box that asks whether you want to replace the field with the value of the current field (see fig. 4.5). If you make a mistake, select the Undo command or press ⌘-Z to reverse your action.

4. Click the Replace button to proceed with the operation or press the Cancel button (or press Return or Enter) to return to the Browse screen without changes.

The Replace operation is one that uses the ⌘-. (period) cursor on your screen. Remember, if you want to cancel the operation, you can press the ⌘-. (period) keystroke.

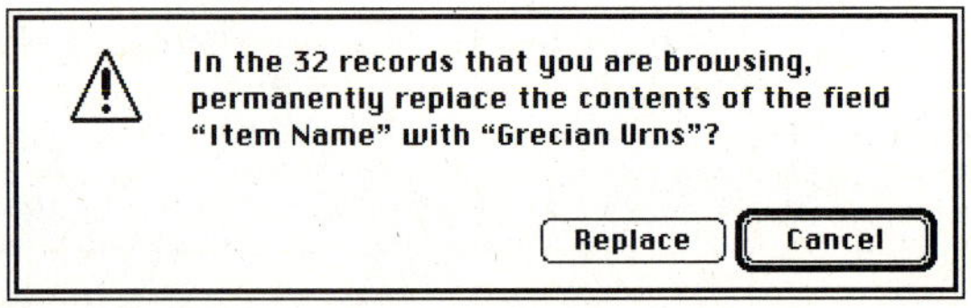

Fig. 4.5
The Replace command alert box.

SPEED KEY

⌘-= replaces the contents of a field in all browsed records with the value in the current field.

FileMaker offers other ways to replace data in multiple records at the same time. You can consider creating a calculation field that will achieve the same results, even a text calculation to edit text, if needed. Consult Chapter 5, "Automating Data Entry," for more information.

Omitting Records

Whenever you want to remove a record from the current browsed set of records, you can use the Omit command on the Edit menu. Omitted records are still contained in your file, but they are no longer contained in the selected set of browsed records with which you are working. Any operation that requires a browsed set of records—summary or calculation fields, printing, or saving a subset of records—will not use the records that you have omitted.

The Omit feature allows you to exclude records, beginning with your current record, and also enables you to specify a number of records that you want to exclude. If you browse record number 5 and specify that 4 records are to be excluded, FileMaker omits records 5 through 8 from your browsed set. The first record omitted is the current record.

Omitting records is particularly useful when you want to exclude a set of contiguous records in a category. Assume that you are assembling a sales report, and you want to exclude a certain time period from consideration. If your file contains daily records in consecutive order, to delete one week's records, you browse the first record in the week and omit seven consecutive records. Or perhaps there is a category of inventory, such as office supplies, that you want to exclude. You can sort by category (see "Sorting Records," later in this chapter), browse the first record in that category, and then omit the number of records in that category.

To omit a record from a browsed set, follow these steps:

1. Make the record that you want to omit from your browsed set the current record. Select the Omit command on the Edit menu or press the ⌘-M keystroke.

   or

   If you want to omit a set of consecutive records, organize the records so that all omitted records occur in a contiguous set and make the first record in that group the current record. Choose Omit Multiple or ⌘-Shift-M. The Omit Records alert box shown in figure 4.6 results.

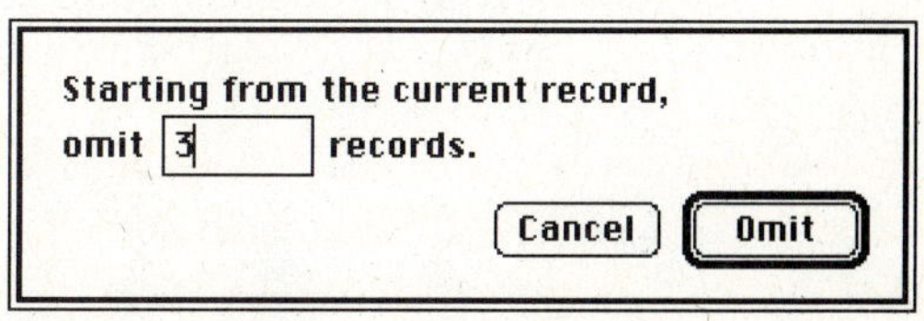

Fig. 4.6
The Omit Records alert box.

2. Enter in the text box the number of records that you want to omit and then click the Omit button. The Cancel button returns the unchanged Browse window.

SPEED KEY

⌘-M removes one record from your current browsed set.

⌘-Shift-M removes multiple records from your current browsed set.

You almost always can omit records by defining a Find operation in a special way. Often, the Omit command turns out to be much easier and faster to implement than figuring out how to structure a Find operation by using the Omit option (the Omit check box in the Find window). Use the Omit option in place of the Omit Records commands when you have a logical exclusion that you can define.

You always can return to the complete set of records in a file by choosing the Find All command from the Select menu. You also can find a set of records by using a Find operation, or you can use a previous Find operation in a session by using the Refind command. Consult "Finding Records," later in this chapter, for details.

If you are working with a browsed set of records, you omit some of them, and then decide you want to include them after all, use the Find command again. FileMaker preserves the last set of criteria in memory and will restore your last found set.

Deleting Records

It's good housekeeping to discard data that you know you will not need again. Smaller files open and close more quickly, calculate faster, and are easier to organize and work with. Unlike omitting records, when the information is still contained in your file, deleting a record permanently removes the record and its associated data from your files. Be particularly careful with the Delete Records command. Be sure that when you delete a record, you will no longer need that data.

To delete a single record, follow these steps:

1. Make the record you want to delete the current record in the Browse window.

2. Select the Delete Records command from the Edit menu or press its ⌘-E keystroke equivalent. The Delete Records alert box appears (see fig. 4.7).

3. Click the Delete button.

   or

   Click the Cancel button (⌘-.) or press Return or Enter to cancel the operation and retain your browsed set of records.

   or

   To delete the record and bypass the Delete Records dialog box, press the ⌘-Option-E keystroke.

Fig. 4.7
The Delete Records alert box.

FileMaker uses the ⌘-D keystroke for the Duplicate command, which makes it unavailable for the Delete Records command. You probably can remember the ⌘-E shortcut if you remember that you are eliminating records.

SPEED KEY

⌘-E permanently removes a record and all its associated data from your file.

⌘-Option-E removes a record and all its associated data from your file, automatically bypassing the alert box.

WARNING

You cannot undo a record deletion, so be particularly careful when you use this feature. The word "permanently" means no recovery is possible. You should use the ⌘-Option-E keystroke that bypasses the alert box carefully. (Do not confuse a *record* deletion, which cannot be undone, with a *text* deletion, which can be undone.)

You also can delete any browsed set of records by using the Delete Found Set command. It deletes the entire browsed set, and all the warnings and restrictions mentioned above apply.

To delete a set of records, follow these steps:

1. Browse the set of records you want to delete.

Do not include in the browsed set any records that you want to retain. Use the Find command (see "Finding Records," later in this chapter) or the Omit command (see "Omitting Records," earlier in this chapter) to remove from the browsed set the records you want to retain.

To delete all records (like having a clone of your file), use the Find All command (if needed) to browse the full set and issue the Delete Found Set command from the Edit menu.

When you delete all of your records in a file, you see a blank Browse window with no fields showing. All your layouts have been retained, just like a cloned file, but they don't show. To see them, create your first record with the New Record command on the Edit menu or press ⌘-N.

2. Select the Delete Found Set command on the Edit menu. The Delete Multiple alert box appears (see fig. 4.8).

3. Click the Delete button to remove the records. Clicking the Cancel button or pressing the Return or Enter key retains your records and cancels the operation.

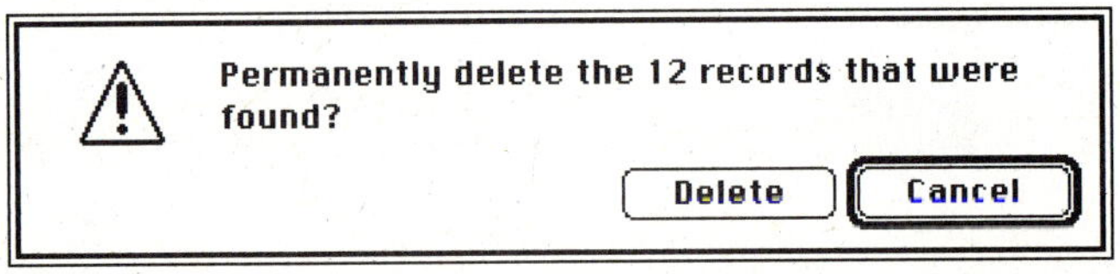

Fig. 4.8
The Delete Multiple alert box.

WARNING

The Delete Found Set command cannot be undone.

If there is any chance that you might want to use the information contained in the records you are thinking of deleting, consider creating an archive file in which to store them. Chapter 15, "Importing and Exporting Data," covers this procedure.

Using the Spelling Checker

FileMaker Pro now includes a spelling checker that aids you both during data entry and while creating the layout. The Main Dictionary (which is available in many languages) and the User Dictionary look up your words electronically. To work conveniently, the dictionaries should be located in the same folder as the FileMaker program or in the System folder. Otherwise, you will be asked to locate them whenever you check spelling for the first time.

The main dictionary exists in a very compressed form; however, all Claris products are capable of sharing the same dictionary. If you are already using a Claris dictionary, there is no need to install the one that comes with FileMaker Pro. The spelling checker will locate the existing Claris dictionary.

To check the spelling of a word at the time of entry, follow these steps:

1. In the Browse mode, type in the questionable word. Then highlight the word.

2. Select the Check Spelling command from the Edit menu and then highlight Check Selection from the submenu.

   The Spelling dialog box appears (see fig. 4.9). Possible solutions will be offered for any words with questionable spelling.

Fig. 4.9

The Spelling dialog box.

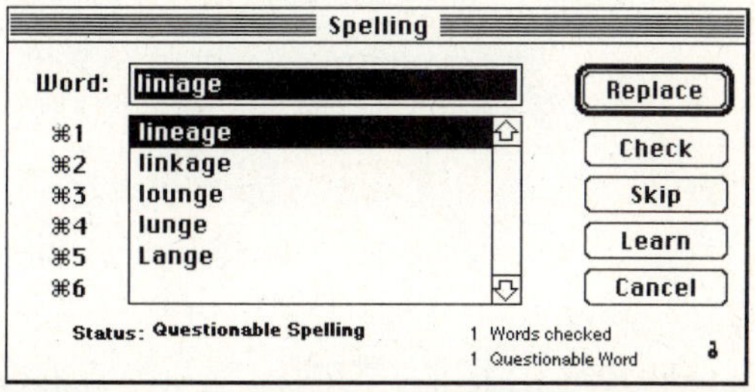

3. If you want to take action on one of the solutions, click on the desired choice (it may already be highlighted).

   Select the following button or one of the buttons listed under step 4:

   Replace button. Clicking this button will automatically insert the highlighted solution in the field box in the Browse window.

4. If the field you chose had multiple words in it, FileMaker will continue to check all of the words and offer suggestions to any questionable spelling. Use the Highlight and Replace button to make any other changes.

   Check button. If you are not sure of your revision, click this button.

   Learn button. If you want to add words to the dictionary, click on the Learn button to insert the highlighted word.

Skip button. Some words may be flagged even though they are spelled correctly (possibly a proper name). To continue without making a change, click on the Skip button.

5. Click on the Done button or choose Cancel if you want to return to the Browse window without making any changes.

The Spelling Options command on the Edit menu allows you to "spell as you type." Instead of selecting the spelling checker when you want to question a word, FileMaker will notify you when a word is in question. Depending on your specification, FileMaker will beep or flash the menu bar to alert you. You then can decide if you want to use the spelling checker.

To activate the automatic spelling checker, follow these steps:

1. Select Check Spelling from the Edit menu and then highlight Spelling Options from the submenu.
2. Choose whether you want the spelling checker to be active while you type and then indicate how you want to be alerted (see fig. 4.10). FileMaker can either beep or flash the menu bar when a word is questionable.
3. Select whether the Spelling dialog box should be automatically placed on the screen or user defined.
4. Click OK.
5. Bcgin your data entry. FileMaker will alert you whenever a questionable word is typed.
6. When a spelling alert appears, correct the word, or to obtain assistance, place the cursor in the correct field and choose the Check Record command on the Check Spelling submenu of the Edit menu.

Fig. 4.10
The Spelling Options dialog box.

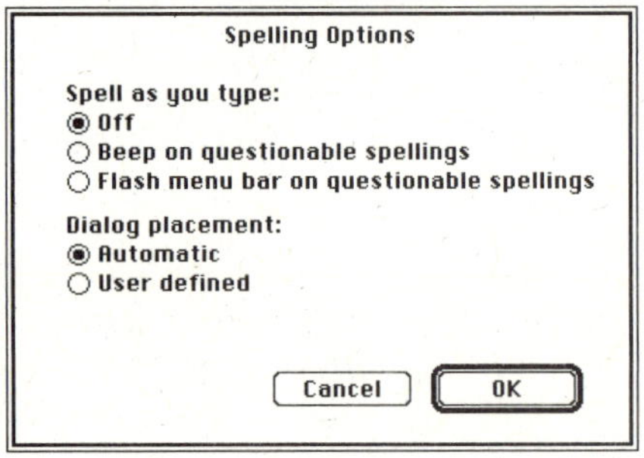

The spelling checker is a feature new to FileMaker Pro.

Changing Defined Fields

You may want to change the name of one of your defined fields, a calculation or entry option, or more rarely, change the field's data type or field attributes. This task is accomplished easily from within the Define Fields dialog box. To display this box, choose the Define Fields command from the Select menu or press ⌘-Shift-D to enter define mode.

Changing Field Attributes

The field attribute defines the type of information that you can store in a field and the set of manipulations that FileMaker can perform on the field. Your first choice for a field attribute or data type is the one you usually will want to stick with. After all, a Picture field will always be a Picture field, and a Date field will always be a Date field. Sometimes you may want to switch a Number field to a Text field, and vice versa. You may want to change one of the basic data attributes to one that FileMaker sums, calculates, or possibly auto-enters.

You can make this change easily, but you need to consider some consequences:

- When changing a Text field to a Number or Date field, an alert box informs you that FileMaker retains only the first 255 characters on the first line. A Return character ends a line. Number fields ignore all alphabetic characters in the index; sorts are based strictly on the numeric entries.
- If you change a Date field to a Number or Text field, you will no longer be able to perform date calculations (see Chapter 5) or sort a field chronologically.
- If you change a Time field to a Number or Text field, you will no longer be able to perform time calculations (see Chapter 5) or sort a field chronologically.
- When you change a Picture field to any other kind of field, you lose all of your graphics data. When you change any other kind of field to a Picture field, you also lose any data it contained. FileMaker always warns you with an alert box.

- When you change any basic field attribute to a calculation or summary field, all data is lost. These fields do not contain data; calculation and summary fields' data automatically is entered by FileMaker. An alert box is posted for this change.

If, by chance, your field contains no data, you do not need to be concerned with any of the previously mentioned consequences.

To change the field attribute, follow these steps:

1. Choose the Define Fields command from the Select menu or press ⌘-Shift-D.
2. Select the field to be changed by clicking on its name to highlight it. Scroll the field list text box if needed.
3. Click the appropriate radio button for the new field attribute or use the command keystroke shortcuts listed next to their names.
4. Click the Change button to accept the change. FileMaker posts the appropriate alert box.
5. To effect the change, click the OK button in the alert box. Clicking the Cancel button returns with the field still selected.

WARNING

When FileMaker says that data will be deleted or replaced, it means that recovery is not possible. *These actions cannot be undone*. It is quite possible to lose an entire file of data in one fell swoop. So, if you fail to read the alert boxes and consider the implications of a field attribute change, you may commit a catastrophic act.

Another operation you may want to perform inside the Define Fields dialog box is to change entry options: auto-entry details, data validation, and lookups. You also may want to change a calculation or summary field formula at some point. Chapter 5 discusses these procedures.

Adding Fields

To add (create) a field to your file, you must define it in the Define Fields box. All the necessary details for creating a file are described in Chapter 3. The procedure here is only slightly different. The difference is that when you create a file, FileMaker automatically prompts you to add fields. In this case, you must initiate the process.

To add a new field to an existing file, follow these steps:

1. Choose the Define Fields command on the Select menu. An insertion point is automatically placed in the field Name text box.
2. Type the new field name.
3. Click the radio button of the field type you want or use the keystrokes listed next to their names. Add any entry options or formulas needed.
4. Click the Create button to enter the field or press the Return key.

   To clear the field Name text box and not create the field, press the Delete key or click Done to exit.
5. Click the Done button to return to the FileMaker window. Your current layout will automatically show the new field in the window. If you switch layouts, you will need to add the new field.

Creating a field or adding a new field to a file is not the same as adding a field to a layout. To add a new field to a layout, you use the Field tool in the Layout window and drag the field onto your layout. FileMaker prompts you to select the field name from a list. For more details, consult Chapter 6.

Changing Field Names

When you change a field name because your data changes or the use for that data changes, several things happen. First, any layout text that FileMaker places on your layout is adjusted to contain the new field name. Second, wherever you have used that field name in a calculation or summary formula (see Chapter 5), FileMaker automatically substitutes the new field name for the old one.

To change a field name, follow these steps:

1. Select the Define Fields command on the Select menu or press ⌘-Shift-D.
2. Select the field name to be modified by clicking on its name in the list of defined fields.
3. Type the new name for the selected field. FileMaker text boxes support these Clipboard commands: Cut (⌘-X), Copy (⌘-C), Paste (⌘-V), Paste Special From Index (⌘-I), Paste Special from Last Record (⌘-'), Paste Special Current Date (⌘- -), and Paste Special Current Time (⌘-;).

4. Click the Change button to accept the change.
5. Click the Done button to return to the FileMaker window and observe your changes.

FileMaker II does not sort field names within the Define Fields dialog box. If you have a long list of field names, you may have to scroll and examine a long list of names to find the one you want.

However, FileMaker Pro enables you to select the Field Order icon to change the order in which the fields are displayed in the Define Fields dialog box (see fig. 4.11).

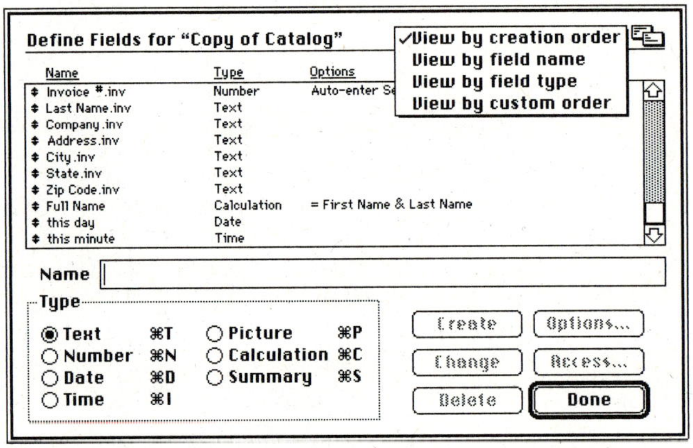

Fig. 4.11
Field order pop-up menu.

A custom field order now can be created at any time. Click on the double arrow to the left of the field name and drag it to a new location (see fig. 4.11).

The capability to customize the field order is a new feature in FileMaker Pro. The Field Order icon also is new.

Deleting Fields

From the Define Fields dialog box, you can delete from your file a field and all of the information it contains. Anytime that field appears in a layout, or if there are associated layout text objects for the field, they will be deleted. For example, in a standard layout, both a field reshape box and a field name in the form of a text object appear side by side. Deleting the field deletes both.

To delete a defined field from your file, follow these steps:

1. Choose the Define Fields command on the Select menu.
2. Select the field name you want to delete by clicking on it to highlight it. Scroll the list if needed. The Field name appears in the Field Name text box.

   If you make a mistake or change your mind, backspace, press the space bar to remove the selection, and make another choice.
3. Click the Delete button to initiate the Delete operation. FileMaker displays an alert box (see fig. 4.12).

Fig. 4.12
The Delete Field alert box.

   Whenever you attempt to delete a field that FileMaker requires in another field—either for a calculation, summary, or lookup—you first must delete the dependent field or remove its reference from the associated formula. FileMaker posts an alert box in which it names the dependent fields in the relationship (see fig. 4.13).
4. To delete the field, click the Delete button in the alert box (refer to fig. 4.12). Clicking the Cancel button returns the Define Fields dialog box, with the field still selected.

Remember, any button in a dialog box that is double-outlined is the default and can be activated by pressing Return or Enter. In figure 4.12, the Cancel button is the choice that will cause the least damage if you err; therefore, it is the default.

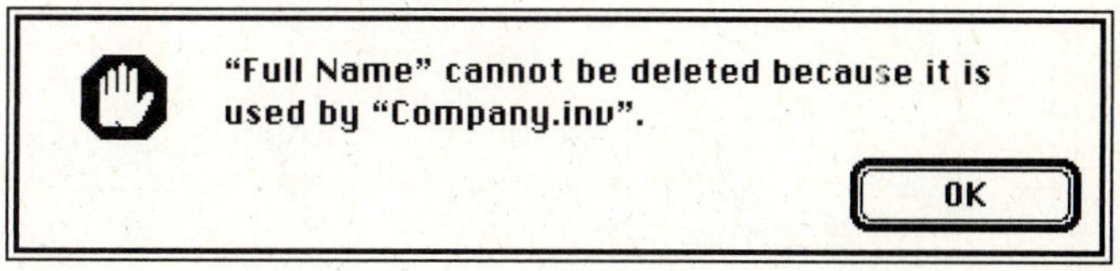

Fig. 4.13
The Delete a Calculated Field alert box.

WARNING

Be careful about deleting a field and all of its associated information; this action cannot be undone.

If you want to retain the information that a field contains, but you don't want the field to appear, delete (remove) that field from a specific layout. You can find details for accomplishing this task in Chapter 6.

Finding Records

FileMaker has a flexible and powerful method for finding information. You select information on the basis of criteria you enter, whether a particular value, a logical expression, or a mathematical formula. FileMaker searches your records to obtain the set of records that match your expression. Your criteria are matched against the index kept by FileMaker for each field involved in the matching process. You can isolate specific pieces of information, select a set of records to browse, based on one or more criteria, or use the Find command to check for accuracy and to eliminate errors and duplications.

The FileMaker Find command supports a set of operators you can use to build your criteria for finding records. When you select the Find command, a Find window appears on-screen. Each field can accept a single criterion, and the total specification for a Find window is called a *request*. Each find can have one or more requests in it, and requests are performed in their order in a find.

You can string find requests together. Each request is in its own window and the order is the order of each window. You move from request 1 to request 2, using the Book and Slide Control Mechanisms, and the Tab and Option-Tab or Shift-Tab keys.

A sampling of the kinds of searches you can accomplish with the Find command include the following:

VALUES:

Exact matches. You can specify that a field contain only the characters specified. For example, typing = *Cool* into the Last Name Text field of your customer file will bring up only customers named Cool. If you want to find Joe Cool, enter = *Joe* = *Cool*; this search also will find Cool, Joe. If you type = *3.14* into a Number field, only records containing 3.14 as an entry will be found; 3.14159 will not be found.

Contains a value. You can specify that a field contain or start with the characters you specify. For example, typing *Cool* into the Last Name Text field of your customer file will find all customers named Cool, COOL, Cooler, Coolest, and so on. Searches are not case sensitive. Typing ***hard drive*** into a Text field will find the entries hard drive, hardly driving, and driven hard, but not HardDrive Cafe. FileMaker searches for each word separately in each field, but order is not important. If you type *3.14* into a Number field, records containing both 3.14 and 3.14159 will be found.

Blank values. You can search for records with blank values in the field you specify by entering the equal symbol (=) only.

LOGICAL VALUES:

Duplicate values. You can search for records with duplicate values in the field you specify by entering the exclamation point (!) only.

Yes or No values. If you defined a Number field as a logical field (see Chapter 6), that field contains a Y or 1 for yes and an N or 0 for no. Type either ***y*** or ***n*** to find records that match those logical values.

MATHEMATICAL FORMULA:

A range of values. You can search a field for values within a range. FileMaker determines whether data falls into a range, based on the ASCII code (see "Sorting Records," later in this chapter). Alphabetic, numeric, and date ranges can be ordered. (For ranges chronologically ordered as serial numbers, see Chapter 3.) For example, if you enter the formula *Cool ... Smart*, entries such as Cool, Smart, O'Hara, and Short will be found. Ranges are inclusive. Entries such as Badger, Bluestein, Sosinsky, Westheimer, 8/27/52, and 3.14 would not. The ellipsis symbol (...) indicates a range.

A mathematical comparison. Using the set of operators < (less than), > (greater than), ≤ (less than or equal to), and ≥ (greater than or equal to), you can define formulas to test conditions for a field.

In a field that shows the balance due for an account, you can search for > 0. Perhaps you want to check for past-due accounts; that is, those accounts that have not been paid 90 days since invoicing. A date calculation, *// – INVOICE date>90*, will find the desired records. The // symbol enters the current day's date.

Time queries can be performed to determine when events happen. A time calculation can be performed to find all sales that occur after 6:00 p.m. To find the results, use *Sales>6:00:00*.

What you find depends on the field type you search. Searching for the current day's date in a Text field will not yield a useful result, because Text fields cannot perform date math. In the section "Entering Criteria," later in this chapter, you will find a much more complete explanation of how to use find operators for a variety of tasks and for all the different field types.

When you find a set of records, you can choose to edit, sort, print, output to another file, delete, or save as a subset the found set. You also can use the Omit command to remove records from a browsed set of records that matched the criteria you entered. You can have any number of find requests linked together in a single search, or you can perform consecutive find operations. All of these options combine to give you enormous control over your search.

Understanding the Find Window

A set of criteria is entered onto a screen called the Find window. This window looks like a blank record in the current layout. Each screen with its associated criteria is called a request.

A Find window is shown in figure 4.14. Many of the window elements common to all Macintosh windows and common to the Browse window already have been introduced. Here, the focus is on the unique elements of the Find window.

Following is a summary of the actions of the unique elements of a Find window:

Find button. Choosing the Find button initiates the Find operation. Alternatively, press the Return or Enter keys to activate the Find button.

Find Operators. The Find operators are operators that you can click to enter into your current entry field. They are the less than (<) operator, less than or equal to (≤), greater than (>), greater than or equal to (≥), Exact (=), Range (...), Duplicate (!), and Today (//).

Omit box. Checking this box omits all records that match the criteria you enter from the found group. It performs a logical NOT operation.

The Find criteria symbols now are displayed in the lower left section of the window. Three symbols were added in FileMaker II: ≤, ≥, and //. The ellipsis (...), which indicates a range, replaces the two periods (..) used in FileMaker Plus. Both range operator symbols, however, still function correctly in FileMaker Pro.

Fig. 4.14
Elements of a Find window.

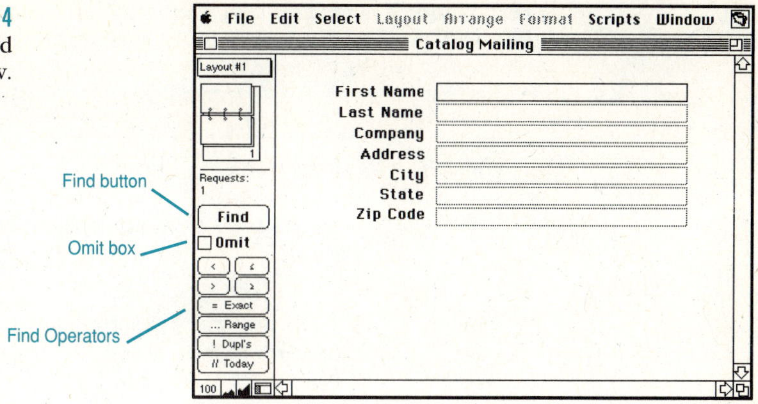

Entering Criteria

To move from entry box to entry box, use the same methods that you learned for the Browse window, discussed in Chapter 3. The fields support text editing and the Clipboard in the same manner as a Browse window.

To enter criteria in a field, follow these steps:

1. Make that field the current field by clicking on it. You can tell where all the fields are if they're not showing by pressing the mouse button.

   Pressing the Tab key selects the first field in the tab order and goes forward in the tab order. Pressing the Option-Tab keystroke selects the last field in the tab order. Use it or the Shift-Tab keystroke to go backward in the tab order.

2. Enter your value or criteria in that field.

SPEED KEY

Tab in the Find window goes forward one field.

Option-Tab or Shift-Tab in the Find window goes backward one field.

Table 4.1 contains a summary listing of the acceptable symbols and operators that FileMaker uses to perform searches, and it also lists their effects on various field types.

In table 4.1, the search criterion value is any character string. A character string that FileMaker indexes is considered a word. For the field types

Text, Number, Time and Date, you also can use these symbols to search for calculation fields with results of each of these four attributes.

Table 4.1
Symbols Used for Search Operations

Symbol	*Text Field*	*Number Field*	*Date Field*
= value	Exact word match *value* for exact match	= not necessary, just type *value* for exact match	= not necessary, just type *value* for exact match
= value = value >	Two words in the same field that match exactly	Not applicable	Not applicable
value (no symbols typed)	Finds words that match or begin with *value*	Finds the numbers that match or begin with *value*	Finds the date you enter as mm/dd/yy
value value (no symbols typed)	Finds two words in the same field that match or finds *value value* string only	Finds *value value* string only	Not applicable
= (only)	Blank field	Blank field	Blank field
value...value	Inclusive range of words	Inclusive range of numbers	Inclusive range of dates
< value	Words alphabetically before *value*	Numbers smaller than *value*	Dates prior to *value*
> value	Words alphabetically after *value*	Numbers larger than *value*	Dates later than *value*
≤value	Words that match or are alphabetically before *value*	Numbers that match or are smaller than *value*	Dates that match or are prior to *value*

Symbol	*Text Field*	*Number Field*	*Date Field*
≥ value	Words alphabetically after *value*	Numbers that match or are larger than *value*	Dates that match or are later than *value*
! (no value typed)	Finds duplicate entries	Finds duplicate numbers	Finds duplicate dates
//	Not applicable	Not applicable	Finds today's date
0/00/0000	Not applicable	Not applicable	Finds invalid dates
00:00:00	Not applicable	Not applicable	Finds invalid dates

Performing Search Requests

This simple find uses two criteria in a single request and illustrates how the Find command operates.

To select a set of records, follow these steps:

1. Open your file and go to any layout that contains all of the fields into which you want to enter criteria.

   After you select matching records, you are free to switch layouts. If you decide to perform the same find again, and a field for which a criterion was defined is missing, FileMaker deletes that criterion in its search.

2. In either the Browse or Layout window, choose the Find command on the Select menu or press the ⌘-F keystroke.

3. In each field, enter the value, logical expression, or mathematical formula that you want to use as criteria.

   In figure 4.15, a layout that tracks the current balance of clients for statements, billings, and past-due accounts is queried for both the number of days since an invoice was issued and for a positive account balance. The Invoice –90 field is a Date field with a date calculation. The underlying calculation formula is Today –90.

Today is a FileMaker operator that enters the current date. Accounts 90 days past due require special handling. For more information, see Chapter 5. When you enter *>0* into both fields, FileMaker supplies you with all of your transactions that require special attention; they are both past due.

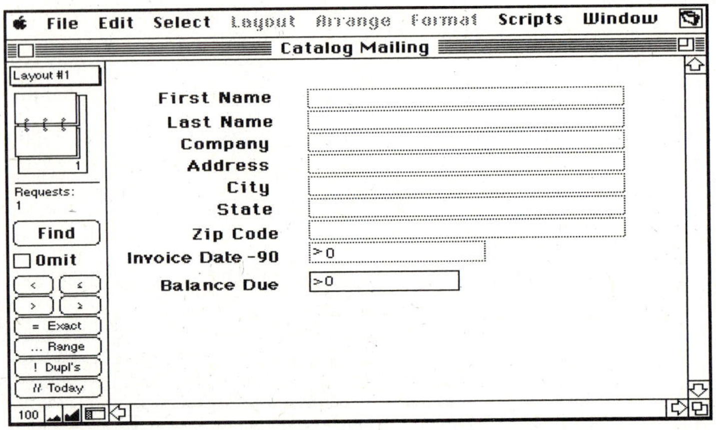

Fig. 4.15
A Find window with two criteria entered and a single request.

4. Click the Find button or press Return or Enter to find the records that match your criteria.

Text fields or calculation fields with text results expand and word wrap to show your complete criterion. All other fields show you only what fits within the field box. To see more of the criterion, you may want to expand the field size in the Layout window.

If you defined a field to Display a List of Values as an auto-entry option (see Chapter 5), a list is displayed when you select the field. Double-click on the entry desired. To use a different value, click once in that field to dismiss the list, and type your entry. You also can use Paste Special from the Edit menu and choose the submenu From Index command (⌘-I) to enter data; see "Using the Field Indexes," later in this chapter.

SPEED KEY

⌘-F, the Find command, creates a set of requests with associated criteria and opens a Find window.

Finds can be fast or slow, depending on the size of your file and how many calculations are needed. To cancel a find in progress when the ⌘-.(period) cursor is on the screen, press the ⌘-.(period) keystroke.

The ⌘-. (period) cursor is a cursor that looks like the ⌘-.(period) keystroke abbreviation. The presence of this cursor on-screen indicates that you can cancel the current operation by pressing ⌘.(period). When a find is completed, FileMaker places you in the Browse window and posts this message in the status area:

```
Records:
  ## (the number of records in your file)
Found:
  ## (the number of records that match your requests)
```

This message shows you the condition of your selected set of records after a find. You can continue to change the browsed set by omitting, editing, adding, or deleting records. The message changes whenever you affect the number of browsed records.

When you enter more than one criterion in a request, FileMaker performs an *exclusive* search operation—the equivalent of a Boolean AND function. Records found must match the criteria entered in each of the fields for the operations you specified; Field 1 and Field 2 must both be true.

You also can select a set of records that do not conform to the criteria entered by checking the Omit check box in the status area of the Find window. Checking the Omit box after the screen in figure 4.15 will find a set of records for which the balance was $0 and that had been paid within the last 90 days. You will not find any other balances, because the database does not contain negative balances. The records found are your better customers with whom you recently did business.

Most often, you will want to perform an *inclusive* search operation—the equivalent of a Boolean OR operation. Include all the records that correspond to Field 1 or Field 2, and so on. This operation is done by creating two or more requests; FileMaker automatically satisfies all requests in a search.

You can define a script that will perform a search for you, and you also can chain together find operations by using scripts (see Chapter 12, "Creating Scripts and Buttons") to form more complex searches. When you define a script, FileMaker retains in memory all of the components (criteria and requests) that you entered in the last search in a work session.

By using the Omit check box with a request, you can perform the equivalent of a Boolean NOR operation: a search that matches one request and not another. If you search with a request for the exclusion of (with the Omit check box checked) *Invoice – 90 > 0* and then use a second request to search for *Balance Due > 0*, you get all the records that have an unpaid balance but are still in your active billing cycle (people you would bill normally without turning their accounts over to your collection agent).

To find records that don't match your request, follow these steps:

1. Choose the Find command on the Select menu or press ⌘-F.
2. Enter the selection criteria that define the set of records you want to *exclude*.
3. Click the Omit check box in the status area. Do this for each request in a find operation.
4. Click the Find button or press the Return or Enter key.

   FileMaker returns you to the Browse screen with all of the records selected that do not match the criteria in your find. If you have some records that you want to exclude from a found set, and they are a small part of your found set, you may find it more convenient to omit these records by using the Omit command in the Browse mode. If so, continue with step 5.
5. Browse any records that you want to remove from your found set and select the Omit Records command on the Edit menu or press ⌘-M.

You might want to select a set of records that conform to one request but do not conform to another request. This is an example of a find with mixed requests: one request and the logical negative of another request. FileMaker processes requests in order, so if you use the Omit check box in the second request to exclude a set of records, FileMaker subtracts the records that match that second request. For example, when you want to find all occurrences of ZIP codes that fall within the range 30000 to 80000, enter *30000 ... 80000* in the Zip Code field of the first request. To exclude ZIP codes between 50000 and 60000, create a second request and enter *50000 ... 60000* in the Zip Code field and then click the Omit check box. When you perform the find, you select records that fall within the ranges 30000 to 49999 and 60001 to 80000.

Editing Requests

If you have defined more than one request in a find, each request occupies a Find window, so you may need to switch requests. In this case, the Book and Slide Control Mechanism are active.

To edit a request, you first must find it. You can find the request by using one of these methods:

- Click on the bottom page of the Book to go forward one request, or press the ⌘-Tab keystroke. Click on the top page of the Book to go backward one request or press the ⌘-Option-Tab or Shift-Option-Tab keystroke equivalents.
- Drag the Slide Control Mechanism to the top of the slide for the first request or to the bottom for the last request or until the desired request number shows in the center page of the Book.
- Drag over the request number in the center page of the Book or double-click to highlight it. Type the number of the desired request and press the Return or Enter key to go to that request.

After you have the correct request screen, enter or edit your selection criteria as desired.

Sometimes you may want to delete a request. If you weren't interested in a subset of found records, for instance, you can modify the find operation to eliminate the request. To delete a request, follow these steps:

1. Make that request the current request.
2. Select the Delete Request command on the Edit menu or press the ⌘-E keystroke.

The Delete Request command functions only when you have two or more requests in a find operation. You cannot undo a Delete Request command.

To duplicate a request, follow these steps:

1. Make the request you want to duplicate the current request.
2. Select the Duplicate Request command on the Edit menu or press the ⌘-D keystroke.

The duplicated request has the next available request number in sequence, and that request screen appears on your monitor. Use the Duplicate Request command when you have a complex screen that you want to edit while keeping the original intact or use it for a series of similar requests.

SPEED KEY

⌘-E, the Delete Request command (in the Find window), removes a request from a find.

⌘-D, the Duplicate Request command (in the Find window), creates a duplicate of your current request.

The Duplicate Request command keystroke has been changed from ⌘-M to ⌘-D, to be consistent with the Duplicate command in the Finder. As a result, the Delete Request command keystroke was changed from ⌘-D to ⌘-E.

Repeating a Request

Because FileMaker retains in memory your last group of requests, you can return at any time in a work session to a set of records that match your last find request by using the Refind command. Any new records you added that match the criteria will be included. Using Refind is different from giving the Find command again, because Find brings back a blank Find window.

To repeat your last selection operation, follow these steps:

1. In either a Browse or Layout window, choose the Refind command on the Select menu or press the ⌘-R keystroke.

   Make sure that all the necessary fields for your search are on the screen before you select this command. If a field for which you defined a criterion is missing from your current layout, FileMaker enters criteria only in the available fields. This prevents you from selecting records with criteria you cannot see, and it can be a source of confusion.

2. Edit your search, if needed.

3. Click the Find button or press the Return or Enter key.

You often will want to return to the *complete set* of records that are in your file. Use the Find All command to do this. The Find All command is active on all three FileMaker windows: Browse, Layout, and Find.

To browse your entire set of records, choose the Find All command on the Select menu or press the ⌘-J keystroke. This method works with whatever type of FileMaker window you currently are in.

⌘-R, the Refind command, returns you to the last find operation you defined.

⌘-J, the Find All command, selects the entire set of records in a file for browsing.

You can select records by information contained in a field that is not displayed or printed (for example, a logical Yes-or-No field). You enter a value into that field to include or exclude a record. If you go to the layout from which you will do your find and place that field outside the print boundary, the field is available for you to see and select with, but does not print.

Using Field Indexes

FileMaker performs one of the fastest find operations of any Macintosh database on the market today. The key to its speed is the way FileMaker uses its index to search for data. When you define a field attribute or data type, you control how that field indexes the data you enter into it. You may want to refer back to Chapter 3 for a further discussion of how fields are indexed. FileMaker matches any value for a field against the index in almost the same fashion that a spelling checker matches words against a standard list of acceptable words.

All fields are indexed using the ASCII code, and character strings are treated as words if they are separated by appropriate separators. Text fields index all characters, and Number fields index all numbers and ignore alphabetic characters. Date fields allow numbers formatted only in date formats, and Time fields allow numbers to be formatted only in time formats. Picture fields are not indexed.

From the Find window, you are not limited to selecting Text, Number, Time, and Date fields and viewing their indexes; you can select calculation fields and view their indexes, as well. Calculation fields index in exactly the same manner as Text, Number, and Date fields, depending on the calculation result. Remember, you learned in Chapter 3 that you cannot select a calculation field in a Browse window, because you cannot enter data into it. FileMaker automatically does that.

Text fields are easier to search and find with because they usually don't require an exact match. They also are often slower to search because they index more entries or characters. When you search for the value 3.14 in a Number field that contains only 3.14159, FileMaker will not find that entry. When you enter *3.14* into a Number field that contains only the entry *Pi equals 3.14*, you get a match for that entry because Number fields index only numeric entries. Similarly, dates stored in the index of Date fields are stored as short dates (such as 4/1/91). FileMaker performs the necessary conversions between date formats to make matches. Whenever you are unsure about what field type to use, define a Text field, because searches are easier and more complete.

To view an index and enter a value into a field, follow these steps:

1. Choose the Find command on the Select menu or press ⌘-F to open the Find window.
2. Select the field for which you want to view an index by using one of the previously mentioned techniques.
3. Select the Paste Special from Index command on the Edit menu, or press ⌘-I. A scrollable window with all indexed words (or acceptable character strings) opens.
4. To enter data into a field, double-click on the word to be entered or click once on the word and click the Paste button.

   To dismiss the index without entering a word, click the Cancel button.

The index feature is a great way to check the accuracy of your data. Suppose, for example, that you view the index for a ZIP code and find that someone entered the letter O instead of the number 0 or the letter l instead of the number 1. That ZIP code shows only a four-digit number. View the index, paste that four-digit number into the Zip Code field, perform a search, and you can isolate the improperly entered number.

You always can tell when an invalid date is entered on a Browse screen because the field contains a question mark. When you are looking for a mistake, it can be inconvenient to search for each record in a large database. To check for invalid dates, enter *0/0/0000* into a Date field or a calculation field with a date result and perform a find operation. Here are some examples of an invalid date: you input data from another file that is not a date, you have a date calculation outside the acceptable range (1/1/0001 to 12/31/3000), or you have a formula for a calculation field that cannot be evaluated (*date 1 – date 2* = negative number).

Sorting Records

As important as selecting data is the capability to organize your data. This involves a *sort* operation. Sorting is done for a browsed set of records and uses the ASCII code (explained in Chapter 3). Sorts are done by field and use the values found in the respective field indexes. You can, therefore, sort Text, Number, Time, Date, and calculation fields but not Picture fields. Picture fields are not indexed.

FileMaker Pro now allows summary fields to be sorted. A sort also can be done by using a custom order based on the field's value list (as a defined entry option).

FileMaker allows sorts by field in *ascending order*, *descending order*, or *custom order*. Ascending order means A to Z for words, 0 to 9 for numbers, and chronological order for dates. Macintosh converts dates to serial dates, which are numbers. Numbers sort before words.

For Text fields with mixed alphabetic and numeric characters, an ascending sort sorts by the first character (numbers first and then the alphabet), then by the second character (numbers first and then the alphabet), and so on. For Number fields with mixed alphabetic and numeric characters, an ascending sort sorts only by the number; FileMaker ignores all non-numeric characters in a Number field, just as it does in the index. Descending order is the reverse of ascending order.

You also can perform *any* level of sort: sort by one field and then the next. Your records are organized by this *sort order*: first by the highest field in the sort order, and then the next, and so on. Consider a sort by ZIP codes first and then by last names. All records with the ZIP code 02165 will be grouped and separated from the set of records with the ZIP code 02168. Then FileMaker sorts each group of two ZIP codes by last name.

To specify a sort, follow these steps:

1. Browse the set of records that you want to sort.
2. Choose the Sort command on the Select menu or press the ⌘-S keystroke.

   The Sort Records dialog box is displayed with a listing of *all* of your defined fields, not just the fields on your current layout (see fig. 4.16).

3. Find the first field in your sort order and click on the Ascending Order or Descending Order radio button, as desired.
4. To place the field in the sort order, click on the field name and then click on the Move button or double-click on the field name.
5. Repeat steps 2 through 4 until the sort order is complete.
6. Click the Sort button, or press Return or Enter to sort the browsed records and return to the Browse window.

or

To cancel a sort in progress, when the ⌘-. (period) cursor is on the screen, press the ⌘-. (period) keystroke.

Alternatively, click the Exit button to return to the Browse screen with your records unsorted.

The following list summarizes the actions of the Sort Records dialog box elements:

Field list. This list shows all defined fields in your file. You cannot choose Picture or summary fields from this list.

Sort order. This shows each field you sort by, starting with the first sorted field at the top, and ending with the last sorted field at the bottom.

Clear button. Clicking on the Clear button removes all fields in the sort order. This button is always enabled.

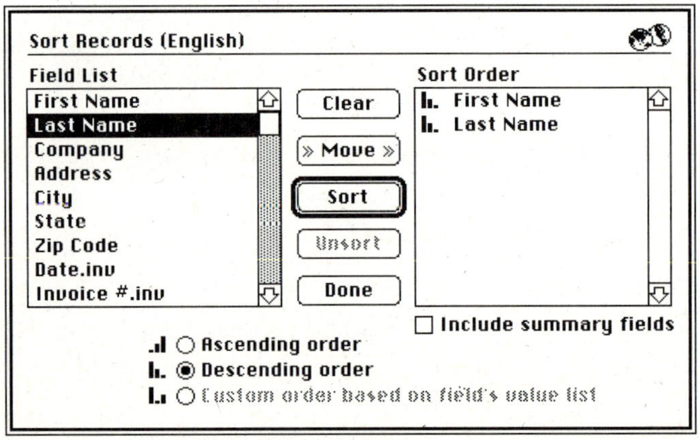

Fig. 4.16
The Sort Records dialog box.

Move button. This button is enabled when a field is selected (highlighted). Double arrows point in the direction of a move. When a highlighted field is in the Field List, click on it to add that field to the sort order. When the highlighted field is in the Sort Order list, click on it to remove that field from the sort order.

Sort button. Click on the Sort button to sort the current set of browsed records and return to the Browse window. This button is enabled when there is a sort order.

Unsort button. Click on the Unsort button to restore the browsed records to their original order and return to the Browse window. This button is enabled only after a browsed set is sorted.

Done button. Click on the Done button to return to the Browse window without sorting your records. FileMaker retains in memory the sort order you specified.

Ascending order radio button. This button is always enabled. Click on it before moving a field into the sort order to sort from bottom to top in the ASCII order.

Descending order radio button. This button is always enabled. Click on it before moving a field into the sort order to sort from top to bottom in the ASCII order.

Custom Order Based on Field's Value List. This button is new to FileMaker Pro. To perform a custom sort, the selected field must contain a value list (specified at the time the field was defined). Records will be sorted by the first entry in the value list, then the second, and so on.

World Icon. FileMaker Pro now has the ability to sort using different languages. Click on the world icon in the upper right of the Sort Records dialog box, and a pop-up menu will produce a list of many languages. Highlight your choice.

Summary Fields box. Summary fields can be excluded or included in the sort process. To exclude, make sure that the box is unchecked; to include, check the box. Summary fields cannot be sorted in a custom sort order.

SPEED KEY

⌘-S, the Sort command, orders a browsed set of records by fields in the sort order you specify.

When you sort a browsed set of records and you return to the Browse screen, FileMaker displays the following in the status area:

```
Records:
   ## (the number of records that are in your file)
Sorted
```

The first record in the sorted order is displayed. If you are working with a subset of the total set of records that you found, the status area displays

```
Records:
  ## (the number of records that are in your file)
Found:
  ## (the number of records in the current browsed set)
Sorted
```

If you want to have a found set of records sorted, however, you should find the records first and then sort them. FileMaker removes a sort order whenever you use the Find or Find All command; the record's normal order is re-established.

You can continue to add to and modify your current set of browsed records. When you create a record, new records are added at the end of any sorted group of records that included the current record on the screen. If your browsed records no longer correspond to your last find requests and sort order, FileMaker displays the following message in the status area:

```
Records:
  ## (the number of records that are in your file)
Found:
  ## (the number of records in the current browsed set)
(Sorted)
```

When you use the Find All command, all records are browsed and the sort order is destroyed. Records return to their natural order. FileMaker remembers the last sort order in a work session so that you can resort without changes by selecting the Sort command and pressing the Return key. You can add sorts to scripts to automate your work (see Chapter 12). The same situation applies when using the Refind command. FileMaker loses the sort order, which you must execute again.

To edit the sort order, follow these steps:

1. Choose Sort to open the Sort Records dialog box.
2. Remove a field from the sort order by clicking on its name to highlight it. The Move button is enabled; click on the Move button to delete the field from the sort order or double-click on the field and it will be removed. All other fields and their order are retained.
3. To erase the sort order, click the Clear button.

or

To restore the unsorted order of your records as you created them, click the Unsort button. You are returned to a Browse window. A Find command also unsorts the records it selects.

Use sorts to create a different sequence of browsed records, such as organizing a mailing list by ZIP codes for a bulk mailing. Certain fields, such as summary fields, require a sorted field that they can summarize (see Chapter 5). You also should sort records so that they can be organized by logical groupings for you to view.

In figure 4.17, you can see the effect of a two-level sort in a sample report. The first sort is by *Division*; the second is by *Quarter*; and both sorts are in ascending order. This report contains one sub-summary field that is keyed to the Division field. Each duplicate value of division is grouped to form a category, and the field sums all values in the Sales field.

Frump Corporation Annual Report

Division	Quarter		Sales (billions)
Air Frump	1		1.45
world's largest	2		1.22
airline	3		1.09
	4		2.34
		TOTAL	**6.10**
Bank of Frump	1		2.45
world's largest	2		3.22
bank	3		1.85
	4		3.55
		TOTAL	**11.07**
Frump Towers	1		0
world's largest	2		0
apartments	3		0.50
	4		0.45
		TOTAL	**0.95**
San Frumpador	1		2.45
banana division	2		3.55
	3		1.60
	4		2.10
		TOTAL	**10.70**
		GRAND TOTAL	**28.82**

January 1, 1991

Fig. 4.17
An annual report with two sorted fields.

Reordering Records

If you can figure out a way to find and sort the records you want to reorder, you can save a copy of your file. Sometimes you will need to retain a complete set of records and move just a record or two. This process is easily accomplished by browsing a record, duplicating it, and then deleting the original.

To reorder records, follow these steps:

1. Browse the record that you want to appear at the end of your browsed set.
2. Select the Duplicate Record command on the Edit menu or press ⌘-D. FileMaker returns the last record in the browsed set to the screen.
3. Return to the original record.
4. Select the Delete Record command on the Edit menu or press ⌘-E and then the Delete button in the Delete Record dialog box. Or, delete the record directly by pressing the ⌘-Option-E keystroke.
5. Go to the next records you want to resequence and repeat steps 2 through 4, until you have the desired sequence.

Reordering takes some planning, and it's tedious with big files, but if you want to, you can reorder an entire file. Beware of duplicating records that do auto-entry for you; you may have to go into the new record to adjust those fields to make them correct for the new order.

The procedure for reordering records is the same procedure that you use to reorder layouts and find requests. The Duplicate Record command has as its counterparts: the Duplicate Layout and Duplicate Request commands in the Layout and Find windows, respectively. The Delete Records command has as its counterparts: the Delete Layout and Delete Request commands, as well. All keystrokes are identical.

In Review

FileMaker uses browse, layout, find, sort, and define modes on the Select menu to protect your data, create operational options, simplify data entry, and minimize operator error.

FileMaker has three Macintosh-styled windows: Browse, Layout, and Find. Elements of FileMaker windows unique to FileMaker were introduced in this chapter, and detailed features of the Browse and Find windows were discussed. Each window contains a status area with a Book and Slide Control Mechanism to move from related window to window.

To move from record to record, use the ⌘-Tab keystrokes to go forward and the ⌘-Shift or ⌘-Option-Shift keystrokes to go backward. You also can click on the pages of the Book to go forward or backward a page, or you can drag the Slide Control Mechanism until the desired record is the current record.

To enter data, you need to select the field and make it the current field. You edit data in fields by using standard text-editing techniques.

The Replace command can replace all values in a browsed set with the current field value. You can copy a record with the Duplicate command, remove a record from a browsed set with the Omit command, and remove records from your file with the Delete Records command.

You change field names, change field types or attributes, add fields, and delete fields in the define mode from within the Field Definition dialog box. Changing field types and deleting fields can cause you to lose data unintentionally, because you cannot change your mind; these operations cannot be undone. Sometimes, however, it makes sense to use them. The implications of these changes were discussed.

FileMaker has a flexible system for finding information and selecting records, based on defining criteria for each field of interest. In the Find window, you create a set of criteria, called a request, and you can string requests together. Finds are used to work with the records you need and are performed based on the contents of each field index. Values, logical expressions, and mathematical expressions may be defined and evaluated.

Records are sorted with the Sort command, based on the ASCII code. Any number of fields may be sorted, in any order.

CHAPTER 5

Automating Data Entry

Much of what makes FileMaker special may be found in this chapter. Here you learn some of the more advanced features that speed up your work, improve your accuracy, and make data entry much more palatable.

All the techniques you have learned so far require that you enter data into your file in one of the five basic field attributes: Text, Number, Date, Time, or Picture. With FileMaker, you also can create two other field types: calculation and summary. Both of these are derived, or logical, fields. A derived field is one that FileMaker automatically enters for you. The program, working with the data contained in the fields you specify, calculates the fields based on a formula that you define. This derived field returns a result that can be text, numbers, or dates.

Much of the power and elegance of FileMaker resides in its capability to do automatic data entry and validation for you. Imagine entering a single piece of information and having that data checked for accuracy and then having a dozen other fields automatically entered, calculated, and summed. If you run a mail-order business, with FileMaker an order might require you to enter only the name of one of your previous customers, the inventory number of the item ordered, and the quantity ordered. All other parts of a complex sales order form—address, pricing, billing, inventory checking, date, sales number, and so on—could be entered by FileMaker. The result is that what would have taken 5 to 10 minutes to do manually can now be done in less than a minute—and much more accurately.

When using a database, few feelings are more satisfying than entering a value into a field and watching FileMaker put data into 5 to 10 other fields automatically. If you follow some of the suggestions contained in this chapter, you will be able to create a file in which two or three entries and a couple of mouse clicks will totally fill out one of your complex forms.

In figure 5.1, you see an example of how to enter an incoming sale. When you create a record, FileMaker assigns a Sales # and enters Today's Date, advancing you to the first field. Double-click on the requested item in the list that is displayed, and FileMaker then enters the Item Cost, advancing to the Quantity field. Enter a quantity, and FileMaker then calculates the Total Sales, advancing to a list of acceptable Methods of Payment. Double-click again, and the cursor advances to the Customer #. Because your customer file is a lookup file, the file is automatically opened with your Sales file. Switch to the customer list, find your customer's number, switch back to your Sales file, and enter that number. FileMaker then enters customer information.

After you begin to understand how much thought goes into creating databases and how valuable they are, you will understand why professional database developers are in such demand. You also will appreciate why a well-written template (see Chapter 13) is a thing of beauty, worth more, perhaps, than the database that serves as its calculating engine.

Using Calculation Fields

A calculation field takes data from fields within a record and, using a formula you define, enters a result. The calculation formula can return either text, number, time, or date results, and can use any number of fields, constants, operators, and functions, which are described in this section. For example, the formula Sale Price * Tax, entered in the Total Price field, multiplies the value in the Sale Price field by the value in the Tax field and enters the result in the Total Price field for every record.

When you are in browse mode, you cannot enter a result into a calculation field—FileMaker automatically enters that result. Also, although FileMaker keeps an index of values for a calculation field, you cannot view that index in a Browse window. You can, however, view the index and search for values in a calculation field by using a find operation, and you can sort those values, too. When you change a calculation formula or change any data in a dependent field, FileMaker automatically updates the calculation field to account for your changes.

Fig. 5.1
Supercharging a FileMaker file.

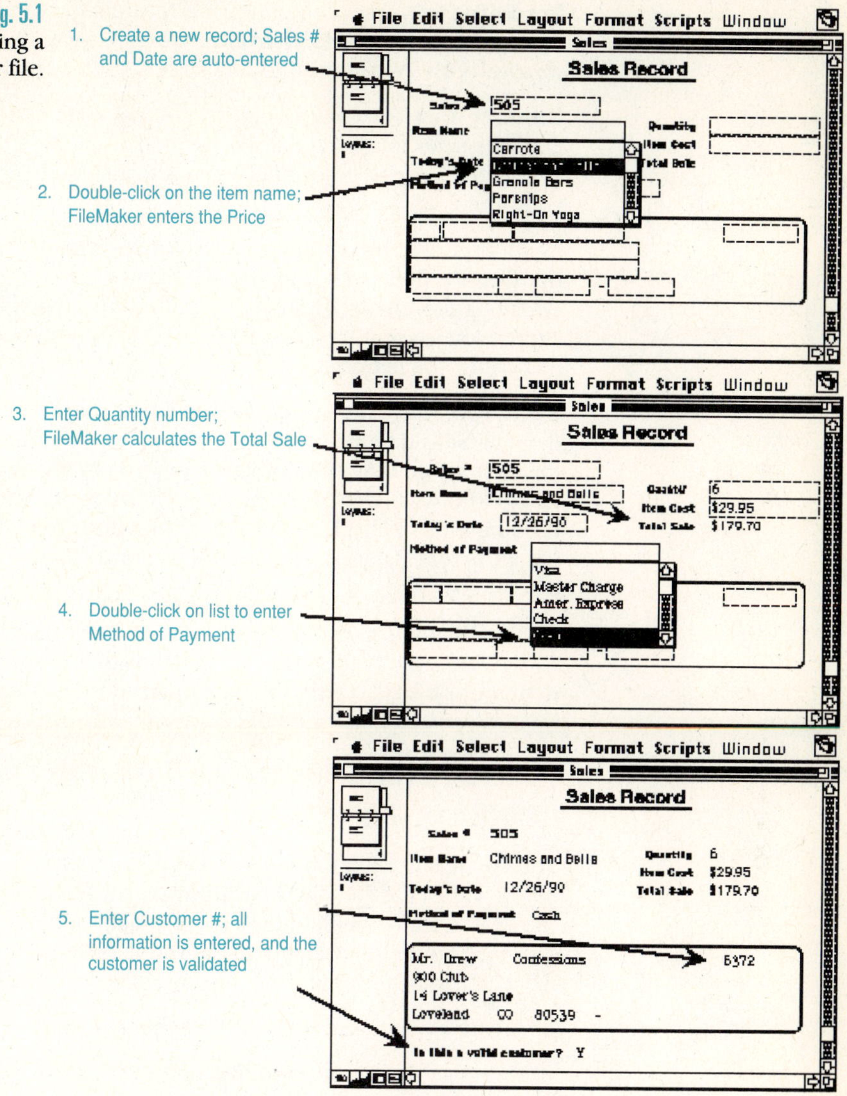

Here are some examples of calculations you may want to define:

Text. You import customer names as a single field from another file. Using the functions Left and Position, you can change Full Name to a first name. *left(Joe Cool,position(" ",1))* returns "Joe."

In another use, you can define an If formula for an action field on a statement. For example, if inventory exists, write *Your product has been shipped.* Otherwise, write *Expect shipment in two to four weeks.*

Number. In a Total Sales field, you define a mathematical calculation for applying sales tax. Total Sales is defined as Sales * (1 + State Tax). The field State Tax is a lookup field that returns a state tax as a decimal equivalent.

As another use, you can do date arithmetic and define the result as a number. To determine the Status of a customer, define that field as Today – Date Invoiced. Then you can use the result in another logic expression, so that if Status ≥ 90, that customer's account is turned over to a collection agency.

Date. You can perform date arithmetic to enter date results. If you define a Ship date field so that it calculates the If function, you get this definition: If Method of Payment = cash, the date entered is Invoice date. Otherwise, the date entered is Today + 30. You also can nest If statements to check a logical field that finds out whether the customer has a Current Balance = 0, and then returns Invoice date as the Ship date.

Time. Calculations can be performed to show time results. If you define a Premium time field so that it calculates the If function, you get this definition: If cost < $10, the time entered is Discount time. Otherwise, the time entered is > 6:00:00.

Defining a Calculation Field

You create a calculation field as you do any other field: in the define mode within the Define Fields dialog box. When you enter a name for the field, specify the field type as a calculation field and click the Create button. You see the Calculation Formula dialog box, in which you define the calculation formula.

To create a calculation field, follow these steps:

1. Select the Define command on the Select menu. The Define Fields dialog box opens.

2. In the Field Name text box, type a field name.

   A name can be 63 characters long. Because you can use calculation field names within the calculation formula of other calculation fields, do not use the following symbols or words:

   + – * / ^ & = ≠ > < ≥ ≤ " " ( ) and, or, not, today

Also, do not use a period or number or the name of any FileMaker Pro function. If you do, FileMaker may try to use the field name as a calculation formula (making the field name impossible to use in a calculation), which is not what you intended.

3. Click on the Calculation button or press the ⌘-C shortcut to set the field attribute.

SPEED KEY

⌘-C specifies a calculation field within the Define Fields dialog box.

4. Click the Create button to create the field. FileMaker opens the Calculation Formula dialog box.

5. Enter the formula into the Calculation Formula text box either by typing the formula or by using the Fields, Operators, and Functions scroll boxes or the keypad. By clicking once on any of these features, you enter them into your formula.

6. To create a repeating field, click Repeating Field with a Maximum of N Values and type the maximum number of times you want the field to repeat. Information on repeating fields appears later in this chapter in the "Field Functions" section. Figure 5.2 shows the dialog box filled out.

Fig. 5.2
Creating a calculation field.

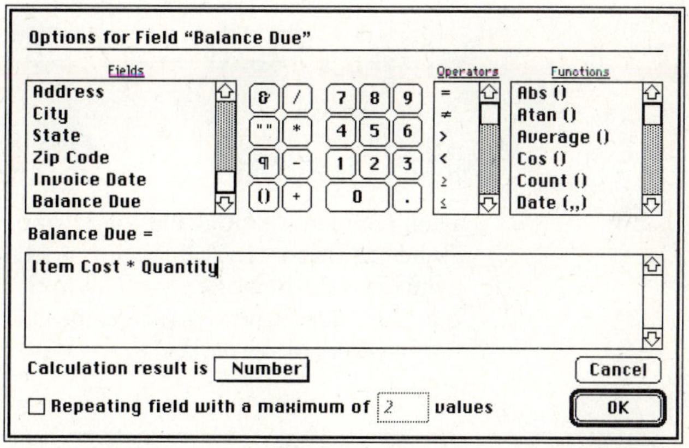

7. Select the Calculation Result type by clicking on the pop-up menu next to Calculation Result and dragging through the choices to find the one you want (see fig. 5.3).

For the same reasons that you are required to set the field type for a basic field type, you must tell FileMaker whether your calculation should be treated as a Text, Number, Time, or Date result.

Although the fields you work with can have certain attributes associated with them, you can use a calculation formula to interpret those results as a different data type, or you can use a function (as you will see shortly) to convert a result from one attribute to another.

8. Click the OK button or press the Return or Enter key to accept the formula and return to the Define Fields dialog box.

9. Click Done.

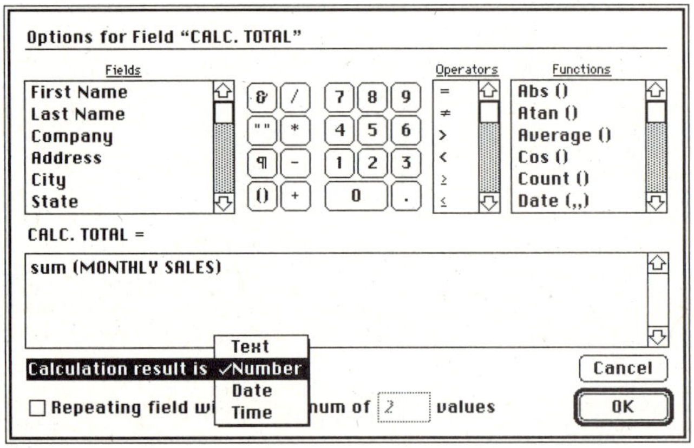

Fig. 5.3
Calculation Options dialog box showing pop-up menu.

The Repeating Field specification has been moved from the Format menu to the Options of the Calculation Formula dialog box.

When you leave the Calculation Formula text box, FileMaker calculates all the entries for that calculation field, as well as any other calculation or summary fields that use that field in their calculations. FileMaker calculates numbers with an accuracy of 15 floating decimal point digits. Your calculation formula is entered under Options in the Define Fields window.

Operations are performed from left to right, with multiplication and division taking precedence over addition and subtraction. By placing operations inside parentheses, you can force those operations to be evaluated first. For example, 4 + 8 / 4 = 6, but (4 + 8) / 4 = 3. When you create a formula that FileMaker cannot evaluate (such as dividing a number by zero), no alert box appears. When you return to the Browse window, however, you see a question mark in the field box.

A summary of the features of the Calculation Options dialog box (shown in fig. 5.2) follows:

Field names scroll box. Click once on the field name, and FileMaker enters it into your calculation formula, left of the insertion point. You can enter a field name from your keyboard, but a separator such as a space character is required for FileMaker to recognize it. You can enter any Text, Number, Time, Date, or calculation field (of any type). You cannot enter Picture and summary fields.

Keypad. Click once on any of the numbers or symbols to enter them into your formulas or type these symbols from your keyboard. You can use the following special symbols:

/	division
*	multiplication
–	subtraction
+	addition
( )	a set of parentheses
&	concatenation
" "	a text constant
¶	a return character
.	a decimal point

Enter all symbols into the formula to the left of the insertion point, except for the parentheses and the double quotation marks. The insertion point is placed between those two symbols to enable further entry.

Operators scroll box. Click once on the symbol you want to enter or type the symbols from your keyboard. The mathematical and logical operations contained in this scroll box are described in the preceding text.

Functions scroll box. Click once on the function you want to enter into your formula or type these functions from your keyboard. The functions contained in this scroll box are described later in this chapter.

Calculation results pop-up menu. Click on the desired data type; the choices are Text, Number, Date, and Time.

Calculation formula text box. This standard Macintosh text box supports the Clipboard and text-editing techniques. Type or enter a formula up to 250 characters long.

WARNING

FileMaker truncates formulas more than 250 characters long when you press OK and then returns you to the text box to edit the truncated formula. If you want to edit the formula, you can move the insertion point by clicking where you want or by using the arrow keys.

OK button. Click this button or press Return or Enter to accept the formula and return to the Define Fields dialog box.

Cancel button. Click or press the ⌘-. (period) keystroke to return to the Define Fields dialog box with the field still selected but without the calculation formula defined.

Editing a Calculation Field

You can edit calculation fields in the same manner that you create them: by going into the define mode and working with the field in the Define Fields dialog box. Fields are selected, deselected, and deleted in the usual manner, as described in Chapter 4.

To change a calculation field, follow these steps:

1. Choose the Define Fields command on the Select menu to open the Define Fields dialog box.
2. Click on the field name desired. Scroll the list, if needed.

From here, you can change the field name and change the calculation result type.

To change the field name, do the following:

1. Edit the highlighted field name in the Field Name text box. This text box supports text editing and the Clipboard.
2. Click the Done button to confirm the name change.

   or

   Click on the Cancel button or press ⌘-. (period) to dismiss the Define Fields dialog box without changes.

To change a calculation result type, follow these steps:

1. Click on the Options button, which is enabled when a calculation field is selected, to open the Calculation Formula dialog box.
2. Scroll through the pop-up menu of Calculation Results and highlight your new choice.

3. Click on the OK button or press the Return or Enter key.

   or

   Click on the Cancel button or press ⌘-. (period) to dismiss the Calculation Formula dialog box without changes.

Changing the field type or attribute has some serious implications, which are discussed in Chapter 4. You may want to review that section before you perform this operation. If you decide to change a basic field attribute (Text, Number, Time, or Date) to a calculation field, you lose all your previously entered data. Be especially careful before you perform this operation. Changing from a calculation field to one of the basic field types, however, retains your data and is not hazardous to its condition.

To change a calculation formula, follow these steps:

1. Choose the Define Fields command on the Select menu to open the Define Fields dialog box.
2. Click on the field name desired. Scroll the list, if needed.
3. Click on the Options button, which is enabled and is the default when a calculation field is selected, to open the Calculation Formula dialog box.
4. Edit the calculation formula as desired. The Calculation Formula text box supports text editing and the Clipboard.
5. Click on the OK button or press the Return or Enter key.

   or

   Click on the Cancel button or press ⌘-. (period) to dismiss the Calculation Formula dialog box without changes.

When you exit the Calculation Formula dialog box, FileMaker recalculates the calculation field, as well as any other dependent calculation or summary fields that use data derived from the calculation field.

Using Calculation Operators

A calculation formula can result in text, numbers, times, or dates. The formula can contain values in the form of constants, field names, or an expression. You can enter text, numbers, times, and dates into a formula as a field of the right data type, a calculation field of the right calculation result type, an expression in the right format, or as a constant. Normally, these values are acted on in some manner in an operation defined by an operator. FileMaker uses symbols to represent operators. Some operations are more complex and are considered functions.

The following are elements you can use to build a calculation formula:

Constants. A constant is a value you enter into a formula. Constants can be text, numbers, times, or dates.

To define a text constant in a formula, enclose a character string inside quotation marks, such as

"23 Skiddoo"

Even if the characters entered are numbers only, FileMaker interprets them as text and can work with them as such. Similarly, you can define a Number constant by entering any number, such as 3.1416. A Date constant can be a date you enter, such as 7/4/91. Date constants also can be returned by a Date function so that they also can be used to enter a date value. For example, Date (8,27,1952) returns 8/27/52, a constant.

When you use field names in each record, they return a value that is used by the expression. Although each record may have a unique value, an operation using a constant is always acted on in the same manner. For a Date field defined as Invoice Date + 30, a date result 30 days later than the invoice date always will be returned.

Field Names. You can use any previously defined Text, Number, Date, Time, or calculation field name as a value in a formula. When using any field in a calculation formula, that field must have the right data type for the calculation result type. You cannot use Picture or summary fields. A summary field calculates results for a group of records; a calculation field requires a single field.

If a field is not the correct data type but is one of the acceptable data types, you can convert that field's data type by using one of the conversion functions described later in the chapter. You also can format fields as repeating fields, and you can define each field to contain multiple values. Repeating fields require special functions and techniques so that they perform properly in a calculation formula. They are discussed later in this chapter.

Expressions. When you define a formula that results in a value, the formula is an expression. Expressions can have Text, Number, Time, or Date results and also can be used as a value for a formula; that is, expressions can be formulas nested inside other formulas. For example, when evaluating the expression

TOTAL SALE = (ITEM COST – DISCOUNT) * SALES TAX,

the term ITEM COST – DISCOUNT, which is the adjusted item cost, is an expression returning a value that is used in a formula.

Operators. Operators include symbols that perform arithmetic (+ – / * and ^), comparison symbols (= > < and so on), Boolean logic symbols (and, or, not), and text operations (& " " and ¶). These operations are defined. You can use decimal points, parentheses, ampersands, quotation marks, and paragraph symbols as operators. See table 5.1 for an explanation of these symbols.

Functions. A function is an operation defined by FileMaker to act on one or more values. Functions are listed in the Function scroll box in the Calculation Formula dialog box and are described in the following section. Functions fall into the following categories: mathematical, financial, repeating field, text, date, time, logical, and data-type conversion.

Arithmetic operators can evaluate values in the form of numbers, dates, times, field names, and expressions, and they return a value, number, field name, or expression that is a valid formula. Comparison and logical operators are evaluated with Boolean logic. Values are acted on to produce a logical result, true or false. In a field containing comparison or logical operators, 1 is calculated for true and 0 for false.

Table 5.1
Summary of Calculation Operators

Operation		*Example*	*Explanation*
ARITHMETIC OPERATORS			
Note: → means "results in" or "returns"			
+	Addition	(2 + 3) → 5 Today + 30 → 1 month hence	Plus sign
–	Subtraction	3 – 2 → 1 (Sale – Item Cost) → Tax	Minus sign
*	Multiplication	2 * 3 → 6 (Sale * 0.07) → Commission	Asterisk
/	Division	(8 / 2) → 4 (Annual Income / 12) → Monthly Income	Slash
^	Exponent	(3 ^ 3) → 9 4 ^ (1/2)) → 2 pi (radius ^ 2) → CIRCLE AREA	Caret symbol; number raised to the power of

continues

Table 5.1 continued

Operation		Example	Explanation
.	Decimal	3.1416	Period; separates integer from modulus
COMPARISON OPERATORS—Returns 1 if true, 0 if false			
=	Equals	(2 = (4 – 2) → 1 (Today =Yesterday) → 0	
≠	Does not equal	(3.14 ≠ 3) → 1 (Today ≠ Yesterday) → 1	Use Option- = keystroke
>	Greater than	(Today > Yesterday) → 1	
<	Less than	(Today < Yesterday) → 0	
≥	Greater than or equal to	(4 ≥ 4) → 1 (4 ≥ 2) → 1	Use Option-> keystroke
≤	Less than or equal to	(4 ≤ 2) → 0 (4 ≤ 4) → 1	Use Option-< keystroke
LOGICAL OPERATORS—Returns 1 if true, 0 if false			
and		(Today ≥ Yesterday) and (Year = 1917) → 0	Requires both expressions be true → 1; else → 0
or		(Today ≥ Yesterday) and (Year = 1917) → 1	Requires either or both expressions be true → 1;< else → 0
not		Today = not (Yesterday or Tomorrow) → 1	Returns 1 when expression is false; else 0

Operation		Example	Explanation
TEXT OPERATORS			
&	Concatenate	Full Name = First Name & " " & Last Name	Joins Joe, space, and Cool into "Joe Cool"
" "	Text constant	"23 Skiddoo"	Treats the value as a text constant; indexed as 23, Skiddoo
¶	Return or end line character	Truly & "¶¶¶" & Joe → 3 blank lines between "Truly"and "Joe"	Use Option-7 keystroke

Using Calculation Functions

A function is a complex operator that condenses two or more separate operations into a single, separate, and streamlined calculation. The 61 functions that you can use are programmed into FileMaker. You can type them or enter them by clicking on the function name in the Function scroll box of the Calculation Formula dialog box. If you have used a spreadsheet before, done some simple programming, or used another database, many of these functions will be familiar. The following sections discuss the available functions.

Mathematical Functions

In the descriptions of mathematical functions that follow, a value is what the function operates on. A value may be the result of other values. Number values can be number constants, the data in Number fields and calculation fields with numeric results, and the data derived from a number result for an expression or calculation.

abs (number). The Absolute function takes a number and returns the absolute value. Positive numbers and zero are unchanged; negative numbers are converted to positive numbers.

Examples: abs (100 – 101) → 1, abs (101 – 100) → 1, abs (Today = Yesterday and Tomorrow = Yesterday) → 0.

int (number). The Integer function takes a number and drops off all places to the right of the decimal place.

Examples: int (pi) → 3, int (–11.1234) → –11.

ln (number). The Ln function returns the base-e (natural) logarithm of the supplied number. The opposite of the Ln function is the Exp function.

Example: ln (2.7182818) → ln(exp(3)) → 3.

log (number). The Log function provides the common logarithm (base 10) of a number. The result can be any positive value.

Examples: log(1) → 0, log(100) → 2.

mod (first number, second number). The Modulus function divides the first number by the second number and calculates and returns the remainder, called the modulo.

Examples: mod (2/28/90 – 2/1/90, 3) → mod (28, 3) → 1, mod (pi, 1) → mod (3.1415..., 1) → 0.1415... The number in the last example is calculated to 15 decimal places and is displayed to as many places as you format the field to show.

pi. The Pi function returns the value of the constant pi (π), or approximately 3.14159.

Example: Pi * 10 → 31.4159.

random. The Random function returns a random number between, but not including, zero and one.

Example: Int(6 * Random) + 1 → 4 or 3, or any number between 0 and 7.

round (first number, number of decimal places). The Round function takes the first number and retains the number of decimal places indicated by the second number. The second number must be a whole number (...1, 0, –1, ...). When the second number is positive, numbers retained are to the right of the decimal point. For a second number that is a negative number or zero, FileMaker rounds the result to the left of the decimal point.

Examples: round (pi, 3) → 3.141, round (pi, 0) → 3, round ((pi * 1000), –2) → round (3,1415..., –2) → 3,100.

The Round function is useful when you want to control the precision of a number that is used to perform calculations and summaries. If you want to retain the 15-digit accuracy but display a number only to a certain number of decimal places, use the Format Number command on the Format menu when that field is selected in the Layout window to set the number of decimal places.

sign (number). The Sign function returns a result that tells you whether a number is positive, negative, or zero. For these two cases, 1 and –1 are returned, respectively.

Examples: sign (2/28/90 – 2/1/90) → sign (27) → 1, sign (2/1/90–2/28/90) → sign (–27) → –1

Text Functions

Text functions produce some of the most useful calculation formulas to be found in FileMaker. They perform calculations on text values that you can enter as text constants, Text fields, or calculation fields, with text results of an expression or calculation formula. When referring to a position, FileMaker uses the first character (the one on the extreme left) as position 1, not 0. The character to the right of the first one is 2; the one to the right of 2 is 3; and so on.

exact (first text, second text). The Exact function compares the two text strings and returns a 1 if they are the same or a 0 if they are not. This function is case sensitive.

Examples: exact (Joe Cool, Joe cool) → 0, exact (Joe & " " Cool, Joe Cool) → exact (Joe Cool, Joe Cool) → 1.

left (text, number of characters). The Left function deletes all characters to the right of the number of characters specified, returning a copy of just the specified number of characters. This function is most useful when you want to extract a portion of a text string. If there are fewer than the number of specified characters, FileMaker enters what it can.

Example: left (Phone Number, 5) → left ("(617)555-0439", 5) → (617).

length (text). The Length function returns a number that is the number of characters in the text string.

Example: length (23 Skiddoo) → 10.

lower (text). The Lower function returns a copy of your text string with all alphabetic characters in lowercase.

Example: lower (5 Bucks) → 5 bucks.

middle (text, number of starting character, number of characters). The Middle function extracts a set of characters within a range of text defined as beginning at the starting position and counting the specified number of characters to the right.

Example: middle ((317)555-2500 ext. 2555, 6, 8) → 555-2500.

position (text, position text, number of starting character of position index). The Position function searches a text string for a character or set of characters that serve as a position index, and it returns the position number of the first character in the index. When position text is not found, FileMaker returns a 0.

Example: position (Name, " ", 1) → position (Joe Cool, " ", 1) → 4.

proper (text). The Proper function capitalizes the first character of each word and places all following characters in lowercase, returning a text string with the same number of characters. Only alphabetic characters are changed. Any indexed item is considered a word. This function is particularly useful to convert names to the correct format. Note that you should not use the Proper function with names such as del Rey.

Examples: proper (23 skiddoo) → 23 Skiddoo, proper (elysian fields) → Elysian Fields.

replace (text, start position, number of replacement characters, new characters). The Replace function takes text and replaces a number of characters, starting at the position you specify. The number of characters you replace can be different from the number of characters that are used as their replacement, resulting in character strings of different length.

Example: replace ((617)555-2910,10,4,3917) → (617)555-3917.

right (text, number of characters). The Right function displays the specified number of characters from the right. This function is most useful when you want to extract a portion of a text string. If there are fewer than the number of specified characters, FileMaker enters what it can. When blank, a blank is returned.

Example: right (Phone Number, 5) → right ("(617)555-0439", 5) → –0439.

trim (text). The Trim function removes any leading or trailing spaces from a character string.

Example: (trim (Last Name) & ":") → (trim (Cool) & ":") → Cool:.

upper (text). The Upper function converts all alphabetic characters in a string to uppercase.

Example: upper (Postal Code) → upper (bs8 1ts) → BS8 1TS

Logical Functions

FileMaker's logical functions are some of the most useful functions the program offers. Use the If function to create conditional statements that will greatly enhance your work. Also, Exact is a text function (see preceding section), but it also is a logical function because it returns a value of true or false.

if (expression, first value if true, second value if false). The If function evaluates an expression for Boolean logic, true or false, yes or no, 1 or 0, respectively. When true, the function returns the first value, and when false, the function returns the second value.

Example: if (Today – Invoice Date ≤ 90 and Balance Due > 0, "Past Due !" Thanks!) → if (2/28/90 – 2/1/90 ≤ 90 and 325 > 0, Past Due!, Thanks!) →

if (28 ≤ 90 and 325 > 0, Past Due!, Thanks!) → if (1, Past Due!, Thanks!) → Past Due!

Nested If statements are particularly useful. Follow the logic of this example:

if ((if (Today – Invoice date ≤ 90 and Balance due > 0), Past due!, Thanks!) = Past due! and (Today – Invoice date > 90), A collection agent will call!, Thanks!) → if ((if (2/28/90 – 2/1/90 ≤ 90 and 325 > 0), Past due! Thanks!) = Past due! and (2/28/90 – 2/1/90 > 90), A collection agent will call!, Thanks!) → if ((if (27 ≤ 90 and 325 > 0), Past due!, Thanks!) = Past due! and (27 > 90), A collection agent will call!, Thanks!) → if (Past due! = Past due! and 28 > 90, A collection agent will call!, Thanks!) → if (1 and 0, A collection agent will call!, Thanks!) → Thanks!

In the example above, you evaluate a third option by using a second If function. You can nest If statements to evaluate any number of possibilities.

Date Functions

FileMaker uses serial dates to perform date arithmetic. Depending on the type of calculation done, the result can be another date or a simple number. Values used in date functions can be numeric constants, number fields, or calculation fields with number results, or the numeric result of an expression or calculation.

date (month, day, year). The Date function evaluates three numbers in the format (#, #, #) and returns a date in the format mm/dd/yy. If either the month or the day numbers fall outside of their normal range (1 to 12 for months, and 1 to 28-31 for days), FileMaker adjusts the year or the month, respectively.

Examples: date (Month, Day, Year) → date (2, 28, 90) → 2/28/90, date (Month, Day + 1, Year) → 3/1/90.

day (date). The Day function evaluates a date and returns only the day portion as an integer between 1 and 31.

Example: day (Month, Day + 1, Year) → day (2, 1 + 1, 90) → 2.

DayName (date). The DayName function returns text containing the name of the weekday upon which the supplied date falls.

Example: DayName(TextToDate("9/24/90")) → Monday.

DayOfYear (date). The DayOfYear function determines a number equal to the number of days since January 1 of the year of the supplied date.

Example: DayOf Year(TextToDate("1/20/1990")) → 20.

month (date). The Month function evaluates a date and returns only the month portion as an integer between 1 and 12.

Example: month (Month, Day, Year) → month (2, 28, 90) → 2.

MonthName (date). The MonthName function returns text containing the name of the month in which the supplied date falls.

Example: MonthName(TextToDate("9/23/90")) → September.

today. The Today function takes no argument (value) and returns the current date at the time of file calculation, based on the date you set for the Macintosh clock. To change the current date, alter it in the Alarm Clock desk accessory.

Example: today → 4/1/91.

The Today function is different from the Paste Date command on the Edit menu (⌘- -[hyphen]). Paste Date is a date stamp that puts the date at the time of its execution permanently into where it is placed. You also can place the Today function in the form of a layout object by placing // on a layout (see Chapter 9).

WeekOfYear (date). The WeekOfYear function returns the number of weeks since January 1 of the year of the supplied date.

Example: WeekOfYear(TextToDate("2/5/90")) → 6.

year (date). The Year function evaluates a date and returns only the year portion. A year is returned as a four-digit integer, even if the date was entered in short form as a two-digit integer.

Example: year (Month, Day, Year) → year (2, 28, 90) → 1990.

Field Functions

A repeating field is a field that can contain several independent values in a single record. To perform proper mathematical manipulation of each of the independent values in a repeating field, you may need to use some of the functions that FileMaker supplies especially for that kind of field, described in the following text. The value field refers to a set of values defined by a repeating field. You can use only a repeating field.

average (repeating field). The Average function sums all values in a repeating field (excluding blank values) and divides it by the number of values to return a number. Average here refers to the arithmetic mean.

Example: average (Marbles) → average (1, 2, 4, 5) → 3.

The Average function, like any FileMaker function, supplies a calculated mean for a set of values within a record. If you want to find the average for values in a field across a browsed set of records, you need to define a summary field, which is discussed later in this chapter.

count (repeating field). The Count function evaluates a repeating field and returns the number of values in that field.

Example: count (Marbles) → count (1, 2, 4, 5) → 4.

If you want to find a count of values in a field across a browsed set of records, you need to define a summary field.

extend (nonrepeating field). The Extend function takes a nonrepeating field and repeats its single value the correct number of times to perform appropriate arithmetic or logic. Use the Extend function when you use a combination of repeating and at least one nonrepeating field in a formula.

Example: The field Sales contains the values (1200, 42000, 1800), and the field Tax contains only the value (0.05).

Then, Sales * extend (Tax) → (1200, 42000, 1800) * extend (0.05) → 60, 2100,90

last (repeating field). The Last function returns the last valid, nonblank value in a repeating field.

Example: Given that ParcelBids is a number field formatted to repeat with 10 values and contains the values 2500, 1200, 1500, then Last(ParcelBids) → 1500.

max (repeating field). The Maximum function evaluates a repeating field and returns the largest value.

Example: max (sales) → 42000.

To find the maximum value in a field across a set of browsed records, define a summary field.

min (repeating field). The Minimum function evaluates a repeating field and returns the smallest value.

Example: min (sales) → 1200.

To find the minimum value in a field across a set of browsed records, define a summary field (discussed later in this chapter).

NPV (interest rate, field). The Net Present Value function is used for repeating fields. It's discussed in the following section.

stdev (repeating field). The Standard Deviation function calculates the standard deviation for the values in a repeating field, returning a number. FileMaker uses the n-weighted average (population standard of deviation) to calculate the standard deviation.

Example: stdev (questions) → 4.0

To find the standard deviation in a field across a set of browsed records, define a summary field.

sum(repeating field).The Sum function calculates the total of all values in a repeating field, returning a number.

Example: sum (invoices) → 36000

To find the sum in a field across a set of browsed records, define a summary field.

summary (summary field, break field). The Summary function extracts the value of the specified summary field for the current range of records when the database is sorted by a break field. The result will be blank if the database is not sorted by a break field. If a summary field is supplied in place of a break field, the Summary function returns the value of the specified summary field for all the records in the database. The file does not have to be sorted for a value to appear.

The Summary function works like summary fields do on printed reports.

Financial Functions

If you have used financial functions in spreadsheets, FileMaker's functions will seem familiar to you. Financial functions are mathematical expressions that use values to return financial information. Financial functions use as arguments number values, such as number constants, number fields, or calculation fields with number results of an expression or calculation. Use decimal format when entering values. FileMaker calculates results to 15 digits and displays the number of decimal places that you specify in the layout mode by using the Format Number command.

FileMaker does not offer an extensive array of financial functions. If you need that kind of a program, investigate power spreadsheets such as Excel, Wingz, or Full Impact.

FV (present value, interest rate, number of periods). The Future Value function calculates a series of equal payments made at equal intervals at the specified interest rate (in decimal form) per period, returning a number.

Example: For an annuity paying $1,000 once a year for 12 years at 8 percent interest, FV (1000, 0.08, 12) → $18,977.13.

NPV (interest rate, field). The Net Present Value function calculates a set of payments from a repeating field (they can be unequal amounts) to be made at equal intervals at a specified interest rate (in decimal form) and returns a number.

Example: A car loan your bank wrote is to be paid back with four annual payments of $1,000 and a fifth payment of $10,000 at an interest rate of 6 percent: NPV (0.06, (Payments)) → $14,937.69.

pmt (amount, interest rate, number of periods). The Payment function calculates the payments needed to return a specified amount at the stated interest rate (in decimal form) per period. Payments are made at equal intervals at the end of each period.

Example: To make monthly payments on a $1,000 furniture loan paid out at 12 percent for 12 months, pmt (1000, 0.01, 12) → 132.70.

PV (amount, interest rate, number of periods). The Present Value function calculates the value of an annuity, a series of equal payments made at equal intervals with a given interest rate (in decimal form) per period, and returns a number.

Example: For the present value of an annuity due when payments of $1,000 are made at 12 percent for 10 years, PV (1000, 0.12, 10) → $5,650.22.

Conversion Functions

Often you want to work with a field in a calculation that is of the wrong data type or attribute. Numbers can be interpreted as simple text strings and dates can be converted to their serial number equivalents. FileMaker includes seven conversion functions for changing the data type in calculations. Values can be fields, results of calculations or expressions, and often number or text constants.

DateToText (date). The Date to Text function reads dates as text.

Example: "On " & DateToText (4/1/90) & " take the money and run!" → On 4/1/90 take the money and run!

degrees (number). The Degrees function converts the supplied number from radians to degrees.

Example: Degrees (atan (1)) → 45. (The term atan is defined under "Trigonometric Functions.")

NumToText (number). The Number to Text function reads numbers as text.

Example: Change a phone number into a text string: "Call" & " " & NumToText ("(617)555-2483") → Call (617)555-2483.

TextToDate (text). The Text to Date function reads text as a date. All characters entered into the text string must constitute an acceptable date format.

Example: TextToDate (Deadline) → TextToDate (1-15-91) → 1/15/91, where Deadline is a Date field.

TextToNum (text). The Text to Number function reads text as a number.

Example: TextToNum (Price) * Sales Tax → TextToNum (500 dollars) * 0.05 → 25, where Price is a Number field.

TextToTime (text). The TextToTime function returns the time equivalent of the supplied text, for use with formulas involving time or time-oriented functions. The text supplied must be in hours/minutes/seconds format (HH:MM:SS). Seconds are optional.

Example: TextToTime("03:59:12") → 3 hours, 59 minutes, and 12 seconds.

TimeToText (time). The TimeToText function returns the text equivalent of the supplied time, for use with formulas involving text or text-oriented functions. The result is always in the format HH:MM:SS.

Example: TimeToText(Duration) → 09:27:10.

Time Functions

Filemaker Pro includes four functions you may find useful for dealing with time.

hour (time). The Hour function returns a number representing the number of hours embedded in a time value.

Example: Hour(TextToTime("10:12:13")) → 10.

minute (time). The Minute function returns a number representing the number of minutes embedded in a time value.

Example: Minute(TextToTime("10:12:38")) → 12.

seconds (time). The Seconds function returns a number representing the number of seconds embedded in a time value.

Example: Second(TextToTime("09:14:37")) → 37.

time (hours, minutes, seconds). The Time function returns a time result with the given number of hours, minutes, and seconds, counting from zero and adding the supplied duration of time to each unit.

Example: Time (3.5,20,32) → 3:50:32.

Trigonometric Functions

FileMaker Pro also includes trigonometric functions that may be helpful to you in your work.

atan (number). The Atan function returns a number, which is the arc tangent of the number supplied.

Example: Atan(1) → 45.

cos (number). The Cos function returns the cosine of the angle supplied. The angle must be in radians.

Example: Cos(1.047) → 0.9998330.

exp (number). The Exp function returns the value of the constant e (the base of the natural logarithm, equal to 2.7182818) raised to the power specified by the supplied number. The Exp function is the inverse of the Ln function.

Example: Exp(1) → 2.71828182845904.

radians (number). The Radians function converts the degrees supplied in number to radians. The parameters of FileMaker trigonometric functions must be in radians. A degree is equal to $\pi/180$ radians.

Example: Sin(Radians(30)) → 0.0091384.

sin (number). The Sin function returns the sine of an angle expressed in radians.

Example: Sin(Radians(60)) → 0.0182760.

tan (number). The Tan function returns the tangent of the angle (in radians) represented by a number.

Example: Tan(.13) → 0.0022689.

Using Repeating Fields

You can create a special kind of field called a repeating field that stores a list of values. Repeating fields enable you to split up related values into a single repeating field that normally would require several individual records to be stored. If you think of a field as a box that can hold some value, then a repeating field is a box with several compartments, each of which can hold a value. You have worked with forms that contain repeating fields, although you may not have realized it. Most invoices or statements that you can buy have separate lines for Item Numbers, Descriptions, Unit Prices, and Prices. You can enter more than one item number, description, and so on, and each entry is considered a repeating field.

Repeating fields are convenient. Creating individual records for each field entry would slow down your file and not provide a good overall picture of your data. It also would be confusing to try to work with individual records. Certain operations, such as summing a field, are awkward across records because you first must find the appropriate records to browse.

Any field other than a Picture field can be made to repeat if you format it that way.

To create a repeating field, follow these steps:

1. Choose Define Fields from the Select menu.
2. Select the field you want to repeat.
3. Click the Options button.

4. Click Repeating Field With a Maximum of N Values.
5. Type the maximum number of times you want the field to repeat.
6. Click the OK button or press the Return key to return to the Layout window.
7. Click the Done button.

Notice that each field has only one small black reshape box on the first line; each repeating field is a single object. A repeating field with five lines is not the same as a field with five lines. Each line in a repeating field holds an individual value, and you can resize the entire field using techniques discussed in Chapter 7. A repeating field retains the attributes of the field from which it was derived, and each repetition has exactly the same formatting characteristics (font, size, style, and so on).

You enter data into repeating fields in the Browse window with the same method that you learned in Chapter 3—using the Tab key, the Option-Tab or Shift-Tab keystrokes, and using the tab order. Each repeating unit in a field supports text editing and the Clipboard. If you reformat a repeating field (on the original layout or on any other layout) so that it doesn't repeat, FileMaker retains all the individual values in your file even if it shows only one.

When a repeating field is used in a calculation formula, the calculation field contains all values that result, even if it is formatted to show only one. Any calculation or summary field that uses repeating fields in its definition will contain all repeating field values even if only one shows. It can be confusing to see all values. Reformat the field to show the needed repetitions.

When you use repeating fields, you must account for the fact that not all operations can use repeating values. When you do calculations—for example, multiply a repeating field by a nonrepeating field—you must use the Extend function on the nonrepeating field, as described in the "Field Functions" section. The functions described for repeating fields are used to summarize values within a record, and they are similar to formulas defining summary fields of the appropriate type for a group of records.

When you sort a repeating field, only the first value (repetition) can be used.

Repeating fields have certain restrictions on their use in summary field definitions and in lookup field operations that you may want to bear in mind. Refer to the two following sections.

Using Summary Fields

A calculation field calculates a result for a specific record only. If you want a calculation for a group of records, you need to define a summary field. In the definition of a summary field, you can use a calculation field.

Many times, calculating the data contained in a single record by using a calculation field is not what you're after. Instead, you need some sort of calculated result for a field across a group of records. To calculate across records, define summary fields. You can use Text, Number, Time, Date, or calculation fields, depending on the type of summary formula you define. Because a summary field is a logical, or derived, field, you never enter data into it on a Browse window. Instead, FileMaker calculates it and updates that calculation whenever data in a dependent field is changed. Also, you cannot export the results of a summary field or format a summary field to repeat.

Defining Summary Fields

You can define several different types of summary fields, including total, average, count, minimum, maximum, standard deviation, or a fraction of the total of the values in the field you specify for the records in a browsed set. Some of these formulas offer additional options; for instance, you can specify that a total be a running total, an average be a weighted average, a count be a running count, or the fraction of a total be subtotaled. These different types and options are explained in the following text.

Use Number, Date, Time, or calculation fields with number or date results for any of the preceding formula types. You can use Text fields for count summaries, which give the number of fields that contain a value. When you use a repeating field, FileMaker uses all the values it contains to calculate summaries.

A new feature of FileMaker Pro is that summary fields can now be included in calculations.

To create a summary field, follow these steps:

1. Select the Define Fields command on the Select menu to open the Define Fields dialog box.
2. Type a field name in the Field Name text box and either click on the Summary button or press the ⌘-S keystroke.

3. Click the Create button or press the Return or Enter key to open the Summary Formula dialog box (see fig. 5.4).

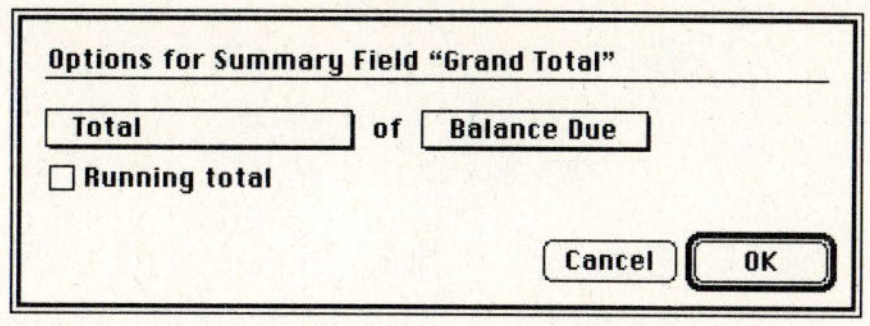

Fig. 5.4
The Summary Formula dialog box.

4. Click and press on the summary option to display a pop-up menu. Scroll through the list to highlight the one you want.
5. Click and press on the field name to display a pop-up menu. Scroll through the list to highlight the one you want. These options are described in detail in the following text.
6. Click in the Running Total box, if desired.
7. Click the OK button or press the Return or Enter key to return to the Define Fields dialog box.
8. Click the Done button.

   or

   Click the Cancel button or press ⌘-. (period) to return to the Define Fields dialog box without creating the summary formula. When you create a summary field, that field shows the summary formula in the Field Name scroll box, along with the first 37 letters of the formula.

FileMaker II only: Depending on your layout, the new summary field may be placed on the Browse or Layout window. If it is not, refer to Chapter 7. Note that if you are using the View as List option on the Select menu, FileMaker does not display a result in the summary field. Turn off this option by selecting the command once again to view your summary field.

SPEED KEY

⌘-S specifies a summary field within the Define Fields dialog box.

Following is a summary of the available options in the Summary Formula dialog box (see fig. 5.4):

Field names pop-up menu. The selected field is the dependent field that your summary field summarizes.

Summary formula pop-up menu. Click on this pop-up menu to choose the formula you want.

Total. The total includes all values in the field being summarized.

Running Total check box. When you check this box, FileMaker provides an accumulating sum, which is the sum record by record. This option is similar to the running total you keep for your checkbook.

Average. Click this option, called Average Of in the Field Name list box, to average all values in the dependent field for a browsed set of records. An average is the sum of all values, divided by the number of values; sometimes it's called an arithmetic mean. Blank values are not averaged. When this is the selected type, you have this added option:

> **Weighted By check box.** When you check this box, a second pop-up field list appears (see fig. 5.5). Your average value is divided by the value found in the field that you specify.

Fig. 5.5
Specifying a weighted average.

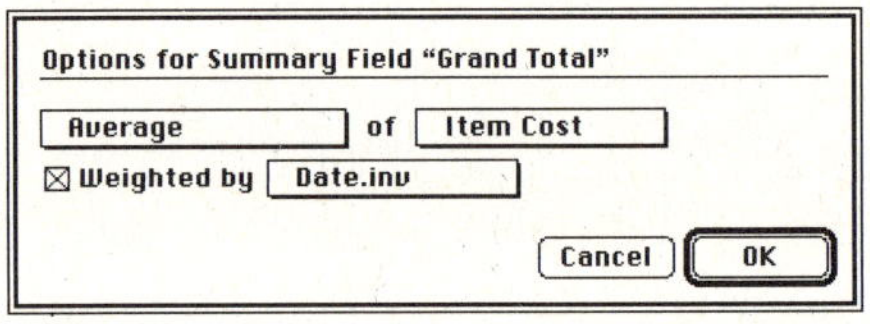

Count. Click this option to show how many values appear in the dependent field for a browsed set of records. Blank values are not counted. You can use Text fields for this type. When this is the selected type, you have this added option:

> **Running Count check box.** When you check this box, FileMaker provides an accumulating count, which is the count record by record.

Minimum. Click this option to show the smallest values in the dependent field for a browsed set of records.

Maximum. Click this option to show the largest values in the dependent field for a browsed set of records.

Standard Deviation. Click this option in the list box to show the variance in the dependent field for a browsed set of records. The standard deviation uses the n-weighted, or population, standard deviation formula in its calculation. Blank values are not considered.

Fraction of Total. Click this option in the Field Name list box to show the ratio of the dependent field being summarized for a browsed set of records to the total of all values in that field. For example, if the dependent field shows sales by salesperson, and this option is checked, the Fraction of Total sales will be shown. You cannot calculate the Fraction of Total for a repeating field. When you select this option, you have the following additional option:

> **Subtotal check box.** When checked, an additional field list pop-up menu is added. To provide subtotals, you first must sort the field to be subtotaled (in the additional list). FileMaker provides the fraction that the field contributes to the subtotal rather than the total. For example, if one field shows sales by salesperson and the second field shows field by item type, a subtotal would show the fraction of the sales per item type by salesperson. Because FileMaker uses only the first value when sorting a repeating field, any subtotal based on that field will be based on the first entry only. You see Fraction of Total Sub-Total when sorted by Field Name in the Field Name list box.

OK button. Click the OK button or press the Return or Enter key to accept the summary formula.

Cancel button. Click Cancel or press ⌘- . (period) to return to the Define Fields dialog box without defining the summary formula.

The records you browse, whether those records have been sorted, and where on a layout you place summary fields can have a profound effect on what is being summarized and the value you see in that field. FileMaker offers some special layout objects called parts that control the action of summary fields. These layout objects are described in detail in Chapter 9.

If you place a summary field in the body section of a record, your summary appears once in each record. For a standard layout, a summary field is placed automatically on each record, enabling you to see a summary of all records browsed. This feature is particularly useful for running totals or running counts, because it enables you to view the overall changes as you change individual data values on the record you're browsing.

In particular, two special parts are useful in summarizing records: the sub-summary and grand summary parts. A summary field, when placed into a sub-summary part, summarizes a group of sorted browsed records. A summary field placed into a grand summary part summarizes all browsed records. If a sales journal for a company is sorted by items, and a summary field is defined to total sales, you can place this summary field into both a sub-summary part to give item totals and into a grand summary field to give the overall totals. It may be useful to view your summary field in the sub-summary part in the Preview window to make sure that it is operating properly. To preview your sub-summary, select the Preview command on the Select menu or press ⌘-U. See Chapter 10 for more details.

At times, you will be interested only in a summary of the data in a file. You can show only summary fields in the appropriate parts in a summary report. You don't see your data contained in the database per se, but you display and output the calculation or summary field of interest.

Editing a Summary Field

You can change the name of a summary field in exactly the same manner you change a calculation field.

To change a summary field to another data type, follow these steps:

1. Choose Define Fields from the Select menu.
2. In the Define Fields dialog box, click on the field attribute you want to change.
3. Type in the new name.
4. Click on the Change button to accept the correction and then click on the Done button.

Unlike changing a calculation field, in which case changing data type retains the data in that field, summary fields lose all calculated data when the field attribute is changed. This loss of data occurs because summary fields are calculated across records, and calculation fields and all other types are attached to each record.

To change a summary field formula, follow these steps:

1. In the Define Fields dialog box, select the summary field name that you want to change.
2. Click on the enabled Options button to open the Summary Formula dialog box or press the Return or Enter key.
3. Click on the Summary Formula pop-up menu and highlight an option.
4. Click on the additional Summary Formula option from the pop-up menu, if desired.
5. Click on the field to be summarized and, if necessary, click on the field needed for the Summary Formula option.

6. Click on the OK button or press the Return key to accept the change.

   or

   Click the Cancel button or press ⌘- . (period) to dismiss the Summary Formula dialog box and retain its original formula.

7. Click the Done button to leave the Define Fields dialog box.

Using Lookup Fields

It's nearly impossible to place into a single file all the information you want to organize. Sometimes it's more logical to organize one set of data into one file, another set into another file, and so on. If the connection between data sets is not essential, you are better off separating them. Smaller files run more quickly, and businesses often separate files such as sales records, payroll, and inventory.

Defining Lookup Fields

For times when the information you want to use is contained in another file, you can define what FileMaker calls a *lookup* field. A lookup field is defined as an Auto-Entry option (discussed later in the chapter) in the Define Fields dialog box. It compares the contents of two other fields, called comparison fields, and when they are equal or they match, FileMaker places the contents of a third field (a reference value) from the lookup file into the lookup field.

If you have separate sales and inventory files, you can define a set of lookup fields that takes the Item Name and compares it in both files. When the value in both fields matches, all the additional item information is copied over from the reference fields of the lookup file into the appropriate lookup fields in the current file. You can use a customer file in exactly the same way. Lookups speed up data entry and add to overall accuracy.

A lookup is a basic implementation of a relational link between files. Although you can buy databases that are totally relational and allow for new files to be synthesized in memory (as described in the Introduction), often just a set of well-planned lookup fields in FileMaker can serve as an efficient solution.

To define a lookup field, follow these steps:

1. Select the Define Fields command on the Select menu to open the Define Fields dialog box.
2. Select the field name for which you want to create a lookup.

   or

   If that field does not exist, create it by typing the new field name in the Field Name text box, selecting the appropriate data type, and clicking the Create button.
3. Click on the Options button to open the Options dialog box.
4. Click on the Lookup Value from a File check box.

   If you already have defined this field as a lookup field and you want to change the lookup, refer to the instructions for changing entry options later in this chapter.
5. Navigate to the file you want to use as your lookup file. Double-click on the file name or click once and click the Open button to dismiss the standard file box.
6. In the Lookup dialog box (see fig. 5.6), click on Copy the Contents Of to show the pop-up menu in the current file and on the value name in the lookup file to use them as the comparison fields.

Note

Field names and field types do not have to match; only the values as compared by the field indexes do. Certain values can transfer, such as number to text, but picture data requires an attribute match.

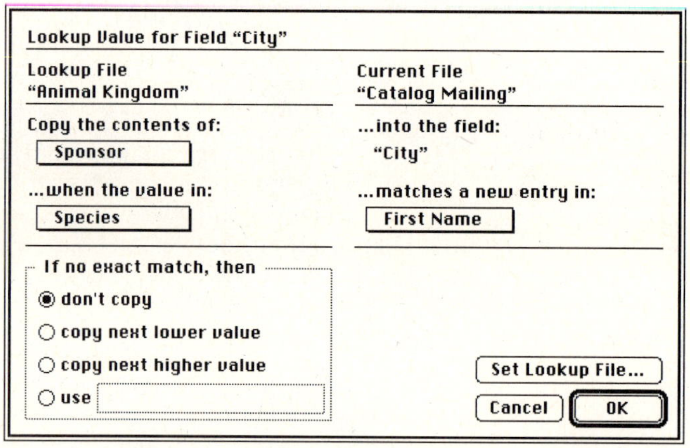

Fig. 5.6
The Lookup dialog box.

7. Click on the field that will supply the referenced value to be entered into your lookup field.

If you make a mistake and want to change lookup files, click on the Set Lookup File button to return to the Open file box, and repeat steps 5 through 7.

8. Click the OK button or press the Return key to establish the lookup. Click on OK again.

If you change your mind and do not want to establish a lookup, click the Cancel button or press ⌘-. (period) to return to the Entry Options dialog box for further changes.

You must keep certain considerations in mind when you establish a lookup. Placing the lookup file in the same folder as the current file will speed up its operation when it opens. Also, FileMaker stores the location of your lookup file as a path name, so if you move the lookup file after the link has been established, the program will not be able to find it.

Tip

To improve speed, use large databases without calculation fields and smaller databases that perform calculations.

Although the size of the database determines, to some extent, the speed of your file, other factors also come into play. Specifically, a large number of calculation fields slows file access considerably. Multiple lookups (described later) to different lookup files particularly slow down the operation of your file as the Macintosh searches the directory for each file name. If possible, keep looking in the same folder your file is in. Using large databases with no calculation fields coupled to smaller databases that perform calculations is a good idea. If performance is still too sluggish, consider breaking your database apart in some logical way—by ZIP codes, alphabetically by last name, or in some other manner.

Because the fields you can use as lookup files have no restrictions, you can use the current file, called a *self lookup*. Self lookups are a great way to automate your database when you have all the information you need in your file. For example, on an invoice when the Last Name fields match for the person to be billed and the person to be shipped to, you can have FileMaker fill in all of the various address and phone number fields that you have already defined.

Matches are made using the field indexes, so FileMaker ignores capitalization and punctuation in a text field and ignores any text in a number field. The first record in a file that has a matching value is used, so if you have duplicate records with the same matching value, make sure that the referenced value is identical as well. You can guarantee this by requiring the referenced field to contain a unique value (discussed later in this chapter). Also, you cannot look up information from repeating or summary fields, but you can place lookups into repeating fields. Because calculation and summary fields are derived (or logical) fields, they also cannot be lookup fields.

If there is no match in the two comparison fields for the values they contain, you have other options available. You can click on the Don't Copy button in the Lookup dialog box, which makes the lookup field remain blank. You also can click on the Copy Next Lower button to enter the next lower value. In this case, FileMaker enters the reference value that is indexed before the one requested for the match, which means words that are alphabetically before, numbers that are smaller, and dates that are earlier than the value are entered. Consider a lookup of a tax rate from a tax table. If the salary for a taxpayer matches exactly the salary in the tax table, FileMaker enters a rate from the rate field. Salaries almost never match, however, because the tax table lists values in $200 increments.

If you use the Next Lower Value option, FileMaker places the next lower tax rate into your client's file. To do the reverse, click on Copy Next Higher Value. If you prefer, you can click on Use and type in any value you like.

The lookup file is opened as a hidden window; that is, its name is enclosed in parentheses on the Window menu and it is retained in memory, but the lookup file does not show on your screen. This approach is used to access easily the lookup file in case you decide to change one of the comparison fields. To check that the lookup worked correctly or to search for additional information contained in a lookup file, activate that file by selecting its name in the Window menu. The lookup file then appears on your screen.

Many times when you work on a file, you need information contained in other files. If this is a regular occurrence with a particular file, consider making the reference file a lookup file. Then the reference opens as a hidden window when you open your file, enabling you to access it quickly. This capability is useful, for example, for linking sales files to inventory files.

You can edit, replace, and delete values entered into a lookup field. When you change the comparison value in your current file, FileMaker changes the lookup value in the lookup field. To have your previously entered lookups updated, you can use the Relookup command from the Edit menu, as discussed in the following section.

Changing a Lookup File

To change a lookup file, you must work within the Entry Options dialog box. You can remove a lookup by clicking on the Lookup check box. FileMaker retains in memory a lookup field's entry options, so that if you change your mind after removing the lookup and you later reinstate it, your comparison fields and referenced fields appear again in the Lookup dialog box.

To change a lookup definition, follow these steps:

1. In the Define Fields dialog box, select the field you want to alter.
2. Click on the enabled Options button to open the Entry Options dialog box.
3. In the Entry Options dialog box, click on the Set Lookup button. FileMaker opens the Lookup dialog box into which you enter your changes.
4. Scroll the field boxes to select the new fields in the lookup or click on one of the following buttons in the Lookup dialog box: Don't Copy, Copy Next Lower Value, Copy Next Higher Value, or Use (and fill in a word).

   If you need to change lookup files, click on the Set Lookup File button and choose the new file name from the Open file dialog box.
5. Click the OK button or press the Return key to accept the changes or click the Cancel button (⌘-.) to retain your previous settings and return to the Entry Options dialog box.
6. Click OK to return to the Define Fields dialog box.
7. Click the Done button or press the Return key to leave the Define Fields dialog box.

FileMaker enters data from a lookup file into your lookup field when the comparison fields match. After that data is entered, you can continue to work with your files and change data. If you changed the lookup file in the interim, or you import records using the Input From command on the Edit menu, your records may no longer match defined lookups.

Usually, you need to enter the comparison value into every lookup field that you might want to update. FileMaker, however, provides a method for accomplishing this task. You can update your file by using the Relookup command on the Edit menu. When you select the comparison field (make it the current field), performing a Relookup updates all the browsed records.

To update lookup values, follow these steps:

1. Browse the records that you want to update.

You might want to update all of your records, any records that you selected with a find operation, or a set of newly imported records.

2. Make the current field the comparison field on which the lookup is based.
3. Select the Relookup command from the Edit menu. FileMaker posts an alert box (see fig. 5.7) that indicates the number of records to be updated.
4. Click the OK button. FileMaker opens the lookup files and updates your records based on the current field.

   or

   Click the Cancel button to retain your file in its previous condition.

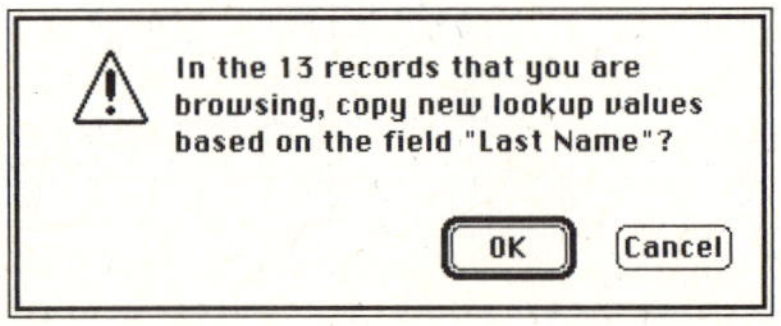

Fig. 5.7
The Relookup alert box.

Specifying Data-Entry Options

Entry options are part of a field's definition and are defined by accessing the Options dialog box from the Define Fields dialog box. There are different types of operations available to you in the Options dialog box (see fig. 5.8).

Auto-enter data. Anytime a field entry requires the current or modified date or time, repeats a value, or requires the use of a consecutive (serial) number (a sequential integer), use this option to speed up data entry and accuracy. If you have a large number of records to create that have a value that falls into one of these three categories, set this option before creating the records and turn it off when you are finished. You also can enter the name of the person who creates or modifies the record. FileMaker inserts whatever name is under the User Name section of the Chooser. Your previously entered values are unaffected by this change; only newly created records change. Remember to enter data in a format that the field accepts.

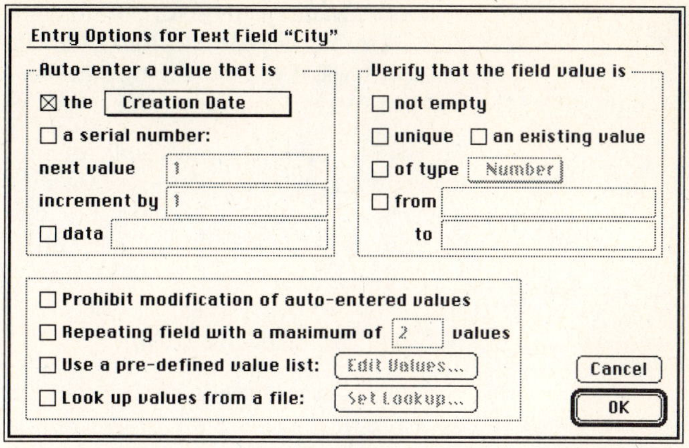

Fig. 5.8
The Entry Options dialog box for a text field.

Examples of situations in which auto-entering data is useful include automatically dating forms or output, using a consecutive number scheme in an invoice file, and ensuring that a letter is signed by the same person or that the same paragraph is always placed in a letter.

Display a list of values. This option enables you to create a pop-up list of values so that you can quickly enter a selection into the field for which the list is assigned. (The mechanics of working with lists on a Browse window are discussed later in this chapter.) The advantage of creating a field of this type is that your list serves as a reminder of accepted values. Even complex values can be entered quickly and accurately in the form you create only once.

One example of a situation in which a list of values is useful is when you want to accept only a certain set of values: abbreviations for states, months, days of the week, or accepted forms of billing. If you work in a large company that uses 12-digit account numbers, a list will be particularly useful.

A list of values now can be formatted to display the list as check boxes, buttons, a pop-up menu, or a pop-up list.

Look up a value. Lookup is FileMaker's implementation of a relational database linkage and was discussed in detail in the preceding section. You enter a value in a field you specify, based on a comparison of values in two fields that you specify. For more ideas on the use of lookups, see Chapter 12. (More information also is given earlier in this chapter.)

Validate an entry. These options enable you to set criteria whereby FileMaker checks your data for validity. FileMaker restricts your entry to those criteria. If you violate the criteria, the program displays an alert box that forces you to accept or deny your entry.

These entry options are available: define a list to choose from during data entry, require a field to contain a value, require a field to contain a numeric value only, and require a field to contain a value in a range. Now you also can specify multiple entry options for a field.

Automatically Entering a Value

You don't always have to enter values manually. FileMaker often can do it for you, if you set up the proper options.

To create an entry option for a field, follow these steps:

1. Issue the Define Fields command to open the Define Fields dialog box.

2. Create or select the field you want and set the attribute to Text, Number, Date, Time, or Picture, as desired.

3. Click the Options button to go to the Entry Options dialog box (see fig. 5.8 again).

4. Click the auto-enter check boxes you want to apply:

   Select the Creation Date to have FileMaker enter the current date. A pop-up menu enables you to select the following options: Creation Date, Creation Time, Modification Date, Modification Time, Creator Name, and Modifier Name. The date is set by the Macintosh clock. This box is enabled for Text, Number, Time, and Date fields only.

   Select a serial number to have FileMaker enter an incremental number. The number starts with the number you place in the Next Value box and increases for each new record you create by whatever number you place next to Increment By. This box is enabled for Text and Number fields only.

   Select Data to auto-enter data into a field. Type the information you want automatically entered. This option places a data entry you define (appropriate to the field type) into your field. This box is enabled for all field types except Picture.

5. If desired, click on Prohibit Modification of Auto-Entered Values to prevent changes being made during data entry.

6. Click the OK button or press Enter to return to the Define Fields dialog box.

   or

   If you want to make any changes, click the Cancel button or press ⌘-. (period). Your previous definitions and settings are preserved.

To place a large auto-enter data value into the Auto-enter Data or Display Values text boxes, create that data elsewhere and copy (⌘-C) or cut (⌘-X) it to the Clipboard. Then place the insertion point in the box and paste (⌘-V) the value. All three commands are on the Edit menu. The Entry Options dialog box supports text editing (most FileMaker dialog boxes now support text editing). This feature is particularly valuable because the Auto-enter Data text box doesn't show all of your entry, nor does it scroll.

Another benefit of the Entry Options dialog box's capability to support text editing is that you can create a list of entries in a database or spreadsheet such as Excel and use the Clipboard to place them in the two text boxes mentioned in the preceding paragraph. Remember that in the text format, a spreadsheet separates each row with a return and each column with a tab, so use just a single column in Excel for your data import.

Displaying a List

Sometimes you want to see a list of values. FileMaker can display the desired values for you if you tell it which ones you want.

To dispay the values, follow these steps:

1. In the Define Fields dialog box, create or select the desired field and set the attribute to Text, Number, Time, Date, or Picture.
2. Click the Options button to go to the Entry Options dialog box.
3. Click the Use a Pre-defined Value list box and fill in the text box, entering a set of values and pressing Return after each value.
4. Click the OK button or press the Enter key to return to the Define Fields dialog box.

   or

   If you want to make any changes, click the Cancel button or use the ⌘-. (period) keystroke. Your previous definitions and settings are preserved.

To display the list of values as check boxes, buttons, a pop-up menu, or a pop-up list, follow these steps:

1. Go to the layout mode by pressing ⌘-L and select the field with a value list.
2. Choose Field Format from the Format menu.
3. To the right of Use Field's Value List to Display Field As, click on the pop-up menu and choose the display method you want.
4. Click OK.
5. Adjust the size of the field on the layout to accommodate the display you chose.

Validating an Entry

FileMaker can help you to avoid entering the wrong type of value or a value outside an acceptable range. This process is called validating the entry.

To validate an entry, do the following:

1. In the Define Fields dialog box, create or select the desired field and set the attribute to Text, Number, Date, Time, or Picture.
2. Click the Options button to go to the Entry Options dialog box.
3. Click the value you want. You can select more than one check box:

   Not Empty. The field cannot be left blank.

   Unique. The field cannot have a duplicate value.

   An Existing Value. The value must match an entry in another record.

   Of Type (Number). The field must be a certain type selected from a pop-up menu: number, date, or type. The value must contain only numbers (digits), a decimal point, or a minus sign. Fields cannot contain letters or a leading zero.

   From...To. Any range—alphabetical, numerical, or chronological, based on the ASCII code you enter—is accepted. You can set a lower or upper bound range only, or you can set a range where both bounds are inclusive.

   From: text box. Indicate the lower bounding value.

To: text box. Indicate the upper bounding value.

4. Click the OK button or press the Enter key to return to the Define Fields dialog box.

   or

   If you want to make changes, click the Cancel button or use ⌘-. (period). Your previous definitions and settings are preserved.

When you enter data that falls outside the accepted values, FileMaker alerts you and requires you to accept or deny the entry.

Note that any entry option you set is indicated by the notation next to the field types. If you set more than one option, FileMaker places an ellipsis (...) following the first option. You can examine entry options by printing the defined fields.

Because entry options apply only to records you created in the current file after they were set, it is possible to have a database that does not match the criteria you desire. This situation occurs with previously created data, or with data that was copied from another file by using the Import command (see Chapter 15) on the File menu. To correct information that doesn't match, use the Find command and select the records that need to be altered. See Chapter 4 for further details.

Entering Data from a List

You also can enter data from a list into a list field, as well as enter data not on a list into a list field. Follow the instructions in this section.

To enter data from a list into a list field, follow these steps:

1. Select the field that displays the list, and that list appears below the field (see fig. 5.9).

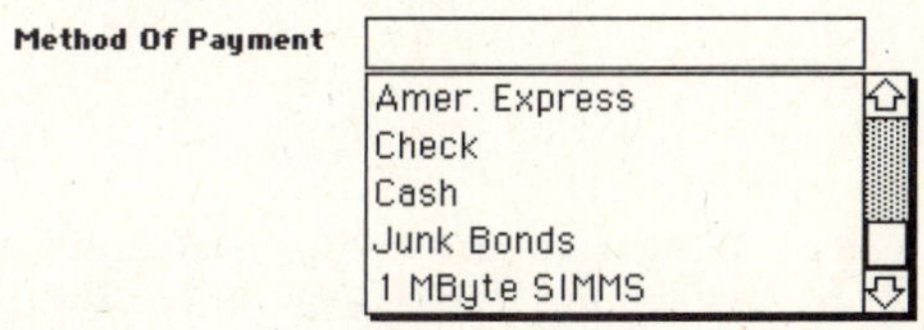

Fig. 5.9
A list field just selected.

   The List pop-up window is the same width as the field size you set in the layout. Up to five entries can be displayed. If there are more entries, FileMaker places an enabled vertical scroll bar. Usually, the list is displayed below the field; however, if the list doesn't entirely fit into the body section of the record, it is displayed above the field.

2. Double-click on the entry desired or click once on its name and press Enter, scrolling if needed.

   You can choose values by typing the first few letters to highlight the entry or by using the up-arrow or down-arrow keys. If a value was previously entered in the field, it is highlighted. If you press the Delete key at this stage, you leave the field blank and go to the next field in the tab order.

3. Either deselect the field and enter the value by pressing the Enter key or move to the next field by pressing the Return or Tab key.

To enter data not on a list into a list field, follow these steps:

1. Select the list field and display the list.

2. Click in the Field box. The list disappears, and an insertion point appears in the field.

3. Enter the data you want.

   If there was a previous value entered from the list, it appears with the name highlighted on the list. Click in the field and use the standard text-editing techniques to modify the field value any way you want.

   If there was a previous value entered not on the list, the entire field is selected with the list showing. Edit the field or delete the entry; press the Delete key or the Clear key on the numeric keypad, if you have one. You also can replace the entry by using the list.

4. Either deselect the field and enter the value by pressing the Enter key or move to the next field by pressing the Return or Tab key.

Checking Data Accuracy

You can use many of the entry options mentioned in the preceding section to check an entry's validity before it's entered. When you enter data that doesn't conform to the entry option, FileMaker warns you with an alert box. You can click the OK button to dismiss the alert box and accept the data, or you can re-enter new data. Of the options mentioned, the ones that are best suited for checking the validity of an entry are the set of options offered by Verify That the Field Value Is check boxes.

These check boxes include Not Empty, Unique, Existing Value, Numeric Type, and From...To Range. Don't forget that you can specify more than one entry option at a time.

Keep in mind that FileMaker uses the index to match values and determine accuracy. With "23 Skiddoo" as a data entry and "23 Skiddoon't" indexed in a Text field, FileMaker will not accept this entry when the option Existing Value Only is checked. This entry would be accepted, however, for a Number field because the index for a Number field tracks only numeric entries. Also, because the index for a Text field ignores capitalization, word order, and punctuation, exact matches may not be found. "Elysian Fields, III" is the same as "Fields, Elysian III."

Entry options are fine for new records you create. How do you check the accuracy of data already in your file or data that you entered into your file with the Import command? For these situations, you need to use the index for each field to check for data accuracy. The best way is to go into the Find window and select the field you want to check. Open the index by using the Paste Special from Index command on the Edit menu or press ⌘-I. Sometimes you can find errors just by examining the index. For example, if a seven-digit phone number includes a letter, the entry will not be seven numbers long because the index for the Number field will show only numeric entries. The incorrect number will stand out. To check for less obvious errors such as duplication or empty fields, use the Find command to select a group of records. Remember also that you can paste index entries into a field in a Find window to aid you.

Changing Entry Options

You can change a defined entry option, add new options, or delete existing options at any time. Data already entered into your file is unaffected by these changes.

To change an entry option, follow these steps:

1. In the Define Fields dialog box, select the field you want to alter.
2. Click on the enabled Options button to open the Entry Options dialog box.
3. Click on any option you want to add; click off any option you want to remove.

   If the option you want to alter requires you to enter additional information into an attached text box, enter it. Remember that text boxes support text editing and the Clipboard. You can tab from text box to text box, and doing this selects an entire text box's contents.

4. Click the OK button or press the Return key to accept the changes or click the Cancel button (⌘-.) to retain your previous settings.

Specifying the Tab Order

When you enter data into a Browse window, you usually go from field to field, using Tab to go forward and Option-Tab or Shift-Tab to go backward. This order, defined by FileMaker, is called the tab order. The tab order for fields is usually from left to right, then from top to bottom—exactly the order that you follow as you read this book. The top edge of a field box defines the top-to- bottom position of that field in the tab order; the left edge of a field box is what determines its left-to-right order.

Consider the Browse window for data entry in figure 5.10. This simulated FileMaker form is labeled for its tab order; numbers within each circle indicate each field's tab order.

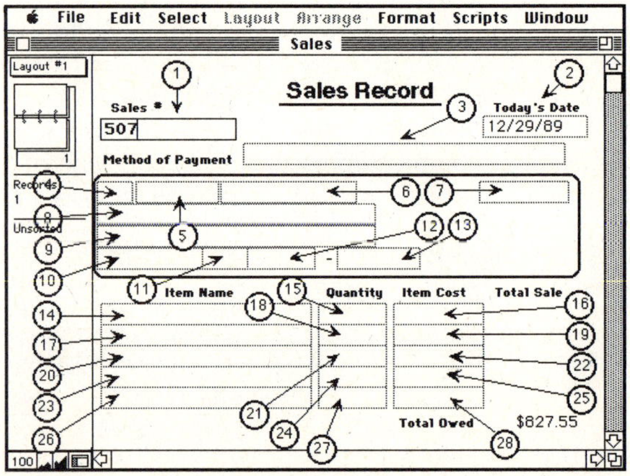

Fig. 5.10 The natural tab order for a complex form.

You should learn several helpful facts here. When this file was defined, fields 1 and 2 were auto-entry fields. When a new record was created, FileMaker entered those fields, placing the insertion point to the right of the entry in Sales # (field 1). Fields 4 through 13 enter customer information (within the rounded rectangle) and are in the tab order you expect. The fields Item Name, Quantity, and Item Cost are repeating fields, with five repetitions. Here you might expect that each field would tab from top to bottom. That is not the case, however. Repeating fields tab one value at a time, left to right, because they are aligned. This standard is particularly useful for forms, because often you want aligned fields to be related to one another—that is, line items. When FileMaker reaches the last field entry, box 28, it returns to the first field in the tab order.

Some features in FileMaker Pro enable you to change the tab order in any way you like. In FileMaker II, a Tab Order dialog box enables you to assign tab groups. If you select a group of fields, you tab through those fields as a unit before moving on to the next field in the order. By adding a layout object to a tab group, you can use that object as part of the tab group and achieve a desired tab order for your group in FileMaker II. FileMaker Pro adds a new scheme for setting the tab order (see fig. 5.11). Now when that command is chosen, each field has its own text box into which you can enter its tab order priority.

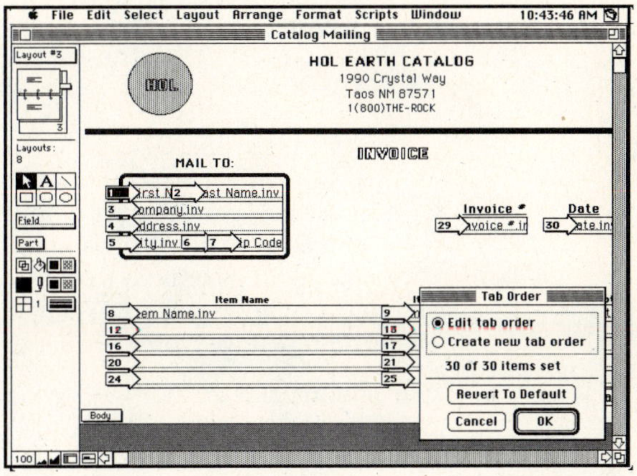

Fig. 5.11
Setting the tab order in FileMaker Pro.

Changing the Tab Order

The natural tab order may not always be what you want. You can change the tab order for a layout by following these steps:

1. Select Tab Order from the Arrange menu.

   The Tab Order dialog box appears with numbered arrows pointing to each defined field. Drag the title bar of the dialog box to reposition it on your screen.

   The numbers inside each arrow indicate the tab order sequence for the layout.

2. Click on either Edit Tab Order or Create New Tab Order.

   Edit Tab Order enables you to renumber the individual arrows. Create New Tab Order removes all the numbers and enables you to set the tab order by clicking the arrows in the order you want.

   To return to the default tab order, select Revert to Default.

If you click an arrow pointing to a repeating field, the arrow starts flashing. While you specify the tab order of more fields, it continues to flash until you return to the same repeating field. The arrow then stops, flashing and the program completes the tab order for the remainder of that repeating field, based on what it has been instructed.

By double-clicking the arrow pointing to a repeating field, the tab order will be vertically instead of horizontally based.

A feature new to FileMaker Pro is the capability to change the natural tab order by using the Tab Order command in the Arrange menu.

In Review

FileMaker provides a set of tools that enable you to automate data entry: calculation and summary fields, auto-entry, data validation, and lookups or links to other files. These tools can greatly simplify entering a complex record. Whenever possible, use these options to eliminate repetitive typing, increase speed, and enhance accuracy.

Calculation fields are derived, or logical, fields that can have text, number, or date results. They use a calculation formula that you define to calculate data. Calculation fields are indexed and can be used for selecting records in a find operation. Because the data is dependent on other fields, however, you cannot enter data into a calculation field on a Browse screen or export that field's data to other files.

A wide variety of mathematical, logical, financial, data conversion, and some repeating field functions are available for you to use to build the calculation formulas used in calculation fields. You also can use values in the form of constants and variables in the form of field names. Field names return values for the specific data that that field in the record contains. When you define a calculation formula, each calculation refers to the data contained in an individual record.

You can format fields to repeat, which creates a list of separate values that can be formatted, entered, displayed, calculated, and summed. Repeating fields are a great convenience for use in forms. They also can be used in calculations but require a special set of functions (discussed in this chapter).

You can define summary fields to summarize the values in a specified field in a group of records. Because summary fields are derived data, you cannot select them in a Browse window for data entry, and the data they display cannot be exported to another file. A number of different summary types are available, including total, average, count, maximum, minimum, standard deviation, and fractions.

The records you're browsing, whether a file has been sorted, and where you place a summary field on a layout have a profound effect on what's being summarized. You can summarize data in each record by placing a summary field in the body section of a layout, or you can use special summary parts to control the action of your summary field. Two summary parts, sub-summary and grand summary, are particularly useful in this regard.

Lookups are relational links to other files. When you establish a lookup field, you compare the values in two other fields that you specify, one in the current file and the other in the lookup file. Matching values in the comparison fields cause FileMaker to enter a value, called the reference value, into the lookup field in the current file. Lookups are singularly useful in automating a database. You can continue to edit data after a lookup and update your current file by using the Relookup command.

Entry options include auto-entering data, displaying a list of values to choose from during data entry, lookups, and various options for performing data validation. Specific entry options include automatic date or serial number entry or entry from a list of values. (In this chapter, you learned about data entry from a field with a list attached.) Other entry options relate to entering values from a range and checking for unique, existing, or numeric values only. Multiple-entry options may be defined for a field.

A natural tab order exists for entering data into fields in a Browse window: first, top to bottom, then left to right. You can change the tab order.

You edit, delete, or change the names or attributes of fields from within the Define Fields dialog box. Use the Options button to access the Calculation and Summary Formula dialog boxes to edit selected fields of the calculation or summary type. Also, by using the Options button and Entry Options dialog box, you can change selected field-entry options.

PART II

Working with Layouts

Includes

USING FILEMAKER PRO

CHAPTER 6

Creating a Layout

FileMaker calls a visual display of data a layout. Layouts control the presentation of data but do not affect how your data is saved. Your data is separate from any layouts you create. You can choose to place any fields in your file on any layout, or you can omit data from a layout to suit your purposes. All your data is still contained in your file, even if you choose not to display any part in a layout, and you can add or remove data from a layout at any time.

The Define Fields command controls the behavior of the data contained in a field regardless of the layout. You use the layout only to change the appearance of the data in each field.

Consider how FileMaker separates your data from your layout and how that layout controls your printed output. Figure 6.1 shows a layout for mailing labels. Although the file contained about 30 fields, you chose only the fields that were needed for this label: First Name, Last Name, Company, Address, City, State, and Zip Code. The remaining fields are in your file, available for use with other forms. When you switch to the Browse window (see fig. 6.2), you see the effect of your layout: the data for the current record appears. Switch to the Preview window (see Chapter 10, "Printing Basics") to see what your labels would look like if you printed them on continuous feed, 8 1/2- by-11-inch stock paper, two labels to a page (see fig. 6.3).

Fig. 6.1
A custom 2 3/4-by-3 3/4-inch mailing label shown in a Layout window.

Fig. 6.2
A single record in the Browse window corresponding to the layout in figure 6.1.

Think of a layout as a form or report; other database programs often use these terms interchangeably, but FileMaker assigns special meanings to each. A *form* is a display of data from a single record, such as an invoice or purchase order. A *report*, on the other hand, is a display of data from a group of records. You can create layouts for various types of labels or envelopes. You don't need to think in terms of committing your data to paper or printing it. If *displaying* the data on your computer in an appropriate format is important, you can create a layout for that purpose. You might need, for example, a data-entry screen for a confidential listing of the personnel records of the employees in your company or for a listing of telephone orders.

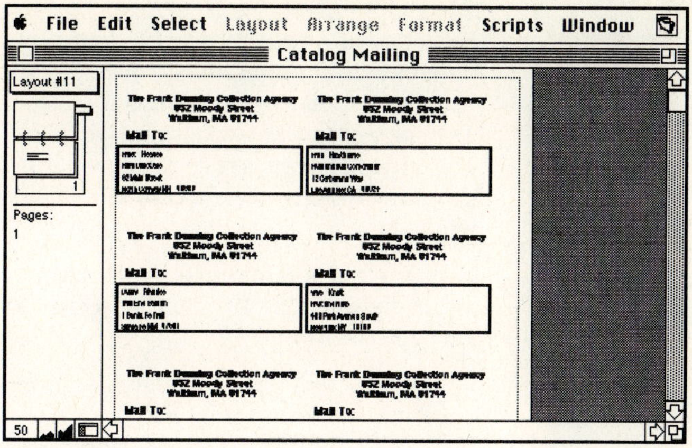

Fig. 6.3
A preview of the printed records of the label format created in figure 6.1.

If you run a business, you can use layouts for mail-merge letters, invoices, statements, mailing and packing labels, monthly summary reports, check printing, and W-2 forms. You could use one file to run your entire business, and, although there are good reasons not to do so, the entire collection of layouts could be attached to a single file. This chapter explains how to create a layout.

Defining Layout Possibilities

Defining a layout is simple. The process is nearly identical to creating records in a Browse window; you even use the same keystrokes. To create and work with layouts, enter the layout mode by choosing the Layout command on the Select menu or press the ⌘-L keystroke from wherever you are in FileMaker. The Layout window appears.

⌘-L, the Layout command, opens the Layout window that corresponds to your current layout.

When you create a file, FileMaker offers you the choice of six different types of predefined layouts: standard, columnar report, single-page form, labels, envelope, and blank. You can use these layouts to create your own display or form. You can create a layout for a single record as a *form*, as a *list* for a report, in *repeating units* for labels, or as a custom size for any purpose you can think of. Sizes from one square inch (1 inch by 1 inch) to one square yard (36 inches by 36 inches) can be accommodated.

You can create and store as many layouts as you want in a file—up to the capability of your disk. You can switch layouts quickly to perform different tasks, duplicate layouts, edit layouts, and reorganize them as you see fit. You can use layouts to make your data perform specific tasks. The *current layout* is what you see displayed in a FileMaker window. The current layout is reflected in what you see in the Browse window, so if you need to see the effect of any changes, switch back to the Browse window.

You now can add buttons to your layouts to provide another way to switch between layouts. See the section called "Adding Buttons to Layouts" in Chapter 12.

Objects that you place on a layout can include text, fields, pictures, graphics, and units called parts. A *part* is a section on a layout that performs a specific function. These objects can be placed with accuracy and formatted in many different ways. You can spruce up your layout with lines, rectangles, and circles. You can change the size of objects, their outlines, and their fill patterns to add emphasis to your work.

If you want to change the way data is displayed in a layout, use the Format menu in the Layout window (see "Formatting Layout Objects," later in this chapter; to change an object's display, see Chapter 7, "Enhancing Layout Appearance").

Understanding the Layout Window

The Layout window contains features similar to other FileMaker windows you have seen so far. In figure 6.4, a standard layout is shown with some of the elements marked that are unique to Layout windows. This section focuses on elements that are common to all Layout windows. In the sections that follow, you will see what differentiates one kind of Layout window from another.

The following list summarizes the elements unique to a Layout window:

Parts. A part is a repeating unit. Some parts repeat once per record, some repeat once per group of records, and some repeat once per page. Each layout requires a part. See Chapter 9, "Preparing To Print," and the text that follows this list for further details.

Field reshape box. This box controls the size and placement of a field and the data it contains. Where you place a field on your layout is where it appears on your Browse window. The small black boxes at each corner are resize—or grow—boxes. You can use these boxes to resize the field.

The field size is set by the reshape box and controls only display and output. If you want to enter data beyond the size of the box, the box expands to accept the information. Note that the name of the field is shown inside a field box.

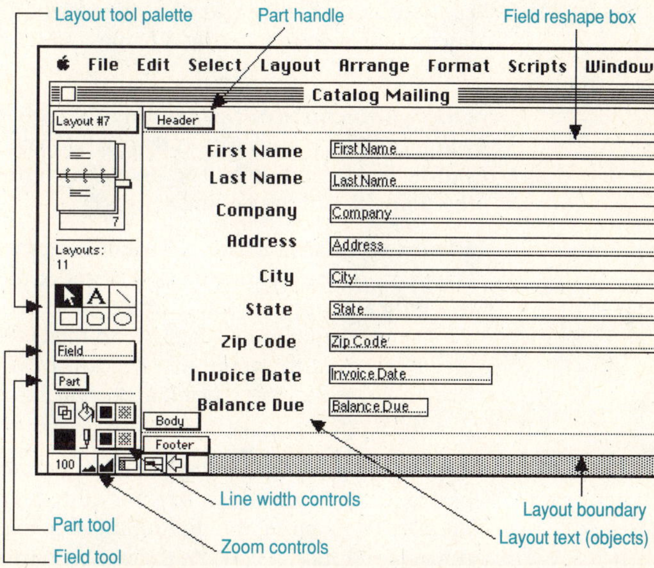

Fig. 6.4
Elements of a Layout window (in the standard layout).

Field tool. Dragging this tool onto the layout creates a field. In the resulting dialog box, you can select which field you want to place. See "Adding Fields," later in this chapter.

Fill controls. The two buttons to the right of the paint bucket icon contain pop-up menus for object fill color and pattern. The box on the left is a sample of the current default settings.

Layout boundary. This boundary indicates the size of your layout, not the page size. When the View as List command in the Layout menu is selected, the layout size governs the number of records that will fit in a Browse window. Otherwise, only one record appears. In either case, you print on a page all the records that the page size specifies. For more details, see "Viewing a List," later in this chapter.

FileMaker indicates the size of your printable area by placing a solid vertical line to indicate the right margin and a dashed horizontal line to indicate the bottom margin. The left and top margins line up with those edges of the layout window.

Layout pop-up menu. Clicking on the layout title above the Book icon brings up this pop-up menu, which enables you to switch instantly to a new layout.

Layout text (object). A text object is text that appears on all records. You create it with the Text tool (the letter A in the Toolbox), and you can select and format text objects with the Format menu. In the standard layout, FileMaker places field names, which are layout text, next to field boxes.

Line width control. This button icon contains a pop-up menu with line width options. Line width is displayed in points. The box on the left shows the current default settings. The number in the middle represents the point size of the default setting.

Layout window indicator. This indicator tells you that you are in the layout mode and it appears as text under the Book icon. In FileMaker II, this indicator appeared at the bottom left corner of the window. (Also, the Layout command is checked on the Select menu.) Remove the status area to show more layout in a window by clicking on this Layout window icon or press the corresponding keystroke again to return the status area to your screen.

Part handle. A part handle labels the part and enables you to resize the part by dragging it until it becomes the desired size. You also can resize the part by dragging the dotted line attached to the part handle. Hold down the Option key while dragging a part to change the part's size and to retain other part boundaries. To remove parts, drag them into the title bar or into other parts above or below the part.

Part label control. Clicking this icon flips the part labels to a horizontal or vertical position in a layout.

Part tool. Dragging the Part tool onto the layout creates a part. In the dialog box that results, you can choose a part type. See the section called "Adding Parts" at the end of this chapter.

Pen controls. This icon looks like a drafting pen. The two buttons to the right contain pop-up menus for line color and line pattern. The sample box on the left displays the current default setting.

Status Panel control. Clicking the Status Panel control icon hides or shows the status panel and its tools.

Tools Palette (Toolbox). The Tools Palette contains tools to create drawn elements. Clockwise from the highlighted Arrow tool are the Text, Line, Oval, Rounded Rectangle, and Rectangle tools (see Chapter 7).

Zoom controls. Clicking this icon enlarges or reduces the image on the screen.

Zoom percentage box. The Zoom percentage box indicates the current percent of magnification. The range available is 25 to 400%.

The following features are new to FileMaker Pro: fill controls, pen controls, layout pop-up menu for the line width controls, zoom control, zoom percentage, and the parts label control. Some of these controls were previously found on menus; now they appear in the Status Panel.

In FileMaker Pro, the T-Square and magnet icons have been removed from the Status Panel area and replaced by the position and size box.

Notice that a Layout window also contains the status area with the associated Book and Slide Control Mechanism. Operations that referred to records in a Browse window or requests in a Find window now refer to layouts. Your current layout is shown in the bottom right corner of the Book icon; the number of layouts in your file also is indicated in the status area.

The layout you are viewing (the current layout) determines the display of your Browse screen and what you can output. If you switch layouts, you browse a different screen and output a different form. The fields you place on a layout control how the data is displayed on a Browse screen. Only fields shown in a Layout window appear in the Browse window. Because a field's data is always in the file (even if the data isn't showing), you can use any calculation or summary field (even if it depends on its data).

Parts are an important part of a layout, and although they make FileMaker more difficult to understand, they give you flexibility in organizing and working with your data. If you have used a word processor, parts may seem familiar to you. Many word processors, such as Microsoft Word, use headers, footers, and title page parts to control page setup. Much of Chapter 9 explains how parts work with fields and how parts are used to set up pages. To better understand the difference between one layout and another, parts operation needs to be explained here briefly.

Figure 6.5, a Layout window with several parts showing, shows how various pieces of a layout come together for a report. From top to bottom, you see a title header, header, leading grand summary, subsummary, body, trailing grand summary, footer, and title footer parts.

The following list describes the parts in a Layout window:

Title parts show up once, at the top and bottom of your first page of output, as the title header and title footer, respectively.

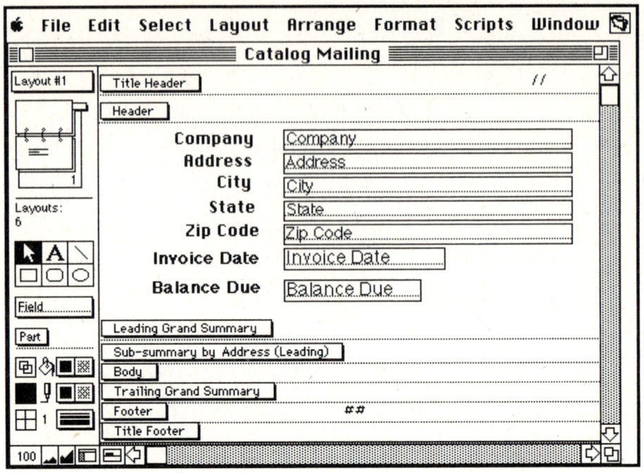

Fig. 6.5
A report layout with several parts.

Header and footer parts show up on all other pages, except the title page (if you have defined title parts).

Body parts are repeated for each record in a browsed set on every page, as room permits, until all have been output.

Sub-summary parts occur whenever a field value changes; therefore, they require that you organize or sort your file by field values.

Grand summary parts occur only once at the end of all your records and after all sub-summaries. It sums the contents of an entire field.

You don't need to understand all the elements of page parts yet. They will be explained in more detail later. You do need to know how the whole process comes together. When you go to the Browse window, you see the number of records that can fit on-screen, which is a function of how large each part is and how many records you are currently browsing. A labeled printout of a Layout window is shown in figure 6.6.

FileMaker enables you to place into your layout certain objects with which you can label a page: page numbers, print date, and record numbers. Notice that the date stamp (//) placed in the title header part occurs only once, but the page stamp (##) placed in the footer part is found on every page except the title page. The Date Entered field contained in the header also is found on every page except the title page. All these parts combine to give you considerable control over the display and output of a browsed set of records (see Chapter 9).

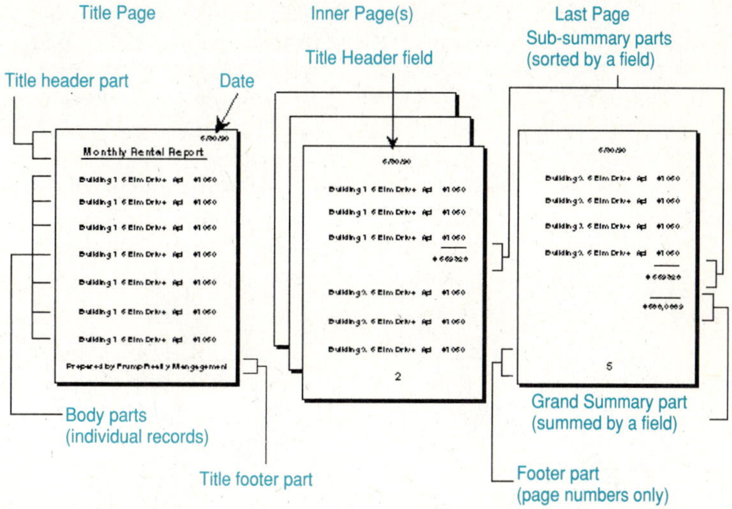

Fig. 6.6
The printout of a Layout window.

Using Predefined Layouts

If you didn't create additional layouts after you created your database file, and you accepted FileMaker's default layout, you are looking at a standard layout. Many of the figures you have seen so far in this book have used a standard layout. If you have another layout on your screen, and if you retained the original standard layout, you always can go into layout mode and switch to the standard layout.

The sections that follow describe the predefined layouts that you can use when you create a layout. Although layouts offer a set of formatted features, keep in mind that you can alter any of these layouts in ways that suit the task at hand. The six layouts are meant to be shortcuts, similar to templates.

Using the Standard Layout

The *standard layout* is the default layout. When you create a file, you automatically create this type of layout. All the fields are placed onto a standard layout in a vertical array. The fields are placed in the order that they are defined from top to bottom, and the name of each field is placed onto the layout just to the left of the field reshape box. The purpose of the standard layout is to show all your fields in a compact manner.

Consider the standard layout shown in figure 6.7. Note that a standard layout contains three parts: header, body, and footer. All fields and field names are placed inside the body of the layout, and the header and the footer are initially empty. You always can add objects to the header and footer later. Each body part defines a single record, and you see only one record in the Browse window. You can change the default configuration of viewing one record at a time by choosing the View as List command (see the section "Viewing a List," later in this chapter). If you do change the default, you see a Browse window with as many records on your screen as the body part permits.

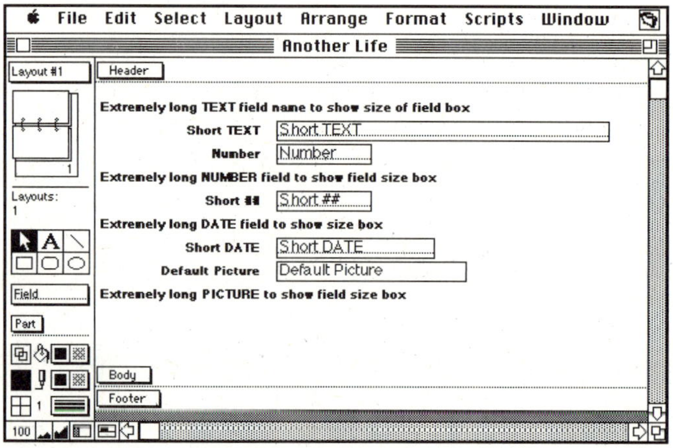

Fig. 6.7
The default configuration of a standard Layout window.

All field reshape boxes are initially one line of text high, using 12-point text as the standard. The length is not dependent on the length of the field names but on the data type (see fig. 6.8). Text fields are made the longest (3 1/2 inches long); Number and Date fields are made the shortest (1 inch long). When you have a long field name, the associated text object overflows into the field reshape box. This situation occurs in the example with the fields whose names start with `Extremely long` (see fig. 6.7). In fact, the field reshape boxes for the Number and Date fields in this category are totally obscured. You can edit, resize, or delete the text objects if you choose (see Chapter 7).

Figure 6.8 shows the Browse window that corresponds to figure 6.7. The field entry boxes appear if you hold down the mouse button.

Fig. 6.8
The Browse window that corresponds to figure 6.7, the standard Layout.

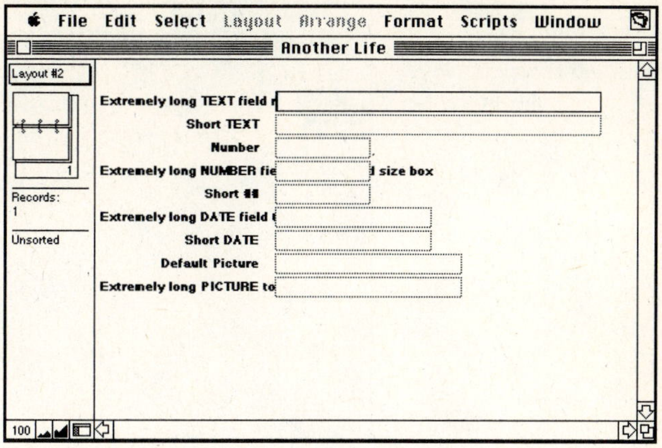

You can continue to work with and edit a standard layout, or you can define additional standard layouts. If a standard layout is on-screen when you define a new field, that field is added to the bottom of the stack, and, if necessary, the body part grows to accommodate the new field. If that field is a summary field, it is placed into the body part, and although it summarizes the dependent field, the summary field appears in each record. To summarize a group of records, place the summary field in a subsummary part. To summarize all records, place the summary field into a grand summary part (see Chapter 9 for more details on using summary parts). Any other layouts in your file, including the standard layout you originally created, are unaffected by newly defined fields.

After the standard layout is created, an invisible grid is turned on to help align fields. The width of the fields is no longer determined by the width of the field names. Instead, width is determined by the field type.

Using the Columnar Report Layout

If you want to see as much of your data as you can at one time, and you have just a few fields, using the columnar report layout is your best bet. A columnar report layout displays your data as a list or an array, similar to a spreadsheet. A typical columnar report layout is shown in figure 6.9. The layout contains three parts: a header, a body, and a footer.

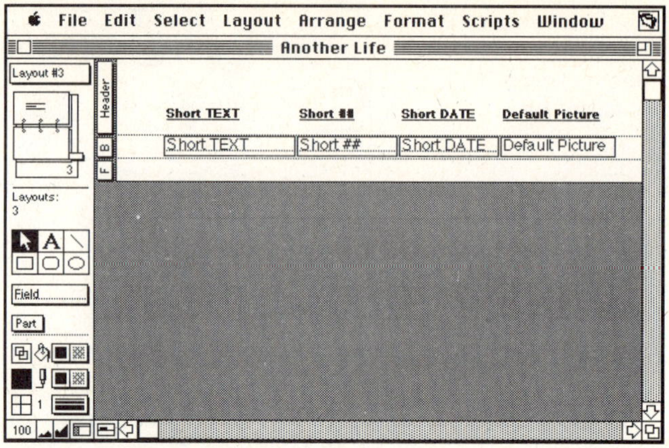

Fig. 6.9
The default configuration for a columnar report layout.

Fields are placed into the body part, and they appear from left to right, in the order that you add them when you create a layout. And when you create a layout, a Field Selection dialog box appears. From this box, you select the fields you want the layout to contain.

If a field is a summary field, it is placed into the body part and, although it summarizes the dependent field, it appears in each record. Again, to summarize a group of records, place the summary field in a subsummary part. To summarize all records, place the summary field into a grand summary part (see Chapter 9). Field names are placed as text objects into the header so that they appear once in your Browse window as field titles.

When the layout runs out of room on the right margin, it starts another line of text objects in the header and field reshape boxes in the body. For this reason, the columnar report layout is useful only for a few fields. As you can see in figure 6.10, more than one line of fields is confusing. The columnar report layout defaults to the width of your previous layout.

In the Browse window, each record is a row, each field is a column, and a field name text object appears as a heading. Although the layout shows one line, you see as many records as the size of your body part allows. In figure 6.11, which is the Browse window corresponding to figure 6.9, 10 records have been created (enough to enable the vertical scroll bar), and the seventh record is selected. Clicking the mouse button selects and shows only one record at a time. The columnar report format automatically turns on the View as List command. (See the section "Viewing a List" later in the chapter.)

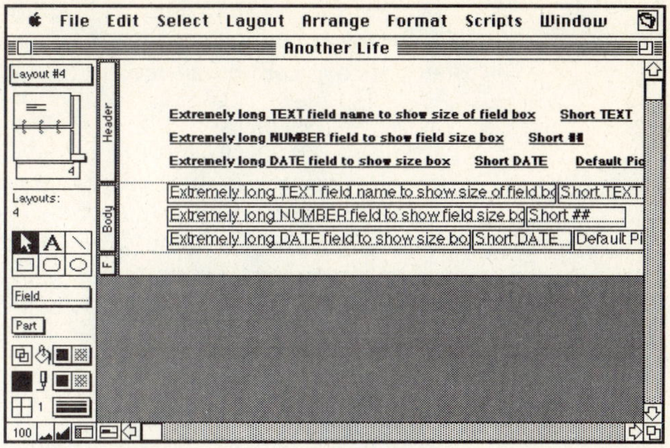

Fig. 6.10
Chaos in the columnar report layout format.

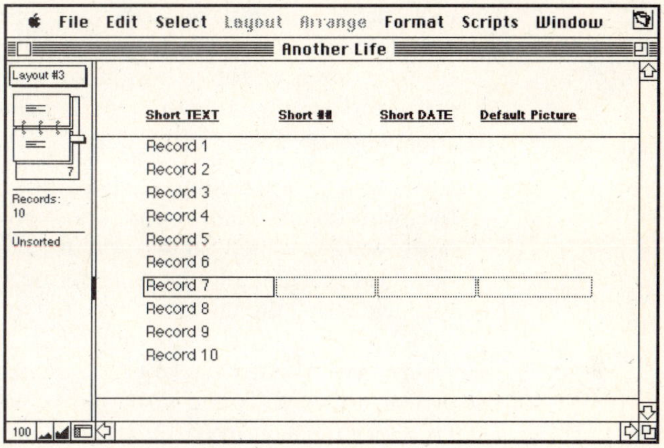

Fig. 6.11
The Browse window of the columnar report layout shown in figure 6.9.

Using the Label Layout

Use the label layout when you want to create a repetitive array of objects. The label layout enables you to specify the size of the unit that will be repeated and the number and arrangement of items in the array. The prototype label is often called a *primitive*. You can use an arrangement with any number of columns, and you can specify that the labels fill from left to right and then top to bottom, or from one column to the next, from left to right. Columns are discussed in the section "Using Columns" later in this chapter. A two-column array was specified in the label preview shown in figure 6.3. Although labels are the most obvious use for this layout, you can use this layout for any repetitive arrangement, such as continuous-feed forms for checks or statements.

The printer you use controls the page sizes available to you, and the page setup you specify controls the label size available to your layout. You select printers in the Chooser DA from the Apple menu (see Chapter 3, "Creating a File"), and you choose the other two settings with Page Setup in the File menu. (For a detailed discussion of printing mailing labels, see Chapter 10; a step-by-step tutorial on creating mailing labels is the subject of Chapter 11, "Quick Start: Creating Mailing Labels.")

Fields you place into the label are stacked vertically, the same way that they are stacked in a standard layout. Space to the right of the primitive is grayed. The default field size is 9 points, and FileMaker stacks as many fields as you want, up to the limit of the height of the primitive. For a one-inch label, this limit is six fields (see fig. 6.12). If you need to add more fields, you must go to the layout first to resize and move fields. If any of your fields are blank, and you want to close the fields by removing blank spaces from top to bottom or left to right, you can use the Show command from the Layout menu to bring up the Sliding Objects command (see Chapter 9).

If you specify one-column (called 1-up) labels, you see only the primitive, with no other label boundaries showing. In figure 6.12, three-up labels were specified, so two additional label boundaries are shown. Scroll to the right, and the page boundary appears as shown in figure 6.12. Note that the margins to the left and to the right of the labels are bunched to the right of the right label. The label stock in the printer is positioned to center the labels on the stock. To see typical label data, browse a record. To see what your printed output will look like, use the Preview command from the Select menu or press ⌘-U to open the Preview window.

Using the Single-Page Form

Use the single-page form to devote an entire page to each record. Each field appears on a separate line in the same order as they appear in the Define Fields dialog box. The field name appears to the left. A single-page form has no header or footer. To create a single-page form, choose New Layout from the Edit menu. Enter a layout name and click on the Single Page Form radio button. Finally, click the OK button.

Fig. 6.12
Three-up Label layout with primitive shown and scrolled right to show the page boundary.

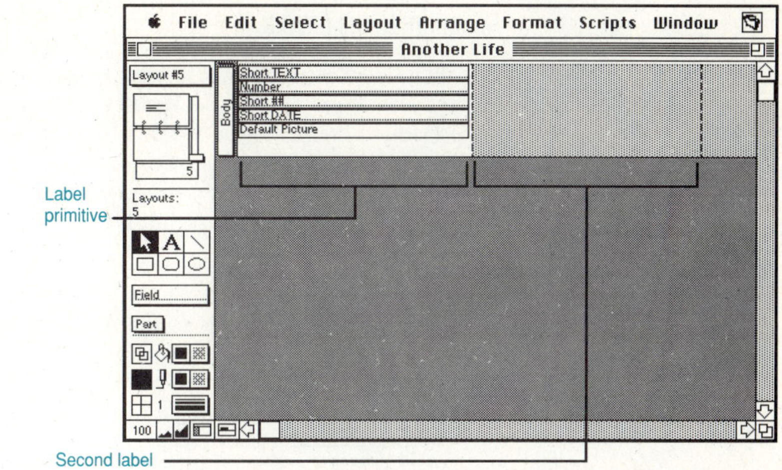

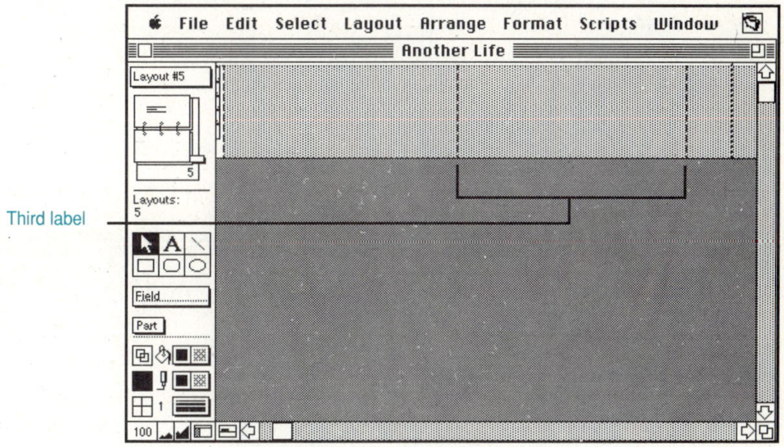

Using the Envelope Form

The envelope form enables you to arrange names and addresses in the type of layout for printing business envelopes. This choice is similar to the label layout. After choosing New Layout from the Edit menu, type a name for your layout and click on the Envelope radio button. After clicking the OK button, the Field List dialog box appears. Select the fields one at a time and click on the Move button after each selection. After all the fields are moved, click the OK button. You then can rearrange or reshape the fields the way you want the information to appear on an envelope.

Using the Blank Layout

Use the blank layout when you want to start with a clean slate, or when it's easier to place your fields and layout objects than remove the ones that are on previously created layouts. The blank layout is useful when you want to create a nonstandard arrangement of objects in a layout. A blank layout also is useful for generating forms or envelopes. In Quick Start: Creating and Using Forms, the blank layout is used to create a form.

The blank layout is created with header, body, and footer parts (see fig. 6.13). As its title implies, the layout is blank. FileMaker bypasses a Field Selection dialog box so that no fields appear on the layout when it opens. The blank layout defaults to the size of a compact Macintosh (Classic or SE) screen.

Fig. 6.13
The blank layout.

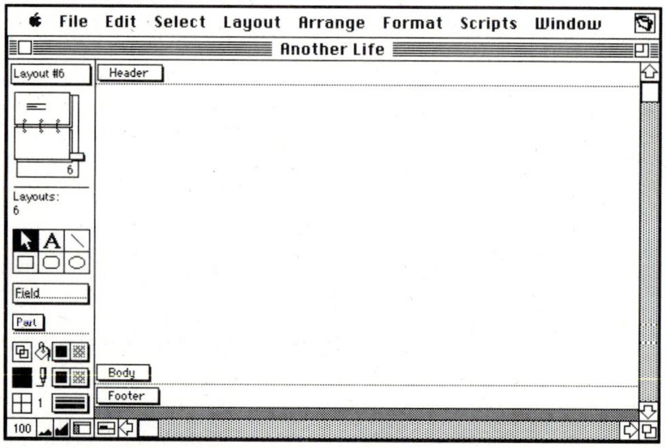

Creating a Custom Layout

This chapter has discussed all six of FileMaker's predefined layouts. These layouts are meant to be only starting places for creating layouts. You can create custom layouts that allow you to generate layouts if you keep the following principles in mind:

- Whatever layout you choose, remember that the number and distribution of the parts on the layout controls how your records are displayed, how your derived (calculation and summary) fields behave, and what your output looks like.
- Consider carefully what parts you want to include or add and what parts you need to delete.

- Pay particular attention to the placement of derived fields, especially summary fields, and to the summary (sub-summary and grand summary) parts.

You can copy and paste much of what you see on a layout by using the Clipboard. You can copy from one layout to another any object on a layout, except parts. In fact, if the field names match, you can copy fields from one file to another. The data underlying the field does not copy (remember that in FileMaker data is separate from display), but all the formatting and definitions copy. This powerful technique enables you to quickly copy aspects of layouts that you like and to generate custom layouts.

One benefit of using templates (see Chapter 13, "Using Templates and Other Resources") is the skill you build as you use the concepts and techniques they include. If you haven't looked at the templates Claris shipped with FileMaker, you should. You can use them as is, and you also can learn how to construct powerful layouts. Instructions for the layouts are attached as separate layouts in each of the files.

FileMaker Pro has two new layout choices: the Single Page Form and the Envelope layout.

Viewing a List

You can specify that a layout appear as a list of records in the Browse window. This list of records is the default choice for the columnar report layout, but you need to select it as an additional option for other layouts. When you choose the View as List command on the Select menu, you see the Browse window shown in figure 6.11. A list display has no effect on what you see in the Layout window; the list display only affects what's displayed in the Browse window. View a list for the same reason you use a columnar report layout: to see many items at once. If each phone number in a directory file is a single record, you might want to view that file as a list when you're looking for someone whose name you know but aren't exactly sure how to spell. If you have a file in which each record stands by itself (a single purchase order, for example), view each record separately.

To view a list of records, follow these steps:

1. Select the Layout command from the Select menu or press the ⌘-L keystroke to open the Layout window.

2. Select the layout you want.

3. Select the View as List command on the Select menu. FileMaker remembers whether you chose the View as List option whenever you open a file and puts a check mark next to the command on the Select menu.

   If the View as List command was checked, this option already has been selected for that layout. Select the command once again to view records singly.

4. Choose the Browse command on the Select menu or press the ⌘-B keystroke to view a display of your records as a list.

The size of the body part controls how many records show on your screen or fit into a printed page for a list.

Using Columns

Just as you can display any layout as a list, you also can choose to display a layout as a set of columns. Choosing Layout Options from the Layout menu opens a dialog box (see fig. 6.14). FileMaker prompts you for the number of columns and for the filling order. You can choose from 1 to 99 columns of records. When you choose the Across First option, records fill row by row, from left to right, and then top to bottom. The Down First option fills fields column by column, top to bottom, and then left to right.

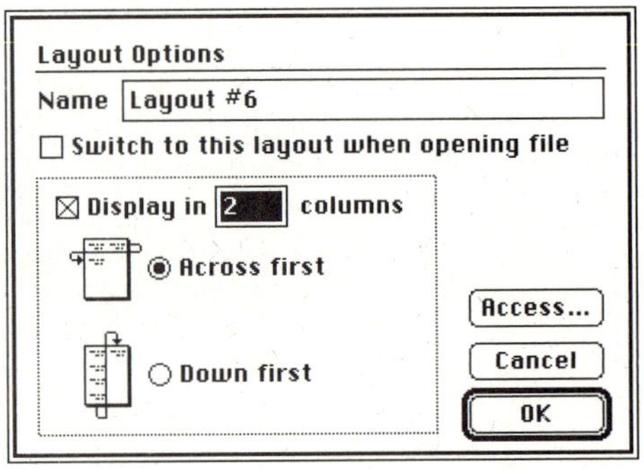

Fig. 6.14
The Layout Options dialog box.

Under Layout Options, you now find the Access button, which enables you to set passwords (in Chapter 16, see the section called "Access Rights").

If you are printing labels, choose the row-by-row option (Across First). Then, if your printer misfeeds or your job is interrupted, you can more easily reprint the job. Another benefit is that the row-by-row option uses the minimum amount of label stock in a print job. When you are printing a directory, choose the Down First option, because readers have a natural tendency to read in columns from top to bottom.

The printer specified in the Chooser DA from the Apple menu and the paper size selected under Page Setup control the number of columns you can have or the number of records that can fit in a row. Like the label layout, the column layout option uses a prototype section, or primitive, in the Layout window to show how all records will look, and it grays out the rest of the layout. Multiple columns are marked with dashed lines to show where they are bounded, and the boundary of the printable area is marked with a solid vertical line.

The View as List option controls what you see in the Browse window, and the Column Setup option controls what you output to your printer. You can select both options at the same time and, provided that your primitive is of the appropriate size, one column will not overlap the next. If the primitive is too large to support the number of columns you chose, part of the primitive is grayed out. If this happens when you preview your output, columns to the right obscure the parts of the columns to the left that they overlap. In the column layout in figure 6.15, the grayed area extends into the primitive. When the Preview window is displayed, the obscured sections are obvious (see fig. 6.16).

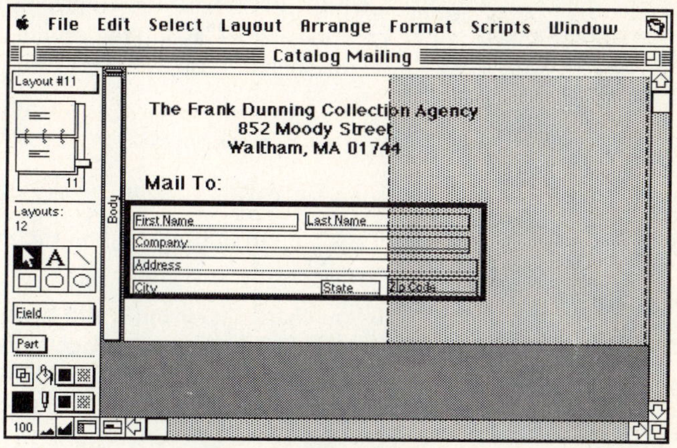

Fig. 6.15
Too many columns specified in a layout.

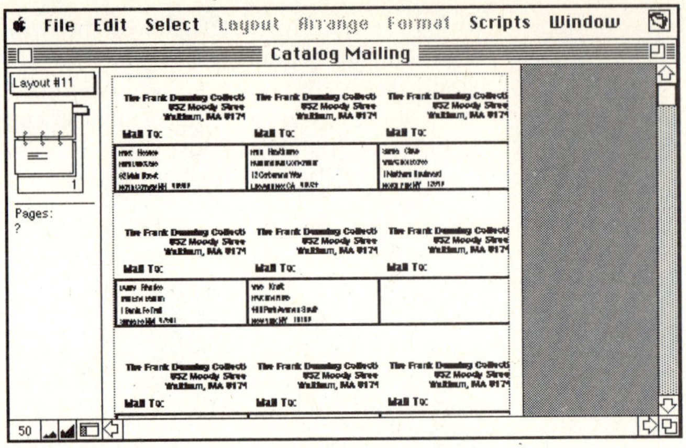

Fig. 6.16
The Preview window corresponding to figure 6.15.

To preview records in columns, follow these steps:

1. Choose the printer you want to use by selecting the Chooser DA on the Apple menu and then selecting Page Setup from the File menu. Specify your options. Refer to Chapter 10 for details.
2. Choose the Layout command from the Select menu or press the ⌘-L keystroke to open the Layout window.
3. Make the layout you want to set up in columns the current layout.
4. Select the Layout Options command on the Layout menu. The Layout Options dialog box (see fig. 6.14) is displayed. If you are creating a label layout, the number of labels across the page is part of the specification of the layout.
5. In the Layout Options dialog box, insert the number of columns you want, from 1 to 99.
6. Click the Across First or Down First radio button.
7. Click the OK button or press the Return or Enter key to accept this specification.

   If you change your mind and do not want to have a column setup or you do not want to change any column setup that may have been specified, click the Cancel button or press the ⌘-. (period) keystroke to return to the layout with your previous setting intact.
8. To view your records in columns, select the Preview command from the Select menu or press ⌘-U. Choose Browse or Layout from the Select menu when you are finished.

You can change or remove a column setup at any time by opening and working with the Layout Options dialog box. Repeat steps 1 through 5 above.

To remove a column setup, click off the Display in "n" Columns box and then click the OK button. To change the number of columns or the manner in which they fill, change the number in the Display in "n" Columns box and click the appropriate fill radio button (if needed). Click the OK button.

If you have specified a layout with the column setup Down First, any sub-summary parts are printed the width of the column. When you create a sub-summary part, and you check the Page Break check box in the New Page dialog box (see the section "Adding Parts" at the end of this chapter), FileMaker starts a new column instead of starting a new page. With the Across First option, sub-summary parts print the entire width of the page; clicking the Page Break check box causes a new page whenever a sub-summary part prints. Remember, sub-summary parts are used to summarize groups of records, and they appear whenever the values in the dependent field change.

Creating a Layout

After a file is established, you have no restrictions on the number of layouts it can have, their type, or their order. If you want to work from a copy, you can duplicate a layout. You can delete layouts, or, by using both commands in sequence, you can reorder a layout's position in your file. If you want to delete the original standard layout from your file, you can, if you retain at least one layout in the file. This section discusses these operations.

Remember that the current layout controls what you can display and output; the purpose of creating a layout is to perform a specific task. Do not be overly concerned with the number of layouts in a file; you do not pay much of a penalty in disk storage for layouts, unless they include a substantial number of graphic images. Also, you pay no real speed penalty for layouts; only the current layouts of active files are loaded into memory for use.

To create a layout, follow these steps:

1. Select the Layout command from the Select menu or press the ⌘-L keystroke to enter layout mode.

Make sure that you have selected the printer you want to use (through the Chooser) and page setup (see Chapter 10).

2. Select the New Layout command on the Edit menu or press the ⌘-N keystroke. The New Layout dialog box appears (see fig. 6.17).

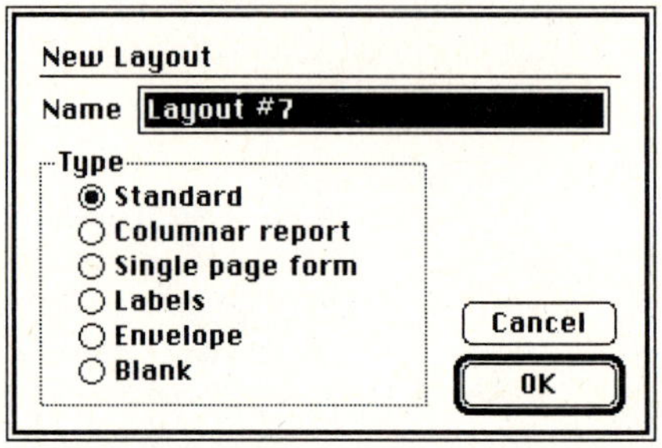

Fig. 6.17
The New Layout dialog box.

3. In the New Layout dialog box, click the appropriate radio button. The standard layout is the default choice.

4. Click the OK button or press the Return or Enter key to continue to create the layout.

   or

   Click the Cancel button or press the ⌘-. (period) keystroke to cancel the operation and to return to the current layout without creating a new one.

SPEED KEY

When you are in the layout mode, ⌘-N, the New Layout command, creates a layout with the next available layout number.

Note that FileMaker automatically turns on the option Align to Grid on the Layout menu to aid you in lining up fields in a layout. To turn off the option, select it again. The process of creating a layout diverges at this point, depending on the type of layout you chose in step 3.

To create a standard layout, follow the preceding steps; no other steps are required. Your new standard layout appears as the next available layout with all your defined fields showing.

To create a blank layout, follow the preceding steps. Again, no other steps are required. Your new blank layout appears as the next available layout with no fields showing.

To create a columnar report layout, follow these steps:

1. Follow steps 1 through 4 above. A Set Field Order dialog box appears on-screen (see fig. 6.18).

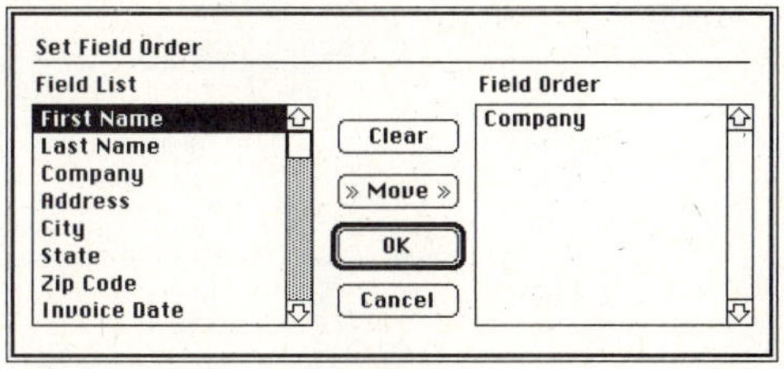

Fig. 6.18
The Set Field Order dialog box.

2. Select the field you want by double-clicking on the field names or click the field name and then the Move button.

   If you make a mistake, click the field name in the Field Order scroll box and then click the Move button to remove it from the field order. Or, click the Clear button to remove all fields from the field order.

3. When the field order is the way you want it, click the OK button or press the Return or Enter key.

   or

   Click the Cancel button or press ⌘-. (period) to cancel the operation and return to the current layout without creating a columnar report layout.

FileMaker creates the layout as the next available layout in your file and opens it on-screen. Fields are placed into the body part of your columnar report layout from left to right in their order in the Field Order scroll box.

If you specified the label layout, the Label Setup dialog box appears (see fig. 6.19). The default choices for an ImageWriter printer are shown. The page setup changes, depending on the options you choose with that command.

Follow these steps to finish the label layout:

1. Enter the number of labels you desire in the Labels Across the Page text box.

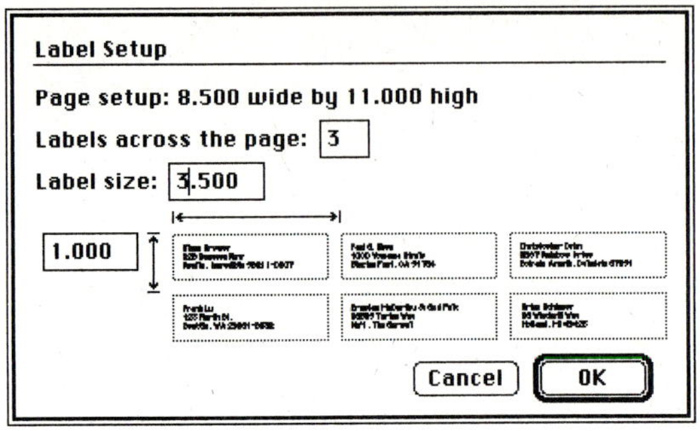

Fig. 6.19
The Label Setup dialog box.

2. Enter in the Label Size text boxes both the width (horizontal bar) and height of the labels you want. Remember that these dimensions go from one label edge to the same label edge of the next label.

3. Click the OK button or press the Return or Enter key to continue to create the layout. The Set Field Order dialog box appears (see fig. 6.18).

   or

   Click the Cancel button or press ⌘-. (period) to return to your previous current layout without creating a label layout.

4. Double-click on the desired field names or click on their names to highlight them and then click the Move button.

5. When the field order is the way you want it, click the OK button or press the Return or Enter key.

   or

   Click the Cancel button or press ⌘-. (period) to return to the previous current layout without creating a label layout.

FileMaker enables you to place only as many fields as the label height allows and posts an alert box if you attempt to place additional fields (see fig. 6.20). For a one-inch label, the limit is six fields. The field order is from top to bottom. If you must place additional fields, resize the fields and move them (see Chapter 7). Use the Field tool to place additional fields on the layout (see the section "Adding Fields," later in this chapter).

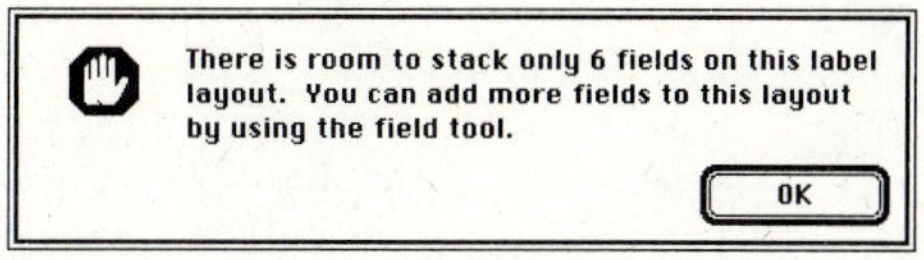

Fig. 6.20
The alert box you see if you try to place too many fields in your label layout.

Switching Layouts

To switch layouts, use the Book or Slide Control Mechanism and keystroke equivalents. Use the same keystrokes for changing records in a Browse window or requests in a Find window.

The easiest way to move from one layout to another is to click on the layout title above the Book. A pop-up menu listing all of the available layouts appears to the right. Scroll through the list and highlight the layout you want.

Another way to move from layout to layout is to choose the Layout command on the Select menu or press the ⌘-L keystroke. Then do any of the following procedures:

- Click on the bottom page of the Book to go forward one layout (a higher number) or click on the top page of the Book to go backward one layout (a lower number).
- Click on the number in the lower right corner of the Book (your current layout) or drag on it to highlight it. Type the number of the desired layout and then press the Enter or Return key to go to that layout.
- Drag the Slide Control Mechanism to the top to go to the first layout or to the bottom to go to the last layout. Drag the Slide Control Mechanism until the desired layout number appears in the Book and then release the mouse button.
- Press the ⌘-Tab keystroke to go forward one layout in the Layout window or press ⌘-Shift-Tab or ⌘-Option-Tab to go backward one layout.

SPEED KEY

⌘-Tab selects the next layout in the Layout window. ⌘-Shift-Tab or ⌘-Option-Tab selects the preceding layout in the Layout window.

Most databases offer some sort of keystroke that enables you to open directly and examine a field's definition so that you can see how it's constructed. FileMaker doesn't offer this feature; therefore, you should have one layout that documents your database. Many templates, including the ones that come with FileMaker, offer this sort of documentation.

Use a layout like the standard layout that contains all the fields in your file. You can check the field's formatting by double-clicking on the field. A Text Format dialog box appears and shows all the formatting for the selected field (see fig. 6.21). You can store notes on the layout itself, or you can create records that you can browse with more information for Text, Number, Time, or Date fields. Calculation or summary fields cannot be entered or explained in the Browse window; you must use a layout explanation for those. When you enter information in the Browse window, you do not have to resize Text, Number, Time, or Date fields. They accept enough information for their explanation. Use layout explanations for Picture fields.

The problem with using the predefined layouts is that the fields in the layout window are only one line high. You can expand the field boxes so that they include enough space for these text explanations: field attributes, entry options, calculations, logic, formatting, or any valuable information concerning the originating point or the destination of the data.

Keep in mind that if you define additional fields, they will be added to a standard layout only if it is the current layout. The original standard layout may not have all the required fields.

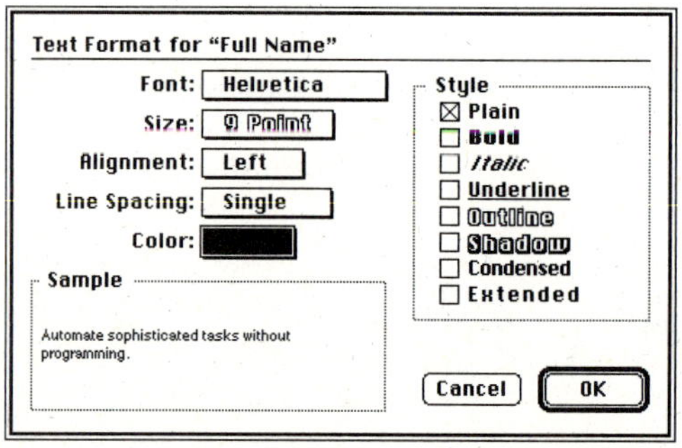

Fig. 6.21
The Text Format dialog box for a selected field.

You also can create scripts or buttons (see Chapter 12, "Creating Scripts and Buttons") to go from layout to layout. Scripts also can be used to reset a number of conditions (such as selected records, sorts, and page setups) to those specified when the script was created.

Duplicating a Layout

At times, you may want to create a layout based on one you already have. If it's less trouble for you to remove objects from an established layout than it is to create a layout, use the Duplicate Layout command to create a copy. You can use the copy to experiment on and to modify without fear of making errors. This approach is a great time-saver.

To duplicate a layout, follow these steps:

1. Make the layout that you want to copy the current layout.
2. Select the Duplicate Layout command from the Edit menu or press ⌘-D.

FileMaker creates a copy of the layout as the last layout in the file and opens it in the Layout window.

Deleting Layouts

You can remove any layout from your file as long as you retain one layout. Because layouts are separate from the data, deleting a layout leaves your data intact in the file.

To delete a layout, follow these steps:

1. Choose the Layout command on the Select menu or press the ⌘-L keystroke to open the layout window.
2. Make the layout you want to delete the current layout.
3. Select the Delete Layout command from the Edit menu or press the ⌘-E keystroke equivalent. You can remember this keystroke if you understand that you are *eliminating* a layout.

   FileMaker displays an alert box that asks whether you want to delete the current layout.
4. Click the Delete button.

   or

   Click the Cancel button or press Return to go back to the current layout.

SPEED KEY

If you use the ⌘-Option-E keystroke instead of the ⌘-E keystroke, you bypass the alert box, and the previous layout appears on the screen.

⌘-E, the Delete Layout command, permanently eliminates the current layout from your file when you are in layout mode.

WARNING Be very careful when deleting layouts. Deleting a layout is permanent: it cannot be undone. For this reason, you shouldn't use the ⌘-Option-E keystroke.

Reordering Layouts

You may want to change permanently the order in which your layouts occur. You can use the Duplicate Layout and Delete Layout commands in tandem for that purpose.

To reorder the layouts in your file, follow these steps:

1. Choose the Layout command from the Select menu or press the ⌘-L keystroke to open the Layout window.
2. Make the first layout in the new order the current layout.
3. Select the Duplicate Layout command from the Edit menu. The new layout appears at the end of the file, and FileMaker opens that layout on your screen.
4. Return to the original layout you used in step 2 and delete it by selecting the Delete Layout command on the Edit menu or press its ⌘-E kcystrokc cquivalcnt.
5. In the Delete Layout alert box, click the Delete button. The layout previous to the current layout appears.
6. Continue to sequentially duplicate and delete each layout in the order that you want.

Use this same procedure to change record order (see Chapter 4, "Editing, Finding, and Sorting Records"). Although this procedure is very tedious for a large number of records, most files don't have that many layouts attached to them.

Editing Layouts

To customize your layout, you can make any number of changes. You can format the data so that it appears the way you want it. You can add items, such as fields, text, pictures, and parts, to match your layout needs. The following sections discuss these changes.

Formatting Layout Objects

FileMaker offers the Text Format, Number Format, Date Format, Time Format, and Picture Format commands to change the display of the attributes associated with a Number, Date, Time, Text, or Picture field. Because they alter the display, in FileMaker lingo they are *formats*, and FileMaker places them on the Format menu. Although you may type 7/25/22 in a Date field, you can have FileMaker display a long date: Tuesday, July 25, 1922. Or, you can format a number to show two decimal places or to display as a percentage.

In this part of the chapter, you will learn how formatting changes the way *data* is displayed. You also can format objects; you can specify the line pattern for a square. These changes use the Format menu but a different set of commands. You also can format an object, for example, to change text's font or style from plain to bold, the point size from 10 to 12, or the alignment from left justified to middle. The changes use commands associated with the Font, Size, Style, and Align Text commands on the Format menu (see Chapter 7).

Numbers

You can format data in Number fields in a variety of ways: with commas, dollar signs, percent signs, and decimal points. You can even define a logical format for a Number field as Yes or No, corresponding to whether the field is true or false (in the Boolean sense), or 1 or 0, respectively.

Tip

Any number format other than unformatted slows down the operation of your file, because your Macintosh calculates them internally.

Numbers that appear on your Browse screen in any field (Text, Number, Date, Time, summary, or calculation) are ASCII characters, so you can use the Format menu to select from Font, Size, Style, and Align Text to change their display. When you create a Number field or a field such as a calculation or summary field that has a numeric result, the additional formatting commands are available to you through the Format Number command on the Format menu.

If, for example, you format the number 1234.56789 as a percent to two decimal places, FileMaker displays the number `1234.56 %` when you enter it or deselect the field. Changing the display of any number entry does not change the data in the file. FileMaker retains a 15-floating-decimal-place accuracy internally, even if it shows the data to only two places.

To format a Number field's data, follow these steps:

1. Choose the Layout command on the Select menu or press the ⌘-L keystroke to open the Layout window.
2. Select the Number, calculation, or summary field with number results to be formatted.
3. Choose the Number Format command on the Format menu or double-click on the field to open the Number Format dialog box (see fig. 6.22).

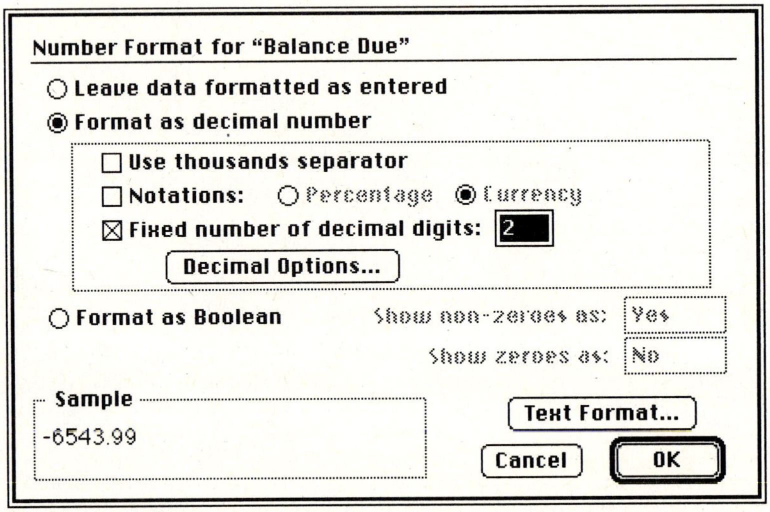

Fig. 6.22
The Number Format dialog box for a selected field.

4. Make your selections by clicking the check boxes on or off and filling in the appropriate text boxes.
5. Click the OK button or press Return or Enter to accept the settings. FileMaker marks your settings with a check mark.

   or

   Click the Cancel button or press the ⌘-. (period) keystroke equivalent to leave the dialog box and return to the previous settings.

To remove or change a number format, follow steps 3 through 5 again.

Double-clicking on a field opens the appropriate format dialog box.

Tip

Before you create a Number, Time, Date, Picture, calculation, or summary field, you can set the formatting and attributes by clicking on a field with the desired properties.

The following list contains the Number Format dialog box elements' actions (see fig. 6.22):

Leave Data Formatted as Entered. Choosing this option displays the characters the way you enter them. Use this setting when you work with a combination of alphabetic and numeric characters in a numeric field. This method enables you to use special characters: $250.25/copy or 1.25.

Format as Decimal Number. Choose this option to round off the number and to display the number of decimal places you place in the text box. You must check this box to turn on these settings:

> **Use Thousands Separator.** Click this option to place a comma after every three digits to the left of the decimal point.
>
> **Notation: Percentage.** Using this option multiplies a number by 100 and places a percent sign to the right of the value.
>
> **Notation: Currency.** Using this option places a dollar sign to the left of a number and places negative numbers inside parentheses.
>
> **Fixed Number of Decimal Digits.** Enter the desired number.
>
> FileMaker retains the accuracy of all the decimal places in a record and uses the decimal places in calculations, but it displays or prints only the number of digits you specify. Typing 0 displays no decimal points, and typing a negative number rounds a number off to the number of places to the left of the decimal place. With a format of –2 decimal places, FileMaker displays the number 2345.6 as 2300.
>
> FileMaker has a Round ( ) function that also sets the number of decimal places (see Chapter 5, "Automating Data Entry").

Format as Boolean (Yes/No). Turning on this option places a logical result Yes or No (Boolean value) in the field. If the field contains a value of 1, Yes, or Y, the value displayed (and printed) is a Yes. If the field contains a value of 0, No, or N, then it is displayed as a No. An empty field or one with non-numeric characters (other than Yes, Y, No, or N) is left empty. Yes/No fields are best used in logical calculations, such as defining a field called Account Active that displays a Yes when the money owed to you is not zero (see Chapter 5).

Dates

You can format data in Date fields by using the Date Format command. This formatting does not affect the data contained in the Date fields, nor any date calculations that you use with them. See Chapter 3 for information pertaining to how FileMaker uses Date fields internally. Special date formats are available to you. Again, using any format for data in a Date field other than unformatted slows down your file's performance.

To format a Date field's data, follow these steps:

1. Choose the Layout command on the Select menu or press ⌘-L to open the Layout window.

2. Select the Date, calculation, or summary fields with the date result to be formatted.

   You also can format date layout text objects that contain the date stamp (//) by using the Date Format command.

3. Choose the Date Format command on the Format menu. The Date Format dialog box appears (see fig. 6.23).

Fig. 6.23
The Date Format dialog box for a selected field.

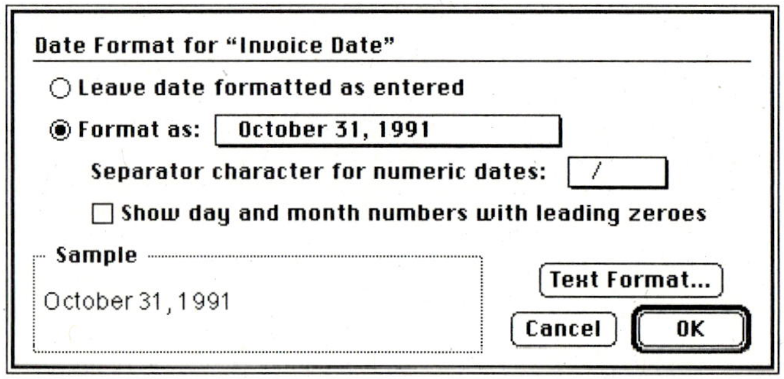

4. Click on your selection.

5. Click the OK button to accept the setting or press the Return or Enter key.

   or

   Click the Cancel button or press the ⌘-. (period) keystroke to return to the Layout window with your original date formatting intact. You can return to the Date Format dialog box later to change or remove the settings, if you want.

Unformatted Date field data displays the characters as you enter them. No calculations or attribute settings are made. The other choices use the following style:

7/22/88
Jul 22, 1988
July 22, 1988
Fri, Jul 22, 1988
Friday, July 22, 1988

Remember that FileMaker can perform date calculations from 1/01/0001 to 12/31/3000, but the program can format dates only in the Macintosh range from 1/01/1904 to 12/31/2039. When you type the date *8/27/90*, FileMaker assumes that you mean the 20th century and formats it as 1990. If you type the date *8/27/890*, the year 1890 is displayed.

Time

Time and calculation fields can be formatted with a time result. You can specify:

12- or 24-hour formats

AM or PM suffix

punctuation between hours, minutes, and seconds

text attributes

A time symbol (::) also is available for use on layouts. Select the symbol, and format it as you would a field.

To format a Time field, follow these steps:

1. Choose the Layout command from the Select menu or press the ⌘-L keystroke equivalent to open the Layout window.
2. Choose the Time Format command from the Format menu. The Time Format dialog box appears (see fig. 6.24).

   You also can double-click a time field to open a Time Format dialog box. If Time Format is dimmed, you cannot apply a time format to the selected fields.
3. Click on the Format As radio button.
4. Use the pop-up menu to choose the format you want.
5. If you want something other than what appears, enter a character in the Unit Separator box. Use a period, slash, or any single character you want.
6. Click on either the 24 Hour or 12 Hour Time Suffix radio buttons.

Note

If you prefer to leave the time the way you entered it, select the Leave Data Formatted as Entered radio button.

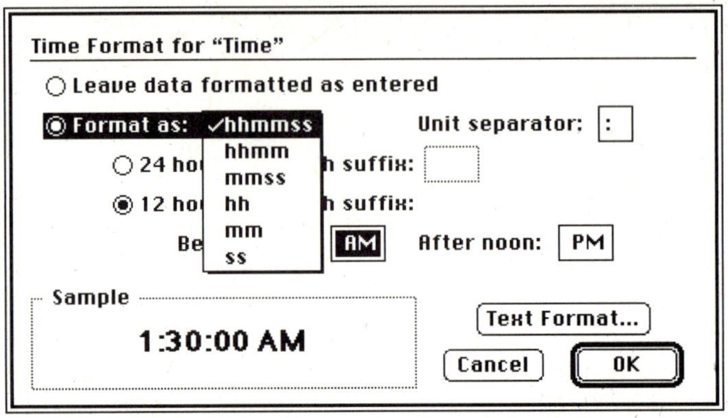

Fig. 6.24
The Time Format dialog box for a selected field.

7. To set the text attributes, click on the Text Format button.
8. Click on the OK button.

Pictures

Pictures that you add to a layout as *objects* appear on every record; pictures entered into a Picture field are data attached to a specific record, and they appear in the record to which they belong. You can change picture data by using the Picture Format command on the Format menu. You can *scale* a picture—enlarging or reducing it—to fit inside a field box, or you can crop it and use just the part of the picture you need. These manipulations are fairly crude, and you may want to investigate the use of SmartScrap and the Clipper as alternatives to using these formats.

To format a Picture field's data, follow these steps:

1. Choose the Layout command on the Select menu or press the ⌘-L keystroke to open the Layout window.
2. Select the Picture fields to be formatted.
3. Select the Picture Format command on the Format menu. The Picture Format dialog box is displayed (see fig. 6.25).
4. Click the desired option.
5. Click the OK button or press the Return or Enter key to accept the settings.

   or

Click the Cancel button or press ⌘-. (period) to return to your Layout window with the previous settings.

Fig. 6.25
The Picture Format dialog box for a selected field.

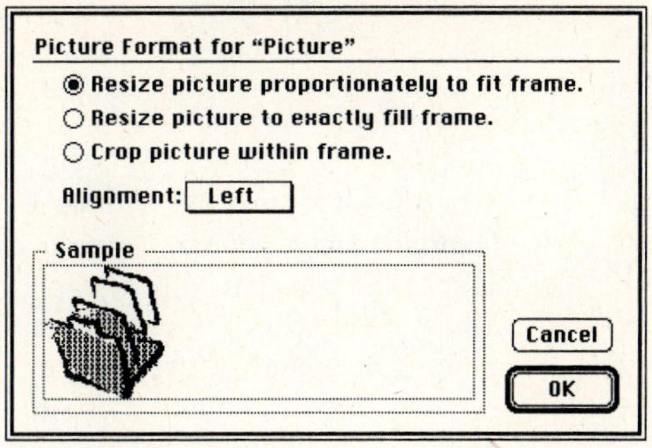

Tip
Use an object-oriented drawing instead of a bit-mapped drawing to increase the speed with which FileMaker displays and outputs your file.

The option Resize Picture Proportionately To Fit Frame is commonly referred to as *scaling*; using this option fits the original image into the available space, filling the space as much as possible without distorting the proportions of the image. Using the Resize Picture To Exactly Fill Frame option completely fills the available space, but image proportion is lost. The Crop Picture within Frame option is used for *cropping* the picture, or cutting off a portion of the image. Figure 6.26 shows the difference between cropping and proportionately resizing an image. The Picture fields contain the same image.

Fig. 6.26
Scaling and cropping a picture.

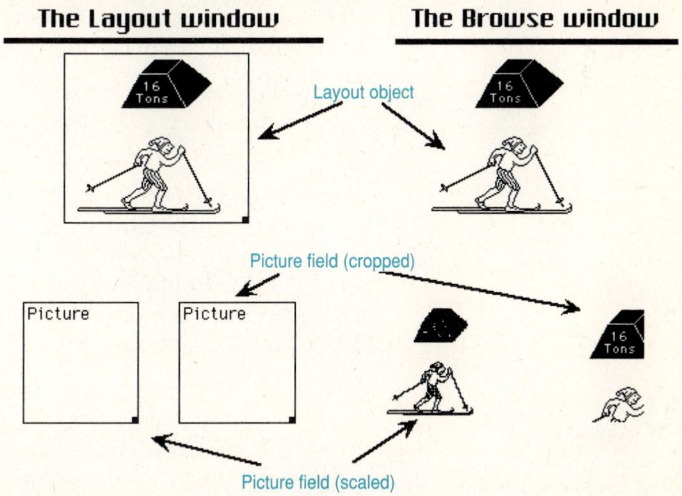

You also can obtain the same two effects (cropping or scaling) with a layout object when you choose either formatting option that the Picture Format command offers. You resize the picture box by using any of the small black reshape handles on the corners (see Chapter 7).

Adding Fields

When you create a file, FileMaker first adds all fields you create to your standard layout. Whatever your current layout, when you define a field, FileMaker automatically adds that field to the current layout style. For all layouts except the columnar report layout, the layout style is a field name as a text object to the left and the field reshape box to the right. A newly defined field in a columnar report layout is added, with a field name in the header part and the field box in the body.

Many times, however, you will want to add a previously defined field to a layout. Use the Field tool on the Layout window for that purpose. By using the Field tool, you can place a field reshape box at any point on the layout and in any part. Although a field's behavior depends on the part in which it's placed, you have no restrictions on the number of times or the position you can place a field on a layout. In certain parts of a layout, a field may not operate properly—the field is inconsistent with what you want to achieve or the result cannot be calculated. When this is the case, FileMaker often grays out the field box.

To add a field to a layout, follow these steps:

1. Choose the Layout command on the Select menu or press the ⌘-L keystroke to open the Layout window.
2. Display the area on the layout where you want to place the field by scrolling the screen if needed.
3. Choose the formatting that you desire by making the appropriate selections on the Format menu.

   or

   Select a field that has the format you desire. FileMaker uses the last selected object's setting when it creates a field. You can format a field at any time.
4. Click on the Field tool and drag the new field onto your layout. You will see a field outline with the baseline extended for accurate placement (see Chapter 7). Note that FileMaker places a field into the part that the field's top boundary is in (see fig. 6.27).

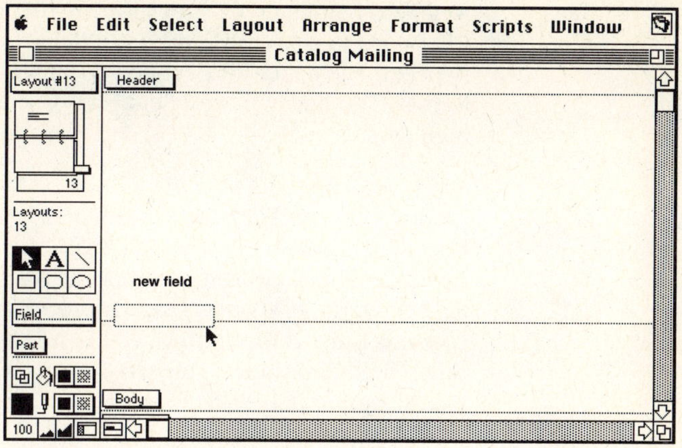

Fig. 6.27
Placing a new field on a layout with the Field tool.

5. Release the mouse button; the field outline is drawn, and the New Field tool dialog box appears (see fig. 6.28). Select the field you want to place by double-clicking on its name and scrolling if necessary. Or, click on the name to highlight it and then click the OK button or press the Return or Enter key.

Clicking the Cancel button or pressing ⌘-. (period) returns you to the layout without placing the field.

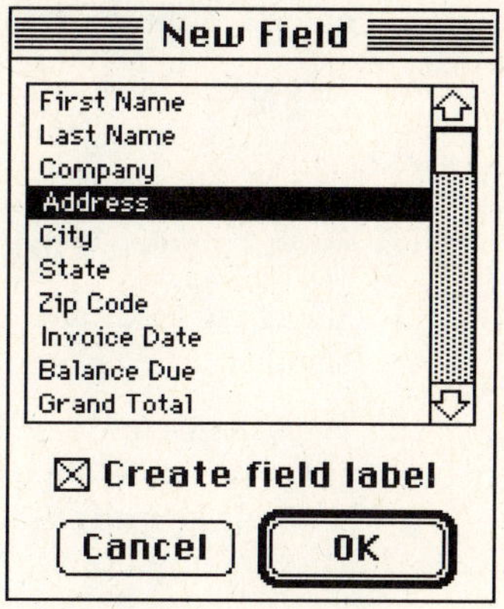

Fig. 6.28
The New Field tool dialog box.

As an alternative procedure to using the Field tool, you can use the Clipboard to cut, copy, and paste fields between layouts and even between FileMaker files, while you retain the full field definition and format. The newly pasted field is copied to the center of your screen and highlighted.

WARNING

Pasting between FileMaker files works correctly only when the field names are an exact match. FileMaker does not check for letter case. A field pasted from another file does not contain any of the field definitions, such as calculations or entry options: the field contains only its formatting. To learn how to copy fields and still retain field definitions, refer to Chapter 15, "Importing and Exporting Data."

To add a field from another file, follow these steps:

1. Select the fields and other objects on the layout you want to paste.
2. Select the Copy command (⌘-C) to place a copy in the Clipboard or select the Cut command (⌘-X) to remove the selection to the Clipboard. Both commands are on the Edit menu.
3. Display the layout into which you want to paste a field.
4. Scroll to the area where you want the objects placed and select the Paste command (⌘-V) on the Edit menu. FileMaker places the objects in the center of the screen.
5. To move selections, click on the Arrow tool in the Toolbox and then drag the selection into position (see Chapter 7).

You also can delete a field at any time by using standard Macintosh techniques. To delete a field from a layout, follow these steps:

1. Select the fields and other objects that you want to delete from the layout.
2. Press the Delete key (Backspace on some keyboards). You also can cut a selection to the Clipboard or use the Clear key (on the numeric keypad) to remove a selection, bypassing the Clipboard.

Adding Layout Text

You use layout text for a variety of purposes. Earlier in this chapter, layout text was added to layouts as field labels. You also can use layout text to type entire letters, document a feature, or provide instructions or a description. Some special text objects available place the current date, page, record numbers, and current time on a layout for printing (see Chapter 9).

The next chapter describes many of the techniques you can use to change text objects: formatting text using the Font, Style, Size, and Align Text commands on the Format menu; cutting, copying, pasting, and editing layout text objects; and moving and aligning layout text. Here, the focus is on adding layout text.

To add layout text, follow these steps:

1. In the Layout window, click on the Text tool in the Toolbox. The cursor changes to an I-beam.
2. Click an insertion point where you want the text object to appear.
3. Type all the characters for your object.

   If you press Return, FileMaker starts a new text object. A text object can be on only one line and can contain up to 250 characters.
4. Click the Arrow tool or any other tool to continue your work.

To edit layout text, do any of the following:

- Click on the Text tool and click an insertion point in the text object.
- Drag a selection.
- Double-click to select a word; drag to extend the range of selection while adding additional words.

Type the new text. Click the Arrow tool or any other tool to continue your work.

To move text, follow these steps:

1. Click on the Text tool to select it. Your cursor changes to an I-beam.
2. Select the text you want to place elsewhere.
3. Select the Cut command from the Edit menu or press the ⌘-X keystroke.
4. Move the I-beam cursor to the position you want the new text object to occupy and click an insertion point.

5. Select the Paste command from the Edit menu or press the ⌘-V keystroke.

To delete layout text, follow these steps:

1. Select the text.
2. Press the Delete key to remove those characters.

To delete the entire object, click on the Arrow tool and use the Arrow cursor to click on the text object and any other objects that you want to delete. Press the Delete or Clear (on the numeric keypad) key to remove the objects from the layout.

Text objects can be formatted by using the same set of commands on the Format menu that are used to format text entered into a Text field. To format a text object, you need to switch to the layout mode; text objects are locked on the Browse window. (Chapter 7 describes the complete range of actions available from the Format menu.)

Adding Pictures and Graphics

At times, you may want to import a picture file from another program for use in your FileMaker document. Importing a picture file is not difficult.

To import a picture file from another program, follow these steps:

1. In the layout mode, click in the Picture field.
2. Choose Import from the File menu.
3. Click on Import Picture File into Current Field.
4. Choose the file type you want from the pop-up menu (i.e., MacPaint).
5. Select the file you want to import. You may need to navigate through the folders to find your selection.
6. Click Open.

Graphics such as scanned images now can be directly imported into FileMaker. A variety of formats, including TIFF and EPS, are possible.

You also can add pictures to a layout as objects or as data into a Picture field. In either case, use the Clipboard to paste pictures. Paste layout objects in the Layout window and paste pictures as data into Picture fields in the Browse window. You can place pictures in any layout part; even a summary part, which requires a dependent field, can accept a picture.

To place a picture on a layout, follow these steps:

1. Choose the Layout command from the Select menu or press the ⌘-L keystroke to open the Layout window.
2. Click on the Arrow tool in the Toolbox, if needed.
3. Place on the Clipboard the picture that you want on your layout by copying or cutting the picture from another place on the layout, from another file, from another document in another program, or from the Scrapbook.

   (For a discussion of the types of pictures that FileMaker can accept, see Chapter 3.)
4. Select the Paste command from the Edit menu or press the ⌘-V keystroke to place the picture on the layout.

   FileMaker places the picture exactly in the middle of the window, with the picture selected. If the bottom boundary of the layout is above the middle of the window, FileMaker places the picture so that it abuts that boundary. The graphic is selected and appears highlighted on the screen.
5. To move the picture to its desired location, drag it to the new location.

To enter picture data into a field, follow these steps:

1. Switch to the Browse window by selecting the Browse command or press the ⌘-B keystroke.
2. Make that Picture field the current field.
3. Choose the Paste command on the Edit menu or press the ⌘-V keystroke.

Depending on the format you choose, the picture is cropped or scaled.

To delete a picture object, follow these steps:

1. In the Layout window, select that object.
2. Press the Delete, Backspace, or Clear key.

To delete a picture in a Picture field, follow these steps:

1. In the Browse window, select the field with the desired picture. A selected Picture field is entirely selected.
2. Press the Delete, Backspace, or Clear key.

FileMaker contains a set of tools in the Toolbox that enables you to create a variety of graphics, such as lines, rectangles, and ovals. You also can change line width, line pattern, and line fill (see Chapter 7 for a discussion of these tools).

Adding Parts

You use parts on a layout to affect the condition of a printed page. Parts are sections of a layout that can be added at any time by using the Part tool in the status area of the Layout window. You can create, resize, and remove parts at any time (see Chapter 9).

All layouts initially come with three parts: header, body, and footer, except the label layout, which can have only a body part or a header and body part, depending on options you choose in the Page Setup dialog box.

You can add a part to a layout. A layout can contain parts in the following order from top to bottom:

- One title header part
- One header part
- One grand summary part above the body part
- Any number of sub-summary parts above the body part
- One body part
- Any number of sub-summary parts below the body part
- One grand summary part below the body part
- One footer part
- One title footer part

To place a part on a layout, follow these steps:

1. Choose the Layout command on the Select menu or press ⌘-L to open the Layout window.
2. Select the layout to which you want to add a part.
3. Click on the Part tool in the status area and drag the part outline to the position it will occupy on the layout (see fig. 6.29). The arrow in the lower left corner points to the added part.

Don't worry about accurate placement; you can move the part later. The kind of part that you can create is determined by its position (see the order shown above). If you change your mind about creating the part, drag the outline off the layout.

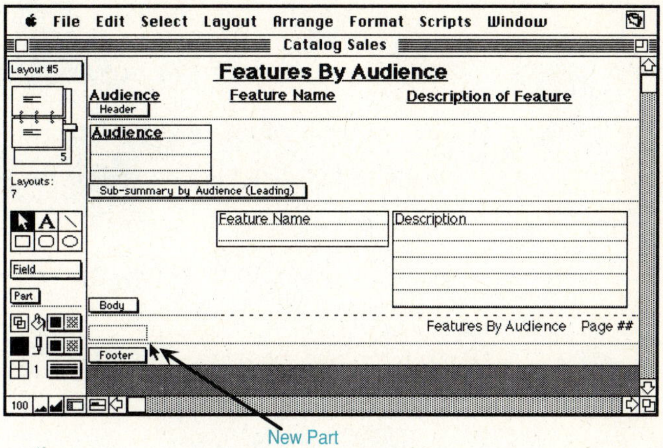

Fig. 6.29
Dragging a new part onto a layout.

4. Release the mouse button to open the Part Definition dialog box (see fig. 6.30). Notice that FileMaker allows you to create only parts that are appropriate to the position where you release the mouse button.

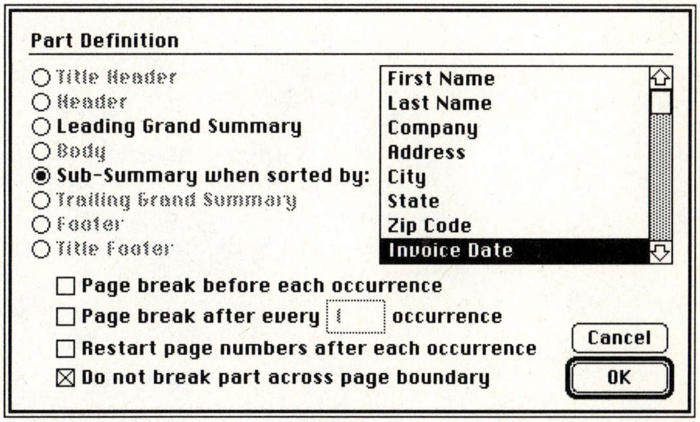

Fig. 6.30
The Part Definition dialog box.

5. Click the button pertaining to the part you want to create.

   If that part is a sub-summary part, you need to specify the dependent field by clicking on the field name. A sub-summary part also offers the option of allowing a page break when a page break occurs. Click on that option's check box, if desired. When a sub-summary occurs above a body, the page break occurs before the sub-summary. When the part is below the body part, the page break occurs after the summary. When you click the page break option for a column setup, a new page is created instead of a new column for the Down First fill pattern.

6. Click the OK button to create the part.

   or

   Click the Cancel button or press ⌘-. (period) to return to the layout without creating the part.

To see whether your part has functioned properly, choose the Preview command (⌘-U) and examine the Preview window. Return by selecting Layout or Browse from the Select menu.

FileMaker labels the part type in the part handle. If the part is a sub-summary part, the name is the field that is summarized. Remember that you have to sort your records by that field to have the sub-summary part perform properly. When the sub-summary part is above the body part, an ellipsis appears at the end of the name to indicate that it will be printed before the records it summarizes. Also, if the Page Break check box is checked, a page break symbol is placed at the end of the name in the part handle.

In Review

Layouts control the display of your data and are separate from the data contained in your file. You create layouts in the Layout window, and you can have any number you want. A Layout window is similar to the Browse and Find windows, but it also has Toolbox, Field, and Part tools. You can use these tools to place objects onto a Layout window, including layout text, fields, parts, and other graphics in the form of layout objects.

Layouts perform specific tasks, such as filling out forms, data entry, and labels. FileMaker offers six types of predefined layouts: standard, single page, columnar report, label, envelope, and blank. Details of their construction were covered in this chapter.

The current layout controls what you see when you return to the Browse window. You can specify that a layout be viewed as a list, and FileMaker fits as many records on your screen as the size of the body part allows. You also can specify that records be printed in columns and filled either Across First or Down First.

Details for creating a layout and moving from layout to layout were covered in this chapter. The New Layout command initiates the process of layout creation, and you move from layout to layout by using the Book and Slide Control Mechanism or by clicking on the layout title and choosing from the pop-up menu.

FileMaker can alter the way data found in fields is displayed. A number, for instance, is stored as a long string, but you can display as many digits as you want. The original number is still retained in full. Number, Date, Time, and Picture fields can be displayed in various formats by using the Number Format, Date Format, Time Format, and Picture Format commands on the Format menu. This type of formatting is different from changing the format of characters by using Font, Size, Style, and Align Text commands on the Format menu.

You can add fields to a layout by dragging them from the Field tool and selecting the field of interest. To add parts, drag them onto the layout with the Part tool.

Click on the Text tool and click an insertion point to type a text object on a layout. To edit a text object, click an insertion point or drag a selection. Graphics may now be imported in MacPaint 2.0, PICT, TIFF, or EPS format (FileMaker uses EPSF as the EPS abbreviation). In addition, graphics may be added to a layout as a picture, or they may be added to a Picture field in the Browse window. The Clipboard is used in either case.

CHAPTER 7

Enhancing Layout Appearance

The predefined layouts that FileMaker provides are good starting places for building layouts, but you often need to alter your layout to suit the task at hand. Many reasons exist for altering a layout: to add or remove information, to place graphics for impact, to accurately place any of the elements of your layout, and so on. This chapter contains explanations for many of the tools that FileMaker provides to aid you in these tasks. This chapter covers the details of the Tools Palette and the many special aids provided by the Layout and Arrange menus.

Adding Objects to a Layout

Unlike some of the changes you can make in FileMaker, editing a layout is relatively forgiving. Most of the changes you make can be undone by using the Undo command found on the Edit menu. You always can work on a copy of your layout, and when you are satisfied with your changes, you can delete the original. You cannot undo, however, a layout deletion. Throughout this chapter, you can assume that changes are reversible unless otherwise noted.

If you have used a draw program such as MacDraw, the draw modules in SuperPaint II, or Canvas, you have some familiarity with the kinds of tools that FileMaker provides. These tools are referred to as objects because they are mathematically described figures with certain properties. When you draw a square on your monitor, for example, you are telling your Macintosh that your shape starts at a specific point; the program draws a line to the three other corners of the square. You also describe the line width, line pattern, and fill pattern of the square with choices you make from the Status Panel. With all those specifications for your square, you can select and change the square's properties, and you easily can move and reshape it. The elements of a FileMaker layout are objects: fields and their reshape boxes, layout text, graphic objects (also called layout objects), parts, and even the page itself.

By contrast, you can create painted images (using a paint program like MacPaint, SuperPaint, or Canvas) to tell your Macintosh to draw a shape by turning pixels on and off on your screen. Pixels are the dots that create the image you see on-screen. If you have a Macintosh II series computer, you can assign shades of gray or colors to each pixel. This type of image is called a bit map because you actually are mapping the image bit-by-bit in a table that your Macintosh stores. FileMaker accepts bit-mapped images as graphics, but FileMaker cannot create bit-mapped images.

Using an object-oriented draw program rather than a bit-mapped draw program means that FileMaker can precisely manipulate objects on the screen, resizing and reshaping the objects, and printing is much sharper. FileMaker draws objects faster than it can draw bit maps. Use bit maps to enhance your layouts, but keep in mind the speed penalty you pay.

Using the Layout Tools Palette

FileMaker provides a set of tools with which you can create objects. In Chapter 6, you learned how you can use the Field tool to add fields to a layout, the Part tool to add parts, and the Book and Slide Control Mechanism to move from layout to layout. In this chapter, you focus on the other prominent element of the status area: the Tools Palette. Figure 7.1 shows the six tools of the Tools Palette: the Arrow tool, Text tool, Line tool, Oval tool, Rounded Rectangle tool, and Rectangle tool. Using the layout tools, you can change most aspects of a layout.

The currently selected tool is highlighted in the Tools Palette, as the Arrow tool is in figure 7.1. The type of cursor you see in the Layout window depends on the selected tool.

Descriptions of the Tools Palette elements follow:

Arrow tool. Click the Arrow tool to select, reshape, or position objects on the layout. This tool performs the function that is performed by what other Macintosh programs commonly call the Selection tool. When the Arrow tool is selected, you see an arrow cursor on your screen.

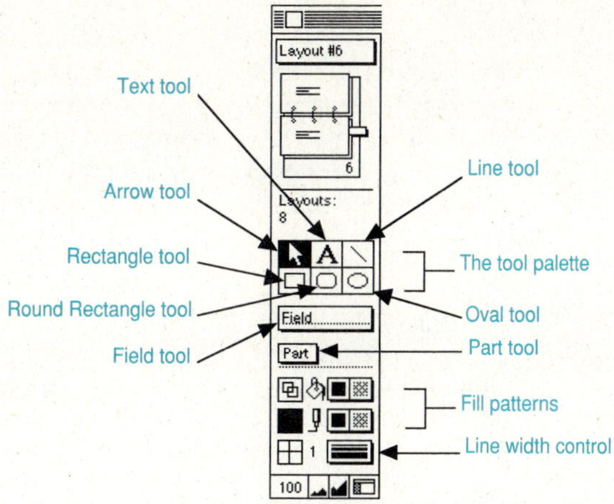

Fig. 7.1
The Tools Palette.

Text tool. Click the Text tool to create or edit layout text. Because FileMaker places the name of the field in the field reshape box, layout text can be confusing. Layout text is an individual graphic object that you can manipulate and format by itself. When the Text tool is selected, the cursor becomes an I-beam. Unless you change text formats, your text assumes the characteristics of the last-selected object.

Line tool. Click the Line tool to create lines on your layout. When the Line tool is selected, your cursor changes to a cross hair. You can specify the width and fill pattern of a line by using the Line Width and Line Pattern tools on the Status Panel. You can make the line horizontal or vertical by pressing the Option key as you draw the line, a process called *constraining the motion*.

Oval tool. Click the Oval tool to create an oval. When the Oval tool is selected, your cursor changes to a cross hair. You can select line widths, line fills, and fill patterns for the oval from choices in the Line Width, Line Pattern, and Fill Pattern submenus on the Status Panel. Press the Option key as you draw to create a circle.

Rounded Rectangle tool. Click the Rounded Rectangle tool to create a rounded rectangle. When you select the Rounded Rectangle tool, the cursor changes to a cross hair. You can select line widths, line fills, and fill patterns for the rectangle. Press the Option key as you draw to create a square with rounded corners.

Rectangle tool. Click the Rectangle tool to create a rectangle. When you select the Rectangle tool, the cursor changes to a cross hair. You can specify line widths, line fills, and fill patterns. Press the Option key as you draw to create a square.

Fill tool. Any object except a line can have a color or pattern in the center, called a *fill*. To set a color, click on the solid box to the right of the paint bucket and drag to highlight the color. The pop-up palette of colors you see depends on the setting of your monitor: black and white, grayscale, or color. To set a pattern, click on the patterned box to the right of the paint bucket and drag to highlight a pattern. Patterns and colors include transparent objects, white, black, and others.

Line fill tool. A line can have a color or pattern, which is called its *stroke*. To set a color, click on the solid box to the right of the pen and drag to highlight the color. The pop-up palette of colors you see depends on the setting of your monitor: black and white, grayscale, or color. To set a pattern, click on the patterned box to the right of the pen and drag to highlight a pattern. Patterns and colors include transparent line (invisible), white, black, and others.

Line width control tool. To set a line width, click on the tool and drag down on the pop-up menu to highlight the desired width. Widths from a hairline to 12 points are shown. The current selection shows numerically next to the tool. The box with the crossed lines displays how the line will look.

Fill tools and line width tools are discussed more fully later in this chapter. See "Formatting Pictures and Graphics."

For information on using the Arrow tool for selection, see "Editing Objects" in Chapter 2. The instructions for creating various objects with the Tools Palette require that you work within the Layout window.

Creating Lines, Rectangles, and Ovals

Lines, rectangles, rounded rectangles, and ovals are great devices for creating many visual effects. You can use them to create forms, to highlight important information, to create rules for tables, flow charts, borders, and so on. The Toolbox has enough power to create simple drawings without leaving FileMaker.

To create a line, follow these steps:

1. Select the Line tool by clicking on it. Your cursor is now a cross hair.
2. Select the line width and pattern you want from the Line Width and Line Pattern pop-up menus, respectively, on the Status Panel. Your choices are indicated with a check mark. See "Formatting Layout Objects" later in this chapter.

   or

Click on an object (other than a text object) that has the format you want.

3. Click a starting point and drag to the end. Holding down the Shift key constrains your motion to the horizontal or the vertical direction.

To create a rectangle or oval, follow these steps:

1. Choose the Rectangle or Oval tool by clicking on it. Your cursor is now a cross hair.

2. Select the options you want from the Line Width, Line Pattern, and Fill Pattern pop-up menus on the Status Panel.

   or

   Click on an object that has the format you desire.

3. Click a starting point and drag to the opposite corner or side.

Note

The use of the Option key to modify a shape is unusual for a Macintosh application. Most applications use the Shift key.

A dotted rectangle indicates the size of your new object before you release the mouse button. Ovals are drawn inside that dotted rectangle. Holding down the Option key constrains your object to a perfect shape: a square from a rectangle, a circle from an oval.

With graphic objects, the lines, rectangles, rounded rectangles, and ovals require that you set their format by selecting choices on the Status Panel. The Line Width, Line Pattern, and Fill Pattern features on the Status Panel are used for this purpose. These choices are shown and discussed later in this chapter in the section called "Formatting Pictures and Graphics." You always can select an object later and format the object to suit your purpose.

The Line Width, Line Pattern, and Fill Pattern features are now located on the Status Panel in FileMaker Pro. These features were previously located on the Format menu.

Editing Objects

To make changes to an object, you begin by selecting the object. You select an object for a variety of purposes: to move, edit, reformat, copy, or delete the object. You can select objects in many of the ways you learned in Chapter 3, either singly or as a range (several) of objects.

To select an object, click on the object with the Arrow tool highlighted. Objects can be field reshape boxes, layout text, or graphic objects such as lines, rectangles, and so on. Parts and the page are not selected and are manipulated in different ways. When selecting a shape, you can click anywhere within that shape.

To select a range of objects, click on one object with the Arrow tool highlighted and then hold down the Shift key while clicking on additional objects. If you want to deselect an object while maintaining your other selections, shift-click once again on that object.

To select a range of objects, drag a selection marquee. Any object the marquee touches is selected. You also can use shift-drag to extend your range of selection.

To deselect all objects, click anywhere in the Layout window outside your selection (but not in the status area or the scroll bars).

To select all objects on a layout, choose the Select All command on the Edit menu or press ⌘-A.

SPEED KEY

⌘-A, the Select All command, selects all objects in the Layout window.

In figure 7.2, you see a variety of selected objects. Notice that all objects, except text objects, have small black reshape handles at each corner. Lines have reshape handles at each end.

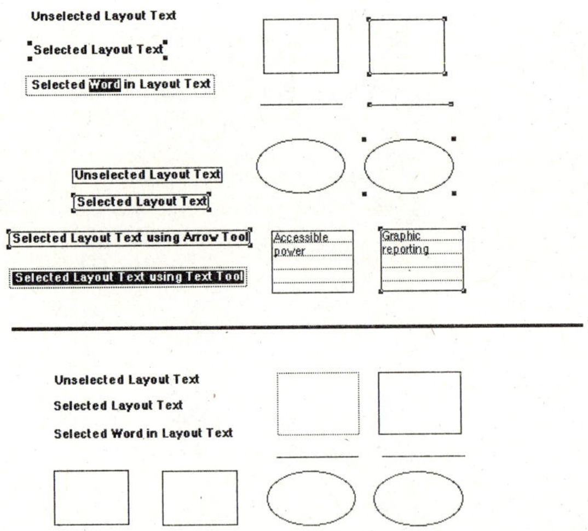

Fig. 7.2
Selected objects on a Layout versus a Browse window.

You can select text objects in their entirety by using any of the methods just described. You also can select any piece of a text object—individual characters, a word, or any set of characters—by using the Text tool.

To select pieces of layout text, follow these steps:

1. Click on the Text tool to select it; your cursor changes to an I-beam.

2. Click on an insertion point at the beginning of the range of characters you want to select and drag either right or left.

To select a word, double-click on it. To extend a range of selected characters, hold down the Shift key and click to establish the new range, or, to add to a range by words, double-click on that word.

The Arrange menu is new to FileMaker Pro. Added features include the Group, Ungroup, Lock, Bring to Front, Bring Forward, Send to Back, and Send Backward commands. The new Tab Order feature is discussed in Chapter 5.

The Align Objects, Alignment, and Slide Objects features existed in FileMaker II, but they were located on different menus.

Grouping Objects

The Arrange menu offers the capability to group and ungroup objects. This feature makes it easy to quickly move, resize, or apply formatting effects to all the objects in the group at once. When objects are grouped, they can be manipulated as a single object.

To group objects, follow these steps:

1. Select the objects you want to group. See the preceding section, "Editing Objects" (use the shift-click method or the selection marquee).

2. Choose the Group command from the Arrange menu or press the ⌘-G keystroke equivalent.

The individual objects no longer have handles, and a boundary appears around the group. The objects now act as one.

New groups can consist of a combination of individual objects and existing groups.

SPEED KEY

⌘-G is the keystroke equivalent for the Group command.

⌘-Shift-G is the keyboard equivalent for Ungrouping objects.

If you want to make changes to an object in the group, you first must ungroup the object.

To ungroup an object, follow these steps:

1. Click on the group to select it.
2. Choose the Ungroup command from from the Arrange menu or press the ⌘-Shift-G keystroke equivalent.

The group is now split into its original parts.

Locking Objects

Locking objects prevents them from being moved or changed. Locked objects can be selected, copied to the Clipboard, or grouped. Locked objects cannot be moved, cut, modified, or aligned to the grid.

Protect entire layouts by choosing the Select All command from the Edit menu and then choosing the Lock command from the Arrange menu. If you group locked objects with unlocked objects, the entire group becomes locked.

To lock objects, follow these steps:

1. Select the object or objects you want to lock.
2. Choose the Lock command from the Arrange menu or press the ⌘-H keystroke equivalent.

The handles on locked objects change from black to gray.

SPEED KEY

⌘-H is the keyboard equivalent for the Lock command.

⌘-Shift-H is the keyboard equivalent for the Unlock command.

To unlock objects, do the following:

1. Select the locked object or objects.
2. Choose the Unlock command from the Arrange menu or press ⌘-Shift-H.

The handles change back from gray to black.

Moving Objects Forward and Backward

Your layout may be made up of overlapping layers of text, fields, and graphics. Each of these objects is on a different layer and some objects may appear in front of or behind others. When these layers overlap, the stacking order affects the appearance of the printed page (see fig. 7.3).

Fig. 7.3
Overlapping layers.

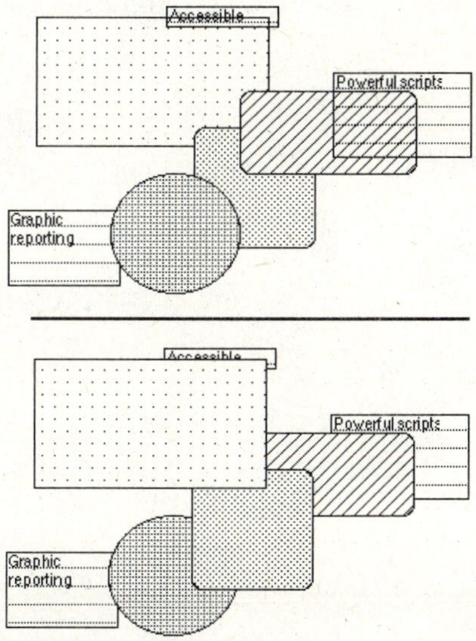

Different looks by using Backward and Forward commands on the Arrange menu

Using the Forward and Backward commands on the Arrange menu, you can control the order of the stacked layers. To change the order, select an object and then apply one of the following commands from the Arrange menu:

Bring to Front. Moves the selected object in front of all other overlapping objects in the stack.

Bring Forward (⌘-Shift-F). Moves the selected object one layer closer to the top in the stacking order of overlapping objects. The selected object changes place with the object in front of it.

Send to Back. Moves the selected object to the bottom of the stack of overlapping objects.

Send Backward (⌘-Shift-J). Moves the selected object one layer closer to the bottom in the stacking order of overlapping objects. The selected object changes place with the object in back of it.

SPEED KEY

⌘-Shift-F is the keyboard equivalent for Bring Forward.

⌘-Shift-J is the keyboard equivalent for Send Backward.

Deleting an Object

You may want to remove an object from a layout. Perhaps you no longer need to include information in a Text field or its text object label.

To remove an object, follow these steps:

1. Select any object to be removed.
2. Select the Cut command on the Edit menu or press the ⌘-X keystroke to place the object on the Clipboard.

   or

   Press the Delete (or Backspace) key or choose the Clear command from the Edit menu to eliminate the object and bypass the Clipboard.

Note

Use this command carefully. After an object is removed, the command cannot be undone.

Moving Objects

Several reasons exist for moving objects around on a layout. You may want to create a form or use a form that already exists (see Chapter 8). In either case, you may want to position elements to match the form. You can move an object, such as a field, off the printable area of a layout so that you can use its data without having the object print.

To move an object, you first select it. Next, you drag the object to a new position. If you have a range or group of objects selected, drag any of the selected objects. All the objects move. You can move an object to any position in a layout; FileMaker includes the object in the part where the top of an object is positioned. For example, a rectangle with its top line in the header part and all the rest of the rectangle in the body part will print just once a page, in the header.

When you move either a field or a text object, FileMaker draws an outline with an extended baseline to aid in accurate placement, if you drag the outline. If you select the object, no baseline is drawn. The baseline is the imaginary line on which all characters sit. When you line up a baseline in two separate fields, their characters are on the same line even if the characters are different sizes. You can tell when two fields line up because both dotted lines merge (see fig. 7.4). You can use this technique to align text objects to fields.

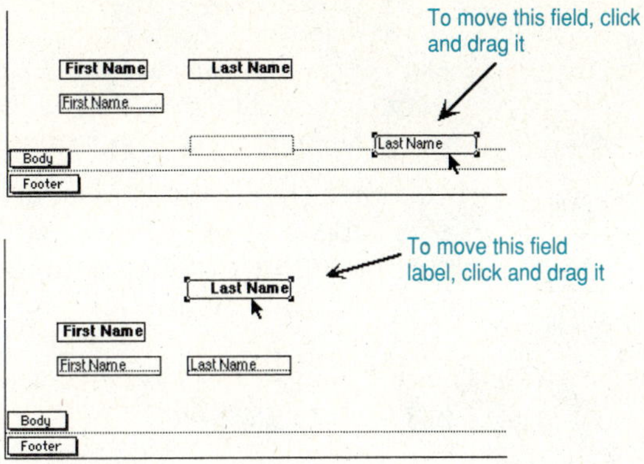

Fig. 7.4
Moving text objects and fields.

When you create a file, an invisible grid is turned on. Your objects align to this grid. You can turn off the grid by choosing the Align to Grid command on the Layout menu. FileMaker has other special features, including borders for text objects and a position indicator called a T-square. These features allow for precision placement (see the following section, "Aligning Objects").

You can change your mind about moving an object. If the move has been completed or if you used the Clipboard to move a selection by cutting it, select the Undo command from the Edit menu. If you are still dragging the object, drag the outline until it reaches the edge of the layout and the outline disappears.

The size box (accessed by using the Size command on the Layout menu) precisely moves objects. The size box is discussed later in this chapter in "Using the T-squares and Size Box."

Aligning Objects

Any form looks sloppy and unprofessional if objects are unaligned. FileMaker provides some special tools to aid you in lining up objects and positioning them precisely. These tools operate in the Layout window. You can use these options—Align to Grid, Gridlines, T-squares, Rulers, Size, and Show Text Boundaries—one at a time or in any combination. If you change a setting for any of the options, FileMaker remembers the setting the next time you open the file.

If you want to align objects with respect to one another (relatively), rather than to a specific position on your screen (absolutely), choose the Align Objects command from the Arrange menu. The Align Objects command can line up objects along their boundaries, center lines, and so on. Aligning objects is discussed in this section of the chapter.

The zoom controls at the bottom left corner of the FileMaker window offer another handy way to position objects. Clicking on the zoom controls enlarges the image on your screen, which enables you to move and align objects precisely.

Using the Invisible Grid

By using the Align to Grid command on the Layout menu, you turn off and on a snap-to grid on your layout screen. With snap-to grid turned on, you can position an object within a few pixels of an imaginary grid line, and FileMaker automatically aligns the object with the grid. The objects seem to "snap to" the grid—as though the grid is magnetized.

You can tell when the grid is turned on because FileMaker puts a check mark next to the command in the Layout menu. To turn the grid off, choose the Align to Grid command again. With the grid off, you can align objects to every pixel on the Macintosh screen in increments of 1/72 inch (0.014"). When the grid is turned on, the standard layout aligns to the invisible grid. When you create a file, that grid automatically turns on.

This grid has 12 increments to an inch (every 0.083"). To change the grid spacing, go to the Layout window and choose the Ruler Setting command. The Ruler Setting dialog box contains a pull-down menu for units and a text box for grid size. You can use the grid to line up fields so that they print in the common spacing of commercial forms, 6 lines per inch (or every two grid snaps per line). If you move or resize an object when the grid is on, the object lines up with the grid.

You can turn off the grid temporarily when you create, move, or resize an object by holding down the Command key while dragging. With the grid off, you can line up new objects to any object. FileMaker sets the grid to line up with the selected object, but FileMaker does not affect other, previously created objects.

Gridlines, a feature new to FileMaker Pro, are the dotted horizontal and vertical lines that aid in alignment. Gridlines correspond to the ruler settings.

Using the T-squares and Size Box

The T-squares help with precise measurement of position and snap-to alignment. When you turn on the T-square, FileMaker draws a horizontal and a vertical line (see fig. 7.5).

Fig. 7.5
The T-square and Size Box.

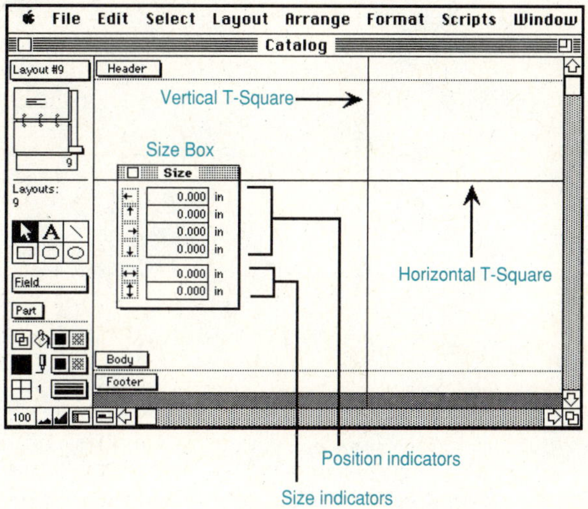

You can position items precisely on a layout by using the size box (see fig. 7.5). The size box indicates the position of the T-square and shows the position, height, and width of selected objects or parts. You can enter new values to reposition or resize an object. You also can nudge a selected object one pixel at a time in any direction with the arrow keys.

To resize an object by using the size box, follow these steps:

1. Select the object you want to resize.
2. Type the desired width and height in the bottom two boxes in the size box.

   Units of measurement are based on the rulers. Ruler settings can be controlled from that command on the Layout menu.
3. Press the Return or Enter key to see the result.

The T-squares are always magnetic. Objects line up with the T-square with the top, bottom, right, or left edge snapped to one or both of the T-square lines. The exact center of an object also can align. Objects that contain baselines—text objects and fields—line up to the horizontal line of the T-square. This feature helps, because if you select a field or text object first and then drag the field or text object, you do not see a baseline. Drag a deselected field to see this feature operate. Figure 7.6 shows these alignment options.

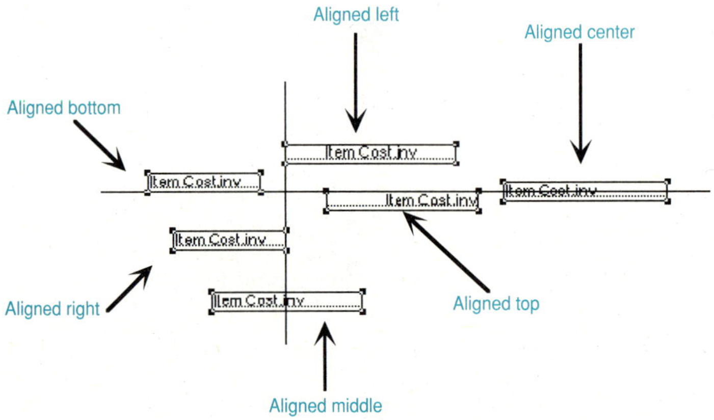

Fig. 7.6
Aligning objects to the T-square.

To use the T-squares, follow these steps:

1. In the Layout window, select the T-squares command from the Layout menu or press the ⌘-T keystroke. The T-squares appear in the middle of the window.

2. Select the Rulers command from the Layout menu. This feature enables you to see the exact position of the T-squares.

3. Select the Size command from the Layout menu. The size box helps you position the T-squares.

Hold down the Command key while dragging or resizing an object to turn off the grid temporarily.

Move the T-square by clicking on either of the T-square's two lines and dragging the T-square to the desired position. Be careful not to click on an area of the T-square that overlaps another object, such as part of a line.

If you make a mistake and want the T-square to return to its previous position, choose the Undo command from the Edit menu or press ⌘-Z to reverse your move. Click anywhere in the layout to deselect any selected objects.

SPEED KEY

⌘-T, the T-square command, turns the T-square off and on in the Layout window.

To position an object using the T-squares and the size box, follow these steps:

1. Select the object you want to position.
2. Choose the Size option from the Layout menu.
3. Determine where you want to place the object and enter the measurements in the Size box.

   Enter the distances from the left edge of the page to the left edge of the object and from the top of the page to the top edge of the object. The distances of the right and bottom edges are computed automatically using the object's width and height.

   The units of measurement are those used by the Ruler.
4. Press the Return or Enter key.

   The object moves to the designated position.
5. Click the close box or leave the size box open if you prefer.

The drag method is another way to use the Size box. Drag the object until the position you want is indicated in the size box.

Changing the Ruler and Grid Units

The rulers and invisible grid offer three choices of units of measure: inches, centimeters, and pixels. (A pixel is one of the little dots that make up the picture on a computer screen.)

To change the ruler or grid settings, follow these steps:

1. Choose the Ruler Settings command from the Layout menu.
2. Selecting the Units box brings up a menu. Choose inches, centimeters, or pixels.

   The selection you make for the Ruler also affects the gridlines and the size box.

   Another way to switch settings is by clicking the intersection of the two rulers at the upper-left corner of the layout.
3. Type the number of units you want in the Grid Spacing box. Choose a unit of measurement from the pop-up menu.

The preset spacing is six pixels. The setting you choose for grid spacing affects only the invisible grid.

4. Click the OK button.

Adding Text Boundaries

The Text Boundaries command is on the Show submenu in the Layout menu. Text Boundaries places a solid rectangle around all layout text so that you can see the edges of the text object. Use this feature to line up objects along a common border, especially to the T-square. Figure 7.7 shows the condition of selected and deselected text objects with the Show Text Boundaries turned on and off.

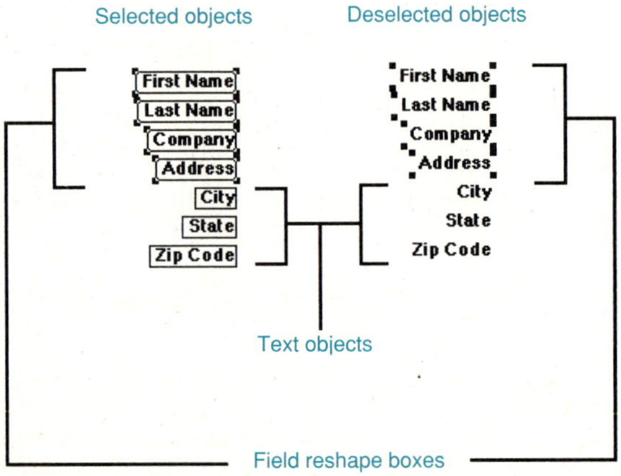

Fig. 7.7

Using Text Boundaries to show the size of a text object and fields.

Field Boundaries

The Field Boundaries option, which places a rectangle around each field, is turned on automatically with a new file. The boundaries help you to align objects. The Field Boundaries control is on the Show submenu in the Layout menu. A check mark means the option is turned on, and solid lines appear around each field. To hide field boundaries, select the option again and the check mark disappears. Field boundaries are never displayed in the browse, preview, or print mode. Instead, field boundaries position objects in the layout mode.

The Show command on the Layout menu is a new feature. Some of the Show submenu options were contained on the Gadgets menu in previous versions of FileMaker. The Show submenu in FileMaker Pro contains Buttons, Text Boundaries, Field Boundaries, Sliding Objects, Non-Printing Objects, and Non-Printable Area.

Sizing Objects

Because on-screen objects drawn by FileMaker are described mathematically, you can resize them without distortion. To resize objects drawn by FileMaker, click on one of the small black reshape handles attached to the object and drag to the desired size. You can resize fields and any object that you can draw from the Tools Palette except for text objects. You also can resize placed graphics or graphics in Picture fields.

Resizing text objects requires using the Size menu (see "Formatting Layout Objects," elsewhere in this chapter). Resizing parts uses other techniques, discussed in Chapter 9.

You may want to resize an object for one of several reasons—to make a line longer so that the line completes an underline of a sentence, to adjust a rectangle used to box text, or to resize a field box. When you create a field or initially place the field on a layout, FileMaker uses a field height of 1 line and a field width that depends on the field type. When you switch from the Layout to the Browse or Find windows, you can enter as many lines as you want into the field, but the field displays or prints only the size of the field on your Layout window. To show more or fewer lines, resize the field reshape box. You can tell the number of lines that will display in a field by the number of dotted lines in the field box on the Layout window.

To resize an object, follow these steps:

1. Click on the Arrow tool.
2. Click on any one of the small black handles in each corner of the object and drag to the desired shape. You can use one of the following options:

    To change only the height or width, hold down the Shift key as you drag the handle.

    To turn a rectangle into a square or an oval into a circle, hold down the Option key as you drag the handle.

If the grid is on, you reshape objects to snap to the invisible grid. If you do not want objects to snap to the grid, select the Align to Grid command on the Layout menu to turn off the grid or hold down the Command key (⌘) while reshaping the object to disable the grid temporarily. The T-square always retains its magnetic snap-to feature.

Chapter 6 shows you how to add graphics to layouts as graphic objects or as data in a Picture field. Acceptable formats for Picture fields are discussed in Chapter 3. Both types of graphics have reshape handles attached to them and can be resized by the technique just described. Depending on the option you choose in the Picture Format command, you can crop or scale the picture.

Also consider whether the picture is object-oriented art or bit-mapped. You can resize object-oriented objects and retain smooth lines, but resized bit-mapped objects often are distorted. Only when you proportionally resize a bit map to specific sizes, like 50% vertical and 50% horizontal, do you get good results.

Cutting, Copying, and Pasting Objects

FileMaker supports the Clipboard for a variety of operations. You can cut and paste objects from one layout to the next, from one FileMaker file to another, or from the Scrapbook or other applications to a layout. You can copy within the layout to duplicate an object. You can cut and paste fields and any other graphical object that you can select (lines, rectangles, and so on). You can select all objects on a layout by using the Select All command and then copy them to another layout.

When you align a set of fields for a mailing label, for instance, you don't have to create the fields again for another mailing label. Just copy the fields as a unit and paste them onto your new layout. Grouping the fields first makes the operation work better. When you paste fields within a file, you transfer all aspects of the field definition. When you paste a field from another file, however, only the formatting of that field transfers. Any entry options, calculations, or summary attached to a field does not transfer to the new file. The only restriction on pasting a field from another file is that the field names match.

You can use the Clipboard for many tasks. You can place a letterhead graphic, move text, create an entire letter in your word processor for transfer to a layout, and so on.

To use the Clipboard to cut and paste graphics, follow these steps:

1. Select the text or graphic that you want to place on the Clipboard. The text or graphic can be in the same layout, another layout, another FileMaker file, an application, or a desk accessory.

2. Select the Cut ⌘-X or Copy ⌘-C command to place the selection in the Clipboard.

3. Open the layout in which you want to paste your selection.

   To duplicate an object on a layout, stay on that same layout. If you're using another application, either quit the application if you're using Finder or switch to FileMaker in MultiFinder. If you're using a desk accessory, click in the Layout window to activate it.

4. To paste text, select the Text tool by clicking on it. Click an insertion point.

   or

   To paste an object, select the Arrow tool.

5. Select the Paste command on the Edit menu or press the ⌘-V keystroke.

When you paste text, the text is placed onto your layout at the insertion point in a manner consistent with the currently chosen alignment. Pasted objects are selected and placed at the center of your Layout window. To move the selected object, drag the object to the desired location.

Formatting Layout Objects

FileMaker contains submenus on the Format menu for modifying layout objects and the display of field entries. Chapter 6 covers some of these submenus. The Number Format, Date Format, Time Format, and Picture Format commands alter the manner in which your Macintosh internally handles data and displays the data. Those commands offer options, such as displaying a number as a percent or displaying the number with a specified number of decimal places, displaying a date in a short or long format, or displaying a picture as cropped or scaled. Because these commands result in changes in the display, FileMaker refers to them as formatting, but they're intimately associated with data type.

In the sections that follow, you will see how to use the other commands on the Format menu to change fonts. These commands include the Font, Size, Style, Line Spacing, Text Color, and Align Text commands. You can accept FileMaker's default settings for characters on your screen, which are for the standard layout (either Geneva 9-point, bold, align left for layout text; or Geneva 12-point, plain, align left for text in fields), or you can change the settings to suit your purpose.

Defaults for graphics are a line width of one point, a line fill of black, and a fill pattern of none (which means that the fill is transparent). Using the Line Width, Line Fill, and Fill Pattern, you can alter the default settings; you can spruce up a layout using these options. In the sections that follow, you will find the necessary instructions for formatting various items on your layout and for modifying layout text.

Anytime you hold down the Command key and click on an object, FileMaker resets the Format menu to assume the formatting that the object has. This program capability means that you can click on an object with the formatting you want and then create an object that has the same format.

Setting text and drawing defaults can be done by choosing settings when no objects are selected. FileMaker Pro applies these default settings to every object that is created until you change the defaults.

SPEED KEY

To reset defaults, ⌘-click the object with the desired attributes.

FileMaker remembers the format of your last-selected object, including all settings on the Format menu. If you want a new object to have the same format as an object that is on your current layout, press the Command key, select the existing object to set the format, and then create the object. This technique works even when you change tools to create different objects or when you change between layouts in a file, but the technique does not work when you change files. Because a field also is an object, you can format a new field instantly by selecting a field with the formatting you want and then creating your new field. This technique can save you a considerable amount of time.

Changing Fonts

The Font command on the Format menu is the key to changing typefaces (see fig. 7.8). Fonts are installed in the system file by using the Font/DA Mover with System 6. You can bypass the artificial limit on fonts (15) by installing either Suitcase II or Master Juggler, which can add the additional resources at start-up or later. System 7 has no limit other than RAM constraints. You may, for example, need more than 15 fonts for desktop publishing. Figure 7.8 shows added fonts. Both utilities allow for literally hundreds of desk accessories as well. Plans for System 7 are for fonts and DAs to be installed by dragging their files into the System folder.

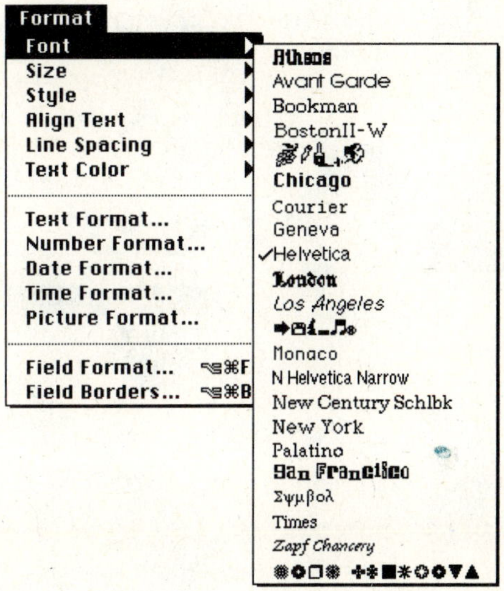

Fig. 7.8
The Font submenu.

FileMaker uses Geneva as the default font. If FileMaker finds Helvetica in the System file, however, the documentation states that FileMaker substitutes that font instead.

A selected font is check marked on the submenu. You can change fonts at any time. Use either the Browse or Layout windows for Text, Number, Time, or Date fields. Layout text objects and calculation and summary fields with text, number, or date results, however, require setting the font in the Layout window alone.

FileMaker has no limit to the number of fonts that you can use in a file. Keep in mind, however, that using more fonts slows down your file's performance as the Macintosh seeks and reads all the needed screen font file tables.

The font menu now displays a sample of how the font will look.

Changing Font Size

The Size command on the Format menu (see fig. 7.9) is the key to resizing text on your screen. In System 6, font sizes installed in your system file are displayed in outlined numbers, just as 9 through 24 points are in the figure. The selected size is check marked on the submenu. Whenever a font size is installed, the font size generally gives a better printed result than an uninstalled size. This situation is particularly true of QuickDraw printers, such as the ImageWriters and the LaserWriter SC. If you use an uninstalled font size that is one-half the size for an ImageWriter and one-third the size for the ImageWriter LQ, you get a better result when printing. PostScript printers draw characters based on outlines, and even though an installed font size generally is better, the difference is not that noticeable.

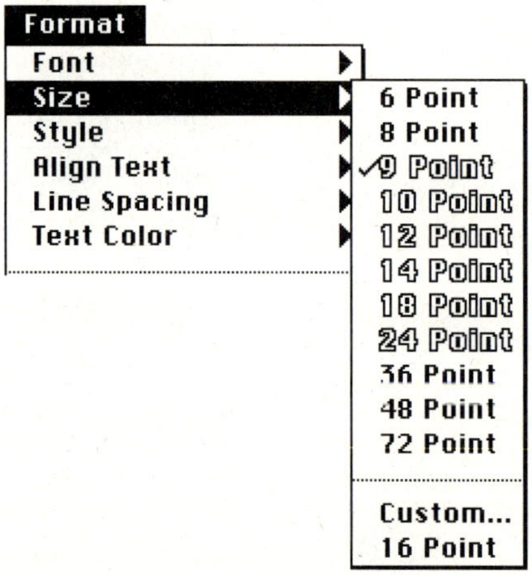

Fig. 7.9
The Size submenu.

Choosing Custom on the Size submenu enables you to format text in a nonstandard font size. You can type in any size from 1 to 127 points. The size you enter appears last on the Size menu.

The Adobe Type Manager and the QuickDraw-based outline fonts that comprise Apple's TrueType font technology in System 7 will offer much smoother on-screen font display and print output. Both will make the selection of font size less critical. Although slightly better results are obtained with installed sizes, the difference will be much less noticeable—even to QuickDraw printers, such as the ImageWriter.

Changing Font Style

The Style submenu (see fig. 7.10) enables you to change the appearance of characters in your font. You can choose normal style (called Plain Text), Bold, Italic, Underline, Outline, or Shadow. You also can choose any combination of styles (with the exception of Plain Text; if you choose Plain Text, the choice removes any other styles you have chosen). Using the Condensed option puts the letters closer together than usual, and using the Extended option spreads them out. You can use the Condensed or Extended options in conjunction with the other style choices.

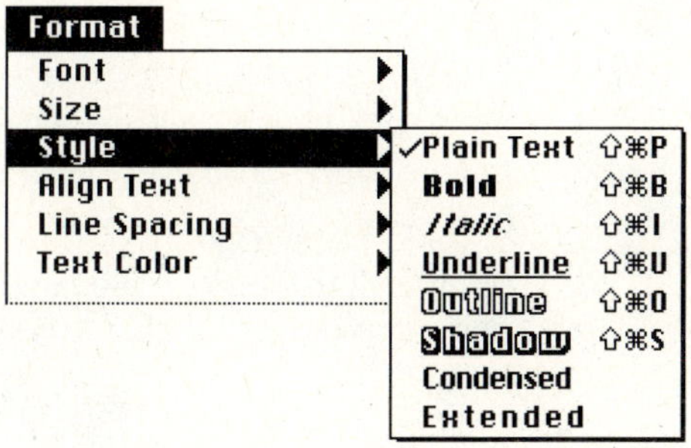

Fig. 7.10
The Style submenu.

SPEED KEY

⌘-Shift-P, the Plain Text command, removes all styles from a font.

⌘-Shift-B, the Bold command, adds the bold style to a font.

⌘-Shift-I, the Italic command, adds the italic style to a font.

⌘-Shift-U, the Underline command, underlines all characters.

⌘-Shift-O, the Outline command, outlines all characters.

⌘-Shift-S, the Shadow command, adds a shadow to all characters.

Aligning Text

The Align Text command from the Format menu produces a submenu (see fig. 7.11) that controls how text aligns, both for data typed into a Text field and for text objects. Alignment applies to all kinds of fields, including Picture fields. You align characters with respect to the field boundaries, or, for a text object, with relation to the position of the original insertion point. You can change alignment only for fields or text objects and only in the Layout window. The three choices offered are

Left, Center, and Right. You can use the ⌘-Shift-L, ⌘-Shift-C, and ⌘-Shift-R keystrokes for the Left, Center, and Right commands, respectively. The only other alignment option usually offered in word processing programs, but not in FileMaker, is justified text. Justified text fills the line from end to end by varying word spacing.

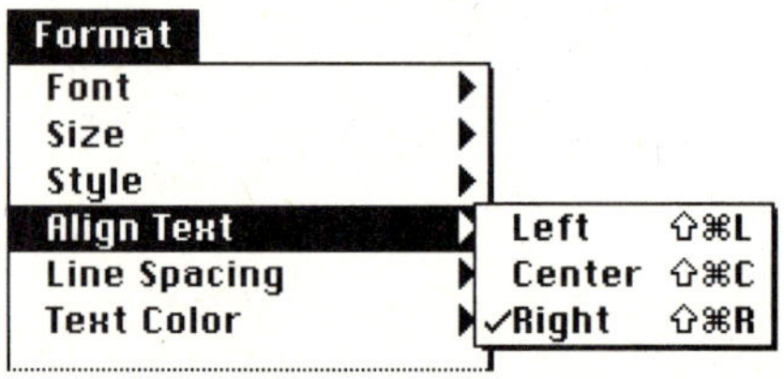

Fig. 7.11
The Align Text submenu.

SPEED KEY

⌘-Shift-L, the Left command, aligns a text object left of the insertion point or aligns characters in a field to the left field reshape box boundary.

⌘-Shift-C, the Center command, centers a text object about the insertion point or centers characters in a field to the middle of the field reshape box.

⌘-Shift-R, the Right command, aligns a text object to the right of the insertion point or aligns characters in a field to the right field reshape box boundary.

If you choose the Left command, text you type flows to the left of the cursor; that is, your original insertion point becomes the left boundary of your text object. Aligning left for fields is the same as left-justified text in a word processor. This alignment is what you usually see printed in a book and is called left-justified, or ragged-right. If you choose the Right command, the cursor stays to the right as you type characters, and your original insertion point becomes the right boundary for a text object. Characters typed or placed in a field set with right alignment are right-justified, or ragged-left. Selecting Center makes the original insertion point the center of the resulting text object.

If you use the Slide Objects command on the Arrange menu to remove unwanted blank fields or spaces, you can use the Center or Right format on an object to prevent it from sliding left. Numbers that are right-aligned to show a column with decimal points remain in a column even if other objects slide left. See Chapter 9 for more details on the Slide Objects command.

Formatting Text

Text you enter into a Text field in the Browse window is like text in a word processor. The text word wraps and supports the full use of the Clipboard. Also, you have complete control over the format of every character in a Text field. This control differentiates a Text field from text objects, which accept only one set of formats and can be formatted only in the Layout window. You can format text characters in a Text field and a text object as a unit in the Layout window. Text objects, however, accept only one format, no matter how much text is selected in that text object. Any special formatting that you set for characters in a Text field in the Browse window override any blanket format that you set in the Layout window; that is, any formatting associated with individual pieces of data override the formatting of the entire Text field.

To format a text object on a layout, follow these steps:

1. In the Layout window, click the Text tool to select the tool.
2. Place an insertion point in that object or select any part of the object.

   As an alternative to these two steps, you can click on the Arrow tool and select the entire text object.
3. Choose the formatting you want from the Font, Size, Style, Align Text, Line Spacing, and Text Color submenus on the Format menu.
4. Deselect the changed text object.

Format a Text field, calculation field, or summary field with a text result by following these steps:

1. In the Layout window, click on the Arrow tool.
2. Click on the Text field to select the entire Text field.
3. Choose the formatting you want from the Font, Size, Style, Align Text, Line Spacing, and Text Color submenus on the Format menu.
4. Deselect the changed Text field.

To change selected characters in a Text field, follow these steps:

1. In the Browse window, select the field you want to edit to make the field the current field.
2. Click an insertion point with the I-beam cursor or drag a selection.

3. Choose the formatting you desire from the Font, Size, and Style submenus on the Format menu. The Align Text submenu is not available to you in the Browse window.
4. Deselect the field by pressing the Enter key or click the cursor outside the field boundary.

Selected characters accept the new formatting, but all other characters in that Text field retain the formatting you set in the Layout window. Any additional changes that you set in the Layout window leave the formatting you set in the Browse window unaffected. Individual characters, however, can be formatted in the Browse window.

Formatting Numbers

Number fields or calculation and summary fields with number results use the same set of formatting commands that Text fields and text objects use. Font, Size, Style, and Align Text menus are used in exactly the same manner as described in the preceding section for text. For information on formatting numbers using commas, decimal places, or percent, or formatting numbers as a logical field, see Chapter 3.

Formatting Dates

Date fields or calculation and summary fields with date results use the same set of formatting commands that Text fields and text objects use. Font, Size, Style, and Align Text menus are used in exactly the same manner as described for text in the section "Formatting Text." For information on formatting dates using short, medium, and long dates of various kinds, see Chapter 6.

Formatting Time

Time fields or calculation and summary fields with time results use the same set of formatting commands that Text fields and text objects use. Font, Size, Style, and Align Text menus are used in exactly the same manner as described for text in "Formatting Text."

Formatting Pictures and Graphics

You can place pictures on your layout screen as a graphical layout object or as a Picture field. Details of file formats that are accepted as entries in a field are discussed in Chapter 3. In general, if you can place a graphic on the Clipboard, you can enter the graphic by pasting it into a Picture field or by pasting the graphic onto a layout as a graphic object. Font, Size, and Style do not apply to either type of picture.

The Align Text command, however, applies to both Picture fields and graphics. If you choose the Resize Picture Proportionately to Fit Frame option in the Format Picture command, the Align command determines where in the box the picture you see is placed (see fig. 7.12). When a field or picture reshape box is smaller than the picture being aligned, the align commands are not used in the same way. The top edge of the picture aligns to the top-left edge of the box, regardless of the alignment chosen. You resize a picture in the normal manner by using the small black handle on the lower right side of the reshape box.

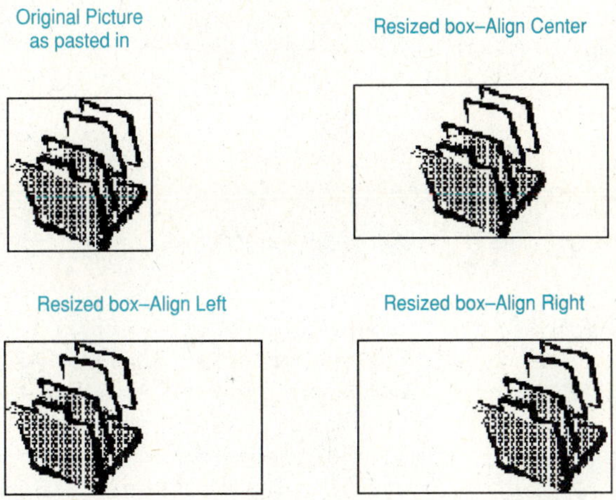

Fig. 7.12
Resizing a graphic with various alignments.

If you want to place text into a Picture field or as a graphic, you can paste or create the text in a paint program and cut or copy the text to the Clipboard as a bit map. When you paste the text into FileMaker, the text is in the form of a picture. Text pasted into FileMaker in this manner loses its font information and is like any other picture.

Graphics that you place on a layout by using the Tools Palette can be formatted by using the Line Width, Line Fill, and Fill Pattern commands. You can get some interesting effects using these submenus, and you can use these shapes to highlight your layouts. In figure 7.13, you can see the effects of changing these three commands on a set of lines, rectangles, and ovals. The appearance of these shapes in the Layout and Browse windows is illustrated. Using fill patterns causes shapes such as circles and squares to fill with a variety of patterns; however, this command has no effect on lines. Instead, the Line Fill feature works with lines.

Fig. 7.13
Drawn graphics from the Tools Palette with a variety of formatting.

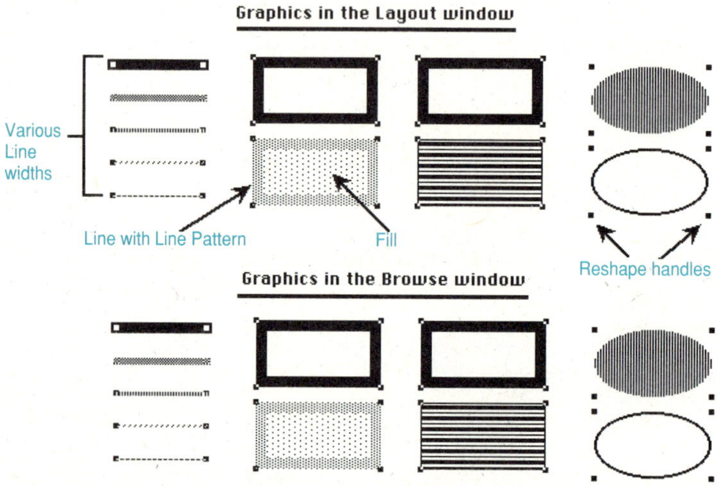

Specifying Line Width

The Line Width pop-up menu is shown in figure 7.14. Line widths refer to line weights, and the available weights are no line, hairline (0.5 points), 1 point, 2 points, 3 points, 4 points, 5 points, 6 points, 7 points, 8 points, and 12 points. Shown as the current line width is the 3-point line. A hairline width appears to be the same as a 1-point line on your screen. If your printer is capable of printing at that resolution (a LaserWriter, but not an ImageWriter), the line prints as a hairline. When printing on an ImageWriter, the line prints as a 1-point line. You can use the Line Pattern command to affect the display of lines.

Specifying Line Pattern and Fill Pattern

The Line Pattern and Fill Pattern submenus (see fig. 7.15) are identical in appearance and operation. Select these options by clicking and holding the small squares to the right of the pen. The difference is that a line pattern fills a line with a pattern; whereas a fill pattern fills the area inside an object with a pattern. In addition to various shades of gray found between black and white, you can choose from a total of 56 patterns. How line patterns appear varies depending on the angle of the line in your layout. You may want to experiment to get the effect you desire.

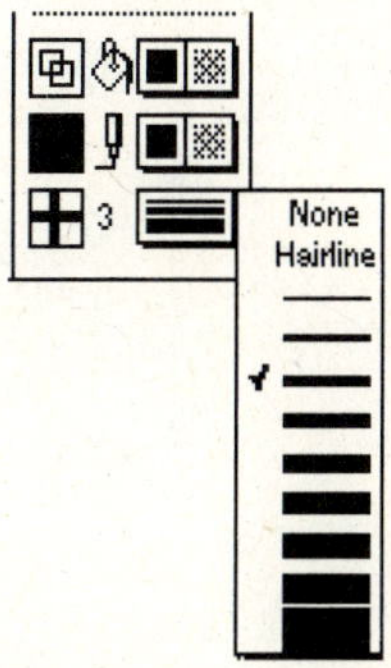

Fig. 7.14
The Line Width tool pop-up menu.

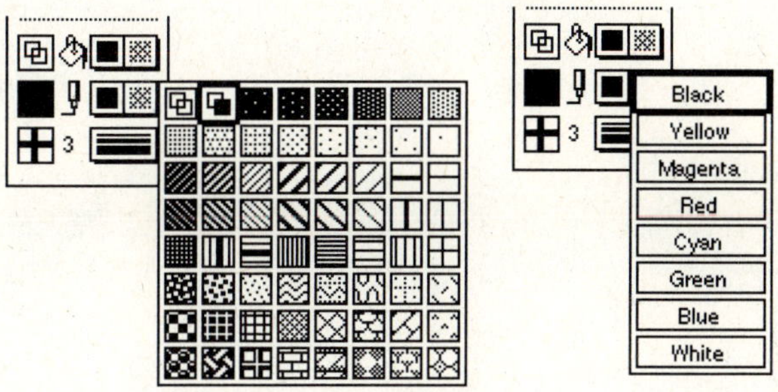

Fig. 7.15
The Line Pattern tool pop-up menu (same as the Fill Pattern menu).

To set the default fill pattern and color of an object, start with a newly created object or with no objects selected. To change an existing object, select it first. Choose the pattern and color from the pop-up menus (see fig. 7.15). The default fill and color are indicated by the left hand square of the two overlapping squares to the left of the paint bucket.

The color and pattern of lines or field borders are determined by the pen color and pattern pop-up menus (see fig. 7.15). To set the default pattern and color, start with a newly created line or field border or with none selected. To change an existing line or field border, first select it. Choose the pattern and color from the pop-up menus.

Field Borders

The Field Borders command on the Format menu opens a dialog box (see fig. 7.16) where you create field borders and baselines for fields on the layout. Field borders are visible in the browse, preview, or print mode.

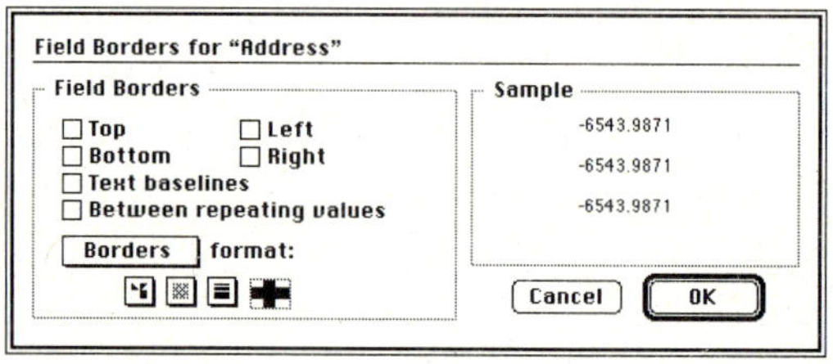

Fig. 7.16
The Field Borders dialog box.

Field Format

The Field Format command on the Format menu opens a dialog box (see fig. 7.17) where you select how to display a field's value list (created during field definition). You also set the number of values from a repeating field (created during field definition) you want shown.

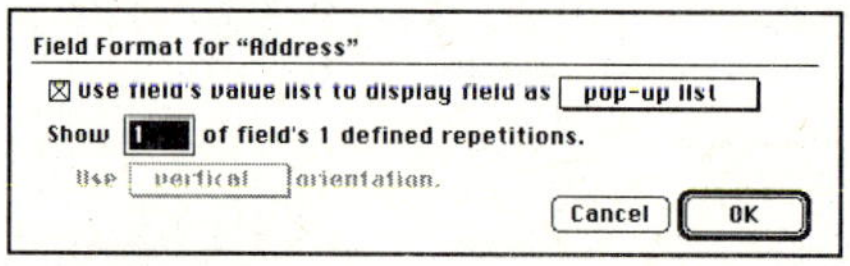

Fig. 7.17
The Field Format dialog box.

The Field Format feature is new. A value list can now appear as a pop-up list, pop-up menu, check list, or as radio buttons.

⌘-Option-F is the keyboard equivalent for Field Format.

⌘-Option-B is the keyboard equivalent for Field Borders.

In Review

The Tools Palette in the Layout window contains six tools: the Arrow, Text, Line, Rectangle, Rounded Rectangle, and Oval tools. The Arrow tool is used for selecting and moving objects. You use the Text tool to create and edit layout text or text objects. The other tools are used to create graphics on your layout.

You select objects in the Layout window by clicking on them after you select the Arrow tool. You can select a range of objects by shift-clicking on them or by dragging a marquee about them. You can select text objects entirely with the Arrow tool. To select pieces of text in a text object, you click an insertion point and drag a selection by using the Text tool. You can use this technique to edit text objects as well.

FileMaker offers some tools on the Layout menu that aid in accurate placement of objects on the Layout window. You can activate an invisible grid with a setting of 12 divisions per inch. This grid is "magnetic" and aligns objects. You also can use a T-square, which aligns objects to it. And you can turn on text boundaries that frame text objects and field boundaries that frame fields.

You resize objects on the Layout window (fields, text objects, and graphics) by clicking on one of the black reshape handles at each corner and dragging to the desired size. Selected objects cannot be resized, only moved. Resizing a field enables you to display or print additional lines of entered characters or more data.

The Clipboard is useful for moving graphic objects around on a layout. Any object that you can select on a layout can be cut to the Clipboard and pasted on another layout. You can even paste fields between files if the names match.

You can format text characters in a field or text objects in the same manner that text in a word processor is formatted. You can select a font, text size, text style, and alignment. Text objects support only one set of formats. You can format a field's data in the Browse window; you format the field itself in the Layout window. A data format overrides a field format.

If you click on an object, the object sets the Format menu to the format of the object. Use this shortcut to create a format for any new object you're creating. Just click on an object that has the format you want.

You can format and place graphics as data in a Picture field or as a layout object. You can apply line widths, line patterns, and fill patterns to graphics that you create by using the Tools Palette.

CHAPTER 8

Quick Start: Creating and Using Forms

In this quick start, you will focus on common problems associated with layouts, use a layout to create a form, and work with an existing commercial form. You create an invoice form and use it to explore some auto-entry options and improve your data entry. You also learn to work with both calculation fields and repeating fields. You explore some of the more important aspects of the Layout window, focusing on the Tools Palette and commands found on the Format and Layout menus. The commercial form simulates a commercial statement form that you can buy at any office supply store.

In this chapter, you learn how to do the following:

- Use the blank layout to define a form
- Work with text objects and the Tools Palette
- Place fields on a layout and position objects accurately
- Format a field's data and display
- Define entry options and calculations
- Use a commercial form
- Print samples

USING FILEMAKER PRO

Creating a Form Layout

The catalog mailing you completed in the first quick start was a success. When customers receive your natural health food catalog, they call to order those great health food items and accessories. Having FileMaker up and running is good because now you need to start automating your paperwork. Because each order requires that you place an invoice form in the shipping box, it makes sense to create a form that your telephone operators can use to take orders. Sometimes database developers create separate data-entry layouts and invoices, but here you will combine the two.

You can use the file from Quick Start 1 to create the invoice. Because you may have made changes to the original file, open and work with a copy of the file. You need to create a layout for the invoice form. Each form is a separate page on 8 1/2-by-5 1/2-inch continuous-feed paper. That is, two pages fit onto one letter-size paper. The best layout to use is the blank layout, because you will be adding fields and graphics as you need them.

To create a blank layout, follow these steps:

1. Launch FileMaker by double-clicking on the FileMaker icon in the Finder or by selecting the FileMaker name in MultiFinder from the Apple menu.
2. Select the Open command on the Edit menu or press ⌘-O to bring up the Open File dialog box.
3. Navigate the file system and open the 60's Nat. Food Emp. folder you created in the first quick start.
4. Double-click on the file named Copy of Catalog Mailing to open the file.

   The Copy of Catalog Mailing file contained two layouts, seven Text fields, and eight customer records in the original mailing. When you last closed that file, you were in the Browse window.
5. Select the Layout command from the Select menu or press ⌘-L to open the Layout window.
6. Select the New Layout command from the Edit menu or press ⌘-N.
7. In the New Layout dialog box, click on the Blank Layout radio button and then click on the OK button or press the Return key.

A blank layout appears on the screen (see fig. 8.1). For information on the blank layout, refer to Chapter 6. A blank layout has three parts: a header, a body, and a footer. Each record is its own form, so you do not need the header or the footer parts in this case. Headers and footers are appropriate when you have a page containing multiple records. To reduce some of the clutter, remove the headers and footers.

Fig. 8.1
The blank layout.

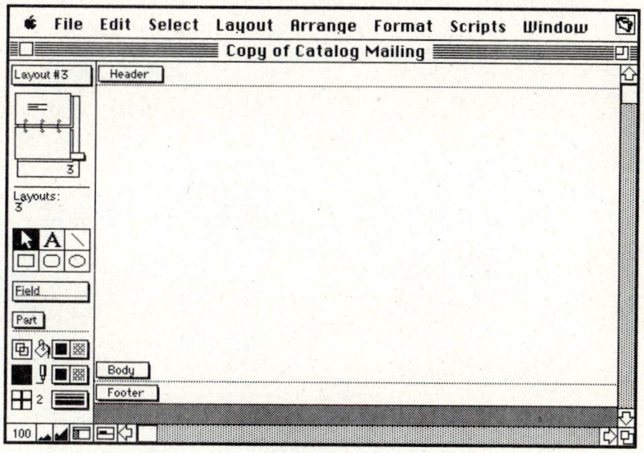

To remove a part, follow these steps:

1. Click on the part handle labeled Header or on the dotted line that marks the header boundary and drag the part into the window title bar.
2. Click on the part handle labeled Footer or on the dotted line that marks the footer boundary and drag the part into the body part.

Only the body part remains in the Layout window. Refer to Chapter 9 for details about removing or changing the sizes of parts.

Setting Up the Page

The page you use is half US letter-size, or 8 1/2 inches wide by 5 1/2 inches long. Since that size is not one of FileMaker's choices, you need to set a custom page size. Use the Edit Paper Sizes option under the Page Setup command to create the dimensions for your custom page.

Note

The printer that you select must be able to accommodate different-sized paper in order for you to use the Edit Paper Sizes option.

To create a page setup for a custom form, follow these steps:

1. Select the Chooser desk accessory in the Apple menu to choose a printer.

   Because you are using continuous-feed, triple-form paper, you need a dot-matrix printer (ImageWriter) to use impact printing. Follow these instructions and, if you have a LaserWriter, don't forget to change back to it when you have completed this Quick Start. If you don't have an ImageWriter, you still can follow along.

2. Click on the ImageWriter icon in the output device box and the printer port (if needed), as shown in figure 8.2. Close the Chooser window.

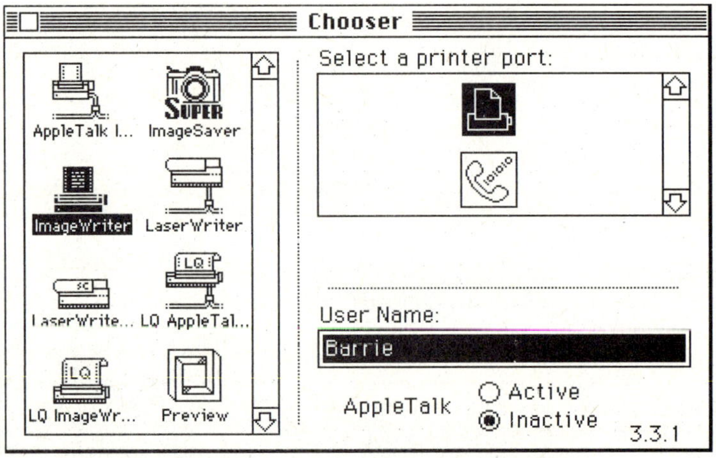

Fig. 8.2
Selecting an ImageWriter printer from the Chooser DA.

3. Select the Page Setup command from the File menu.
4. In the Edit Paper Sizes portion of the dialog box, enter the page size for the Invoice form. Enter *Invoice Form* in the Name text box, *8.500* in the Width box, and *5.500* in the Height text box (see fig. 8.3).
5. Because the forms are continuously fed and don't require top and bottom margins, click on the No Gaps Between Pages radio button.
6. Click on OK to accept your specifications.

Refer to Chapter 10 for more details about setting and using different paper sizes.

Fig. 8.3
Creating the paper size of the invoice form.

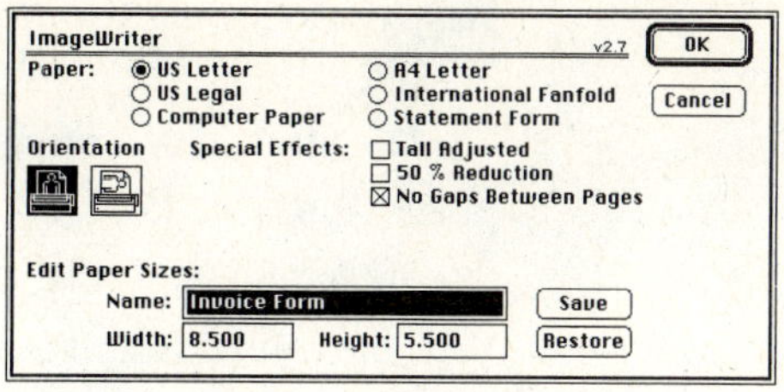

Designing a New Form

You need to place a letterhead and logo on the form. To create a letterhead and logo, type a set of text objects for each of the lines in the address and create a graphic by using some of the tools in the Tools Palette. Don't worry about where you type on the layout—you can use the T-square later to position them accurately. When you first create a file, an invisible grid is turned on. Open the Layout menu and look to see whether the grid is check marked. If so, select the Align to Grid command again to disable the command. You do not need the Align to Grid command right now.

To type the text objects for your layout, follow these steps:

1. Click on the Text tool (the letter A in the Tools Palette). Your cursor changes to an I-beam.
2. Make the following selections from the Format menu by selecting the appropriate commands to format the first line of text:
   - Select Geneva from the Font submenu (Geneva may be checkmarked already).
   - Select 14 Point from the Size submenu.
   - Select Bold from the Style submenu or press the ⌘-Shift-B keystroke.
   - Select Center from the Align menu or press the ⌘-Shift-C keystroke to produce centered text.
3. Click an insertion point somewhere in the middle of the layout and type the first line of text: *HOL EARTH CATALOG*.
4. Click an insertion point directly below the `HOL EARTH CATALOG` text object.

5. Make the following selections from the Format menu by selecting the appropriate commands to format the second line of text:

   - Select 12 Point from the Size submenu.
   - Select Plain from the Style submenu or press the ⌘-Shift-P keystroke.

6. Type the second line of text for the address: *1990 Crystal Way.*
7. Click an insertion point directly below the street line and type the third line: *Taos NM 87571*.
8. Click an insertion point directly below the city line and type the fourth line: *(505)THE-ROCK.*

Each of these lines should be separate text objects.

To place the address in the top center of your form, use a device called the T-square, which is found on the Layout menu.

To accurately place objects on a layout, follow these steps:

1. Select the T-squares command on the Layout menu. FileMaker checkmarks the command.

   FileMaker draws a perpendicular set of lines on the center of the layout, called a T-square.

2. Select the Rulers command from the Layout menu.

   Both a horizontal and vertical ruler appear.

3. Select the Size command from the Layout menu.

   The size box appears; you may move the size box anywhere on the screen by dragging the title bar.

4. Select the Arrow tool, click on the vertical position line of the T-square, and drag until the ruler and size box show the T-square to be 0.125" from the top and 4.250" from the left.
5. Click on the Arrow tool and then select all four of the text objects. Select the objects by clicking where there are no objects in the layout and then dragging a selection marquee around all the objects.

   or

   Select objects by clicking on an object, holding down the Shift key, and clicking on other objects.

Note

When you drag the arrow anywhere on the T-square, a dotted line indicates the movement on the ruler, and the exact position appears in the size box.

6. Click on any of the selected text objects and drag them so that they are centered about the verical line of the T-square and the top of the top line touches the horizontal line of the T-square (see fig. 8.4).

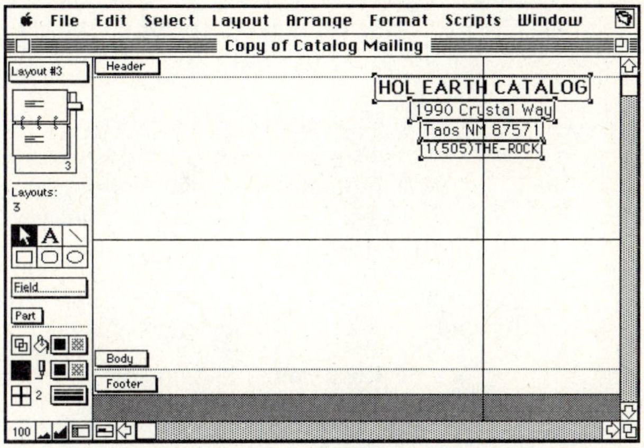

Fig. 8.4
The heading for the invoice form.

Suppose that you just noticed that you have given the wrong area code for the phone number—it should be an 800 number. Also, the phone number would look better if it were smaller in size.

To edit a text object, follow these steps:

1. Click on the Text tool in the Tools Palette; your cursor changes to an I-beam.

2. Drag over the area code, `(505)`, to select the area code.

3. Type the new area code, *(800)*, in place of the existing area code.

4. Change the size by selecting 10 Point from the Size submenu on the Format menu. You also can change the format of a text object by selecting the text object with the Arrow tool and making selections from the Format menu.

You want to use a simple logo on your form; the planet earth with the word HOL on the planet. Create the logo using the Oval tool in the Tools Palette and one additional text object.

To create the logo, follow these steps:

1. Click on the Oval tool in the Tools Palette. Your cursor changes to a cross hair.

2. On the Status Panel, make selections that are appropriate to the circle you want.

   Select the single line (one point) from the Line Width submenu on the Status Panel. The single line is found just below the word `Hairline`.

   Select the color black on the Line Pattern submenu.

   Select the color gray from the Fill Pattern submenu.

3. Click anywhere on the layout. Hold down the Option key and drag a circle about the same size as your address (0.875"). (Use the numbers shown in the position indicators and subtract the top from the bottom or the right from the left to drag the correct circle size.) The Option key constrains an oval to a circle.

4. Click on the Arrow tool. Click on the circle to select the circle and drag the circle up to the top left corner of the layout.

5. Click on the first line of the address to select the format used.

6. Select Outline from the Style submenu on the Format menu or press the ⌘-Shift-O keystroke.

7. Select the Text tool, click in the center of the circle, and type *HOL* (see fig. 8.5).

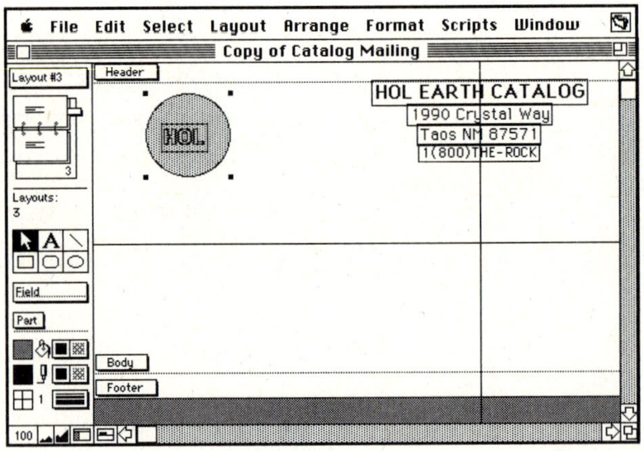

Fig. 8.5
The complete letterhead.

If you need to center this text object, click on the Arrow tool and drag the text object to the desired position in the center of your logo.

Two additional elements are needed to finish the letterhead: a line separating the address and a text object for the word INVOICE.

To draw a straight line, follow these steps:

1. Click on the Line tool in the Tools Palette; your cursor changes to a crosshair.
2. Select the settings for the line on the Status Panel.

   Choose black for the Line Pattern, if needed.

   Select the six-point line, the eighth choice down on the Line Width submenu.
3. Hold down the Option key to draw a straight line and click a starting point about one inch down from the T-square vertical position line and about 0.25 inch in from the left of the layout edge. Drag to the right until you come to within about 0.25 inch of the solid vertical black line that marks the page boundary.

Don't worry about exact placement or size. You can resize the line by selecting the Arrow tool, holding down the Option or Shift key (so that the line is straight), and dragging on the small black reshape handle at the right edge of the line. To move the line vertically with the Arrow tool, hold down the Option or Shift key and drag the line into position.

To add the INVOICE title (a text object), follow these steps:

1. Click on the Text tool.
2. Click on the word HOL in the logo to set the Format menu.
3. Anywhere on the layout type the word *INVOICE*.
4. Select the Show Text Boundaries command on the Layout menu to see the boundaries of each text object.
5. Click on the Arrow tool and drag the new text object into position just below the line (see fig. 8.6).

You can find detailed information about the Tools Palette in Chapter 7.

Working with Fields

The invoice you are preparing requires several new fields that are not currently in your file. To reduce the drudgery of entering data, you can ask FileMaker to do much of the work. This process involves setting auto-entry options for many of these fields. Begin with some simple field options: a field that auto-enters the date and one that enters a serial number for each invoice you create.

Fig. 8.6
Placing the INVOICE title.

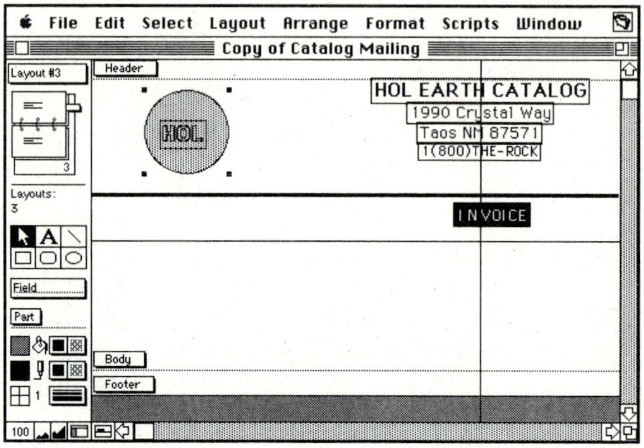

To create an auto-entered Date field, follow these steps:

1. Choose the Define Fields command from the Select menu.
2. In the Define Fields dialog box, type the name *Date.inv* in the Field Name text box; click the Date radio button or press ⌘-D.
3. Click the Create button to create the field.
4. Click the Date.inv field to select the field (see fig. 8.7).
5. Click the Options button. The Entry Options dialog box appears.
6. In the Options dialog box, click the Creation Date check box in the Auto-Enter a Value That Is box (see fig. 8.8). Choosing this option automatically enters today's date when you create a record.
7. Click the OK button to return to the Define Fields dialog box.

To create a serial number field, follow these steps:

1. Type the name of the new field, *Invoice #.inv*, in the Define fields text box.
2. Click the Number radio button or press ⌘-N.
3. Click the Create button to create the field.
4. Click the Invoice #.inv field to select the field.

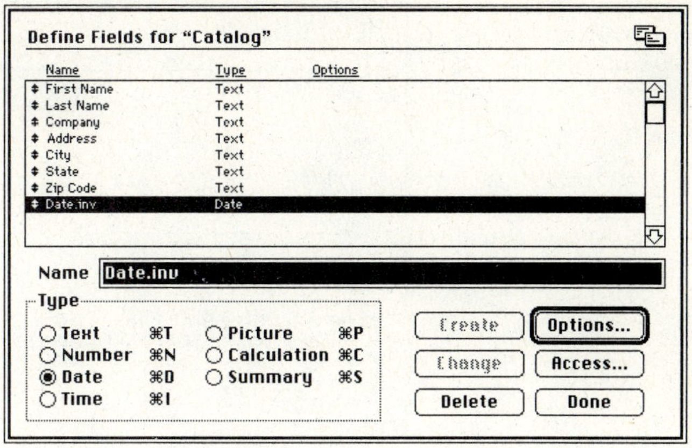

Fig. 8.7
Selecting the newly defined Date field.

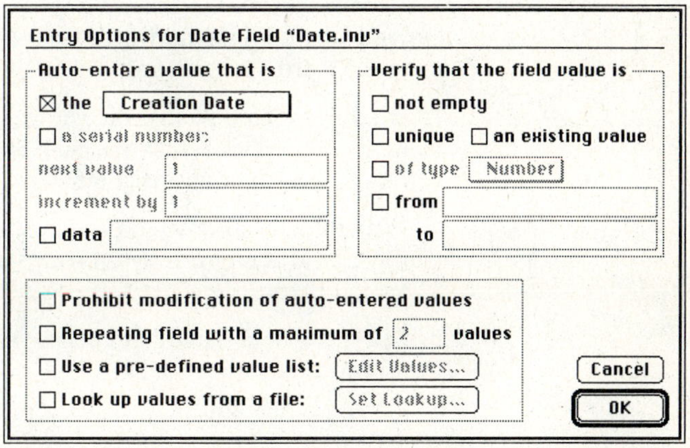

Fig. 8.8
Setting an auto-entered Date field.

5. Click the Options button to open the Options dialog box.
6. Click in the Serial Number text box and, in the Next Value box associated with the Serial Number, enter the number 100.

   FileMaker enters `100` for the serial number of your first record and increases this number by one for each new record.
7. Click the OK button to return to the Define Fields dialog box. This box now shows the two new fields you created (see fig. 8.9).
8. To place the fields and return to the layout, click the Done button.

For more information about auto-entry options, refer to Chapter 5.

Fig. 8.9
Two new fields with auto-entry options.

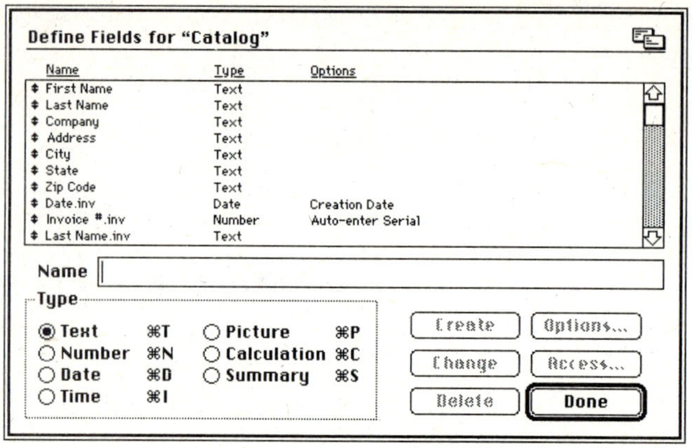

Notice that FileMaker automatically placed the new field on the current layout and labeled the field with a text object to the left. Now, move the fields to their proper position.

1. Set the T-square so that the vertical position (horizontal component) of the T-square is at 2.500" and the horizontal position (vertical component) is at 6.500".

   Remember to refer to the size box and ruler settings. If neither of these guides is currently on your screen, select them from the Layout menu.

2. Select the field names and reformat from the Format menu as follows:

   Choose 12 Point from the Size submenu.

   Choose Underline from the Style menu or press the ⌘-Shift-U keystroke.

   Choose Left from the Align Text submenu or press the ⌘-Shift-L keystroke.

   These three changes make the labels more noticeable and easier to edit.

3. Edit the two field labels to remove the inv suffixes, using the techniques you have learned.

4. Move the two fields and the text objects that label them into the positions shown in figure 8.10.

Fig. 8.10
The final position of the Invoice #.inv and Date.inv fields.

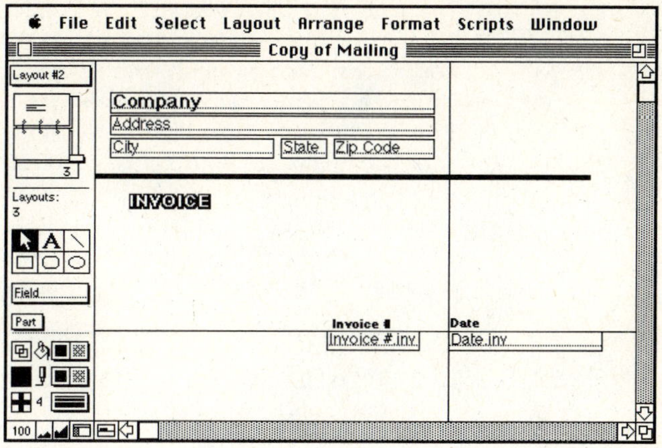

The invoice form requires an address. If you have the customer information in your file, after you enter the name you can have FileMaker fill in the rest of the fields. Begin by defining new name and address fields for this layout. Then set up a link, called a *lookup* (see Chapter 5), between your customer information and your invoice layout. Normally, you will want your customer file to be separate from your invoice file, but here the single file serves double duty.

To create name and address fields, follow these steps:

1. Choose the Define Fields command to open the Define Fields dialog box.
2. Enter *First Name.inv* in the Field Name text box. Then click the Text radio button or press ⌘-T.
3. Click the Create button to create the field.
4. Create the following fields, repeating steps 2 and 3 using the following information:

Last Name.inv	Text field
Company.inv	Text field
Address.inv	Text field
City.inv	Text field
State.inv	Text field
Zip Code.inv	Text field

If you created a link between the Last Name and Last Name.inv fields, when you enter Smith as a last name, you always will get the first customer named Smith in your file, because FileMaker stops at the first occurrence of the name. Marshall Smith's name would be the same as Ben Smith. To circumvent this problem, create two index fields that serve as the match. Both fields, which are called Full Name, take the entire contents of First Name and Last Name fields and concatenate (or join) them using a calculation. Do the same for the invoice name fields. Then, when the Full Name and Full Name.inv fields match, FileMaker auto-enters for all address fields by using a lookup.

To create the two calculation Full Name fields, follow these steps:

1. Type Full Name in the Field Name text box and click the Calculation radio button or press ⌘-C.

2. Click the Create button to create the field. The Calculation Formula dialog box opens.

3. Click on Calculation Result Is and select Text from the pop-up menu.

4. Type the formula *First Name & Last Name* in the Calculation Formula text box (see fig. 8.11).

   You also can enter this formula by clicking on the field names in the list and the operators in the keypad. Generally, this method is a more accurate way to enter the formula. The ampersand (&) is the concatenation operator. The Calculation Formula text box supports text editing, so experiment if you like.

5. Click the OK button to define the calculation and return to the Define Fields dialog box.

You create the second field, Full Name.inv, in the same manner, except the calculation formula is now First Name.inv & Last Name.inv. Repeat steps 1 through 5 to create this second field. Now you can create the lookups for all the address fields that use these two index fields. For detailed information about calculations, refer to Chapter 5.

To create a lookup, follow these steps:

1. Select the Company.inv field by clicking on the name of the field and then clicking the Entry Options button.

2. In the Entry Options dialog box, click on the Lookup Value check box and then click on the OK button. Both items are at the bottom of the dialog box.

FileMaker places an Open File dialog box on your screen. In this case, you use the same Copy of Catalog Mailing file for your lookups. A lookup that uses the same file is called a *self-lookup.*

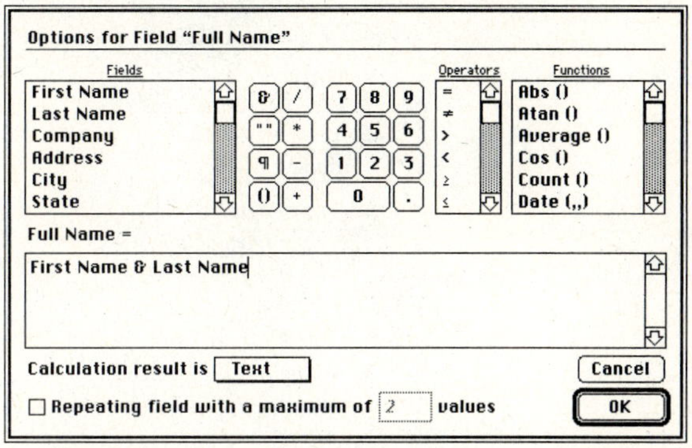

Fig. 8.11
Entering a calculation formula.

3. Double-click on the Copy of Catalog Mailing file name or click once and then click the Open button.
4. In the Lookup dialog box, click on the following field names:

   In the When the Value In scroll box, select the Full Name.inv field.

   For the Matches a New Entry In scroll box, select the Full Name field.

   For the Copy the Contents Of scroll box, select the Company field.
5. Click OK.

Figure 8.12 shows the results.

Now, when the two index fields match, Company.inv will have the same information entered that is found in the Company field with the same full name. Names such as "Santa Claus" will appear as "SantaClaus" in those fields, but now they are indexed together. One problem, however, exists with this match. FileMaker performs the calculations only for new records. Your previous customer records will not have any entries in the Full Name field. You will attend to that issue in the next section.

To set the other address fields for the same lookup, repeat the preceding procedure for the following fields: Address.inv, City.inv, State.inv, and Zip Code.inv. Remember that the two indexes are the matching fields, and the referenced values are the fields of the same name without the suffix. When you are finished, your new fields will be listed in the Define Fields dialog box (see fig. 8.13).

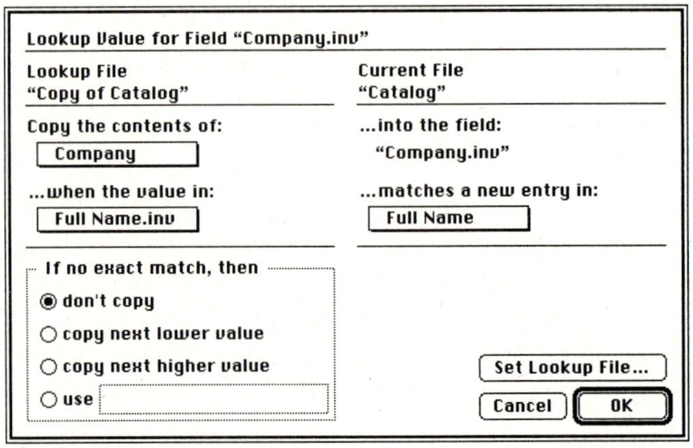

Fig. 8.12
The lookup definition for the Company.inv field.

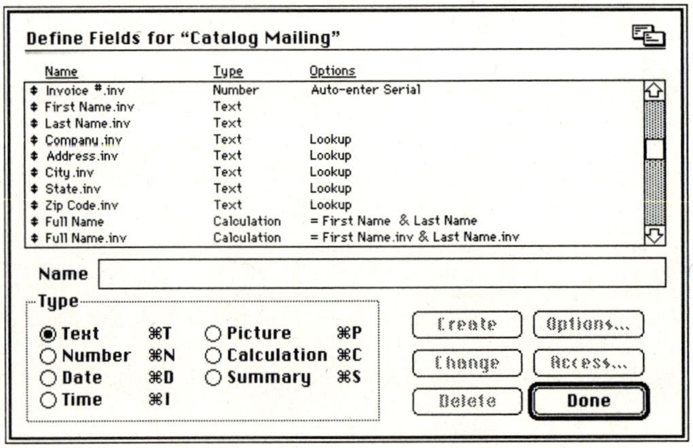

Fig. 8.13
The new invoice customer fields definitions.

Click the Done button to return to your invoice form layout. FileMaker has entered all the new fields for labels on the current layout. To rearrange these fields into a more appropriate customer label, you delete the text objects, resize and move the fields, surround them with a rounded rectangle, and label the customer information.

To create the customer label, follow these steps:

1. Click on the Arrow tool and select all the text objects that serve as field labels, as well as the Full Name and Full Name.inv fields.
2. Delete the selected objects by pressing the Delete key.
3. Resize the fields by holding down the Shift key and dragging the small black handle at the lower right corner of each of the field reshape boxes.

   The Shift key constrains your movement to the horizontal or vertical. Make the fields one line high and of appropriate size.
4. Position the fields by dragging them so that they look like the fields in figure 8.14.

   Move them as a unit to line them up. You may find the T-square helpful in this regard. Don't worry about exact position, but they will look best when the center of the label lines up with the top of your Date.inv and Invoice #.inv fields.
5. Click on the Rounded Rectangle tool and select the following choices on the Status Panel:

   Select 4 Points (sixth choice down) for the Line Width.

   Select black from the Line Pattern submenu.

   Select None as the Fill Pattern.
6. Drag a rounded rectangle around the label fields.
7. Click on the Text tool and select the following choices from the Format menu:

   Select 12 Point from the Size submenu.

   Select Bold from the Style submenu.

   Select Left from the Align Text menu.
8. Click an insertion point above the label and type *MAIL TO:*.
9. Center the MAIL TO text object above the label.

   You are now at the point shown in figure 8.14.

   You need to enter some fields in order to accept the items that are ordered and to calculate subtotals. Because you have a mail order business, you don't need to define a sales tax field. You will add the grand total field in a moment.

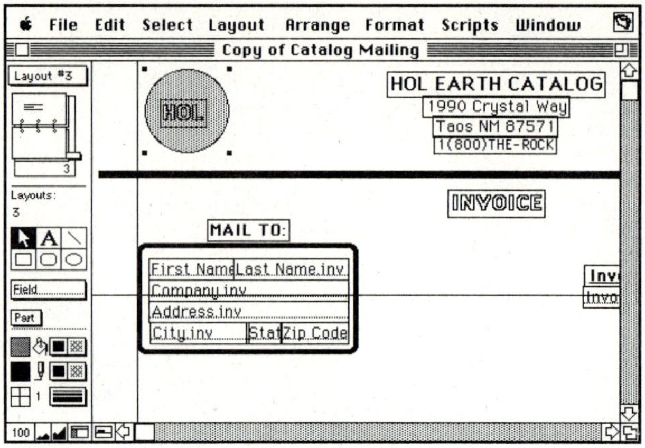

Fig. 8.14
The customer label on the Invoice Form.

To define the item fields, follow these steps:

1. Choose the Define Fields command to reopen the Define Fields dialog box.
2. Type *Item Name.inv* in the Field Name box, click the Text radio button, and then click the Create button to create the field.
3. Repeat step 2 and create three more fields:

Item Cost.inv	Number field
Quantity.inv	Number field
Subtotal.inv	Calculation field

   When you click the Create button to create the Subtotal field, enter *Item Cost * Quantity* in the Text field of the Calculation Formula dialog box.

   Click the Number radio button for the Calculation Result and click the Create button to create the Subtotal.inv field and to return to the Define Fields dialog box.
4. Click the Done button to return to the layout.

   To clean up the layout, you need to align and format these fields as repeating fields.

To resize and align the line item fields, follow these steps:

1. In the Layout window, drag the vertical position line of the T-square down to 5.500". Use the Ruler or Size Box to determine the exact position.

2. Drag the body part handle down to snap to the vertical position line (see fig. 8.15). This line is the length of your form. The form gives you room to work and acts as a guide to show how much room you have.

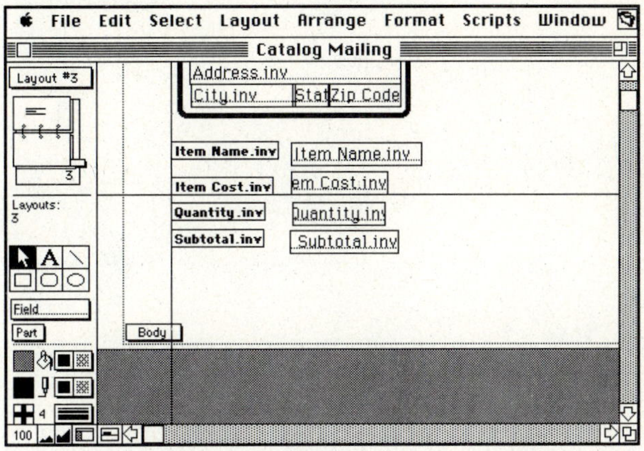

Fig. 8.15
Setting the bottom boundary of the form.

3. Move the vertical position line of the T-square back up to 3.750".
4. Resize and align the following field reshape boxes and their associated field label text objects into position as shown in figure 8.16: Item Name.inv, Item Cost.inv, Quantity.inv, and Subtotal.inv.
5. Edit the text objects to remove the inv suffixes and center them above the fields they label.

   Don't worry about exact size or position. Use steps 4 and 5 to practice your technique. Remember to resize by using the Shift key. If you make a mistake, use the Undo command from the Edit menu or press ⌘-Z to restore its previous condition.

To create repeating fields, follow these steps:

1. Choose Define Fields from the Select menu and highlight the Item Name.inv field.
2. Click on Options.
3. Click on Repeating Field with a Maximum of n Values. Type the number *5* and click the OK button to create the repetitions.
4. Repeat steps 2 and 3 for the each of the following fields: Item Cost.inv, Quantity.inv, and Subtotal.inv.

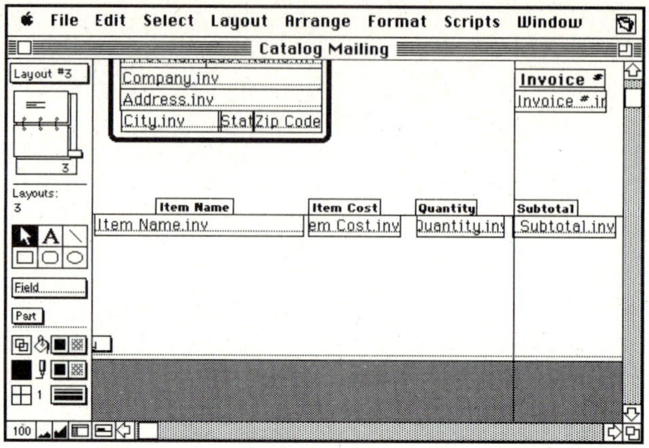

Fig. 8.16
Placing the line item fields.

The repeating fields are shown in figure 8.17.

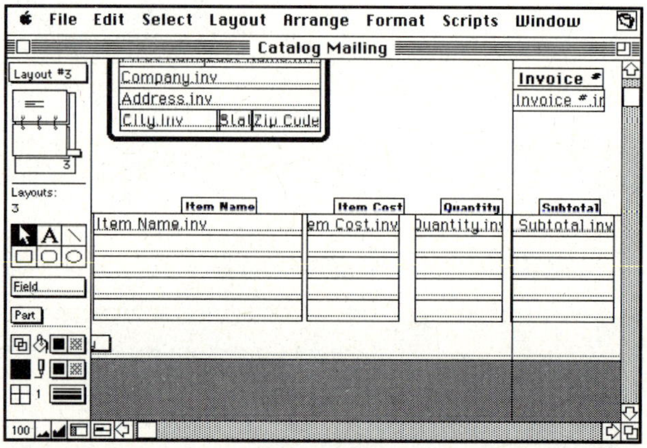

Fig. 8.17
Repeating line item fields.

You need to add the last field, the Grand Total.inv field, which calculates the sum of all of the Subtotal.inv entries. To add the Grand Total field, follow these steps:

1. Choose the Define Fields command from the Select menu or press the ⌘-Shift-D keystroke.
2. In the Define Fields dialog box, enter *Grand Total.inv* in the Field Name text box.
3. Click the Calculation button or press ⌘-C.

4. In the Calculation Formula dialog box, enter *sum(Subtotal)* in the text box. Then click the Number radio button for the calculation result.

5. Click the OK button to return to the Field Definition dialog box. Click the Done button to return to the invoice layout.

6. With the Arrow tool highlighted, select the Grand Total.inv field and resize and move the field so that the field appears as shown in figure 8.18.

7. Select Bold from the Style submenu on the Format menu so that the field stands out.

8. Edit the Grand Total.inv text object to remove the inv suffix. Move that text object into position.

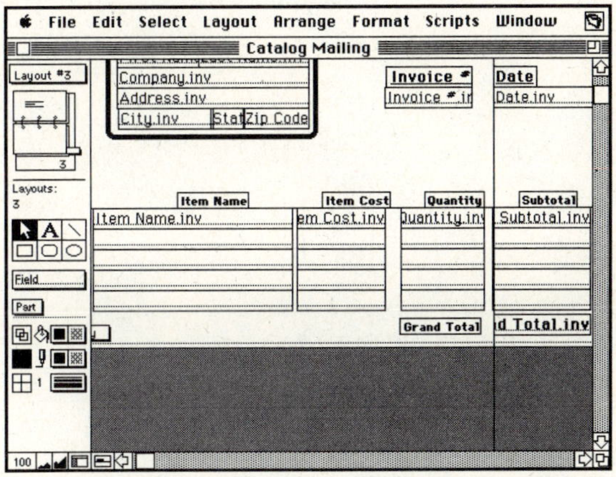

Fig. 8.18
Placing the Grand Total field.

One more entry option makes a helpful aid in data entry. You can create a list of items that your company sells. Then, when you are ready to enter an item in the Item Name.inv field, you can just select from a list.

To attach a list of items to a field, follow these steps:

1. Choose the Define Fields command from the Select menu or press the ⌘-Shift-D keystroke.

2. Click on the Item Name.inv field to select the field. Click on the Options button.

3. Click on the Use a Pre-defined Value List check box. Enter the following items into the Display Values box, which now appears (see fig. 8.19):

   4 MByte SIMMS

   Carrots

   Chimes and Bells

   Grecian Urns

   Gold Bars

   Keeper Crystal

   Click OK to accept the list.

4. Click the OK button to return to the Define Fields dialog box. Click on the Done button to return to your layout.

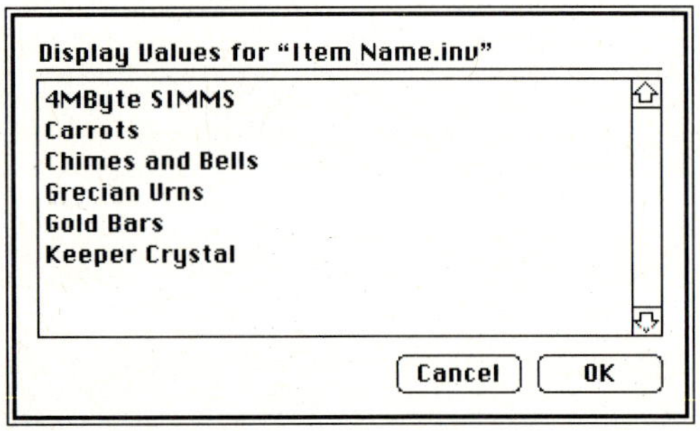

Fig. 8.19
Setting a list of values for a field.

Entering Data

You still need to make changes to help you when you enter data. First, you need to create a set of records so that the Full Name field has the name of all your customers in the field and so that the lookup works properly. Also, you can control the order in which you fill out fields by setting a new tab order. Finally, you should check that your fields operate properly by entering some dummy records.

To fill the Full Name field with the names of all your customers, follow these steps:

1. Switch to the second layout in the file by clicking on the top page of the Book or dragging the Slide Control Mechanism. The second layout is the columnar report layout shown in figure 8.20, which contains eight records.

Fig 8.20
The columnar report layout.

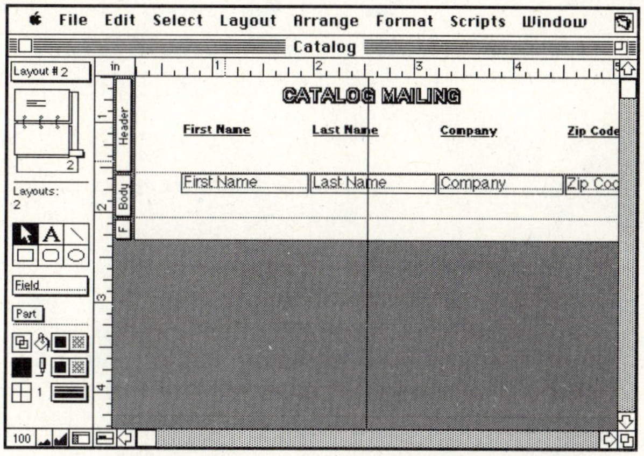

2. Choose the Browse command on the Edit menu or press ⌘-B to open the Browse window as a list.
3. Click on the first record in the window (any entry).
4. Select the Duplicate Record command from the Edit menu or press ⌘-D.
5. Click on the second record in the list (any entry) and repeat step 4.

   Continue creating duplicate records for all the remaining records (numbers three through eight). When finished, you will have 16 records. If you had established a lookup in another file, you wouldn't have to duplicate these records. The lookup would be properly established at the time of field definition.
6. Choose the Layout command or press ⌘-L to return to the layout window.
7. Click the bottom corner of the Book to make the invoice form your current layout. The invoice layout is layout number 3.

You can control the order and selection of fields to be entered by changing the tab order (see Chapter 5). This order selects fields in the order they occur from left to right, then top to bottom. The top edge of a field reshape box is considered the top boundary of the field; the left edge is the left boundary.

To check that your invoice performs correctly, you need to enter data for a couple of records.

To enter data, follow these steps:

1. Choose the Browse command on the Edit menu or press ⌘-B.
2. Create a record by selecting the New Record command from the Edit menu or by pressing the ⌘-N keystroke.

   Notice that FileMaker has entered today's date in the Date.inv field and the invoice number in the Invoice #.inv fields. Because you created eight new records, and now a ninth, FileMaker entered `108` into the invoice field. Also, the current field is now the first field in the tab order, the First Name.inv field. Examine the tab order by tabbing through the fields. Return to the First Name.inv field when you are finished.
3. Enter *Frost* into the First.Name.inv field. Then press the Tab key to advance to the Last Name.inv field.
4. Enter *Heaves* into the Last Name.inv field. Press the Tab key.

   FileMaker auto-enters all the remaining fields in the MAIL TO label when you advance to the Company field.
5. Tab through the label until you get to the first Item Name.inv field. A list of values (items) appears (see fig. 8.21).
6. Double-click on the item Grecian Urns to enter the item into the field and advance to the Item Cost.inv field.
7. Enter the price *39.95* in the Item Cost.inv field. Press the Tab key.
8. Enter the quantity *3* in the Quantity.inv field. Press the Tab key. You are advanced to the second line of the Item Name.inv field.
9. Double-click on the item Keeper Crystal to enter the item into the field. You can scroll the list or type the first few letters (*Kee*) to bring Keeper Crystal into view.
10. Enter the price *99.95* in the Item Cost.inv field and then press the Tab key.

11. Enter the quantity *1* in the Quantity.inv field. The result is shown in figure 8.22.

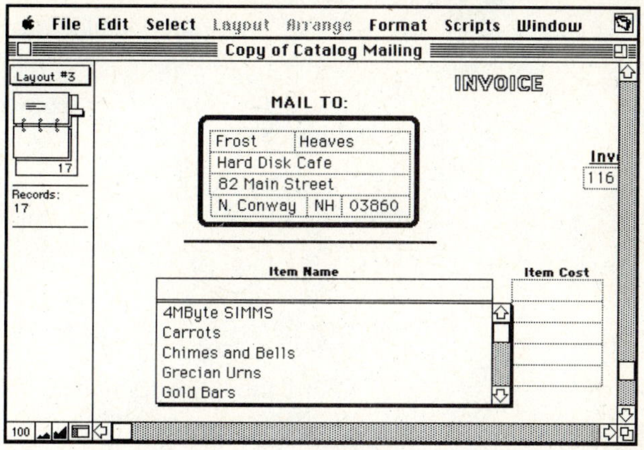

Fig. 8.21
The display values dialog box for the Item Name.inv field.

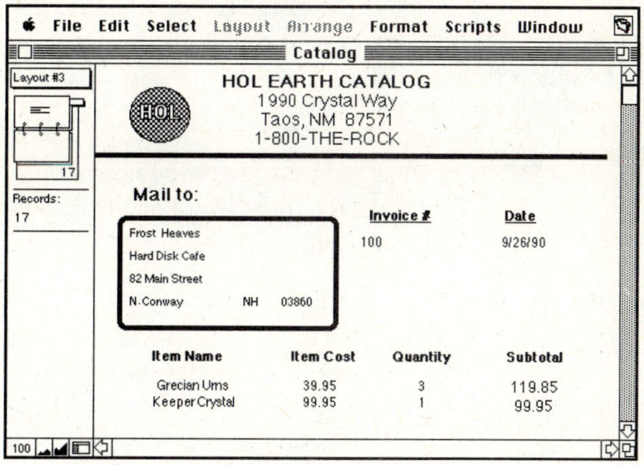

Fig. 8.22
The entered data in the first invoice form.

Frost Heaves now has his order! You might want to scroll the window to look at the Grand Total.inv field to see that FileMaker calculated the sum. The field has a total, but the field is not formatted correctly. The total only shows one decimal place. The sum would look better if the sum displayed a dollar sign and was aligned properly. Likewise, the Subtotal.inv and the Item Cost.inv fields would look better.

To format a field's data, follow these steps:

1. Choose the Layout command or press ⌘-L to return to the Layout window.

2. With the Arrow tool highlighted, select the Item Cost.inv, Subtotal.inv, and Grand Total.inv fields.

3. Select the Number Format command on the Format menu or double-click on any one of the fields. In the Number Format dialog box, make these choices:

   Click the Format as Decimal Number radio button.

   Click the Use Thousands Separator, Notations, and Fixed Number of Decimal Digits check boxes.

   Enter *2* in the text box.

   Click the Currency button (if needed).

The completed Number Format dialog box appears as in figure 8.23.

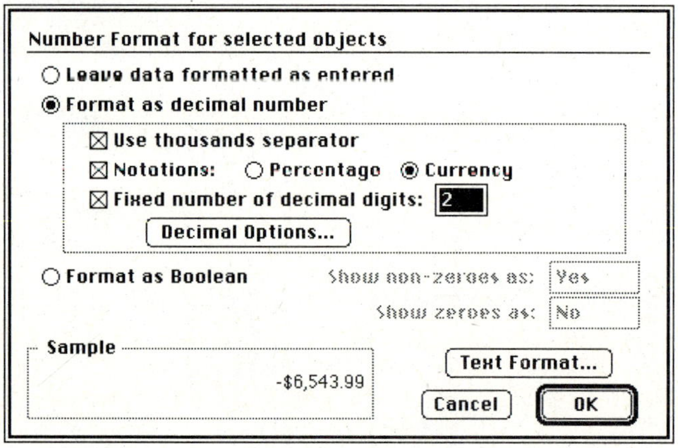

Fig. 8.23
The Number Format setting for your dollar Number fields.

4. Click on the Text Format button in the Number Format dialog box.

5. Select the Right command from the pop-up menu under the Alignment option.

   This choice right-aligns your text.

6. Click the OK button to return to the layout.

7. Select the Quantity.inv field.

8. Select the Center command from the Align Text submenu on the Format menu or press ⌘-Shift-C.

   When you return to the Browse screen, all those fields look more professional (see fig. 8.24).

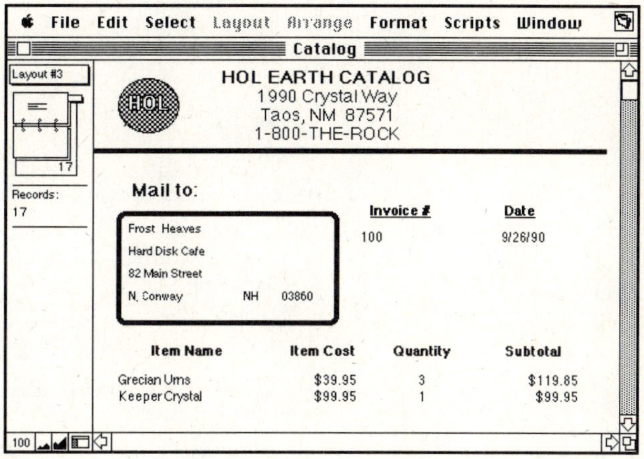

Fig. 8.24
The completed first invoice.

9. Choose the Browse command from the Select menu or press ⌘-B.

   Enter another record or two on your own. Santa Claus just called and ordered some bells and chimes. He also wanted those 4 MByte SIMMS for good children with Macs.

Working from a Prepared Form

Sometimes you might need to use the data in your FileMaker file to enter data onto a prepared form (see fig. 8.25). This task is not as difficult as you might think. You need to know only where all the fields will be placed, how big their reshape boxes must be, and how to place existing fields onto a layout by using the Field tool. This section shows you how to carry out these tasks.

In figure 8.26, you see a statement form for the Hol Earth Catalog. Usually, you will want a separate file for this type of form, but for the sake of brevity you can use the same file and invoice forms you have just defined for this exercise. The approach uses a ruler to measure position on the form and the T-square to place the fields accurately.

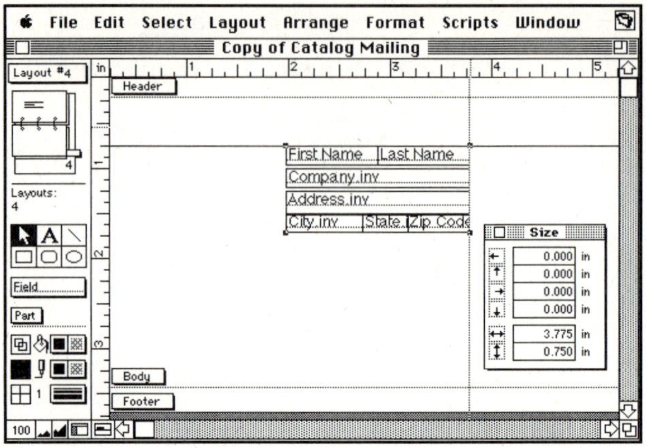

Fig. 8.25
An existing commercially made form.

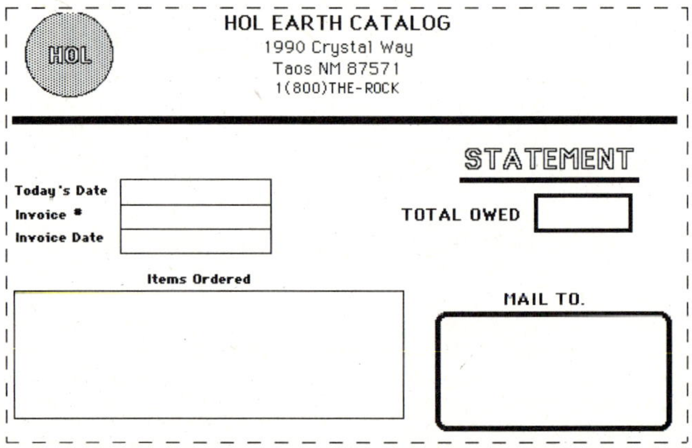

Fig. 8.26
The statement form for the Hol Earth Catalog.

To place fields onto an existing form, follow these steps:

1. In the Layout window, select the New Layout command from the Edit menu or press the ⌘-N keystroke.
2. Click the Blank Layout radio button in the Create a Layout dialog box and then click the OK button.
3. Drag the header part handle into the title bar of the window to remove the header part.
4. Drag the footer part handle into the body part to remove the footer part.

5. Select the Page Setup command from the File menu to set the size of your form.

   Most forms are on standard width paper, such as 8 1/2 inches wide. For this exercise, the form is 8 inches wide. An ImageWriter printer is still selected, so the standard margins are 1/2 inch.

6. In the Edit Page Sizes portion of the dialog box, enter the following settings:

   Type *Statement Form* into the Name text box.

   Type *8.000* into the Width text box.

   Type *4.500* into the Height text box.

7. Click the No Gaps Between Pages check box so that the option is on. Click the OK button to return to your layout.

8. Use the Book or Slide Control Mechanism to return to the invoice form you created in the preceding section.

9. With the Arrow tool highlighted, select all the fields in the MAIL TO label.

10. Choose the Group command from the Arrange menu.

    This step keeps all the label parts together and makes it easier to rearrange the position. When you move one part, the entire group of parts moves together.

    If you find you need to edit any one of the parts later, you need to select the Ungroup command from the Arrange menu.

11. Select the Copy command from the Edit menu or press ⌘-C to place those fields on the Clipboard.

12. Return to your statement form layout and select the Paste command from the Edit menu or press the ⌘-V keystroke.

13. Select the T-square command from the Layout menu; position the T-square so that the vertical position is at 3.750" from the top, and the horizontal position is at 5.000" from the left. Use the Size box indicators to help you place the T-square. This is the position of the customer label fields.

14. Drag the body part handle so that the body part is at, or below, the 5.500" vertical position on the layout.

15. With the Arrow tool highlighted, drag the group of label fields so that they are positioned as shown in figure 8.27.

You have just learned one technique for moving fields onto a layout—the Clipboard (see Chapter 7). Try using this technique to move the Item Names.inv field (a repeating field with five repetitions) from the invoice form layout to the statement form layout. You need to set the T-square to 3.750" vertical and 0.750" horizontal. You also can place fields directly by using the Field tool (see Chapter 6).

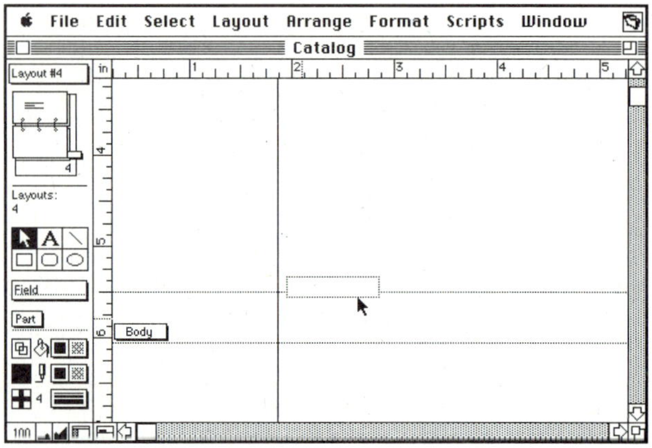

Fig. 8.27
Positioning pasted fields to the T-square.

To place a field directly on a layout, follow these steps:

1. While on the statement form layout, set the T-square to 1.750" horizontal, 2.750" vertical.

2. Click on the Field tool in the status area and drag a field outline onto the layout so that the field outline snaps to the T-square.

3. Double-click on the Invoice #.inv field name in the scroll box shown in figure 8.28.

   or

   Click once and then click the OK button or press the Return key.

You can try to place additional fields by using the techniques in the preceding three steps. For Invoice Date, use the Date.inv field and set the T-square to 1.750" horizontal, 2.875" vertical. For Total Owed, use the Grand Total.inv field and set the T-square to 6.000" horizontal and 2.750" vertical. For Today's Date, you might want to practice creating a field with the auto-entry set to today's date, as you learned earlier. Set the T-square to 1.750" horizontal, 2.375" vertical. Figure 8.27 shows placement against the T-square.

Fig. 8.28
Selecting a field to place on a layout.

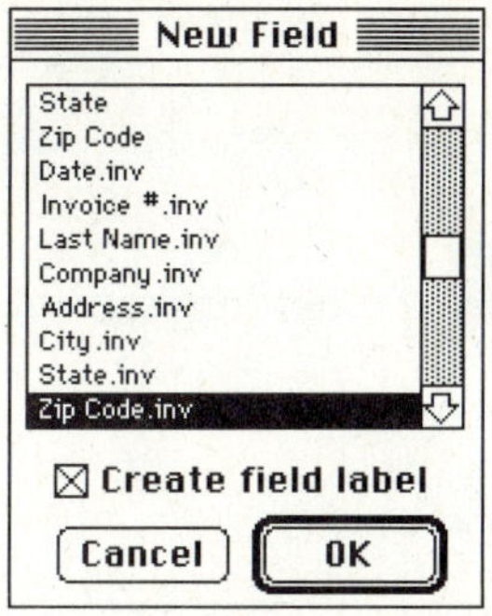

If you have a scanner and know how to operate it, try the following approach.

To use a form as a template, follow these steps:

1. Repeat steps 1 through 7 of the procedure to place fields onto an existing form.
2. Scan the image of the form shown in figure 8.25.
3. Import the file as a PICT (preferred) or TIFF file into a paint program like MacPaint 2.0, SuperPaint II, or Canvas.
4. Clean up the form a little so that you can clearly see where each of the fields is to be placed.
5. Copy the form as a picture to the Clipboard, using the Copy command from the Edit menu (⌘-C) in your paint program.
6. In FileMaker, select the Paste command from the Edit menu or press ⌘-V to place the form as a picture on your layout.
7. Place the fields onto the layout and resize them as needed, as you learned in the preceding set of instructions.
8. When finished, click the Arrow tool select the picture of the form and then press the Delete key.

Notice that this approach enables you to insert fields without worrying about where you should place them on the layout. Drag the field boxes to the appropriate place above the form and reshape the field boxes as needed. When you are finished, the picture of the form is gone. This approach is particularly good for a complex form.

Printing

Check to see that you set up your forms correctly. Often you cannot judge by looking at a form, particularly if your screen is smaller than the form itself and you have to scroll around. You always can preview your form (see Chapter 10) to see whether all the data looks correct. The reduced view gives you a pretty good idea of the overall quality of any form you create. To be on the safe side, in this section you print your statement form and check to see that all the fields line up properly.

To print your statement form, follow these steps:

1. Choose the Browse command from the Select window or press ⌘-B.
2. Turn on your ImageWriter and insert paper (if needed).

   Select the Chooser desk accessory from the Apple menu and click on your printer's icon before printing.
3. Select the Print command from the File menu or press ⌘-P.
4. In the Print dialog box, select the following:

   Click the Blank Record radio button.

   Click the Boxes radio button.

   Refer to figure 8.29 for the settings for an ImageWriter.
5. Click the OK button to initiate printing.

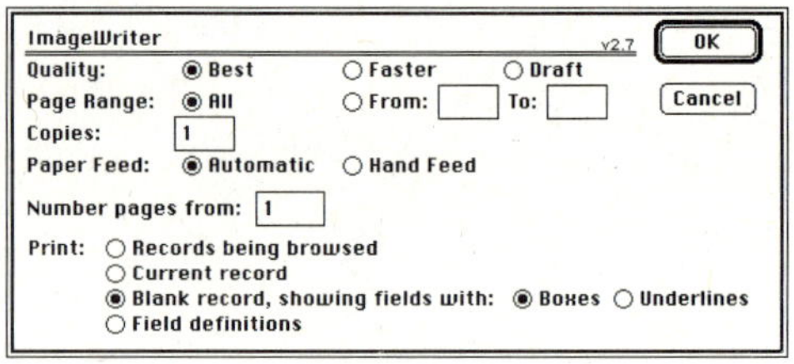

Fig. 8.29
Printing field boxes to check for position.

Compare the printed form to figure 8.25 to check that the field boxes match up properly. If you like, practice printing a few records or try printing your invoice form. To print a set of browsed records, you first need to perform a find operation. Refer to the first Quick Start or Chapter 4 for details. Chapter 10 contains detailed printing information.

PART III

Printing

Includes

USING FILEMAKER PRO

CHAPTER 9

Preparing To Print

You use parts on a layout to control where information appears on a Browse window or on the printed page. The first part of the printing preparation process involves using the Layout window to control where items appear. This chapter focuses on understanding the relationship between parts and the printed page. You learn how to place, rearrange, remove, and resize parts to achieve your goals. You also learn how fields behave when placed in specific parts. Chapter 9 is an extension of topics relating to layouts that you learned about in Part II.

Some other specialized layout tools are described in this chapter as well. FileMaker offers a Slide Objects command for eliminating blank fields, spaces, or parts. This command is valuable in printing any repeating layout objects, such as fields or parts. Using the Slide Objects command cleans up printed matter, such as letters, labels, directories, or any other project for which you use FileMaker.

To aid you in setting up a printed page, FileMaker offers options for placing layout objects, options that will print page numbers, the time, the date, and record numbers on the page. Although they are specialized layout text objects, their placement affects not only where on the page they occur but also how they operate. This chapter explains how to create and place these elements.

Understanding the Relationship of Parts to Pages

All FileMaker layouts use a device called a part to control what you see on your Browse window and what gets printed on a page. A part is a section of a layout, and each layout must contain at least one part.

You have complete control over the parts on your layout. You can add a part using the Part tool (see Chapter 7). You can remove a part (see "Creating and Deleting Parts" later in this chapter). You also can change a part's size individually (see "Changing Part Sizes" later in this chapter) or relative to the part below it so that you can fit more or less information on a page.

You can make some parts, such as sub-summary parts, repeat any number of times on a page. Other parts, like headers and footers, occur once a page; still other parts, such as title headers and title footers, occur only once on the first page of a report. Additionally, FileMaker offers summary parts—the sub-summary and grand summary parts. All parts are described in detail in the sections that follow.

To summarize the relationship of parts on a layout to a page, remember these points:

- Title header and title footer parts print once on the title (first) page at the top (header) or bottom (footer).
- Header and footer parts print once at the top (header) or bottom (footer) on each page, except the title page, when title parts are defined.
- Sub-summary parts above the body print once for each category of values in the sorted field on which the part is based. Below the body, they print below each category. By specifying a column style in the Layout Options dialog box that is available from the Layout menu, you can break for a new page or a new column after each category.
- Grand summary parts above the body print once before all records. Grand summary parts below the body print once after all records.
- Body parts print once for each record, up to the limit of the page size; then a new page begins, until the last record is printed for a list layout. Individual layouts produce separate pages for each body part.

- A specified print job is called a *report* in database terminology, and a report can be one page long or several pages long. Remember, a report usually is the output of more than one record, and a form uses one record only. Consider the layout in figure 9.1 and the figure's associated output shown in figure 9.2. A header and a footer occur at the top and bottom of the page. Each record is a body part, and several of them print. Because a sub-summary part is placed below the body part on the layout, the sub-summary parts print after each body part. The grand summary is placed directly above the footer and prints just once, after all records have been printed.

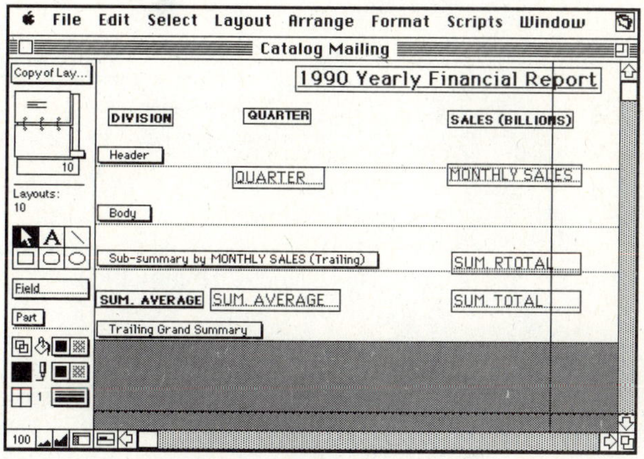

Fig. 9.1
A layout for an annual report.

Body Parts

A body part is displayed and printed once for each record. Any unit of information you want to appear for each record must be placed in a body part.

Headers and Footers

You can use headers and footers to set the top and bottom sections on every page. You can create blank headers (or make part of the header blank) to set the margins. Dates, page numbers, or the time often are placed in the headers and footers. Headers are particularly useful for storing company or personal letterheads.

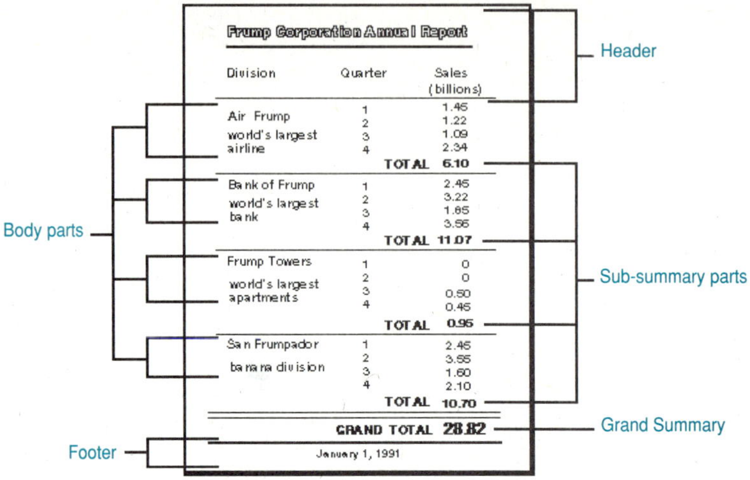

Fig. 9.2
The printed form of an annual report.

You see each record individually and the body part appears once, unless you use the View as List command on the Select menu. In the latter case, the body part becomes a repeating unit, fitting as many body parts on a page as possible. Changing the body size changes the space accorded each record. Any space before or after a body separates one record from the next. You don't always need to have a body part, but if you don't have one, you don't see a record's data in the display or output.

Title Headers and Footers

Use title headers when you want a special set of headers, footers, or both to appear on the first page of your printout. You can incorporate both title headers and footers on the same layout as regular headers and footers to achieve a title page. Title headers appear at the top of a layout; title footers appear at the very bottom of a layout.

Usually, you will want to place the report title, name and address information, and dates in the title header. Often, the title header is a good place to store an attractive graphic to introduce a reader to the subject. Use layout text objects to achieve these goals. Use the // date layout object, for example, if you want to print the date. If you want to print the time, use the :: time stamp layout object.

To print a report with no records on the first page, use a second layout with a blank body part. Make sure that you print page numbers in the second layout, indicating in the Print dialog box that you want to start with page number 2. The first layout is for the title page, and the second layout is for the first page of the report.

Sub-Summary Parts

A sub-summary part summarizes a group of records using a field you specify. For a sub-summary part to work properly, you need to sort the records by the dependent field. Every time a value in that field changes, a new sub-summary part is placed on the layout.

Consider, for example, a sales record for a company of sales representatives. You can define a sub-summary part that is dependent on a Month field. When you sort that field, you get a sub-summary part appearing for each group of monthly records.

You also can place a sub-summary part on your layout that is dependent on a Salesperson field and sort both the Month and Salesperson fields. Consider the simple columnar report layout with two sub-summary parts and one grand summary part (see fig. 9.3). To sort the fields, you place the Month field first (at the top of the list) in the sort order, then the Salesperson field. You then will get a sub-summary part not only when the value in the month field changes, but every time the value in the Salesperson changes each month (see fig. 9.4). Maybe you want to know how your sales break down by item each month—the process is exactly the same.

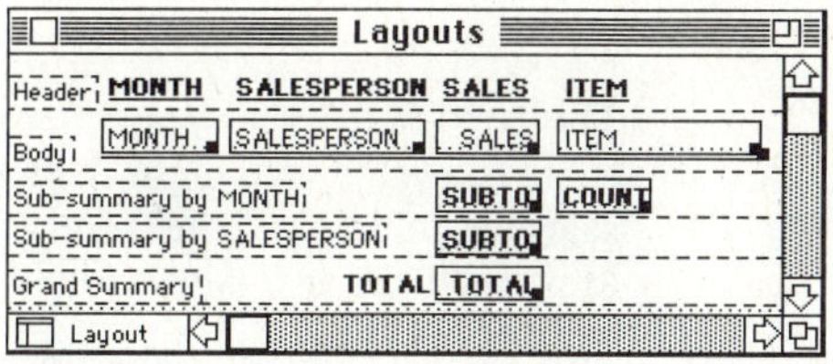

Fig. 9.3
A columnar report with summary parts and summary fields.

Note that the sub-summary parts do not show if you are using a layout as a list. You see sub-summary parts only in the Preview window or in printed output.

Fig. 9.4
The sorted records in the Preview window showing all summary parts and fields.

MONTH	SALESPERSON	SALES	ITEM
February	Carol	$13	Carrots
February	Carol	$15	Fruit & Nuts
February	Carol	$125	4 MByte SIMMS
		$153	
February	Gina	$50	Crystal
		$50	
February	Shirley	$20	Grecian Urns
		$20	
February	Thelma	$5	Hol Milk
		$5	
		$228	**6**
January	Gina	$30	Chimes & Bells
January	Gina	$12	Hol Wheat Bread
January	Gina	$295	Gold Bricks
		$337	
January	Shirley	$295	Gold Bars
		$295	
		$632	**4**
	TOTAL	**$860**	

You can place only summary fields and text labels in sub-summary parts. Date, Time, Text, and calculation fields placed in sub-summary parts display in the Preview window but do not print. Summary fields summarize the records that you now have sorted and broken up into groups (see Chapter 5 for a discussion of summary fields). You can have any number of summary fields in a particular sub-summary part, and FileMaker has no limit to the number of sub-summary parts. In fact, the only penalty you pay is file speed, because summary fields are calculated fields, not intrinsic data in your file.

Consider the summary fields in the two sub-summary parts in figure 9.4. The Total field in the sub-summary by Salesperson part occurs whenever there is a value change in the Salesperson field; that is, for every set of salesperson's sales. FileMaker totals the Sales field, and the part occurs as many times as a new salesperson appears in the month.

That same Total field, when placed in the sub-summary by Month field, totals the Sales field for the group of records defined by each of the two months shown, so even though the Total field has the same definition, the placement of the field in each of the two sub-summary parts leads to a different action. The Count field counts the number of item entries in each month. Each of the two sub-summary by Month parts appears only twice. The Total field in the grand summary part totals the Sales field for all records.

What happens if you don't use a layout that is displayed as a list? Figure 9.5 shows the same layout that was used in figure 9.3. Now, even when you don't sort the records, the parts appear in the Browse window. And when you do sort them, the summary fields appear and function properly. Compare what you see in each window in figure 9.5 with what you obtained in figure 9.4.

Fig. 9.5
The Browse window of records sorted and unsorted in a layout that displays individual records.

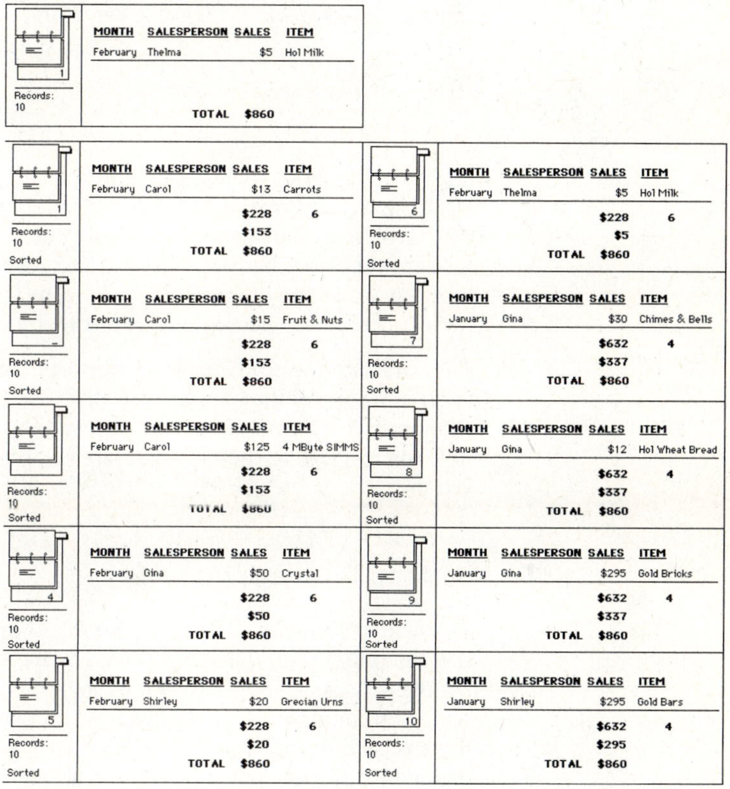

Grand Summaries

A grand summary part is placed before or after the body part and summarizes all records. Regardless of where they're placed, any summary fields in grand summary parts summarize the entire group of records that you are browsing. The summary can be all records, a group of found records, or a single record. The sorted order makes no difference. In figure 9.4, the Total field in the grand summary part always appears, and the Total field always shows the same value. Had a find operation selected some of the ten records in those examples, the value in the Total field would have changed.

A summary field placed in a grand summary part always is displayed in the Browse and Preview windows. The field also is printed. Notice in the preceding examples that the same summary field added to both the grand summary and sub-summary parts yields an overall view and a category breakdown, both at the same time.

Manipulating Parts

In Chapter 6, you saw how the Part tool is used to place a part on a layout and how to specify different part types. Depending on where in the layout you drag the new part outline, FileMaker restricts the parts that you can create to parts that are appropriate to that location. You can add parts at any time, as you see fit. You also can remove and resize parts; the sections that follow show you how.

The part identification labels are now selectable. Parts are easily manipulated by dragging the part label or dividing line while holding down the Command key. Part labels can be moved out of the way into a vertical position by clicking the new part label icon (next to the left scroll arrow).

Creating and Deleting Parts

To create a part, click on the Part tool and drag an outline of the part handle to the desired height on the layout. Although the new part handle is constrained to the left edge of the layout, your arrow cursor is not—you can drag the part border where you want it. When you release the mouse button, you are prompted to make a selection in the New Part dialog box. If you change your mind about creating the part while you are dragging the outline, drag the outline off the window. If you change your mind after the dialog box is displayed, click the Cancel button to dismiss the dialog box.

You remove parts by dragging them into the part above them one at a time. You cannot, however, remove the last part on a layout. To remove a part, follow these steps:

1. In the Layout window, select the Arrow tool by clicking on the tool. Your cursor is an arrow.

2. Select the part label and press the Delete key.
3. A dialog box appears and asks whether you really want to delete the part. Select the Delete button.

   or

   Choose the Cancel button to go back without deleting the part.

If you change your mind about removing a part, use the Undo command from the Edit menu or press ⌘-Z to restore the removed part.

When a part contains objects, you can press the Option key before you drag the part so that the objects remain in the same location on the layout. This feature does not work for the bottom part. The bottom part must be empty to be removed.

You can replace a part by creating a part in exactly the same location as the part being replaced.

Changing Part Sizes

The overall size of parts (the combination of all their sizes) determines how many records you can fit onto a layout and how much space is reserved for headers and footers. You can change the size of parts to allow additional space for more fields, larger graphics, more records, and so on.

You change the size of parts by dragging them up or down, either using the part handle or the boundary of the part. You can change a part size individually, leaving all other part sizes unchanged. By pressing the Option key, you can change the size of the part relative to the part below. Pressing the Option key and dragging leaves the sum of the height of both parts the same; the resized part either takes from or adds to the size of the part below, depending on the direction of your drag.

To resize a part, follow these steps:

1. In the Layout window, click the Arrow tool.
2. Click on either the part handle or the part's boundary to drag the part to the desired location.

You can use the T-square to position a part exactly. Because the T-square is magnetic, the part snaps to the T-square.

Press the Option key before dragging the part either to resize the part relative to the part below or to move the part boundary through any objects on the layout.

If you change your mind about resizing a part, use the Undo command from the Edit menu or press ⌘-Z to restore the part to its previous size.

Holding down the Option key resizes a part and leaves the objects that the boundary traverses in the same location on the layout. This feature can be useful when you want to include an object in one part and not another. Remember that the top edge of an object defines which part that object is included in. To see the edges of layout text, use the Show Text Boundaries command. If you do not hold down the Option key, you cannot move a part boundary past any object; that is, the object blocks movement of the part boundary.

Changing Part Sizes To Set Margins

Most Macintosh programs offer a set of options within the Page Setup dialog box to control page margins, so you may be surprised to learn that FileMaker doesn't offer these settings. FileMaker uses the minimum margins your current printer offers as the margin settings, and you are expected to work with these. Remember that you change printers from the Chooser DA (see Chapter 10 for details). You do, however, have control of margins by changing your layout to incorporate blank space at the top, bottom, right, and left.

FileMaker marks the printable area of a layout by placing a solid vertical line for the right edge and a dashed horizontal line for the bottom edge. These lines do not show the edges of the paper, rather they delineate the printable edges—that is, they show you where the margins are. If a body is too large to fit on a page, the horizontal dashed line shows you where the body will be split. These lines are shown in figure 9.6.

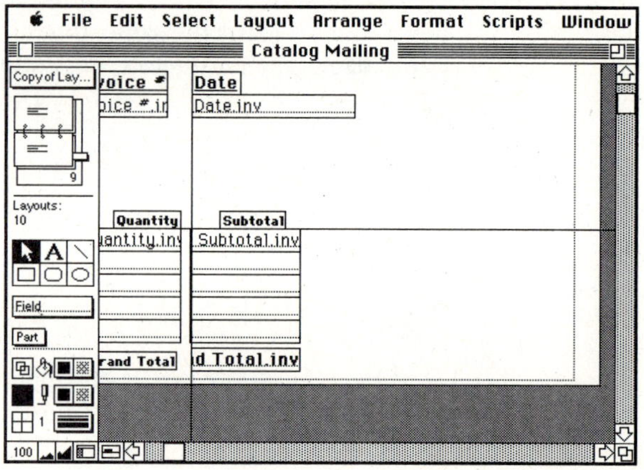

Fig. 9.6
The page boundaries.

From the Layout menu, choose Non-Printable Area from the Show submenu. A dotted line marks the nonprintable area (margins).

When you select an object, the upper four measurements in the size box indicate the object's position relative to the edge of the page. Thus, the T-square measurements now show the distance from the top and left edges of the page rather than the edges of the printable area.

If you have only body, header, or footer parts, follow these steps to set a top and bottom margin:

1. Change the body portion of the layout so that the body portion is a page height or the page height minus the height of the headers and footers.

   You change the body by resizing the body parts, which is done by dragging the boundary. Page height is what you have in page setup. To see what fits on a page, preview it.

2. Move all objects on the body down for the top margin and up for the bottom margin. If you don't move the objects, you cannot resize the part.

To set a top or bottom margin, you can use a blank header or footer part. Use the Slide Objects option to slide up blank parts and then include an object of any kind in the header or footer in the nonprinting area. Because sub-summary and grand summary parts print after header, footer, and body parts are printed, you do not need to worry about them for the purpose of top and bottom margins. Remember, to adjust part sizes, use the Option key to move past objects or first move the objects themselves.

To set a right and left margin, adjust all objects on all parts so that they do not print beyond the margins you desire.

Tip

Remember that you can use the T-square and size box to locate positions from the top and left edges of the paper sizes you choose.

To print a long, multipage form, use a single body that is the same number of pages as the form. FileMaker places horizontal dashed lines at the end of each page, and you can use these as guides for placement of objects. You can place any object you want to go on the first page above the first dashed line; place the ones to go on the second page above the second dashed line; and so on. The Preview command from the Select menu is helpful to visualize how this works.

If you are using the T-square to adjust the horizontal positions of an object on a page and you go below the first page, you must subtract the page height plus each additional margin you add. For ImageWriters, page 2 requires subtraction of 11.25 inches and page 3 requires subtraction of 22.75 inches, because the margins are 0.25 inches each.

When setting up a layout, any object within the printable area prints and can be previewed. You can place objects on a layout outside the printable area, however, and this capability is useful for several purposes. Fields that are to be used only for sorting, indexing, or finding records can be placed outside the printable area. You also can use a field outside the printable area as a scroll guide. Get into the habit of using the Preview command from the Select menu (⌘-U) to examine your output before printing or to check quickly the results of changes you have made on a layout.

Enhancing Output

FileMaker offers some special layout options that can enhance the appearance of your output. These options include a Slide Objects feature for removing blank spaces and parts, and some additional layout objects for placing page numbers, the current date, current time, and record number on your printed page.

Removing Blank Spaces

If you want to see all the data in a field, you need to make the field as large as the largest field entry. Otherwise, the entry is truncated. In some cases, you will want each record to appear in exactly the same amount of space. By not choosing to slide parts up when blank, each record is the same size.

Most often you will want to close up the open space and fill it with additional data. With mailing labels, for example, you want all the blank spaces in fields to close up and all the blank fields to be ignored. Using the Sliding Objects command under Show from the Layout menu, you can remove unwanted spaces or blank fields or parts.

To remove blank spaces, follow these steps:

1. In the Layout window, choose Show from the Layout menu. Select the Sliding Objects command from the submenu.

2. Highlight all the fields you want affected. Choose Select All under Edit or press ⌘-A, if desired. Next, choose Slide Objects from the Arrange menu.

3. In the Slide Objects dialog box (see fig. 9.7) check the type of slide action you want. You can select any combination.

Sliding Left. Using this option removes all blank spaces in a field that is left-aligned and moves the field that is on the same line flush with the field. For fields to slide left, they all must have their top edges aligned at the same level. If a field is blank, the space is closed up by the field to the left. Pictures, lines, rectangles, ovals, Picture fields, multiple line Text fields, and right- and center-aligned fields do not slide left.

Sliding Up Based on All Above. Blank fields are removed when you choose this option, and the fields below the blank fields are moved up to fill the space.

Sliding Up Based on Only Directly Above. This option is enabled only when the Sliding Objects Up option is checked. Check this option if you want different sized parts when you remove blank lines. Header and footer parts (including title ones) do not slide up; they preserve the margins.

4. Click the OK button or press the Return key.

If you change your mind, click the Cancel button or press ⌘-. (period) to dismiss the dialog box and retain your previous settings.

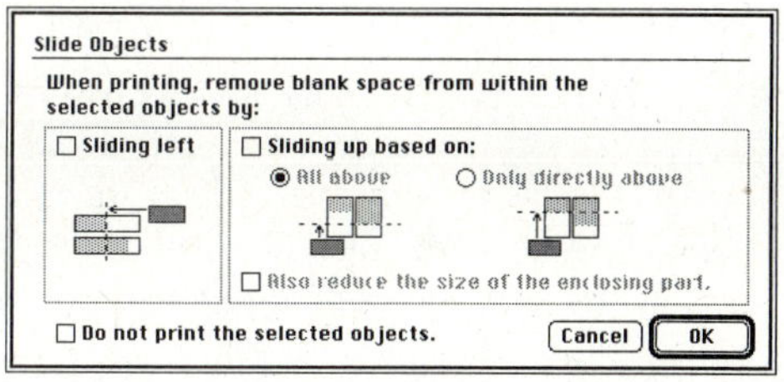

Fig. 9.7
The Slide Objects dialog box.

When you select a Slide Objects option, FileMaker check marks the option in the Show command submenu on the Layout menu and remembers the setting for each layout. Also, repeating fields are treated like individual separate fields for the purposes of slide options. You can remove or change the Slide Objects option by clicking off all settings or adding or removing settings of your choice. To check the effects of the Slide Objects command, preview or print the file.

When objects slide left to fill in a blank field, they fill in all white space, including any spaces between the objects.

For examples of the effects of the different slide options, refer to figures 9.8 through 9.10. Notice that in figure 9.10 the lines separating each record move up when the Sliding Objects Up option is chosen.

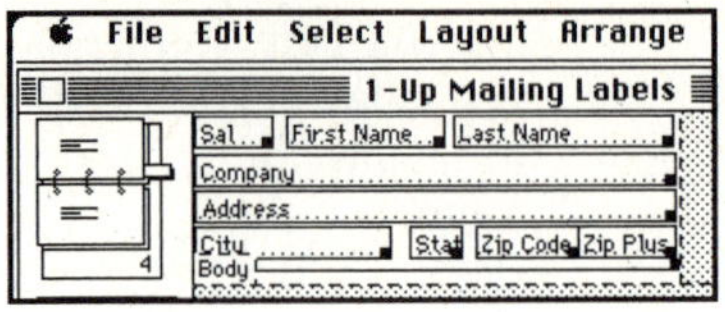

Fig. 9.8
The current layout.

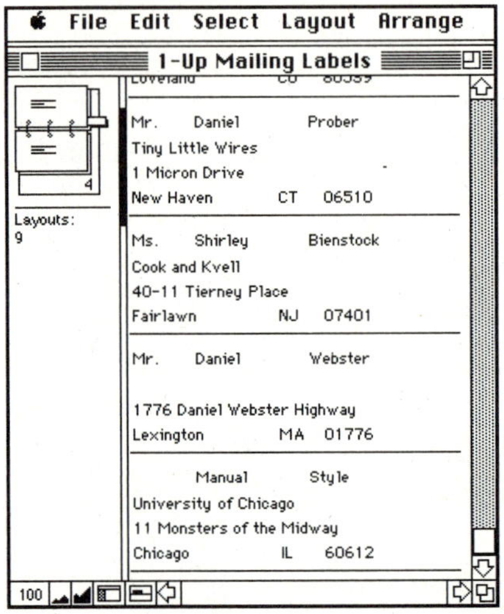

Fig. 9.9
Without using the Slide Objects options, records print as they appear.

Some of the new features of the Slide Objects command in FileMaker Pro include the capability to select individual objects to slide, to slide different objects in different directions, to reduce the size of the part, and to designate objects as nonprinting.

When using the option Sliding Left, you can prevent fields from closing up by formatting them as either right- or center-aligned.

Note

Slide Objects was found on the Gadgets menu in FileMaker II; it is now on the Arrange menu.

Adding Time, Date, and Page Numbers

FileMaker provides a means for specifying page numbers, record numbers, current time, and current date. These elements are specified by symbols typed as layout text. To use these elements, type any of the symbols as a text object. These symbols do not need to be their own text objects; FileMaker recognizes them within any text string that makes up a text object. Use the T-square to place objects accurately on a layout.

Fig. 9.10
Using Sliding Object Up removes a blank line and space between fields.

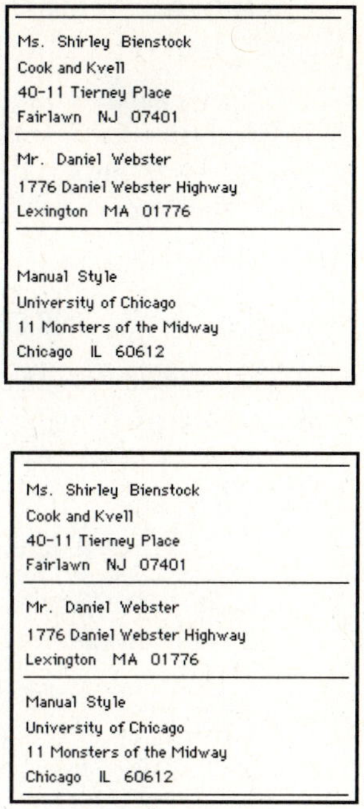

Placing the Page Number on a Layout

Multipage documents benefit from the use of page numbers. FileMaker uses a special layout text object (##) as a placeholder to assign the position of a page number. You can format this page number as you would any text object.

To place the page number on a layout, follow these steps:

1. Click on the Text tool and click an insertion point where you want the page number to be placed.
2. Type the symbol ## (two number signs) within that text object. Or, choose Paste Special from the Edit menu and then select Page Number from the submenu.

   If you type - ## - on your layout, you will see — 1 — in the Browse window or on your printout.
3. Use the Format menu Font, Size, Style, and Align Text options to format the page number.

Optional: In the Print dialog box, enter the starting page number in the Number Pages From text box. The number 1 is the default.

This option enables you to use FileMaker output as pages in the middle of a report or a document created in another application. Chapter 15 explains how to import data from other programs and how to export data to other programs.

Placing the Current Date on a Layout

Multipage documents also can benefit from including the date. FileMaker uses a special layout text object (//) as a placeholder to assign the position of the date. You can format the date as you would any text object.

To place the current date on a layout, follow these steps:

1. Click on the Text tool and click an insertion point where you want the current date to be placed.
2. Type the symbol // (two slashes) within that text object. Or, choose Paste Special from the Edit menu and then select Current Date or Date Symbol from the submenu.
3. Use the Format menu Font, Size, Style, and Align Text options to format the those aspects of the date.
4. Use the Date Format command from the Format menu to format the date ("7/25/22" or "July 25, 1922," for example).

FileMaker uses the date set in your Control Panel and defaults to an unformatted date. You will see a date style such as `August 27, 1991` on your Browse window or printout. You can change this format to any of the allowed date formats: short, medium, long, and so on (see Chapter 6).

Do not confuse the date layout object (//) with the date stamp keystroke ⌘- (hyphen). The former displays the current date (today's date), and the latter displays the date when you pressed the keystroke. Sometimes you can use the Today function in a calculation field in place of the // text object. The Today function is discussed in Chapter 5.

Placing the Current Time on a Layout

Your documents also may benefit from inserting the current time. FileMaker uses a special layout text object (::) as a placeholder to assign the position of the current time. You can format the current time as you would any text object.

To place the current time on your layout, follow these steps:

1. Click on the Arrow tool and click an insertion point where you want the current time to be placed.
2. Type the symbol :: (two colons) within that text object. Or, choose Paste Special from the Edit menu and then select Current Time or Time Symbol from the submenu.
3. Use the Format menu Font, Size, Style, and Align Text options to format the current time.
4. Use the Time Format command from the Format menu to format other aspects of the time.

FileMaker uses the time set in your Control Panel and displays the time in the form `3:54 PM`. You cannot see the current time on your Browse window, only in the Preview window or on printed output.

Placing the Record Number on a Layout

You can place a record number on a layout, too. FileMaker uses a special layout text object (@@) as a placeholder to assign the position of the record number. You can format the record number as you would any text object.

To place the record number on a layout, follow these steps:

1. Click on the Text tool and click an insertion point where you want the record number to be placed.
2. Type the symbol @@ (two "at" signs) within that text object. Or, choose Paste Special from the Edit menu and then select Record Number from the submenu.
3. Use the Format menu Font, Size, Style, and Align Text options to format the record number.
4. Use the Number Format command from the Format menu to format the record number.

You can see record numbers only in the Preview window or on printed output. FileMaker numbers each record in a browsed set in their found or sorted order. Depending on where you place a record number sign, you can achieve different effects. If you place a symbol in the body, each record is numbered consecutively. If you place a symbol in the header, the first record number on that page appears on each page of output. Similarly, placing the symbol in the footer of a layout displays the record number of the last record on the page.

In Review

To print a report, whether a single page or several pages, you need to set up the pages on a layout and then specify how you want the pages printed. Layouts, through the use of parts and layout objects, offer you several essential printing options.

A part is a device that controls what you see displayed and printed. Headers and footers control top and bottom margins; title parts occur once on the first page and displace any normal headers and footers. Body parts print or display once per record in sequence for a list or on a separate page when viewed individually. Sub-summary parts print when a field value changes for a group of records; grand summary parts are printed and displayed for all records.

The edges of the printable area on a layout are set by the printer you selected in the Chooser DA. You can set additional top and bottom margins through the use of headers and footers. You can set additional left and right margins by moving objects on the layout to achieve the necessary white space. You can choose either to show the nonprintable area, or to show only the printable area. These choices affect what you see in your position location in the size box.

To remove blank spaces in left-aligned fields, use the Slide Objects command to slide objects left. The Sliding Objects Up option removes blank fields and, if check marked, also enables you to set an option to remove blank parts from a layout. The Sliding Parts Up option resizes parts to remove blank space. These Slide Objects options are useful for creating attractive output with the maximum amount of data on a page, or for creating more attractive mailing labels.

By placing special symbols as layout text objects, you can add date, time, record numbers, and page numbers to your printed output. Within a text object, type // for the date, :: for the time, @@ for the record number, and ## for the page number. The Paste Special command from the Edit menu also enables you to insert record numbers, times, dates, and page numbers automatically.

CHAPTER 10

Printing Basics

Building on concepts you learned in Chapters 6 through 9, this chapter assumes that you have set up your layout correctly and are ready to print. You learn how to preview output in the Preview window, use the print options available through the Print command, print to an ImageWriter or LaserWriter, and print mailing labels. Chapter 11 (Quick Start), provides detailed step-by-step instructions for printing mailing labels.

Reviewing the Printing Process

FileMaker prints output using the current layout and the set of records that you are browsing. You can print all the records you are browsing, or just the current record. To specify a print file, follow these steps:

1. Choose your printer and output port from the Chooser desk accessory in the Apple menu.
2. Switch to the layout you want to print.
3. Organize your records into the group you want to print by finding and sorting them, if necessary.

   or

If you want to print a single record, make that record the current record. If you want to use a blank record, any record with the desired layout can be the current record.

4. Select the Page Setup command from the File menu and choose a setting for the paper size.

   FileMaker defaults to US Letter size. If you need another size, or a custom size, consult "Setting Paper Sizes" later in this chapter.

5. Choose any additional options and click OK.

   The Page Setup dialog box is set by the printer or other output device driver that you place in your system file, and it may differ from printer to printer. Options are discussed in the sections called "Setting Up the Page," "Printing on an ImageWriter," and "Printing on a LaserWriter," elsewhere in this chapter.

6. Select the Preview command from the Select menu or press ⌘-U to open the Preview window and view your output. Refer to "Previewing Output," later in this chapter, for details.

7. Select the Print command from the File menu or press ⌘-P. To accept your previous settings and bypass the dialog box, press ⌘-Option-P.

The Print dialog box offers four important options that are discussed in detail in the "Printing" section later in this chapter.

To cancel printing while in progress, press ⌘-. (period) while the ⌘-. cursor symbol is on-screen.

FileMaker tells you how many pages are being printed and how many pages are left to print and updates the numbers as needed. If you print a large database regularly, you may want to use Backgrounder, the background printing utility that Apple supplies with your system software (for LaserWriters), or a dedicated print spooler, such as SuperLaserSpool. Print spoolers work by creating a print file on disk and lining up the files to be printed in a print queue. As one print job is completed, the next one is sent to the appropriate printer. To use Backgrounder, MultiFinder and Apple Talk must be active; therefore, you need one of the AppleTalk-capable LaserWriters. Most networks, such as TOPS, offer a print spooler utility built into the network. Consult your network documentation for details.

The following sections discuss options you can set when you select the Print command.

Selecting Your Printer

When you first print a layout, you must specify your printer (or output device). FileMaker can output QuickDraw print commands (the standard Macintosh graphics drawing language), and these commands can be interpreted to PostScript, the page description language of most laser printers. As long as you can see an icon for your output device in the Chooser DA, you know that the device driver file has been placed into your System folder.

If you have ever set up a boot disk or installed new system software, you may have noticed all the icons that look like and have the same name as your printer. These icons represent device driver files. A device driver is a program that interprets print commands for your specific printer. Additionally, if you are using a laser printer or are on a network, you need to have all the appropriate network files, which also are device drivers, in your system folder. The Macintosh comes with a built-in network called AppleTalk, which enables you to connect printers and other Macintoshes to your own computer. You cannot actually connect to a LaserWriter without using AppleTalk for the connection, and if you have an ImageWriter on an AppleTalk network, you need to choose the AppleTalk button first and then the AppleTalk ImageWriter icon in the Chooser window. Make sure that you have the correct printer driver files and network files (if needed).

To choose a printer, follow these steps:

1. Select the Chooser DA from the Apple menu, as shown in figure 10.1.

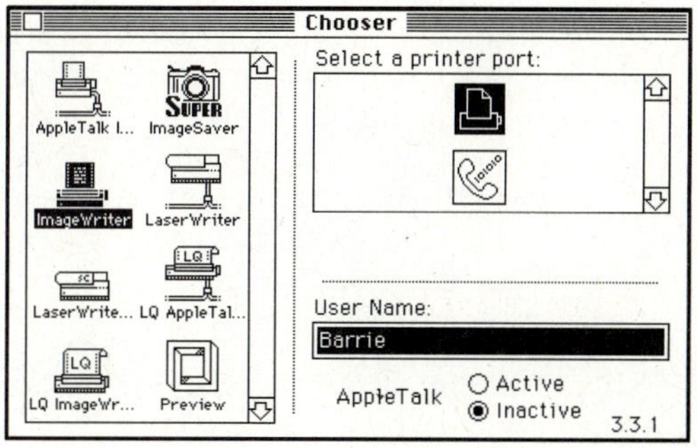

Fig. 10.1
The Chooser DA.

2. Click the icon in the left scroll box for the output device that you want.

   or

   If your printer is on a network, click the icon for the network device driver. If the printer is on an AppleTalk network, just select the printer driver. If the printer is connected to a server (and not your computer), then select the server so that you can print and hope that the server has the correct software to enable you to print your document.

3. Click the printer port in the top right scroll bar.

   When you are on a network, the printer port scroll box changes to indicate the structure of the network and the choices you need to make. You may be prompted with additional dialog boxes and choices, some asking for passwords. Consult your network manager or documentation for details.

4. Click the AppleTalk Active radio button, if needed. (You need to use AppleTalk if you are using a LaserWriter or PostScript device, or if your computer is on a network.) Your Macintosh may prompt you to turn AppleTalk on or off or to switch output ports.

5. Enter your name in the User Name text box.

6. Click the Close box on the Chooser window to dismiss the Chooser.

Setting Up the Page

The options you can specify in a print file are determined by the capabilities of your printer. Printers have different minimum margins, font settings, smoothing options, scaling (sizing), and so on. This section covers the general options offered in the Page Setup dialog boxes for the Apple printer known as the LaserWriter SC. The specific Page Setup dialog boxes for the ImageWriter and for the LaserWriter NT and NTX are discussed in "Printing on an ImageWriter" and "Printing on a LaserWriter," respectively.

Figure 10.2 shows the Page Setup command on the File menu, for the LaserWriter SC that is current to Systems 6.0.x. The LaserWriter SC is a QuickDraw laser printer that does not contain a PostScript interpreter, as most other laser printers do, so it is considerably cheaper than other Apple LaserWriters (NT and NTX). Apple's plan to enhance QuickDraw as an output format, however, makes it a viable option for a printer purchase. Other laser printers in this category are the General Computer Personal Laser Printer (PLP) and Hewlett-Packard LaserJets (for which PostScript cartridges are available). Apple's Personal LaserWriter comes with or without PostScript and is highly regarded, as is Texas Instrument's PS17 PostScript laser printer. One other QuickDraw printer, highly regarded, which delivers 300-dpi resolution at near ImageWriter prices, is the Hewlett-Packard DeskWriter, which uses quiet inkjet technology to achieve these results.

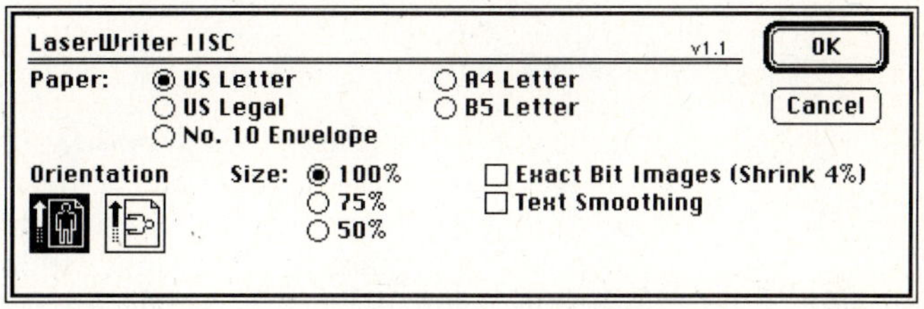

Fig. 10.2
The Page Setup dialog box for the LaserWriter II SC.

With any printer, you set the paper size (type) by clicking the appropriate radio button in the Page Setup dialog box. Additionally, you can create a custom paper size in the Paper Sizes dialog box for certain printers, such as the ImageWriter. When you enter a custom size, that choice appears in the Page Setup dialog box, replacing any previous selection. If you have selected the Envelope (#10) button and then enter a new custom paper size, for example, the new size replaces the Envelope (#10) radio button.

All printers offer the choice of portrait or landscape orientation. Portrait orientation is the normal, vertical printing mode; you select this orientation by clicking on the standing man icon. Landscape orientation is the horizontal printing mode; you select it by clicking on the sleeping man icon.

Most printers also offer scaling options that enable you to reduce or enlarge proportionately the picture size on printed output. Font scaling works well with PostScript printers, but fonts often scale poorly with QuickDraw printers using Systems 5 and 6, because the resolution used for the font is 72 dpi and not the 300 dpi of laser printers. System 7 with its system of outline fonts, which are described by mathematical equations and so enlarge and reduce well, is expected to improve font scaling dramatically for QuickDraw printers.

Finally, laser printers support special smoothing options to improve line quality and the correlation between screen and print images. Dot-matrix printers can support continuous-feed paper and No Gaps Between Pages options. For details on your printer's capabilities, consult your printer manual.

FileMaker stores in memory the settings you specified in the most recent Page Setup dialog box. Chapter 12 explains how you can embed the page setup options as part of a script.

Setting Paper Sizes

Only dot-matrix printers can support variable page sizes (the ImageWriter II, for example) and activate the Edit Paper Sizes command under the Page Setup command on the File menu. When specifying a page size, you make your selection within the Edit Paper Sizes portion of the Page Setup dialog box (see fig. 10.3). You also can create a customized output to replace whatever has been selected in the Page Setup dialog box. One example of when you might need to create a custom paper size is when you are using a custom form or label.

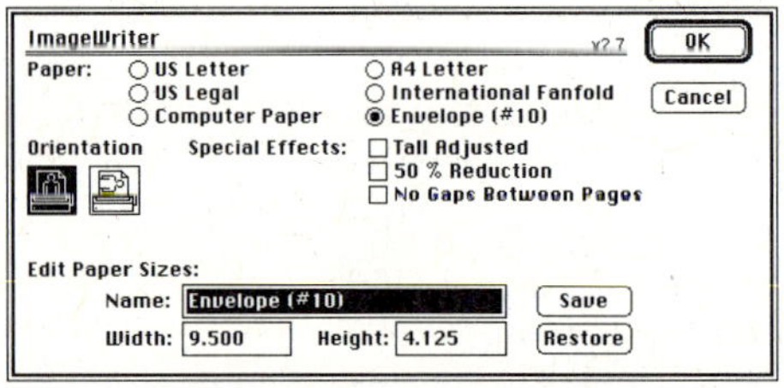

Fig. 10.3
The Page Setup dialog box for an Imagewriter printer.

Printers that do not support variable page sizes (such as the LaserWriter series) do not enable the Edit Paper Sizes command. In other words, you cannot choose this portion of the Page Setup dialog box.

To set a custom paper size, follow these steps:

1. Select a printer in the Chooser DA that supports a variable page size.

2. Select the Page Setup command and either click on one of the choices (e.g., Envelope) or enter the following information in the dialog box:

- The name of the custom size in the Name text box
- The width of the paper in inches in the Width text box
- The height of the paper in inches in the Height text box

Press the Tab key to move from box to box.

3. Click the OK button to create the custom size you specified.

   or

   If you change your mind, click Cancel.

The height for labels is measured from the top of one label to the top of the next; width is measured from the left edge of one label to the left edge of the next. For paper, the page height setting can eject a page or advance to the same position on the next sheet of continuous-feed paper; it indicates the end of your page. Additionally, although U.S. versions of FileMaker use inches as the default measurement preference, foreign versions may use metric measurements. Paper sizes are restricted to any set of dimensions from 1 inch square up to 36 inches square.

Previewing Output

Before you print, you need to organize your browsed records, set up the desired layout, specify the page size, and set any additional page setup options. Previewing your output to see how it will look when printed is always a good idea.

Some parts and fields may not appear in the preview because they are placed off the printable area, and the actual size of elements on the layout is almost always different from the size they appear to be on your layout. Imagining how all parts of a file will be placed, how they will repeat, and whether they are all the correct size can be difficult. File-Maker gives you some guides to help you determine the answers to these questions, such as the boundary markers in the Layout window that show the sizing of the part and page margin lines that show the printable area. The preview mode helps you visualize how your output will look.

To display your data to get a clearer view of how the repetitive units are arranged, use the Preview window, which displays exactly what your printer will print. You should use the Preview window when setting up your layout and when preparing to print.

To preview your output, follow these steps:

1. Select the Chooser DA and click the output device or printer you want to use.
2. From either the Browse or the Layout window, select the Preview command on the Select menu or press ⌘-U.
3. Examine the page by scrolling the window. If you have more than one page, click the Book page numbers to go to the display of the next printed page. Or, enter a page number in the Page Number text box and click the Page button to go to that page.
4. To exit, choose Browse or Layout from the Select menu.

Figure 10.4 shows a Preview window.

The Zoom feature is new to FileMaker Pro. The zoom control is located in the lower left corner and may be used to reduce or enlarge the Preview window. The zoom range is from 25% to 400%.

Fig. 10.4
The Preview window.

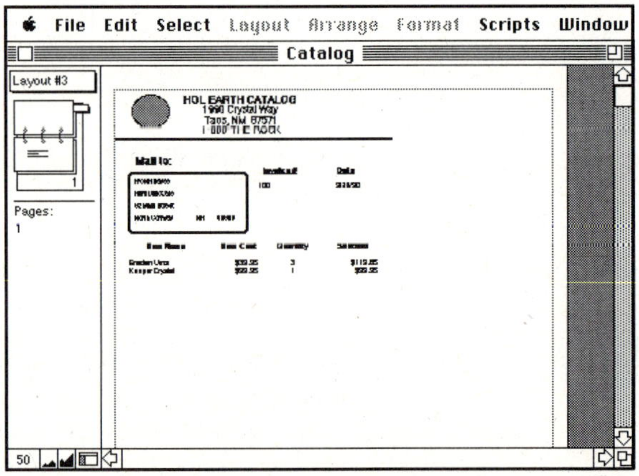

⌘-U, the Preview command, displays the Preview window.

Printing

After you have previewed your file, you are ready to print. To print, select Print from the File menu or press ⌘-P. FileMaker displays a dialog box that enables you to set a number of options. If you are satisfied with your previous print settings, you can bypass the Print dialog box by pressing ⌘-Option-P.

SPEED KEY

⌘-P, the Print command, prints a file you specify, using the options you set.

⌘-Option-P, the Print command, prints a file, bypassing the Print dialog box and using the choices previously set.

Typical settings for all printers enable you to make selections for print quality, page range, number of copies, and type of paper feed. Each printer driver changes the FileMaker Print dialog box, and you need to consult your printer manual for detailed information regarding some of these settings, such as how print quality and print resolution—normally measured in dots per inch (dpi) or lines per inch (lpi)—are achieved. Some options are specific to FileMaker and deserve further discussion here.

A word about print resolution: the dpi measurement indicates the number of elements, or dots, that a printer can print in one inch. For a dot-matrix printer, that is the number of tiny wires that hit the ribbon. For an inkjet printer, it is the size of the inkjet that hits the paper. Dot-matrix printers average about 120 dpi, although some dot-matrix printers (the 24-pin variety) can produce a higher resolution. Inkjet printers often match laser printers in print density (300 dpi), although some laser printers are beginning to go beyond the 300 dpi rating. Fancy imagesetters (professional typesetters) can go up to 2500 dpi. The other measurement mentioned, lpi, is an alternate term that describes how many lines a printer can print in an inch. A newspaper uses about 70 lpi; a glossy magazine might use 150-180 lpi.

Figure 10.5 shows the Print dialog box for the LaserWriter SC. Refer to the sections on "Printing on an ImageWriter" and "Printing on a LaserWriter" for details on the ImageWriter II and the LaserWriter NT and NTX, respectively.

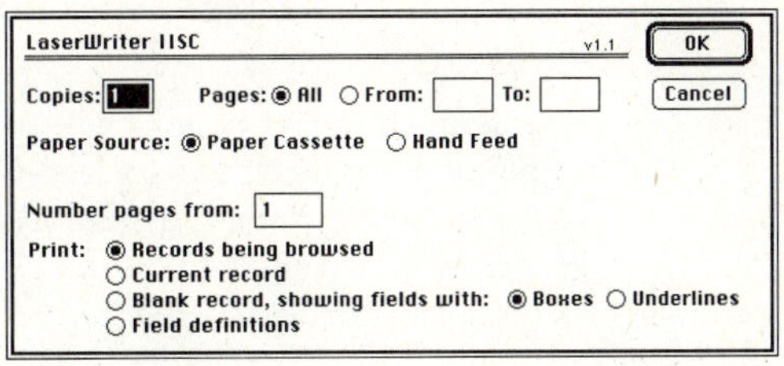

Fig. 10.5
The Print dialog box for the LaserWriter SC.

The following is a summary of some of the features available in the Print dialog box shown:

Quality. Best, Faster, and Draft are modes used by impact printers that affect printer speed and quality, or resolution. Best is the highest quality output but the slowest speed, and Draft is the fastest speed but the lowest quality; Faster falls in between them. LaserWriter printers print to their maximum resolution and are not adjustable. Draft gives you the standard single strike font built into the ImageWriter. Your output will look nothing like your screen, and you will get no graphics. (This option, therefore, does not appear in figure 10.5.)

Pages. This setting enables you to specify a range of pages within a FileMaker file. The page count is affected by the size and the number of the records you browse. Use All to print the entire set of records or use the From and To text boxes to fill in the range of pages you want to print.

Number Pages From. This text box enables you to enter a page number, other than 1 (the default), to begin numbering your pages. Page numbers are placed on your output where the layout text symbol ## was entered.

Print. These four options offer different ways of using your browsed set of data, current record, or layout.

Records Being Browsed. Your current set of records are printed in the order they occur.

Current Record. Only the record on your screen prints, even if you are browsing additional records.

Blank Record, Showing Fields With. Creates a form with each field either boxed or underlined.

Field Definitions. All fields are printed, along with their names, types, and all entry options you have defined.

These Print dialog box options are discussed in detail in the sections that follow.

Filling in a range of pages enables you to print just a part of your browsed set without having to omit records. This option works particularly well when you are using records as individual pages; for example, as forms. You then can continue using all the records in your browsed set later in your work session.

You also can print from the Finder, but this method is rarely the best choice. FileMaker uses the last layout you used before you closed the file to print your data. For this option to be useful, you should know which layout you used last; you also must print all records in the file, all blank records, or all field definitions. When you specify the current record, FileMaker prints the first record in the file regardless of the last browsed record you saw before you closed the file.

To print from the Finder, follow these steps:

1. Click the icon of the FileMaker file you want to print.
2. Select the Print command from the File menu. Your Macintosh launches FileMaker and displays the Print dialog box.
3. Select the options you want to use and then click the OK button or press the Return or Enter key.

Printing Records

You can print all records in a file, all records in a browsed set, or only the current record. When you print a set of records, FileMaker uses the order of the selected records to create the print job. In this manner, you can create reports, summaries, and entire directories.

To print an entire file, follow these steps:

1. Open the file. If it is open, then close it and open it again. By closing the file and then reopening it, you see all the records. An alternative is to use the Find All command, which is a quicker method.
2. Select the Find All command from the Select menu or press ⌘-J to browse all records.
3. Select the file from the Finder and print it from the Finder.
4. Specify the Print Records Being Browsed selection in the Print dialog box. Click OK or press Return.

To print all browsed records, follow these steps:

1. Use the Find command to select all desired records.
2. Sort the records, if needed. Otherwise, FileMaker prints them in their natural record order.
3. In the Browse window, use the Omit command to refine your browsed set.
4. Select the Print command (⌘-P) from the File menu.
5. In the Print dialog box, specify the Print Records Being Browsed selection. Click OK or press Return.

In some cases, you can refine your browsed set by printing only a range of pages, as the preceding section explains.

Printing a current record is useful for filling out a form such as a statement or invoice for your business. You print a single record by opening it on your screen. You do not have to find, sort, or omit records to browse and print a single record.

Printing a single record is the best way to make sure that your file is operating correctly. You can make sure that all objects are in the correct location and that all fields and parts are operating correctly. You may be able to identify problems by looking at the Preview window, but getting an overall view is difficult, especially when you are working on a 9-inch Macintosh screen.

Printing a single record is recommended for ensuring that your file is operating properly before you commit to a substantial print job. Specify the Current Record option in the Print dialog box.

Printing Blank Records

You can use FileMaker to print a blank record with all fields boxed or underlined. Use this option when you need to create a blank form. You do not have to draw lines or boxes; FileMaker does it for you, but you can add extra drawn objects on the layout. If you are keeping a purchase order file, you can create forms to distribute to your purchasing agents for them to fill out before entering the data into FileMaker. Or, you can quickly create a small note paper for your secretary (or your boss) for telephone messages.

Figure 10.6 shows how a mailing label layout is transformed into a printed mailing label with the Boxes or Underlined Fields options for printing a blank record. Underlines are drawn from the extreme left edge of the left field on a line to the extreme right edge of the right field on the same line, and all intervening spaces are filled in (this is true only when fields are aligned on exactly the same bottom line). Field boxes are printed true to their location, but with a slight space between fields. All lines are 1 point wide.

If you need modest forms backed up by a substantial database, use FileMaker. If you need to generate professional-quality forms on the Macintosh, you should investigate PostScript draw programs, such as Adobe Illustrator 88 or Aldus Freehand; page layout programs, such as Aldus PageMaker; or more specialized packages made especially for forms, such as SmartForm Designer, TrueForms, FastForms (a good, low-cost solution), or InFormed Designer (a good, high-end solution).

Fig. 10.6
A mailing label layout printed as a blank record with fields boxed and underlined.

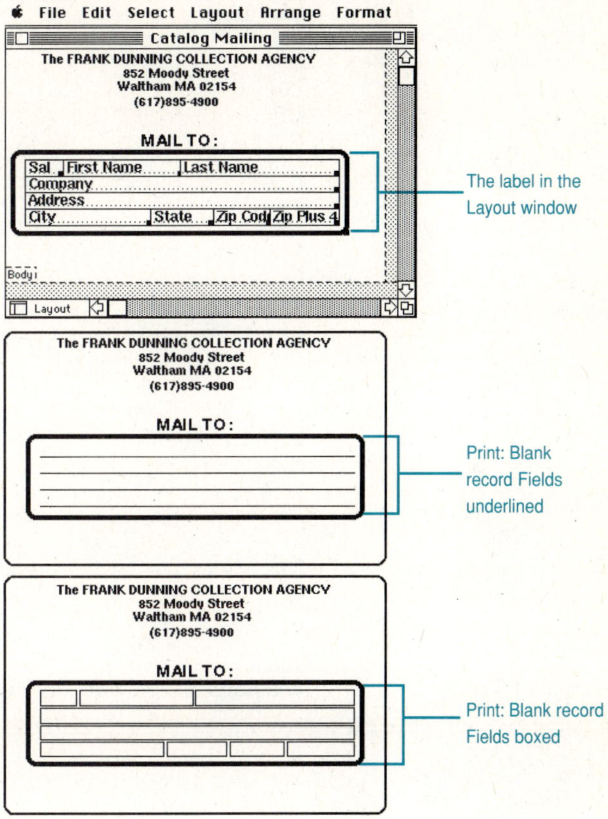

Printing Field Definitions

You also can print a list of your field definitions. Along with the field names, you can display their data types (or attributes), any calculation or summary formulas you have defined, and any specified entry options. You should print this list for every file you have. From the overall view of your fields, you can see whether you have made any little mistakes. All fields are listed, including any problems that FileMaker has flagged (with an error message) in the field definition.

You cannot preview the field definitions, only print them. Figure 10.7, a printout of the field definitions for the invoice form you created in Quick Start 2 (Chapter 8), is shown here as an example.

Field Name	Field Type	Formula / Entry Option
First Name	Text	
Last Name	Text	
Company	Text	
Address	Text	
City	Text	
State	Text	
Zip Code	Text	
Date.inv	Date	Auto-enter today's date
Invoice #.inv	Number	Auto-enter serial number: 116
First Name.inv	Text	
Last Name.inv	Text	
Company.inv	Text	Lookup: "Company" in Copy of Catalog Mailing" when "Full Name.inv" matches "Full Name"
Address.inv	Text	Lookup: "Address" in Copy of Catalog Mailing" when "Full Name.inv" matches "Full Name"
City.inv	Text	Lookup: "City" in Copy of Catalog Mailing" when "Full Name.inv" matches "Full Name"
State.inv	Text	Lookup: "State" in Copy of Catalog Mailing" when "Full Name.inv" matches "Full Name"
Zip Code.inv	Text	Lookup: "Zip Code" in Copy of Catalog Mailing" when "Full Name.inv" matches "Full Name"
Full Name	Calculation (Text)	= First Name & Last Name
Full Name.inv	Calculation (Text)	= First Name.inv & Last Name.inv
Item Name.inv	Text	List: 4MByte SIMMS Carrots Chimes and Bells Grecian Urns Gold Bars Keeper Crystal
Item Cost.inv	Number	
Quantity Inv.	Number	
Subtotal.inv	Calculation (Number)	= Item Cost * Quantity.inv
Grand Total.inv	Calculation (Number)	= sum (Subtotal.inv)

January 18, 1991 Copy of Catalog Mailing

Fig. 10.7
The printed listing of all the field definitions for the invoice form created in Quick Start 2.

Printing on an ImageWriter

The ImageWriter II is a medium-resolution dot-matrix printer that uses a Toshiba print engine; it is assembled and sold by Apple. (An engine is the mechanism that advances the paper and marks it in the right places.) Best Draft is about 78 dpi. An impact printer, the ImageWriter uses pins to strike a ribbon, which transfers the image to the paper, making the printer suitable for printing multipart forms. The ImageWriter is a QuickDraw printer. In Systems 5 and 6, QuickDraw required installed bit-mapped fonts at the size you specified to deliver good output, or a font twice as large as a substitute. Installing outline fonts by using Adobe Type Manager and the promised outline fonts in System 7 dramatically improves the quality of the ImageWriter's output by mathematically scaling the type to size.

You must have an ImageWriter printer driver in your system folder; if you plan to use your printer on an AppleTalk network, you need the AppleTalk ImageWriter driver as well, and a special hardware connection. You need a cable and a board that is installed in your ImageWriter II or LQ printer. The earlier models cannot support this option. You do not need the LocalTalk system connector if you are connecting just one computer and one printer. These drivers appear in the Chooser when they are installed. System 6 does not include a print spooler for background printing for an ImageWriter. You may need to purchase a print spooler such as SuperLaserSpool if you want this feature.

Figure 10.8 shows the Print dialog boxes for the ImageWriter. The ImageWriter II allows output of any length and any width, up to the size of its carriage. You therefore can set a custom paper size by using the procedure discussed earlier in "Setting Paper Sizes." Paper can be fed one sheet at a time by using a sheet feeder mechanism that you can purchase separately from Apple, or you can use continuous-feed paper for automatic feeding. Generally, automatic feeding works best for long print jobs, but the sheet feeder is convenient for letterhead stationery. With continuous-feed paper, you can select the No Gaps Between Pages option, but make sure that you have left enough space for the top and bottom margins. Using the No Gaps Between Pages option causes the printer to print to the end of a page and then immediately start printing a new page. Printing with gaps ejects the page.

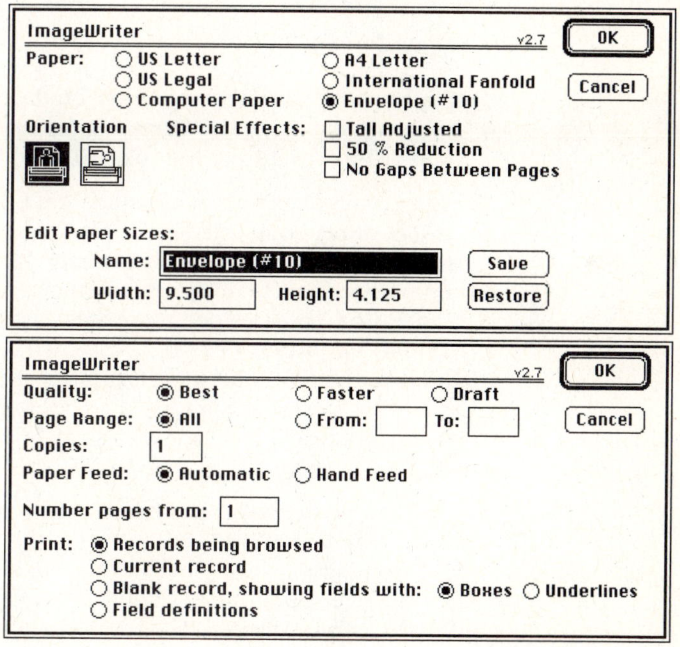

Fig. 10.8
The ImageWriter Page Setup and Print dialog boxes.

You can improve the quality of your output by using good quality stock and properly inked ribbons. For users with heavy print volume, the MacInker ribbon re-inker by Computer Friends is economical. Even new ribbons benefit greatly from this treatment, and each ribbon can be used many times over for pennies' worth of ink.

The ImageWriter provides some special effects that you set in the Page Setup dialog box. The 50% Reduction option enables you to fit additional data onto one page of output. This option gives you half-sized output, but for bit-mapped fonts it results in some distortion as well. The scaling is much better for outline fonts. Normally, scaling ImageWriter output does not result in clean output (unlike the LaserWriter series). The Tall Adjusted option enables the ImageWriter to correlate better with images on your Macintosh screen at 72 dpi by scaling it around 4 percent. This correlation is usually most useful for picture output only.

Printing on a LaserWriter

The LaserWriter series uses a Canon print engine and is assembled by Apple. LaserWriters use a laser beam to place a magnetized image on a rotating drum. Ink in the form of toner (plastic particles) is attracted to the image on the magnetized drum. As the paper rolls over the drum, the image is transferred to the paper with a resolution of 300 dpi. A fuser uses heat to bond the ink to the paper.

The various LaserWriters have different embedded instruction sets (on ROMs, or read-only memory chips) inside the printer and on memory options. LaserWriters are like miniature computers; they contain a microprocessor and memory, and they do a certain amount of their own processing, primarily defining page descriptions. The LaserWriter SC is a QuickDraw printer without a PostScript interpreter chip inside the printer. The NT model adds PostScript and is network-ready; the NTX, a highly regarded laser printer, provides additional features that also make it network-ready. You can upgrade an SC to an NT, and an NT to an NTX.

The LaserWriter requires a LaserWriter printer driver in the system folder. When this printer driver is installed, it appears in the Chooser DA. You must have AppleTalk connected to your printer to print to a LaserWriter, and if you use another network, AppleTalk connects to that network. This connection is not needed for the LaserWriter II SC. Refer to your printer and network manuals for further details. You can use the background printing feature of the System software in Version 6 to spool print files to a LaserWriter, but much better versions of print spoolers, such as SuperLaserSpool, are available.

Figure 10.9 shows the Print dialog boxes for the LaserWriter NT or NTX. You cannot set a custom size page for a LaserWriter. Choose paper sizes from the choices offered in the Page Setup dialog box. Remember that laser output requires at least 0.5-inch margins on all sides, so plan accordingly.

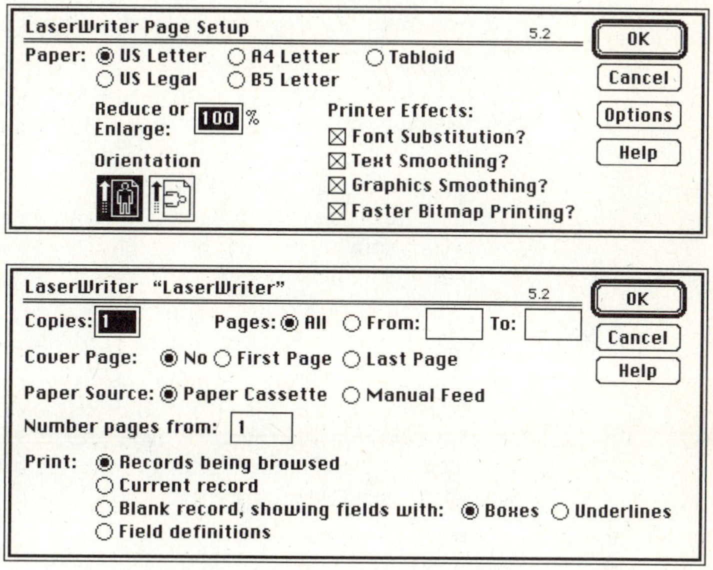

Fig. 10.9
The LaserWriter Page Setup and Print dialog boxes.

This Page Setup dialog box offers some options specific to LaserWriters. You can enter any number you want in the Reduce or Enlarge text box, and the LaserWriter NT and NTX generally give excellent results, scaling your graphic to the size you specified. PostScript fonts and graphics are mathematically described, object-oriented graphics and scale well, as opposed to bit maps, which scale properly only at restricted size multiples. Furthermore, a set of Printer Effects are turned on as the default. A LaserWriter substitutes fonts, for instance, when it cannot find in its memory or on the computer's hard drive the font you specify in your layout. Some smoothing functions and a faster bit-mapped printing option that are available are useful but not important. For further details, consult your printer manual.

Using Other Types of Printers

A print technology similar to laser printing, based on liquid crystal shutters, offers superior quality output. The original printer in this class was the CrystalPrint printer; the same technology is now offered by about half a dozen other manufacturers. You also can get laser-quality resolution from the Hewlett-Packard DeskJet inkjet printer. PostScript interpreters, such as Freedom of the Press—software packages you can buy—are now on the market and offer the possibility of adding PostScript to a printer without a hardware upgrade. You may want to look into these options, especially if cost is a factor.

You can create what amounts to a printed disk file of your database file by using a print-to-disk utility, the best of which is SuperGlue II. This program takes your print file from FileMaker and converts it to a disk file. You can use SuperGlue II to get around the proliferation of various graphics formats (PICT, EPS, TIFF, and so on) because it captures all these formats and enables you to view and work with them. SuperGlue II is compatible with color images and works on all Macintoshes, from the Macintosh Plus up.

SuperGlue II also is singularly useful for large databases, because text and numbers can be extracted as ASCII characters, which is the basic data structure microcomputers use. You can take the numbers or text from the file you created and find, extract, and dump them into any other Macintosh program. What's important is that you can create a file either as a graphics image or as a text file with various delimiters (characters that separate data entries).

Printing Mailing Labels

The label layout sets most of the options you need when you print labels: repetition across a page, column setup (across first), slide objects, and so on. As a convenience, use a label layout whenever you can.

If for some reason you want to create your own label from a blank layout, follow this procedure:

1. Choose Edit Paper Sizes from the Page Setup command from the File menu and, depending on your label size, create a custom label or accept one of the preset sizes. Use any size that is a multiple of your label height, up to 36 inches (the larger the better).

2. Click the No Gaps Between Pages option in the Page Setup dialog box for continuous label stock. Leave it turned off if you are using label sheets with margins.

3. Select the Slide Objects command from the Arrange menu if you want to close up blank space and lines. Do not choose the Sliding Part Up option; it results in misaligned labels.

4. Select the Layout Options command from the Layout menu. Select Display in n Columns and insert a number. If you use 3-up labels—printing with 3 labels across the sheet—choose the Across First option. The Down First option wastes label stock whether your print job runs correctly or not. For 1-up labels, a Column Setup option need not be selected.

5. Test print a page of labels on paper. Your printer may require that you adjust the paper position, and you can see whether your labels will print in the correct position.

When printing labels on an ImageWriter, buy the best quality label stock you can find and never roll label stock back through the platen on an ImageWriter. A label may peel off and get stuck on the platen, costing you a trip to the repair shop. Specify the largest multiple of your label height that can be accommodated, up to 36 inches, in the Page Setup dialog box.

When you specify No Gaps Between Pages, the ImageWriter ejects the first page and prints the next page. If this option is not specified, you can print on the top and bottom labels of each page, and no pages are ejected. The ImageWriter forces 0.25-inch top and bottom margins, and your labels usually print right to the edge. Adjust the printer to accommodate the label thickness (check your printer manual for details).

For standard 1-inch labels, 1-up labels have no special advantage over 3-up labels. The 1-up labels are only slightly less likely to jam and slightly easier to respecify in a print file if your print job is interrupted for some reason.

The next chapter, "Quick Start: Creating Mailing Labels," gives a step-by-step explanation of how to create and use mailing labels on an ImageWriter.

When printing labels on a LaserWriter, follow these tips:

- Buy label stock designed for use with laser printers. (Avery labels are a good choice.) Unknown brands of labels may melt in your printer and cause you much grief.

- Specifying a larger printable area in the Page Setup dialog box may enable you to print additional labels on the page.
- Refer to your printer manual for instructions on how to feed label stock into the printer; some printers require manual feeding.
- In the Page Setup dialog box, click the Options button and set the Larger Printable Area to on.
- If the Paper Size is US Letter and the label setup is 3 columns, choose Across First (assuming that you are using a 3-up label sheet).
- Set the header part at 0.513 inches from the top (vertical position), and the bottom of the body part at 1.513 inches from the top. The label layout printable area extends in from the left edge (the horizontal position) at 3.013 inches.

Printing labels on a LaserWriter has some definite advantages. The LaserWriter is much faster and quieter than an ImageWriter; the labels do not jam in the printer; and laser output looks much spiffier. On the negative side, the sheets of labels are warm when they emerge from the printer, so they curl up and may not stack well in the output tray. Another possibility is that the labels may melt in your printer. Also, labels for laser printers are generally more expensive than bulk labels for impact printers.

Troubleshooting Printing Problems

Printing is usually a straightforward process, but occasionally you may encounter some difficulties. By using some of the procedures in this section, you can circumvent many of these problems.

Systems 5 and 6 use the Chooser DA. Open it and check the choices you want. If your printer is not functioning properly, make sure that you have correctly specified the printer in the Chooser. Sometimes respecifying the printer solves your printing problems.

Even if you have specified the printer correctly, mixing the wrong version of the Chooser with a particular System version can cause printing problems. Chooser Version 3.3.1, for example, should be used with System 6. Always check the Chooser and your system software documentation before you begin a print job, because the Chooser affects other choices you can make.

If you are still experiencing printing problems, check the wires that connect your printer to your network or to your computer. AppleTalk connectors are notorious for disconnecting, and a partially connected printer may not work at all, or it may print gibberish. Also, software glitches can cause your printer port to malfunction temporarily: connecting your printer to the modem port, even temporarily, can restore your printer. (The modem port is functionally the same as the printer port.) Try switching back to the printer port when you reboot your machine.

Another possible cure is to turn your printer off and on once to reset it, or reboot your computer to reinitialize it. ImageWriter printers have a self-test mode to check whether the hardware is operating properly.

In Review

You can print all the records in a file, the records you browse, the current record, a blank record, or field definitions by using the Print command. The options and page sizes available to you, and therefore the appearance of your output, are controlled by your printer.

To print, you must choose a printer, organize the records of interest, select a paper size, set up the page, and specify the type of print job you want.

You create custom paper sizes in the Page Setup dialog box. Any size within the printer's capabilities, up to 36 by 36 inches, is available. Custom sizes can use impact printers such as the ImageWriter, but LaserWriters require that you accept a preset paper size.

Use the Preview window to examine your output before printing; it shows you a sample of how your printout will appear. Many aspects of a layout function properly only in output and need to be viewed in this way. Printing an individual record to make sure that your file is operating properly also is valuable.

CHAPTER 11

Quick Start: Creating Mailing Labels

Your company, Children of the 60's Holistic Natural Health Food Emporium, has just completed the new spring catalog of its products, the *Hol Earth Catalog*. Now you are ready to create the labels you need to mail the catalogs to your customers. In this quick start, you will create 1-inch mailing labels (1-up and 3-up). This quick start provides the basic steps to use any printer for this task and uses an ImageWriter as an example to help you follow along for practice. Having a directory of your customers can be helpful, so the last section shows you how to create a simple directory using a label layout and some additional parts.

In this quick start you will learn to

- Choose a printer, select a paper size, and set up the page
- Create label layouts and a directory layout based on your labels
- Place fields on the label and copy fields to another label
- Use the Slide Objects feature to improve your output
- Preview your work
- Print your labels

This sequence is normal for printing any form, and you will follow these steps for each label until the steps are second nature to you. You can use either of the two files you have worked with in previous quick starts, because they already have the needed fields.

To begin, open the Catalog Mailing or the Copy of Catalog Mailing file by double-clicking the file icon in the Finder or by selecting the Open command (⌘-O) from within FileMaker.

If you want additional practice, you can create a file with a standard layout and a few records. To create this file, you need the following defined Text fields: First Name, Last Name, Company, Address, City, State, and Zip Code. If you need help creating and opening files and defining new fields, refer to Quick Start 1 or Chapter 3.

Specifying Settings for Mailing Labels

Selecting a printer imposes some settings that you need to follow in addition to this quick start. Different printers have different margins, for example, and only continuous-feed printers can create custom paper sizes. Click the ImageWriter icon, even if you don't have an ImageWriter. You can always preview your work during the quick start and then switch to your own printer later. Defining additonal fields in a file is not a problem; you use only the ones you need.

To select a printer, follow these steps:

1. Select the Chooser DA from the Apple menu and click the icon for the ImageWriter.
2. Click the icon for the printer port you use.

   If your computer is on a network (see Chapter 17) with access to an ImageWriter, select the ImageWriter.
3. Close the Chooser DA by clicking the Close box.

For more information about printers and the options they offer, refer to Chapter 10.

Labels sometimes require a custom page size; other times you can use standard paper sizes. In Quick Start: Creating and Using Forms, you learned how to edit paper sizes in the Page Setup dialog box to create a custom size for the statement form, and you still may have that size selected if you opened the Copy of Catalog Mailing file. To print on letter-sized sheets of labels for the 3-up labels you create in this quick start, you need to set the page size as US Letter.

To choose a paper size and page setup, follow these steps:

1. Select the Page Setup command from the File menu.

2. In the Page Setup dialog box, click the US Letter radio button, if needed. A LaserWriter does not allow custom paper sizes; therefore, the Edit Paper Sizes text box is unavailable. To use custom paper sizes, choose the ImageWriter from the Chooser desk accessory.
3. Click on the No Gaps Between Pages check box to select this option and then dismiss the dialog box by clicking OK.

Creating a 3-Up Label Layout

FileMaker provides a label layout that you can define in the New Layout dialog box. The 1-inch labels you create in this quick start use this layout, which is a convenience; when you choose it, FileMaker makes some menu selections for you that speed up creating the layout.

To create a 1-inch, 3-up label layout—three labels across the page—follow these steps:

1. Switch to the Layout window (if needed) by choosing the Layout command from the Select menu or by pressing ⌘-L.
2. Choose the New Layout command on the Edit menu or press ⌘-N.
3. In the resulting New Layout dialog box (see fig. 11.1), click the Labels radio button.

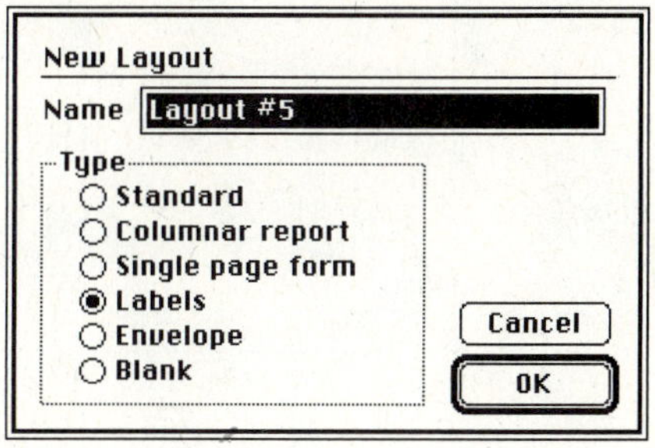

Fig. 11.1
Setting a label layout in the New Layout dialog box.

4. Click OK or press Return.
5. FileMaker posts the Label Setup dialog box (see fig. 11.2).

   Accept the defaults: 3 for the number of columns, 1 inch for height, and 2.5 inches across for label sizes for an 8 1/2-by-11-inch page size. Remember that a 1-inch label is actually 15/16 inch high. The other 1/16 inch is the space before the next label.

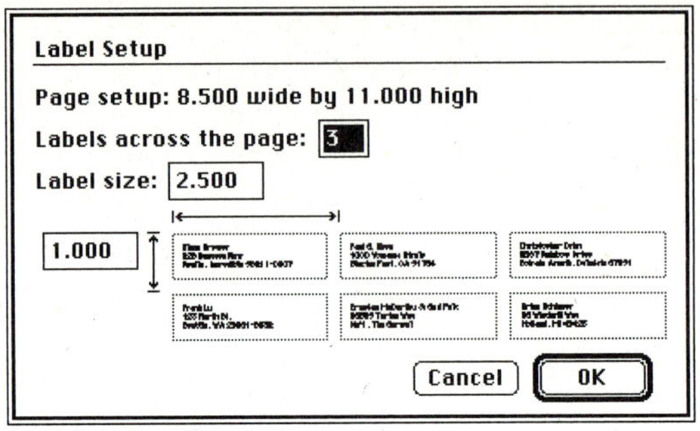

Fig. 11.2
The Label Setup dialog box.

6. Click OK or press Return.
7. In the resulting Field Order dialog box, double-click the following fields in the scroll box: Sal, First Name, Last Name, Company, Address, and City.

   or

   Click a field name and then click the Move button to place the field in the list, as shown in figure 11.3. Follow the same procedure for each field.

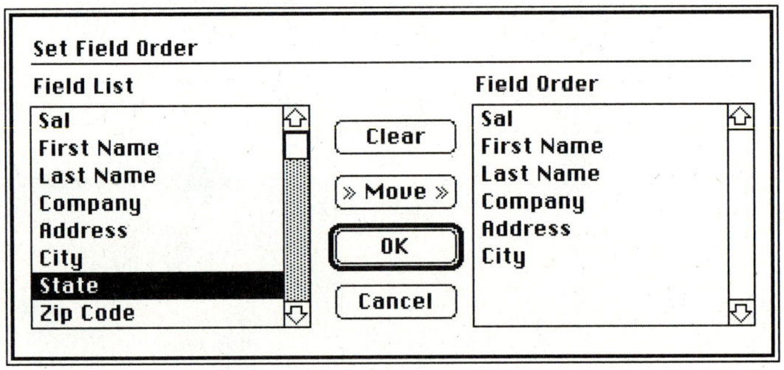

Fig. 11.3
The Set Field Order dialog box with the six allowed fields.

   If you make a mistake, click Clear to remove the list or click a field name in the Field Order list and then click Move to remove it. Because the order in the list determines the order (top to bottom) in the layout (initially), make sure that the sequence is correct.

8. Double-click the State field name.

FileMaker beeps and posts the alert box shown in figure 11.4. Only six fields can fit on a 1-inch label in the default font size of 9-point Geneva (or Helvetica). You have to rearrange the layout to fit the additional desired fields.

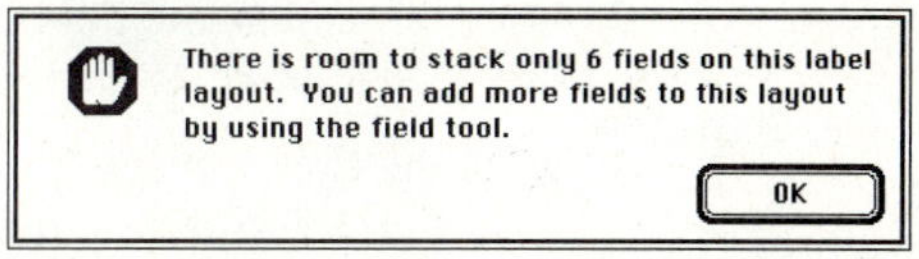

Fig. 11.4
The "6 fields on a label" alert box.

9. Click OK or press Return to dismiss the alert box and return to the Field Order dialog box.
10. Click OK or press Return to dismiss the Field Order dialog box and go to the Layout window shown in figure 11.5.

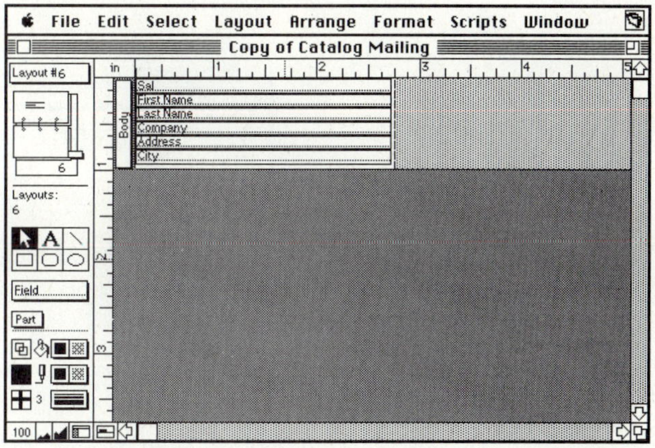

Fig. 11.5
The 3-up label Layout window.

FileMaker stacks your six fields. Dotted vertical lines show you the limits of each of the three labels on a line. If you scroll the window to the right, you can see the solid vertical line marking the page boundary.

You need to include the State and Zip Code fields on the layout. To include these fields, you need to place the field names on the same line, resize them, and line them up. The Shift key constrains your resizing and constrains your dragging motion to perfectly horizontal or vertical (whichever direction you move first).

To set up the fields in the positions you want them, follow these steps:

1. Resize the First Name field by pressing the Shift key and dragging left on one of the small black reshape handles to make it narrower. Drag until you have room to fit both fields on that line.

2. Drag the Last Name field so that it lines up horizontally with the First Name field.

3. Drag the Company field so that its top edge aligns with the bottom edge of the First Name field and the left edges align.

4. Drag or resize fields more precisely by holding down the Shift key as you drag or resize.

   Move the Address field so that its top edge aligns with the bottom edge of the Company field.

5. Move the City field up to the fourth line and resize it so that the layout now looks like the layout shown in figure 11.6.

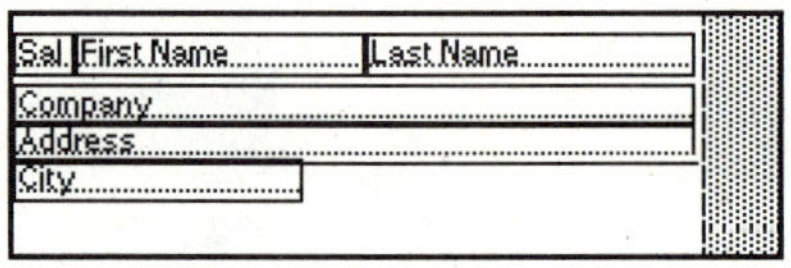

Fig. 11.6
The 1-inch label with the first six fields in position.

6. Add the remaining two fields (State and Zip Code) by clicking Field in the Status Panel and dragging the new fields onto the label.

   When you release the mouse button, FileMaker displays the New Field dialog box (see fig. 11.7).

7. Double-click the field name `State` or click the name to highlight it and then select OK and press Return.

8. Move the State field into the position shown in figure 11.8.

9. Repeat steps 6, 7, and 8 to add the Zip Code field. Your layout should now look like figure 11.8.

You now have the layout in the correct form. Switch to the Browse window; a record appears like the one shown in figure 11.9. Notice that all fields are separated by the amount of space you would expect from the layout. The label in the Browse window has extra space that you don't want printed. The Slide Objects setting removes the extra space.

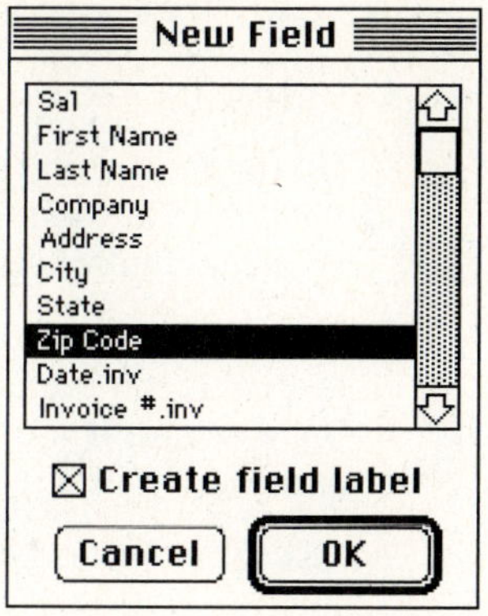

Fig. 11.7
The New Field dialog box.

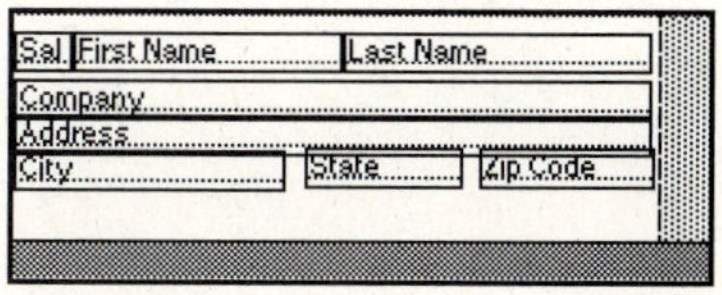

Fig. 11.8
The completed label.

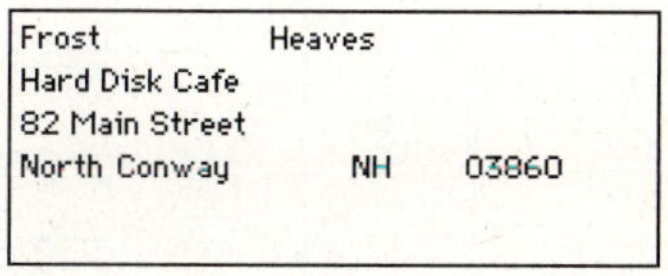

Fig. 11.9
A sample of the newly created label.

To use the Slide Objects command do the following:

1. Choose Select All from the Edit menu or press ⌘-A.
2. Select Slide Objects from the Arrange menu. In the Slide Objects dialog box, choose the Sliding Left and Sliding Up Based on Directly Above options. For more details, see "Removing Blank Spaces" in Chapter 9.
3. Click the OK button.

To see the effect of the Slide Objects command, preview your labels.

One sheet of 1-inch labels holds 33 labels—eleven labels in each of three columns. You can create more records and view your output in the Preview window (see Chapter 10).

To preview the labels, follow these steps:

1. Choose the Browse command from the Select menu or press ⌘-B.
2. Go the the eighth record in the file or any other record that is filled in. You want to see a full page of labels, so you need to create additional records.
3. Press ⌘-D to create records until the third record is on your screen. If you prefer, you can enter actual data instead of duplicating a record. If you just want practice, however, duplicate one record.
4. Select the Preview command from the File menu or press ⌘-U.
5. Click the Zoom control box; the Preview window resembles figure 11.10.

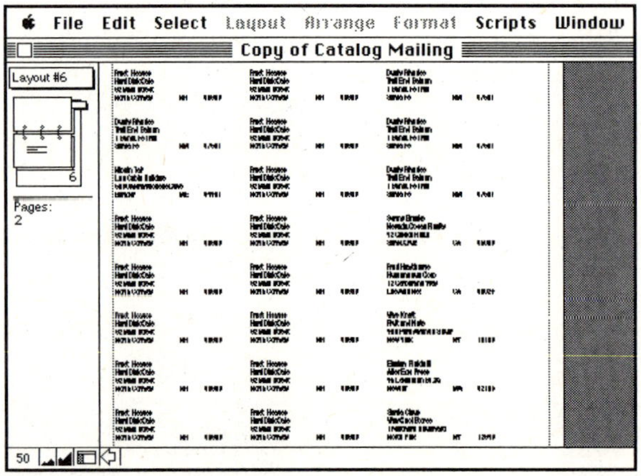

Fig. 11.10
A page of 3-up labels in the reduced view of the Preview window.

6. Click a page of the Book to see the next page or drag the bookmark. Your third record appears on the second page. The number of pages available for preview appears right below the Book.
7. Click Exit to return to the Browse screen.

Printing Your Labels

If you have an ImageWriter, you may want to test print your labels. You don't need label stock; just use regular US letter-size paper. You already have set the page size; therefore, if your labels are perfectly aligned in the printer, FileMaker prints all the labels you specify and then ejects any partially filled page.

The following instructions for printing labels are for the ImageWriter. To print labels on a LaserWriter, see Chapter 10.

1. Select the Page Setup command and enter a check mark in the dialog box in the No Gaps Between Pages check box.
2. Click OK or press Return.
3. Select the Print command from the File menu or press ⌘-P.
4. In the Print dialog box, check for the following:

   Turn on the print quality Best or Faster button.

   Turn on the Page Range All button.
5. Click OK or press Return.

FileMaker prints your labels.

Creating 1-Up Label Layouts

The steps involved in creating a 1-up label format are the same as for 3-up labels. In this section, you learn a shortcut for creating a label quickly.

To create a 1-up, 1-inch label, follow these steps:

1. Access the Layout window by choosing the Layout command (⌘-L).
2. Select the New Layout command on the Edit menu or press ⌘-N.
3. Click the Label Layout radio button and click OK.
4. In the Label Setup dialog box, enter *1* in the Labels Across the Page text box.
5. Leave all other settings the same and click OK to dismiss the dialog box.
6. FileMaker opens the Field Order dialog box. This time, dismiss this box by clicking OK. The blank 1-up label layout appears.

Notice the difference between the 1-up and 3-up labels. When you scroll right in the 1-up label layout, you don't see any dashed vertical lines because only one column prints. Refer to Chapter 9 for more information about margins and setting up a page by using layouts.

Because you already have created a layout with all the fields and layout objects in the correct size and in the right places, you can cut and paste the fields into your new layout.

To cut and paste the fields, follow these steps:

1. Return to your 3-up label format, using the Book or Slide Control Mechanism, or click on the Layout title and highlight your choice.

2. Choose the Select All command from the Edit menu or press ⌘-A to select and highlight all fields on the layout.

3. Select the Group command from the Arrange menu or press ⌘-G. Using this feature treats all the individual fields as one unit and makes the label easier to work with.

4. Choose the Copy command (⌘-C) on the Edit menu.

5. Return to the 1-up label layout, using the same choices as in step 1.

6. Select the Paste command (⌘-V) from the Edit menu.

   All the fields appear in the window, as shown in figure 11.11.

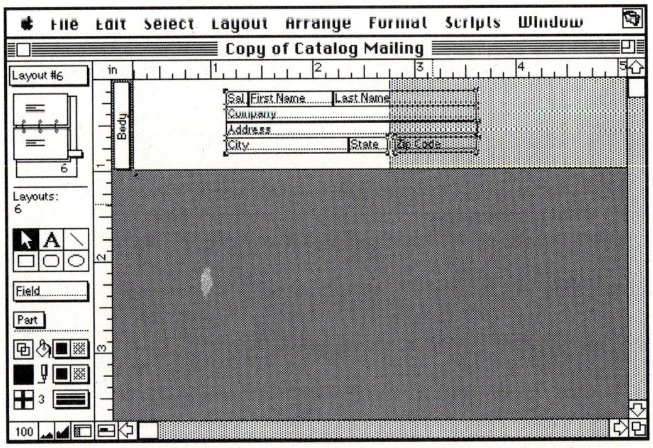

Fig. 11.11
The pasted fields in the 1-up label.

7. Drag the fields to line them up with the top and left margins of the label. To allow a little room for error, center the fields in the label. Click anywhere else in the window to deselect them.

   In general, you should center your labels in a layout. Centering gives you more margin for error as labels are fed through your printer.

All the steps of carefully resizing, moving, and adding fields have been simplified by using copy and paste. Chapter 7 describes this technique in detail.

If you are creating 1-up labels without creating 3-up labels first, check the Edit Paper Sizes in the Page Setup dialog boxes to make sure that you selected US Letter size paper and made your choice for the No Gap Between Pages feature.

8. Select the Preview command on the Select menu or press ⌘-U to see the Preview window (see fig. 11.12).

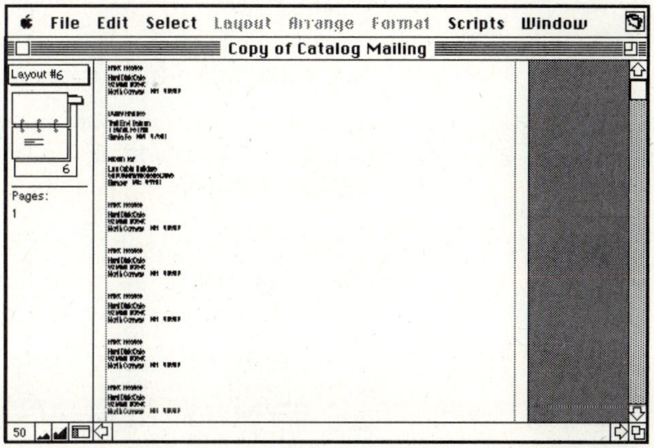

Fig. 11.12
A page of 1-up labels in the Preview window.

9. Choose ⌘-L to return to your Layout window.

10. Press ⌘-Option-P to bypass the dialog box and accept your previous settings.

Creating a Directory from Your Labels

One of the most satisfying tasks you can perform in FileMaker is creating a directory. In fact, you have already done most of the work necessary for creating a directory. In this section, you take your 3-up label layout and modify it by adding some parts to create directory pages.

To create a directory, follow these steps:

1. Return to your 3-up label layout by clicking on the Book in the Layout window.

2. Select the Duplicate Layout command from the Edit menu.
3. Select the Layout Options command from the Layout menu.
4. In the dialog box, click the Down First radio button, and then click OK to dismiss the dialog box.

   Retain the default 3-across column format, although it's more traditional to read down for a directory. Return the Edit Paper Sizes and Page Setup settings to US Letter size. For the directory, you will use header and footer parts to set the margin, so leave the No Gaps Between Pages setting turned on.
5. Select the Page Setup command from the File menu.
6. In the dialog box, click on the US Letter radio button. Click off the No Gaps Between Pages check box and click OK to exit.

You can print your directory now, but you can make your directory much more attractive by adding a header and footer, along with layout objects for numbering pages and records and giving the date.

To add layout parts, follow these steps:

1. Choose the Page Setup command from the File menu and click off the No Gaps Between Pages check box; click the OK button.
2. Center all the fields in the layout by selecting the group and then dragging it into position.
3. Click the Parts tool in the status arca and drag a part above the body part, above all the fields on the layout.
4. Click on the Header radio button in the Part Definition dialog box, as shown in figure 11.13, and then click OK.

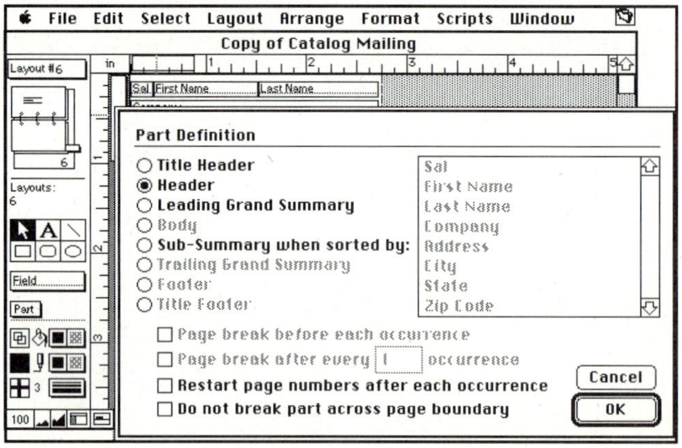

Fig. 11.13
Adding a header to the layout.

5. Position the header part 0.750 inches from the top edge so that the vertical position indicator in the status area reads 1.000". To change a part size, click the handle or the boundary and drag it.

6. Repeat steps 3 through 5, dragging a footer part below the body, positioning it at 0.750 inches, and centering the horizontal T-square at 0.50 inches, as shown in figure 11.14. If you need help using the Rulers and size box to position objects, refer to Chapter 7.

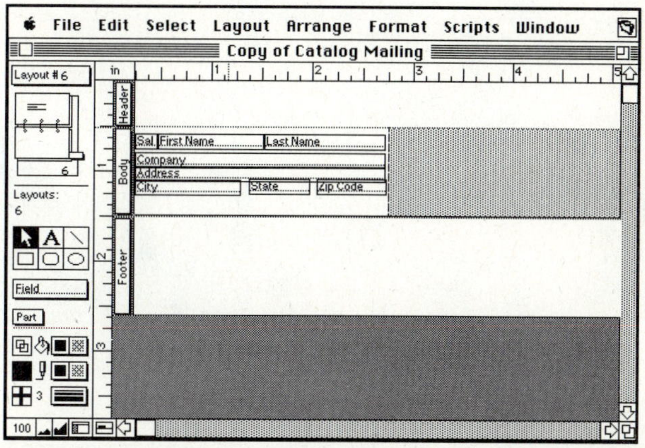

Fig. 11.14
The positioned header and footer.

Now, add a title, page numbers, the date, and some lines to serve as borders to spruce up the directory.

To add these additional elements, follow these steps:

1. From the Format menu choose the following:
   - 1 Point from the Size submenu
   - Bold from the Style submenu
2. Click the Text tool, click an insertion point in the header, and type *CUSTOMER DIRECTORY*.
3. Move the vertical T-square to 5.000 inches and click the Arrow tool, as shown in figure 11.15.
4. Drag the text object so that it is centered above the horizontal position line, resting on the vertical position line.

5. Move the T-square so that the horizontal position line is in the center of the footer (0.500 inch).
6. Click the Text tool, click an insertion point in the footer, and type the symbol // for the date.
7. Click the Arrow tool and drag the date layout object so that it rests above the horizontal T-square near the left edge of the layout, as shown in figure 11.15.

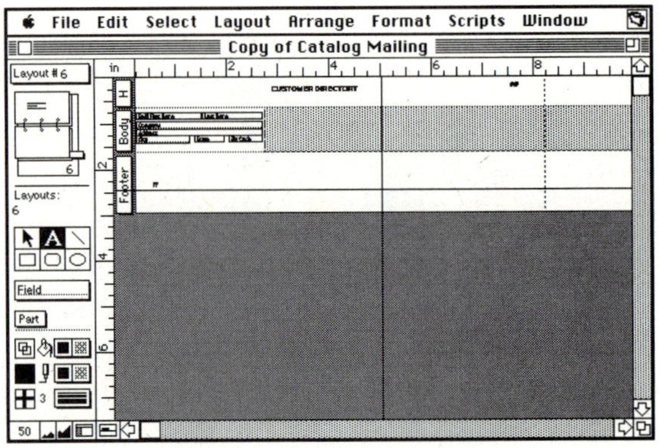

Fig. 11.15
The directory layout.

8. Repeat steps 6 and 7, creating a layout object for the page number. Type ## and position it above the T-square near the right page margin.

   The right printable edge is a vertical line that you may have to scroll right to see, as Chapter 9 describes. Chapter 10 provides information about layout text for the current date, page number, record number, and current time.

9. Click the Line tool, hold down the Shift key, and drag some 1-point wide lines (the default) to the right and below the fields in the body part. These lines will separate the records.
10. Select the 4-point line from the Line Width submenu on the Format menu (the sixth choice down).
11. Hold down the Option key and drag a line across the bottom of the header part. You are now at the stage shown in figure 11.15.
12. Select the Preview command from the Select menu or press ⌘-U to view your directory pages. A sample is shown in figure 11.16.

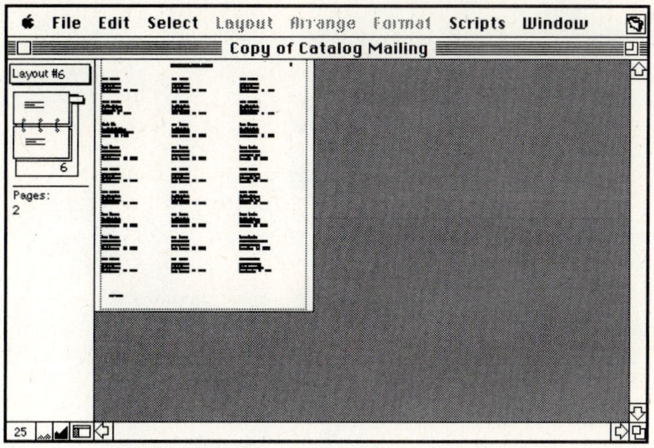

Fig. 11.16
A directory page in preview.

13. When you are finished, return to either the layout or browse mode by choosing ⌘-L or ⌘-B.

Your directory looks great! You can print a page for practice.

PART IV

Advanced FileMaker Features

Includes

Creating Scripts and Buttons

Using Templates and Other Resources

Quick Start: Creating a Summary Report

Importing and Exporting Data

Managing Files

Using FileMaker Pro on a Network

USING FILEMAKER PRO

CHAPTER 12

Creating Scripts and Buttons

Your files normally are task-oriented. One business file might store the results of a catalog mailing, another might contain a customer list, and a third might hold sales information. If you use FileMaker at home, perhaps you might inventory a record, stamp, or coin collection. For most FileMaker applications, data often is used for multiple tasks, so layouts are helpful. Layouts are like different costumes worn by the same person at different functions: your data describes what each piece of the costume looks like, and the layout controls where each item is placed.

You use layouts in a file differently from one another. Perhaps your statement layout is intended only for current customers who owe you money. You then find that particular set of customers, sort them by ZIP code, and print the statement on 8 1/2-by-5 1/2-inch triplicate statement forms. You might use another layout to advertise a promotion for your best customers, sort customers by money spent and ZIP code, and then print their letters on letterhead paper. Still another layout might generate 1-inch mailing labels or labels for cartons. Each layout requires different finds, sorts, page setups, and data import or export instructions, among other things.

If you do any task frequently, you spend a lot of time reproducing the conditions for a layout to perform its function. Worse yet, you can forget what conditions you should use, or someone else can change those conditions when using the file. You can write detailed instructions, but they cannot speed up the work. FileMaker offers you a better way, using a feature called a script. Scripts remember your settings and can re-create the conditions of your file with a keystroke or menu command.

Defining a Script

A *script* is a small program within FileMaker that returns your layout to a specified state, issues some commands (such as printing or previewing a file), or both. When you perform an operation such as a find, a sort, an import/export, a page size or setup specification, or a print command, FileMaker reserves a place in memory to store the settings. You already have learned the Refind command (for restoring a file to conform to your previous Find request). Many of FileMaker's best shortcuts or power user techniques use these stored choices and command options to automate tasks.

After you change a setting, the previous setting is gone. When you close or open a file or change layouts, all the settings are lost. You can attach only one temporary set of settings to your file, and you must create the settings every time you need them.

All database and spreadsheet programs suffer from the problem of how to return to a specified file state, and all solve it in different ways. One common solution is to define a small program, called a macro, that executes when you press a keystroke or give a command. In their simplest form, some macro programs are nothing more than keystroke recorders that record the keystroke, and the program writes the programming code for you. If you have used the MacroMaker program that Apple includes with the system software, you know what a macro is. More complex macro programs are AutoMac III, QuicKeys 2 (a great product), and Tempo II, and you certainly can use any of these utilities to perform tasks in FileMaker.

The more powerful databases and spreadsheets offer more complex solutions to repetitive task automation. If you have used the spreadsheet Microsoft Excel, you might know about its powerful macro language. Wingz uses scripts, as does HyperCard. The dBASE Mac database offers the dBASE programming language, as does FoxBase. 4th Dimension has its own scripting language. You learn these languages, write your own code, and have control over most aspects of these programs. These programs can automate repetitive tasks (such as making a payroll), help you run your business more efficiently, or bring more organization into your life.

With scripts for storing settings, FileMaker takes an intermediate approach between macros and complex automation programs. In a sense, a FileMaker script is like a macro, except keystrokes and settings are defined as the current state of your file when you define the script. No programming language is necessary because all you do is select the current conditions for FileMaker to remember.

You may have found, for example, a set of records, sorted them, switched to a new layout, and then previewed the results. You can store these actions in a script. If you have a file with many layouts, you can define scripts to reach one special layout. If you have several different find requests with any set of criteria you need to remember, store each request in a script. Scripts don't have to be complex to be useful, and the number of possible scripts is unlimited. Because you can name scripts, you can remember their tasks easily. Linking scripts to perform complex operations is discussed later in this chapter.

Suppose that you get a phone call from Elysian Fields, who orders a Grecian Urn. You pull down a script called Order Entry, and a screen appears for recording the sale. You need to check inventory to make sure that the urns are in stock, so you pull down the Inventory Listing script. The warehouse has plenty of urns, so you pull down the Invoice script to open that layout for generating the form. All these steps are accomplished in seconds. If you did not have scripts and the customer wanted another item, you would be lost trying to return to the original data-entry screen.

Creating a Script

Creating a script is easy. You just perform or specify all the operations that are necessary to get you to the stage you want FileMaker to remember. If you are storing only a find request, create the request or perform that find.

After you specify or perform an operation, it is stored in memory. You can create a sort order without performing a sort. (If you want to specify a sort for a script without changing the file, you don't have to perform a sort.) Also, you can specify an import/export order without performing it. If, however, you need to switch to a specific layout, you must make that layout the current layout. You can choose which of the current conditions you want FileMaker to remember by checking them in the Script dialog box; only your selections are remembered.

To create a script, follow these steps:

1. Open a file and perform all the steps you want to store in the script. Perform any one of the following operations:

    - Go to a specific layout
    - Specify a page setup
    - Specify an import or export order and perform that operation
    - Specify a find request and perform that find
    - Specify a sort order and perform that sort
    - Specify a print job and perform that print procedure

    You can set all other script features without specification.

2. From the Browse, Layout, or Find window, select the Define Scripts command from the Scripts menu. FileMaker posts the Define Scripts dialog box shown in figure 12.1.

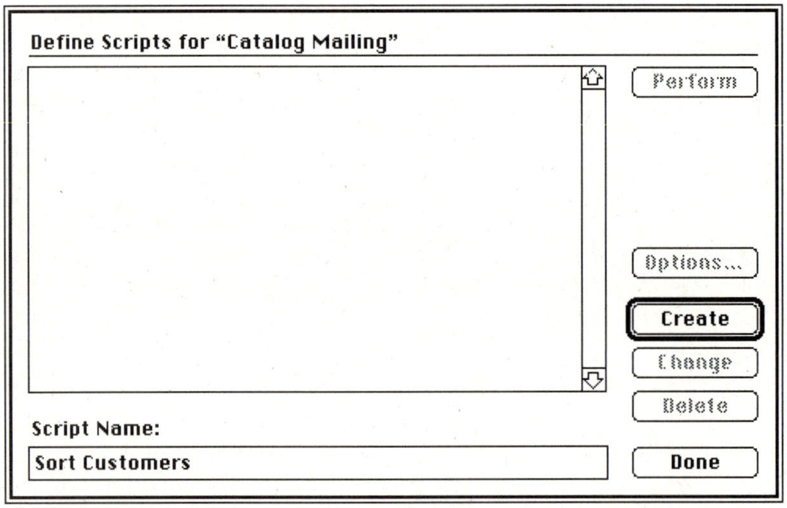

Fig. 12.1
The Define Scripts dialog box.

3. Enter the name of your script in the Script Name text box, using standard Macintosh text-editing techniques. You must give the script a unique name. FileMaker alerts you if you try to give a script a currently existing script name.

4. Click the Create button, and FileMaker posts the Definition for Script dialog box shown in figure 12.2.

   All the options in the Definition for Script dialog box are described in detail later in this section. Figure 12.2 shows the defaults.

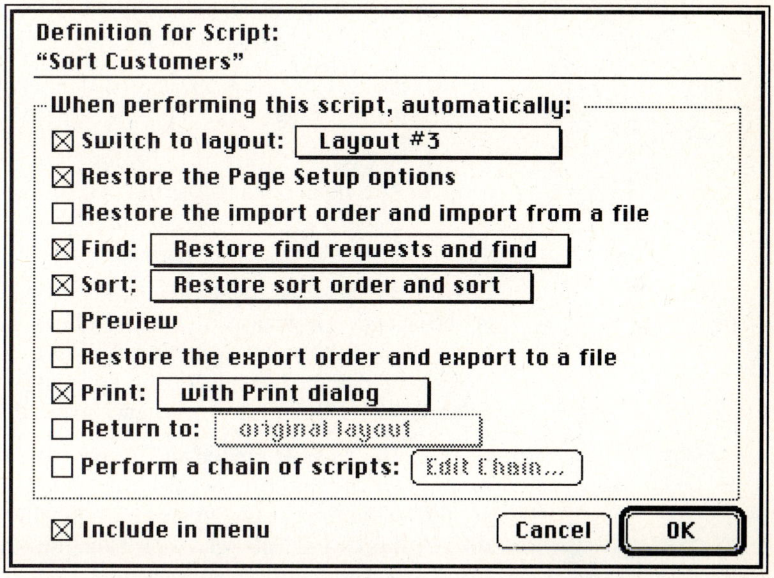

Fig. 12.2
The Definition for Script dialog box.

5. Click the check boxes on or off so that FileMaker performs all the operations you want.

6. Click the Include in Menu check box if you want to add the new script to the Scripts menu.

7. Click the OK button to return to the Define Scripts dialog box.

   If you change your mind and decide you don't want the script, click the Cancel button and the script is not defined. Remember that when you execute the script, Filemaker performs any operation whose setting you leave turned on. If you want to store a setting, but not perform it, create another script that contains that setting.

8. Click the Done button or press the Return key to return to your original file window.

FileMaker adds your new script to the bottom of the Scripts menu. The top ten scripts are numbered ⌘-1 through ⌘-0.

Scripts now can switch layouts and link to any other scripts in any order. Scripts also can pause during Find and Sort or print and bypass the Print dialog box.

The features that you can embed inside a script are listed in the Definition for Script dialog box. A summary of their actions follows.

Script Name. This box is a standard Macintosh text-editing box. Type the new name in here.

Switch to Layout. Opens the current layout when the script is performed. This layout always opens regardless of its position in the layout order, because FileMaker has an internal layout number that it references with this script.

Restore the Page Setup Options. Retains and restores, when the script is performed, any options that are in effect in the Page Setup dialog box at the time of the script definition. Use this setting for any special paper sizes you created or to select from the preset page sizes. Refer to Chapter 10 for more information about page setup.

Restore the Import Order and Import from a File. Retains the import order and other import specifications (such as data types), whether they are the last import performed or just specified but not performed. When the script is run, FileMaker asks for the import file name and then posts a dialog box that indicates the import order, file format (for Text, BASIC, or SYLK formats), and a choice of adding or updating current records. For more information about importing data from a file, refer to Chapter 15.

Find. Enables any of the following four Find options:

> **Find All.** Returns the entire set of records in your browsed set to its natural file order. This option is the equivalent of the Find All command on the Main menu under Select.
>
> **Go To Find and Pause.** Enables you to temporarily change the search criteria that are stored with the script.
>
> **Restore Find Requests and Find.** Restores all the criteria and requests of your last find operation, whether you performed it or just specified it. When the script is run, it performs the find operation.
>
> **Restore Find Requests and Pause.** Restores the search criteria to what is stored in the script.

Sort. Enables any of the following four sort operations:

> **Unsort.** Unsorts all the records you have browsed through into their natural file order.
>
> **Go To Sort and Pause.** Permits you to temporarily change the sort order that is stored with the script.
>
> **Restore Sort Order and Sort.** Stores the sort order in effect at the time of script definition, whether it has been performed or only specified. When the script is run, it sorts all your browsed records by that sort order.
>
> **Restore Sort Order and Pause.** Changes the sort order back to what is stored in the script.

Preview. Opens the Preview window, which enables you to view the way your export will look. If you have checked the Print box, however, FileMaker prints your records before you preview them. To preview before printing, define two linked scripts, with the second one doing the print job.

Restore the Export Order and Export to a File. Retains the export order and other export specifications, such as data type, whether these exports are the last exports performed or are just specified. When the script is run, FileMaker asks you for the export file name and then posts a dialog box that indicates the export order, file format, and a choice of whether the export values are formatted or unformatted. For more information about exporting data to a file, see Chapter 15.

Print. Does not depend on the last print job specified or performed. A pop-up menu displays two choices:

> **With Print Dialog.** Displays the Print dialog box at the time of printing.
>
> **Without Print Dialog.** Prints automatically without displaying the Print dialog box.

Return To. After performing the script, returns to the layout you choose from the pop-up menu.

Perform a Chain of Scripts. Enables you to link scripts or to separate tasks within one larger script. Linking scripts enables you to form complex scripts; separating tasks enables you to perform sequential operations. By defining one script to preview, for example, and a second to print, you can overrule FileMaker's tendency to print first and then preview.

Include in Menu. Places the script by name in the Custom menu and numbers that script with ⌘-1 through ⌘- 0, in order of its creation. Any additional scripts are listed on the menu as they are created. For information about reordering scripts, see "Modifying a Script" later in this chapter.

OK Button. Creates the script that you have just defined and returns you to the Define Scripts dialog box.

Cancel Button. Returns you to the Define Scripts dialog box without creating the script.

If you have to perform a task, such as printing statements, you might want to define a script by using these steps:

1. Go to the statement layout and make it the current layout.
2. Select the Find command and find all compared accounts.
3. Sort by ZIP codes (to save money when you mail your statements).
4. Give the Page Setup command and change the page setup to that required by your form. Now you're ready to define your script.

To define your script, follow these steps:

1. Select Define Scripts from the Scripts menu.
2. Enter a name for your script. When you give the Define Scripts command and define a new script, you want only three check boxes selected:
   - Restore the Page Setup Options
   - Restore Find Requests and Find
   - Restore Sort Order and Sort
3. Check the Include in Menu check box because you generally will want to add a script to the menu for easy selection.
4. Select one of the next two optional check boxes, if you want:
   - Check Print to print automatically, without displaying the print dialog.
   - Check Switch Back to Layout to return to your previous layout; choose the previous layout name.

If you own one of the macro programs mentioned in "Defining a Script," you can embed a FileMaker script within a macro to accomplish even more complex tasks than those that are available to you normally. You can even use this approach to link scripts together with other scripts while performing operations in between. Macro programs enable menu commands to be selected by a keystroke or to be part of a sequence of commands.

Performing a Script

To determine whether a script operates correctly, try it. If, however, you are performing a step that changes the current condition of your file and its permanent condition, you might want to work on a copy of the file before attempting the script. An example of such a command is the Import Records command, which adds records to your file.

To perform a script, follow these steps:

1. Open the file and perform any tasks that are not included in the script definition.
2. Select the script from the Scripts menu. If your script has a command keystroke equivalent assigned to it (⌘-1 through ⌘- 0), press that keystroke.

Alternatively, you can do the following:

1. In the Browse, Find, or Layout window, select the Define Scripts command from the Scripts menu. FileMaker opens the Scripts dialog box.
2. Click to highlight the name of the script.
3. Click the Perform button. If you change your mind about performing the script, click the Done button to return to your FileMaker window.
4. Continue your work, performing any other operations (such as Omit) that are not included in the script's definition.

If you need to delete or modify a script, or change the script order, refer to "Modifying a Script."

Linking Scripts

Linking scripts enables you to perform complex operations not normally available within a single script. You can complete any operation that requires multiple finds, sorts, prints, importing/exporting, and so on with linked scripts. A linked script enables you to preview and then print a file.

To link scripts together, follow these steps:

1. When you create the script, click the Perform a Chain of Scripts check box in the Definition for Script dialog box. FileMaker opens the Set Execution Order dialog box (see fig. 12.3).

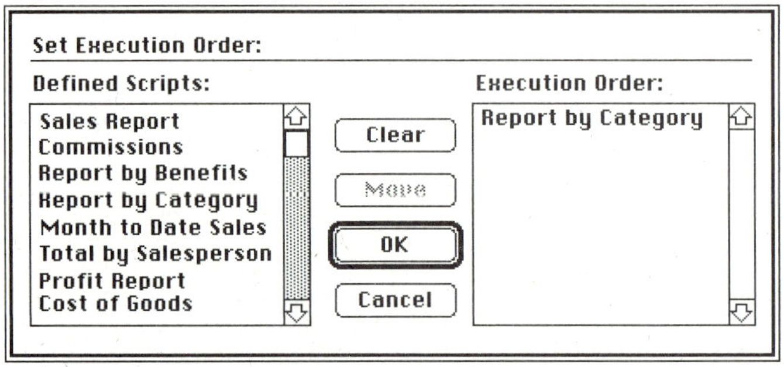

Fig. 12.3
The Set Execution Order dialog box.

2. Double-click on the script name. You also can click on the name of the script you want to perform next, to highlight it, and then click the Move button. Click OK when the list is complete.

   If you change your mind about performing the script, click the Cancel button or press the ⌘-. (period) keystroke to return to the Definition for Script dialog box; then click off the Perform a Chain of Scripts check box.

3. Click the OK button in the Definition for Script dialog box to return to the Scripts dialog box.

   FileMaker adds your new script to the bottom of the script listing. If you do not want to define the script, click the Cancel button, and the script is not defined.

4. Click the Done button to return to your original file window.

Modifying a Script

If you find that your script does not operate correctly or if your needs for that script change, you can retain that script but alter its action with the following procedure.

To change a script, follow these steps:

1. Open the file and perform any steps or specify any settings (sort order, find request, import/export order, and so forth) required to modify the script.
2. In the Browse, Layout, or Find window, select the Define Scripts command from the Scripts menu or press ⌘-H.
3. In the Define Scripts dialog box, click on the script name to highlight it. Edit the name in the usual way and then click on the Change button. (Editing the name enables the Change button.)
4. Click on Options. The Definition for Scripts dialog box opens, with all of the settings from your previous definition checked. You can change the following information:
   - Turn off or on any settings from the previous definition
   - Remove or add any linked script
   - Remove the script from or add it to the Scripts menu
5. Click the OK button.

   When you click the OK button, FileMaker posts a Change Script dialog box (see fig. 12.4). Depending on what changes you made, FileMaker either enables the Replace or Keep button or disables them both and dims them on the screen.

Fig. 12.4
The Change Scripts dialog box.

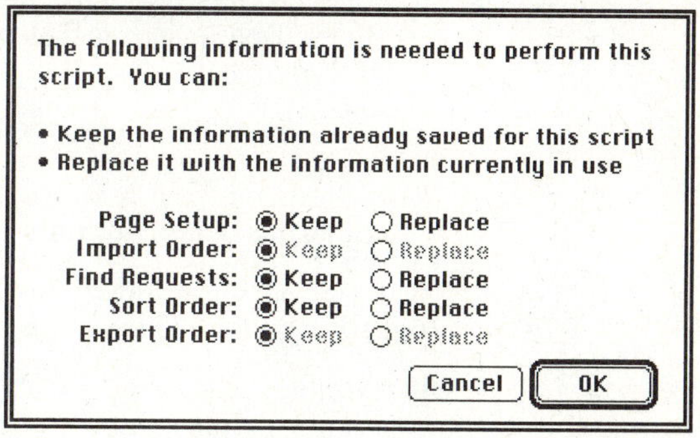

6. To retain the same settings from the previous Definition for Scripts, click on the Keep radio buttons, if needed.

Usually, the Keep radio button is left on as a default choice. To replace a setting with the one currently specified or performed at the time you change the Definition for Scripts, click the Replace radio buttons.

7. Click the OK button or press the Return or Enter key to return to the Define Scripts dialog box.

   If you change your mind about altering the script, click the Cancel button, or press ⌘-. (period).

8. In the Define Scripts dialog box, click the Done button to return to your window; click the Perform button (or press the Return key) to run the script.

Deleting a Script

Not only will you add scripts to FileMaker; from time to time you probably will want to delete scripts. You might want to remove clutter from the menu; you might find the task a script performs no longer necessary; or you might have a better script to supersede one that is on the menu.

To delete a script, follow these steps:

1. In the Browse, Layout, or Find window, select the Define Scripts command from the Scripts menu.

2. In the Define Scripts dialog box, click on the script name you want to remove.

3. Click the Delete button. FileMaker posts the Delete Script alert box shown in figure 12.5.

4. Click the Delete button or press the Return key.

If you change your mind about a deletion, click the Cancel button or press ⌘-. (period) to return to the Define Scripts dialog box.

When you delete a script, FileMaker removes it from the Scripts dialog box and the Scripts menu.

Fig. 12.5
The Delete Script alert box.

When you delete a script, that script and all its settings are gone forever. You cannot undo this action.

Reordering Scripts

Create scripts in the order that they are to be executed in your work. Listing those scripts in order on the Scripts menu is particularly valuable for reminding you of all the tasks to be accomplished. Then, when you need to perform a set of tasks, you do them one at a time. You must reorder scripts if you need to move them around on the Scripts menu. As you create scripts, you may want to move some scripts to the end of the menu and replace the ones to be moved in sequence.

To reorder scripts, follow these steps:

1. Choose Define Scripts from the Scripts menu.
2. Drag the script by double-arrow (left of the name) to the new desired position.
3. Click Done. The script command numbers change automatically.

The reordering occurs in the Define Scripts dialog box by dragging the double-arrows to new positions. Figure 12.6 shows the Scripts menu before and after reordering the scripts.

Fig. 12.6
Scripts menu before and after reordering the scripts.

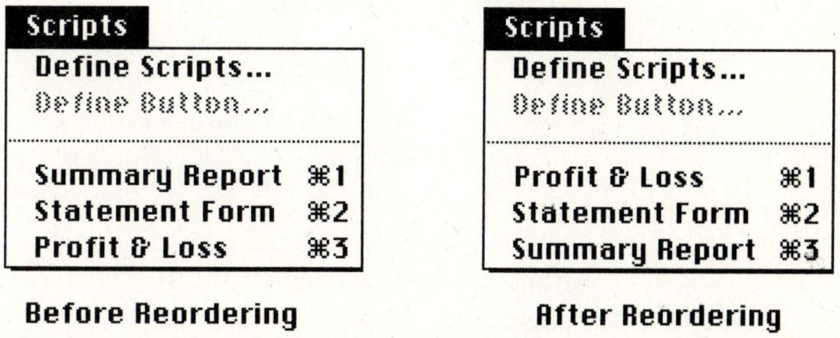

Adding Buttons To Execute a Script or Command

FileMaker Pro enables you to create interactive buttons on your layout to perform scripts or carry out commands. You can either select one of the button graphics provided for you by Claris as part of their button file or create your own. You can create buttons to perform commands such as find, sort, print, switch layouts, or any menu command. Commands can be carried out with or without displaying their associated dialog box.

Anything on the screen can be a button; you define an action and attach it to any object on a layout. A button can look like other Macintosh buttons or you can use text, fields, and graphics to create any look you want. You can even use cut and paste to move buttons to new locations.

To create a button, follow these steps:

1. Choose the Layout mode from the Select menu or press ⌘-L.

2. Select any text or graphic object you want to designate as a button. Fields cannot be used as buttons.

   A file of button graphics is contained in the FileMaker Pro templates folder. You can use any of these buttons to add to your layout. Select the one you want, copy it to the Clipboard, and then paste it into your layout. If you prefer, create your own buttons by using graphic objects or by typing layout text. The Status Panel contains all the tools you need to design graphic objects (Tools Palette, line width controls, fill controls). Refer to Chapter 7 for hints about graphics.

3. Choose Define Button from the Scripts menu. The command is dimmed unless you select an object.

4. The Define Button dialog box appears (see fig. 12.7).

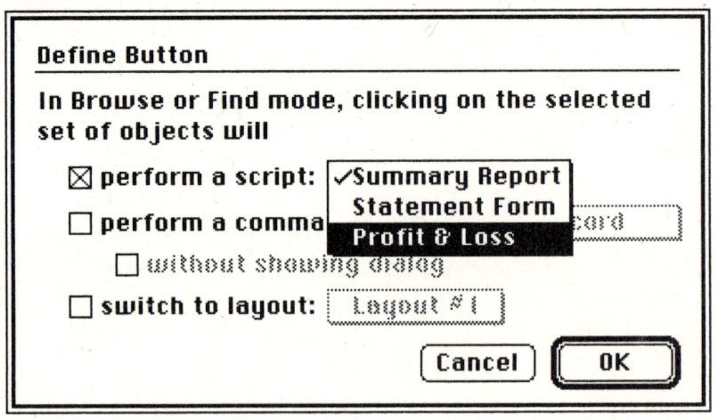

Fig. 12.7
The Define Button dialog box.

5. Select the task you want the button to perform.
6. Click the OK button.

The selected object turns into a button. At any time you can choose the Button submenu from the Show command on the Layout menu. All defined buttons are in gray outlines (see fig. 12.8).

Fig. 12.8
Example of buttons created on a layout.

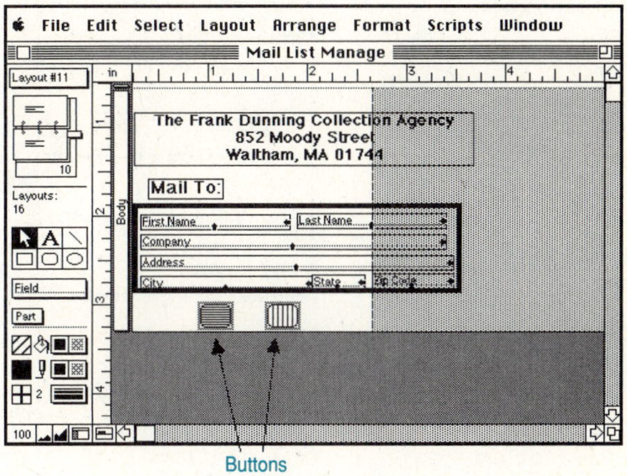

A summary of the options of the Define Button dialog box follows:

Perform a Script. Enables you to perform a script. Click on this option and then choose a script from the pop-up menu.

Perform a Command. Enables you to select any FileMaker Pro command from the pop-up menu (see fig. 12.9).

Without Showing Dialog. Executes the command without showing the dialog box.

Switch to Layout. Enables you to choose any layout from the pop-up menu.

To use the Buttons template collection, follow these steps:

1. Locate the FileMaker Pro Templates folder in the FileMaker Pro application folder.
2. Open the file called Buttons by double-clicking on its icon.

   A button menu appears that lists the different categories of buttons available. To see a collection of buttons, click on the category you want to view.

3. To use any button, select it and choose Copy from the Edit menu or press ⌘-C.

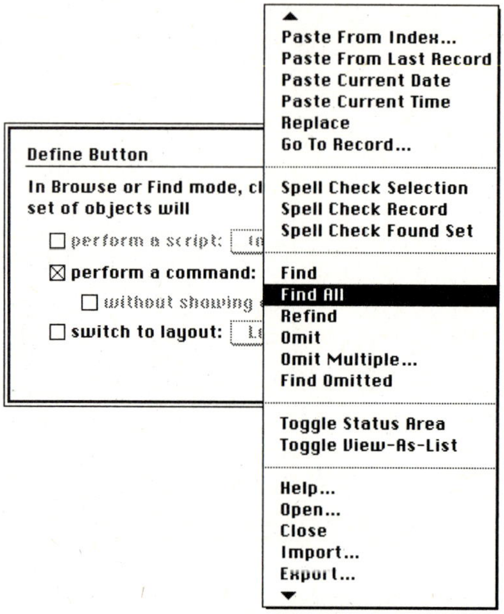

Fig. 12.9
Assigning menu commands to a button from the pop-up menu in the Define Button dialog box.

Note

If you want to use more than one button, you can use the Scrapbook to move them. Refer to your Apple manual for Scrapbook instructions.

4. Return to the layout where you want to use the button. If necessary, choose Open or press ⌘-O to open the file. Then use the ⌘-L keystroke to move to the layout mode.
5. Select Paste from the Edit menu or press ⌘-V. The chosen button appears in the middle of your screen.
6. Use the Arrow tool to drag the button to the desired location.
7. While the button is still selected, choose the Define Button command from the Scripts menu and follow the preceding steps to define the button.

Creating buttons and defining them to perform scripts or commands is a feature new to FileMaker Pro.

In Review

A script is a single command that you define to restore a currently displayed group of settings. You can accept all the settings or just the ones you need.

Scripts can store a number of important operations, such as the current layout, a find or sort operation, page setup, and input and output operations. Previewing or printing a file can be part of a script. You can link scripts, and you can return to your original layout when a script is finished executing.

You can have as many scripts as you want, and you can change their settings, add new ones, and delete them at any time. You can add scripts to the Scripts menu.

Creating buttons in layouts adds power to your database. You can define a button to perform a script, execute a FileMaker command, or switch layouts.

CHAPTER 13

Using Templates and Other Resources

A *template* is a FileMaker file or set of files that contains all the underlying structure needed to organize your work for a specific task. Templates are "canned" databases that contain all the fields, definitions, entry options, layouts, and scripts needed to perform the task for which they were designed. You need supply only the data that is specific to your situation.

You can create your own templates from scratch, or you can buy them from a commercial source. In this chapter, you find some sources of these FileMaker files. Because these files are FileMaker files, you have all the power of FileMaker to alter and refine the file's structure to suit your needs. This chapter introduces you to the tasks you can accomplish in FileMaker.

Defining a Template

Any FileMaker file that another person can use is a template. Templates can be a single file or a set of files that are used for a specific purpose. If a template file requires the use of other files to operate correctly, then the collection of files is considered part of the template.

For example, if you have a set of template files that automate a business's procedures, you may want to have one central file that collects customer or account information. Other files can use the information as lookup information. Structuring a set of templates in this manner permits you to enter the information once, and the information can be used several times. Each file in the set (purchase orders, sales, and inventory) is a template, and they all work together as a template set. In this chapter, no differentiation is made between a single file and a set. A template file (or file set) is created to service a specific need that a user may have.

Figure 13.1 shows a commercial offering, The Small Business Retailer, which is discussed later in the chapter. The offering comprises a set of template files that form a template set. Organizing a business by using centralized data gives you the opportunity to create consistent data that can be used throughout all the operations indicated in figure 13.1. You can create interlocking files this way, or you can use the skills of a professional as a starting place. Templates offer you all these options.

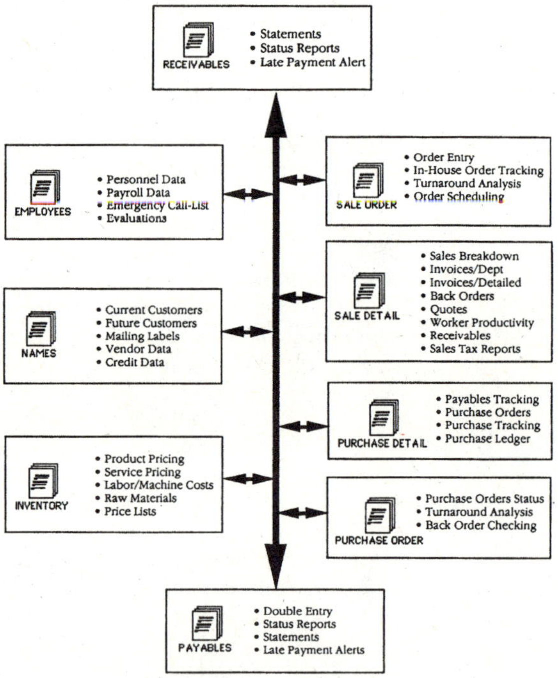

Fig. 13.1
The Small Business Retailer file chart.

When you want someone to use a template file, you often want that file to contain only their information and not your information. Many templates, therefore, contain no records, just the underlying structure of a file. In some situations, however, the person developing the template, the *developer*, wants some of the information that the user needs to keep in that file. Return to the example of a set of templates used to run a business. The developer does not want to include data in a purchase order file, but the developer may want to have a lookup file as part of the template set. For example, the developer may include a lookup file that automatically fills in the ZIP code when you enter the name of a city.

You easily can create a template from any existing FileMaker file by deleting all your records (using the Delete Multiple command). Because a file with no records is a clone, an alternative is to use the Save a Copy command on the File menu to create a clone of the file (see Chapter 3). Either way, the entire structure of the file is left intact: all field definitions, all scripts, and all layouts are unchanged.

When you give that file to another user, the user can employ the file by filling in only the user's own data. This versatility is, after all, what makes a template file valuable. Although a clone is, by definition, a template, remember that not all templates are clones. A template that contains data records is not a clone, but a clone may be a template.

Be certain that when you clone a file for use as a template, you have the right to do so. Most commercial template manufacturers allow you to customize freely the files that you purchase. Often, the developers explicitly tell you in the fine print whether you can make changes. The templates that came with your copy of FileMaker are not copyrighted, and Claris encourages you to use the templates in your own work (see "Using FileMaker Templates" later in this chapter). If you are working with a file created by someone else, however, be sure to check on your rights and limitations in using the file.

Templates save you time in a variety of ways. They impose a consistent structure on your data and your output. After you create a form or report and set up the report for printing, you never again need to perform the exercise. If you have a file that contains lookup data, you can use that file's data for other file lookups because it has the same field name and definition. These tasks are possible because you have a consistent data structure.

Templates also add to your data-entry accuracy because the templates often have considerable auto-entry and data-validity checks. Anytime you automate a function, you decrease the number of keystrokes required and increase the speed and accuracy of your work. You can use the skills and techniques of FileMaker experts to provide you with these features, and you can build on those techniques. Data accuracy is even more important than entry speed, and you can use all the tricks you have learned to have FileMaker enter data for you.

Altering the template can be as simple as removing the layout text that labels the template and replacing the layout text with information suitable to your own application. If you run a company, you can use your company name and logo in place of the ones that were on the template.

You may want to create a template structure for a variety of reasons. Creating a template structure for a large organization establishes a common structure for your data, documents, and output. All templates can use exactly the same field names so that data is easily imported or exported, and using the same layout enables you to create professional reports and forms with consistent styles.

Because of the power of FileMaker, you can have a power user or a developer set up a file that benefits all FileMaker users in a work group. Even if they don't know about a feature like data validation, the feature can be built in for their use. The expert user that oversees the file can assign passwords to protect the file and to limit what each user can do. Protecting files is described in more detail in Chapter 16.

You don't need to be in a large organization to create a template. Any task that requires an organizational structure that you need to reuse for a similar purpose is a good subject for a template. If you are a professional author or researcher, you can create a bibliography that organizes each book or research project into a separate set of files and creates your output in a similar style for each project. One layout can generate a table of contents, and another can be used for an index. A script can be used to organize all the records used for each chapter, and perhaps another can be used to bill your grantor or publisher for the time you spent on the project. After you have created the template, you can use the template over and over again. The data-entry Browse window for the Bibliography file included with the Claris templates is shown in figure 13.2.

Using FileMaker Templates

You don't have to start from scratch if you want to create a set of templates. Claris includes a set of templates with every copy of FileMaker. By all means, dust off your copy of those templates and use them as a starting place for your work. They contain some useful layouts and ideas that you may find valuable in your future work. They also are part of the purchase price of the program and are explicitly provided to you for alteration, with no copyright restrictions. Figure 13.3 shows the template files that are shipped with FileMaker Pro.

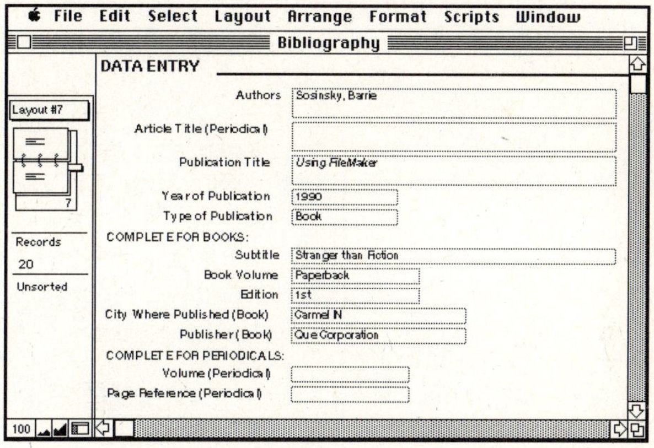

Fig. 13.2
The data-entry screen for a Bibliography file.

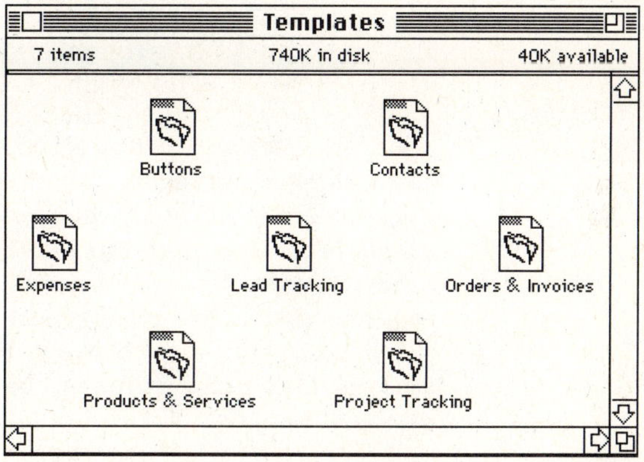

Fig. 13.3
The FileMaker Pro template files.

To use one of these template files, double-click on the file icon in the Finder to open the file or use the Open command from within the FileMaker program. The templates in the Claris set contain some sample records so that you can see how your file will look after you enter the data. To use these files for your own purposes, change the data in the sample records to make them your own and create as many new data records as you require. You enter data into these files as you do any FileMaker file.

Each file has several different layouts. One layout contains information on that template and different ways it can be used. The noteslayout for the Service Order/Invoice template is shown in figure 13.4. Printing out the field names and definitions by using the Print command feature (described in Chapter 10) may be useful to see what fields the templates contain and how they are related to one another.

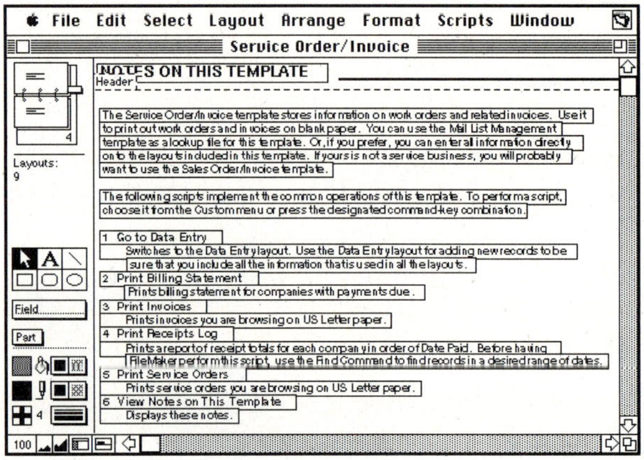

Fig. 13.4
The notes layout for a template.

The Claris FileMaker templates contain a central mailing list that serves as a lookup file for the other template files. Some of the additional files use a lookup as a central repository for commonly used data so that the data only has to be entered once. Sales order/invoice, service order/invoice, checks, purchase orders, expense reports, fixed assets, proposals, membership, and bibliography files demonstrate the range of tasks for which you can use templates. All files may not be valuable to you, but each contains useful scripts and layouts that you can modify for your personal use.

Creating Your Own Templates

When you create a template of your own, think clearly about the different features that you want to include in the file. What tasks are you trying to accomplish? If there is more than one task, how do these tasks relate to one another? Creating a list or an outline defining your needs may be useful. When professional developers are trying to create a structure for a database file (that's what a template is), they usually construct a flow chart. Creating a flow chart may enable you to create a similar set of field names and definitions, and the exercise also helps you to decide how to separate different, but related, tasks into separate related files.

As you build and work with templates, consider the suggestions made in Chapter 1. Your ultimate goal is to enter data accurately, eliminate redundancy, and automate repetitive tasks to the limit of the tools that FileMaker provides. Whenever possible, use auto-entry techniques, data validation, and calculation and summary fields to have FileMaker enter and calculate data for you. Lookup files, fields, and scripts are valuable aids for template users. Remember to test your file with a few sample records to check that the file is operating correctly.

Try to name all the related fields in your templates with the same name and define them in the same way. This organization enables you to use your templates in a consistent and logical manner and eases your task when you cut and paste fields from one layout and file to another. People using your database will understand how the related files were constructed.

Template files commonly have a data-entry screen. Figure 13.5 shows the Layout window for the data-entry screen of the Contacts file from the Claris set of templates. A data-entry screen prompts the user to enter all the needed information into the file, but other layouts may have only a subset needed for a specialized task. If that layout is accessed by a script (see script 1), the layout is easily found.

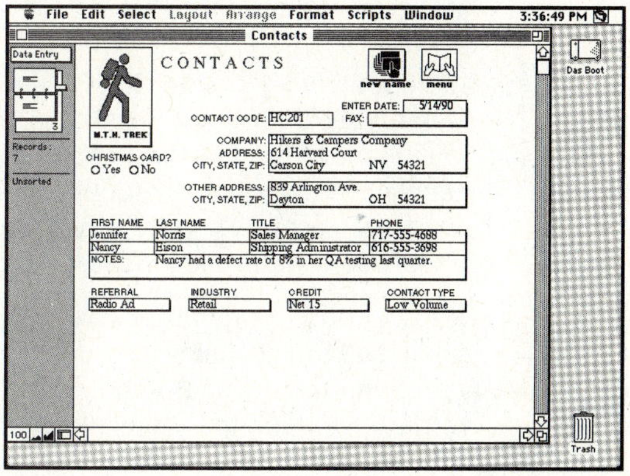

Fig. 13.5
The data-entry window for the Claris Contacts template.

Separating tasks into different files is often a better approach than trying to make a single file do multiple tasks. By using separate files, you can clearly assign each individual record in that file to some set of data that relates only to that task. If you have a file that stores both purchase orders and statements, remembering which records belong to which task can be difficult. When you define auto-entered serial numbers, they can become corrupt, and you may be forced to create "work-arounds" to access the data relating to the different tasks. You don't need separate files for layouts that use the same fields and data, but if the data varies, you need to separate the layouts in separate files. A set of mailing labels used for several different purposes is one example of several layouts sharing the same file.

Lookup information is a valuable auto-entry tool to use with templates. You can create a file containing data to be used by other FileMaker file lookup fields. Files of this type are not normally referred to as templates; they are more commonly called *lookup files*. The Contacts file was the lookup file for the Claris set of templates.

If you have a lookup defined in your template set, the lookup is opened when you enter data into a field that relies on the closed lookup file. Lookups are a great method for keeping handy the information that you may need in your work. Create a lookup, and your lookup file opens at the same time as your current file, which enables you to examine data that you use in your templates. Lookups are discussed in detail in Chapter 5.

Tip

Keep the structure of a lookup file simple. Do not create fields that have auto-entered or calculated data, because they significantly slow down a file's data-access time.

You want your lookups to be as fast as possible. Most professional developers often use lookup files that contain only a couple of fields of data; the files are deep in the amount of data the file contains (number of records), even if the files are narrow in the types of data they contain (number of fields).

Many sources of lookup data can be used, but the most important lookups are undoubtedly the data sets you create. The Elk Horn Library (publisher of *The FileMaker Report*) offers a set of reasonably priced templates for various functions in FileMaker file format. You can purchase a set of ZIP code files that covers the entire United States or an alphabetic-to-numeric lookup.

FileMaker has a straightforward importing function (see Chapter 15), so using data in FileMaker format is not a necessity. You can buy data stored in other formats and import that data into FileMaker to create your own lookup file. Excellent sources are the Heizer Software catalog and the on-line information services. See Appendix D, "Product Index," for references to information services. Companies that rent or sell lists in database format are listed in your local telephone book and in the 800-catalog of the telephone company under the category "Mailing Lists." The world of data is available to you right at your keyboard: all you have to know is what to ask for and how to ask for it.

When you create a template, try to assign scripts to the various tasks you want to accomplish. All high-quality templates make heavy use of scripts to automate various aspects of their use. Perhaps the easiest way to determine the power and elegance of a particular FileMaker template is first to examine the scripts that the file contains. Some scripts contain relatively simple actions: switching layouts, initiating a find, or creating a custom paper size and page setup. Others perform complex actions that may require chaining scripts together. Scripts are productivity enhancers, and you should use them in your work.

The only way you can store a find request, sort order, import or export order, paper size, or page setup is to create a script to store that information. When you pull down the lists of scripts from the Scripts menu, the real function of the template is there for you to examine. Test your template to make sure that it works after you enter a few records; perform all the scripts available in the template.

A good plan for the use of scripts is to have a script that takes you to a layout that stores notes about your template. A second script then takes you to a data-entry screen that makes certain you enter all the requisite data into your file. Additional scripts should be defined around each task you want to accomplish. Because each layout usually is defined to accomplish a task, you should have at least one script for each of the layouts in your file to aid that layout in its task.

Consider the Scripts menu of a FileMaker file constructed to track and manage your checking account (see fig. 13.6). One screen enables you to enter data; a script switches to that layout. The second script switches to a layout that stores notes on the file to remind you of all the different settings of each output and the purposes of each layout. Additional scripts perform various functions associated with your account: printing various forms (such as checks or deposits), updating your records and printing an account summary, and exporting your records to a spreadsheet for analysis.

The Define Button command also is under the Scripts menu. Buttons are layout objects linked to scripts or commands that execute the specified scripts or commands. Anything you want can be a button. The Templates folder that comes with FileMaker Pro gives you many predefined buttons and a whole file of button graphics that are a valuable source of inspiration. Just select the one you want, copy it to the Clipboard, and then paste it into your layout.

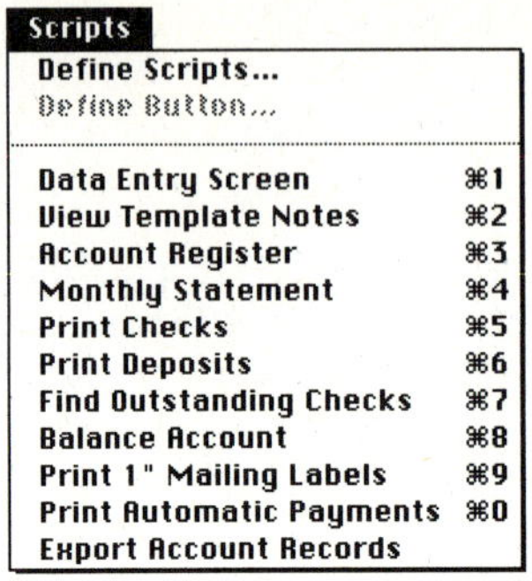

Fig. 13.6
The Scripts menu showing a set of scripts for a checking account database file.

Editing a Template

Because a template is a normal FileMaker file, you can alter it like any other FileMaker file. You can customize templates for your own personal use. Remove the company logo, name, and address and replace them with your own logo and information. Editing any other layout elements that personalize your template also is a good idea. These replacements are simple and are accomplished easily by using techniques you already have learned.

You may require special output beyond what each template provides you. A template is a starting place, but if you have a form that you need to use, you always can add the form to your template file. You can customize layouts by moving fields around or by changing the paper size and page setup to accomplish your tasks.

Always remember to store tasks in scripts. If a script was defined previously for output that you have modified, you need to change the script. Run the script embedded in the script, adjust the settings associated with each command, and store your new settings in a newly defined script. Don't forget to delete the original script.

Reviewing Some Template Ideas

In the sections that follow, you find some examples of tasks you might want to tackle with FileMaker. When examining these examples, try to think of ways you can use FileMaker in your own life and how your approach might borrow from these examples.

Creating Mailing Lists

A mailing list functions as a Rolodex file, and a mailing list is a common template defined in FileMaker. Most template sets offer mailing lists. The advantage to using FileMaker for this particular application is that FileMaker is a good program for finding specific pieces of information, has faster searches, and is flexible in the type of output it delivers.

You easily can use FileMaker to organize your personal telephone numbers and addresses, although many more specialized tools are available, such as Address Book Plus, Focal Point II, and SideKick. These programs offer calendar and time scheduling features, which FileMaker doesn't offer, and these features may be important to you. You can use FileMaker, however, to duplicate these features by adding desk accessories, such as Disk Tools II, to supplement the phone dial feature from Disk Tools II's Phone Pad DA or the daily calendar from the Calendar DA. Specialized desk accessories, such as QuickDex DA, offer many of these features. QuickDex DA is a database in its own right.

Creating Mailing Labels

You can create a single file that contains all your mailing labels, but normally this is not desirable. If your mailing labels are not tracked by a serial number, attach the mailing labels to the files in which they are most often used. In a set of files for different business functions, each file can have its own one-inch mailing labels or large label. When the label becomes a tracked item, you need to create a template file to track the labels you send out.

Remember that you don't have to re-create any labels that you have previously created for other files. If you followed this book's suggestion of naming all fields with the same name, you can cut and paste the fields from one layout to another layout in a new file. For more information about labels, refer to Chapters 10 and 11.

Creating a Card File

FileMaker is an excellent tool for organizing a Rolodex-style file, and you may want to define a template for this use. Each record is an individual card, and you are free to output your records to card stock. In office supply stores, you can find continuous-feed card stock in various sizes that you can use to create a card file. If you are printing a mailing, you can use card stock made for use as a post card, and if you have a business, you can have FileMaker print your business mailing permit in the appropriate place.

You also can use FileMaker as a card file for storing and displaying graphics. Each record might hold a graphic image of an artwork in a museum and an explanation of the art. Because FileMaker accepts pictures in the standard Macintosh formats in both black-and-white and color, you can keep an attractive card file in this format.

To display a moving display of records in a card-type file, you can define a MacroMaker, QuicKeys, AutoMac III, or Tempo II macro to switch records automatically every few seconds. This feature can be useful in real-estate offices and business or product presentations. More specialized presentation products available include Microsoft PowerPoint, Aldus Presentation, and CA-Cricket Presents, but you certainly can use FileMaker for this type of application without much additional effort.

Using FileMaker To Make a Book

By using FileMaker's list and column-setup features, you easily can create a directory of products or items and then publish it as a book. At the end of Quick Start: Creating Mailing Labels, you saw how to adapt the label layout for that purpose. When Nashoba Systems originally published the FileMaker manual, FileMaker was used to create all the pages. FileMaker is an excellent application for database publishing of pages that are defined by regular page-layout output.

FileMaker also has a feature called *signature imposition*. In a printed sheet used for a bound book or magazine, the page plates for the printed pages need to be arranged in a specific order, depending on their position in the final piece. Signature imposition enables the correct order to be defined within FileMaker directly. Both PageMaker and QuarkXPress do not have this sophisticated desktop publishing function yet. For complete details, see "Printing Directories & Signature Imposition," by S.C. Kim Hunter, in issue 23 (September 8, 1989) of *The FileMaker Report*.

Using Purchased Templates

Descriptions of some of the templates currently offered for FileMaker by various companies are in the sections that follow. Most of the commercial templates are provided *as is*; the publisher expects the user to assume the burden of knowing FileMaker and adapting the templates to the user's own needs. Some of the developers offer limited free support; others require support fees. You need to ask about support policies when you purchase a commercial template.

If you have a complex task and want to use FileMaker, starting with a commercial template may not be appropriate. You might consider hiring an outside developer to ease your burden. The outside developer can create a template closely designed for your needs. Most of the companies listed in the sections that follow are developers themselves or keep active lists of professional FileMaker developers. A developer can serve as a consultant to your project or can be involved actively in the construction of your FileMaker database. Expect to pay a professional hourly fee when hiring such a person.

The FileMaker Report and Elk Horn Library

The Elk Horn Library offers a set of templates for various uses and lookup files that you may want to use for creating your own templates. They cover a range of subjects, from a landlord's "Tenant Record-Keeping" system to a "Personal Assets" file. The catalog is currently limited in scope, but offerings are modestly priced.

The same publisher produces *The FileMaker Report*, a newsletter especially written about FileMaker by knowledgeable users and developers. Some of the articles are basic in their theme; some are tutorial in their nature; and many are written by developers on special topics and applications of the program. If you are interested in extending your capabilities in FileMaker as much as possible, this newsletter can be a valuable resource. Ten issues are published each year, and the cost of these newsletters is reasonable.

Gradient Resources

Gradient Resources publishes a set of interlocking templates for small businesses and for professionals responsible for time billing and expense management. The library of templates, which can be purchased separately or as a group, includes two sets of template files called

BillThatJob! and Easy Invoice. The BillThatJob! templates are for professionals who do time billing and track each project by item (see fig. 13.7). The templates create reports and invoices. Easy Invoice enables a business to track and manage sales while using related lookup files you create for customer information (1-2-3 Contact) and inventory (PriceList). Additional templates include an expense log (AutoExpense), a general ledger (Legerdemain), and an order-entry and management system (Order Processing). A template called 1-2-3 Merge Letter enables you to create merged letters with FileMaker by using your client listing.

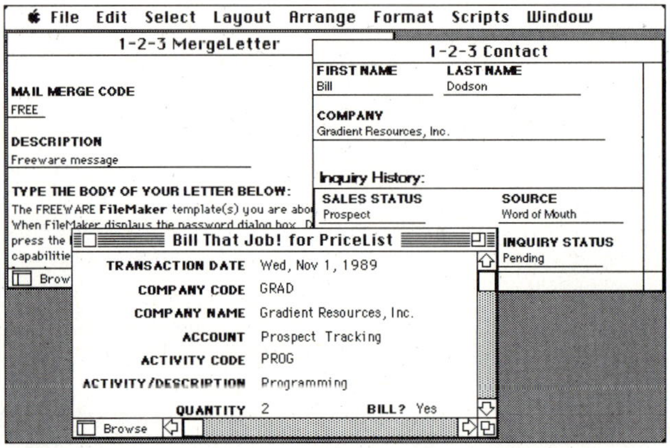

Fig. 13.7
The Gradient Resources BillThatJob! template set.

The Gradient Resources catalog is a new enterprise by a well-known FileMaker developer, and the catalog is constantly adding related templates. The templates in the catalog can be customized for your business needs. If you need more sophisticated support, Gradient Resources offers specialized developer services and on-site training.

Innovative Synthesis

Innovative Synthesis is the company run by the author of this book. The company specializes in creating custom FileMaker templates for businesses, particularly networked database solutions. Innovative Synthesis offers FileMaker developer services and on-site training. The company maintains an active developers list for more specialized and complex projects.

MacPsych Billing

BHC Publishing offers a set of FileMaker templates called MacPsych Billing. The templates automate the billing process for psychiatrists, psychologists, and psychiatric social workers. The program automatically looks up DSM-IIIR diagnoses, CPT-4 procedures, and includes a Universal Insurance Form for quick processing. The program is flexible enough to be used for weekly or monthly billing cycles.

Of Counsel Software

Of Counsel Software is designed for the individual practitioner of law or the small law firm specializing in residential or commercial real estate closings. These templates use FileMaker to track the closing process and to create closing documents. Of Counsel Software's goal is to make the lawyer's life easier by automatically producing cover letters, accounting for escrow monies, tracking the closing process, and creating documents for closing. This software is a combination of a Rolodex for attorneys' names and an accounting package and document generator that enables a secretary to complete many documents associated with real-estate closings by filling in the information screen and printing appropriate forms when needed. Of Counsel Software can be customized easily and modified according to each jurisdiction's need and the needs of localized practice. Currently available templates include HUD-1 forms and closing statements, which are not included in this package.

OrderTrak

OrderTrak is a set of FileMaker templates developed for manufacturers' representatives by Database Associates to track orders, customer service information, and sales commissions (see fig. 13.8). OrderTrak efficiently organizes and automates information by manufacturer, customer, sales representative, and shipping date.

The report structure includes a number of powerful scripts that instantly report daily, weekly, and monthly sales; and year-to-date and year-to-year reports for each sales representative, each item line, and the overall organization progress. OrderTrak automates lookups from customer and manufacturer address files; purchase orders and back order information, by means of SKU-style number description card files; and manufacturers' F.O.B. points and terms. OrderTrak Output follows standard commercial forms or can be adapted to your company's custom forms.

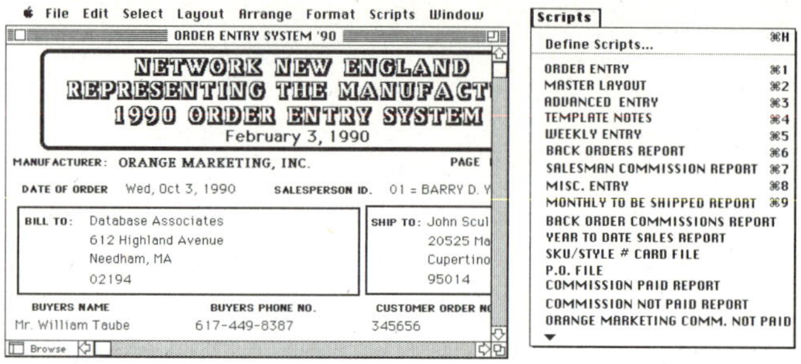

Fig. 13.8
The OrderTrak order-entry management system.

Database Associates provides training, on-line support, and product customization for OrderTrak on a per-case basis.

If you manage a sales organization with item- and sales-tracking needs, then OrderTrak can be a valuable set of templates for your business.

Small Business Retailer

Packer Software sells a product called The Small Business Retailer (SBR), which is a set of FileMaker templates combined with customized scripts that can be used in a retail business. A Sale Order template, along with the Sale Detail template, creates invoices, shipping tags, envelopes, or mailing labels. Other templates include Purchase Order and Detail templates and templates for Employee, Inventory, Accounts Receivable, and Accounts Payable. All the templates relate to each other (see fig. 13.1 again). A sample screen showing three of the related files for a sale is shown in figure 13.9. The whole set is sold as a single package.

SBR is a flexible solution to your business needs. With your knowledge of FileMaker, you can adapt the templates to suit your own personal needs. To operate SBR, you need to be familiar with FileMaker, which is the underlying computing engine. SBR locks out users who cannot pass a quiz indicating that they know FileMaker, thereby preventing an employee from making accidental changes. The documentation assumes that you have some knowledge of FileMaker and deals primarily with features of SBR. SBR is not a canned solution to all business needs. You should expect to do some work customizing SBR to your needs, but SBR represents a fine starting place for a small business.

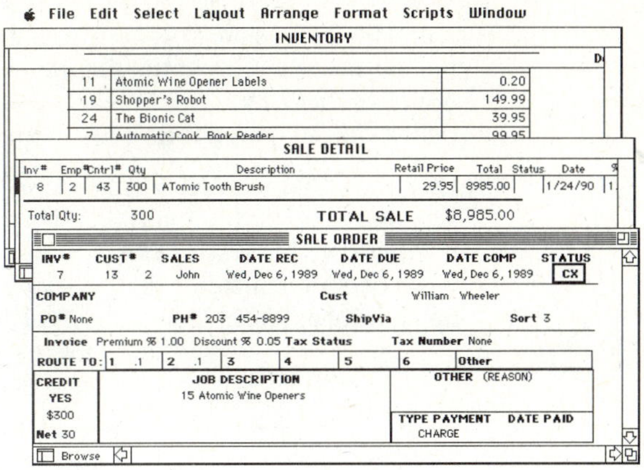

Fig. 13.9
Related sales and inventory files from The Small Business Retailer.

In Review

A template is a FileMaker file (or set of files) with an underlying structure in place for a specific set of tasks. A template is a canned database to which you add your own records.

Templates can be generated easily from existing files by deleting all records or by creating a cloned copy of that file. Clones are a copy with no records, and by definition a clone is a template. You can construct templates from scratch or buy one from a commercial source.

Templates save you time and effort and create consistent data structures and professional output. FileMaker templates are often adaptable to your own specific purpose, so buying a template can save you considerable time. Creating a template can be an excellent learning experience.

Try to build as much automation and data validation into your templates as FileMaker allows. Use of auto-entry techniques, lookup files, and calculation and summary fields speed up data entry and cut down on operator error. Opt for accuracy over speed when a choice is necessary.

Lookups are a very valuable template feature. Most template sets store central data in a lookup file. The best lookup files centralize nonrepetitive data into files that are typically deep and narrow. The files are deep in terms of the amount of data or number of records, and narrow in terms of the types of data or number of fields they contain.

Using scripts is the easiest way to determine quickly the power of a template. Scripts are task-oriented, so an examination of the scripts in a file quickly shows what the file was designed to do. When building a template, define a script for each task you repeat. For even greater ease, define buttons to perform scripts or commands.

Every task that requires a separate set of data should be set up as a separate file. You track certain forms (like invoices and purchase orders) by their own internal tracking numbers, so use separate files for those types of data. For forms that are not tracked (like mailing labels), create an additional layout in any file you choose.

CHAPTER 14

Quick Start: Creating a Summary Report

In this final quick start, you define a *summary report*, in which only derived data is shown. Most beginning users have difficulty understanding how and when to use calculation and summary fields. In particular, the combination of summary fields and their placement in various parts, although flexible, can be confusing. This quick start is designed to help you grasp these concepts.

Creating reports is one task that you may perform often, and redefining all the necessary settings is tedious. A script is the key to doing repetitive tasks. Scripts are FileMaker's only way to store finds, sorts, and page setups. This quick start helps you create a script for practice and capture the script as a button.

In this fourth quick start, you do the following:

- Define and place summary fields
- Find and sort your records
- Create a summary report
- Define a button

USING FILEMAKER PRO

Creating a Year-End Summary

Tax time is coming, and your accountant needs a summary of your yearly sales. Now that the Children of the '60s Holistic Natural Health Food Emporium's records are set up in FileMaker, sales summaries are easy to create. You will create a summary report with all the monthly sales totals.

In order to work with the sales figures, you need to enter the data for each month's sales. This information is given to you on the 28th day of each month by your accountant, who gives you the monthly total. You enter the data in the Day field, the sales amount in the Monthly Sales field, and the month in the Month field. The first thing you need to do is create the fields.

To define the needed data fields, follow these steps:

1. Launch FileMaker and select the Open command from the File menu or press the ⌘-O keystroke.
2. Open the Copy of Catalog Mailing file by double-clicking on the file name.
3. Select the Layout command from the Select menu or press ⌘-L. Make the layout the current layout by choosing it from the pop-up menu on the Layout title bar.
4. Select the Define Fields command from the Select menu or press ⌘-Shift-D to open the Field Definition dialog box.
5. Type *Day* into the Field Name text box; click on the Date radio button and then click the Create button.
6. Repeat step 5 and create a Text field called Month.
7. Repeat step 5 and create a Number field called Monthly Sales.

Adding Summary Fields

Summary fields enable you to perform calculations on a field of a group of records. This capability differentiates summary fields from calculation fields, which perform a calculation on any number of fields in an individual record. Continue working in the Define Fields dialog box and define the summary fields that serve as the basis for your summary report.

Three different summary fields are defined: Sum.Average gives the average amount for a field in a set of records; Sum.RTotal shows how your sales are changing every time a field's value changes and gives a running total; and Sum.Total shows the overall sum of all values in a field.

To create the summary fields, follow these steps:

1. Enter *Sum.Average* into the Field Name text box, click on the Summary radio button, and then click the Create button.
2. In the Summary Formula dialog box, select Average from the pop-up menu on the left, click the Monthly Sales field name in the scroll box, and then click the Create button to return to the Define Fields dialog box.
3. Enter the name *Sum.RTotal* in the Field Name text box, click the Summary radio button, and then click the Create button to return to the Summary Formula dialog box.
4. Click the Running Total check box, the Monthly Sales field name, and the Create button to return to the Define Fields dialog box.
5. Repeat steps 3 and 4 and create a field named Sum.Total that is the total of the Monthly Sales field.
6. Click the Done button to return to the Layout window. Select the Layout command from the Select menu (if needed).

Creating the Layout

Each report requires a layout that is separate from every other report. Think of a report as a form; you can use the same report layout for a different report, but only if you retain the same form for your output.

To create a summary report layout, follow these steps:

1. Select the New Layout command from the Edit menu or press ⌘-N.
2. In the New Layout dialog box, click the Columnar Report radio button, and then click the OK button.
3. Scroll to the bottom of the Field List box and double-click on each of the six new fields you just created—Day, Month Monthly Sales Sum.Average, Sum.RTotal, and Sum.Total—to move them into the Field Order.

4. Click the OK button to return to your columnar report layout, the sixth layout in your file.

5. Remove the footer part by dragging the bottom dotted line of the footer into the part above. This step is optional, but removing the footer part simplifies the process later.

A body part repeats for each record in your report. You need a summary part to define a group of records, so you should add a trailing grand summary part to your layout below the body part. Any summary field placed in the trailing grand summary part calculates over all browsed records for the field you specified in the definition.

Remember that where you place summary fields affects what is summarized. A trailing grand summary part uses *all* records. Other parts work with specific groups of records, as you will see later in this chapter. Chapter 10 describes how using parts and summary fields together offers tremendous flexibility.

To add a trailing grand summary part, follow these steps:

1. Click on the Part tool in the status area of the Layout window and drag the part outline below the body part.

2. In the Part Definition dialog box, click the Trailing Grand Summary radio button and then click the OK button.

3. Click on the Arrow tool in the Toolbox and position the new fields as shown in figure 14.1. Be careful to place the top of each field box in the body part as shown. FileMaker uses the top edge of a field box as the indicator when placing a field in a part.

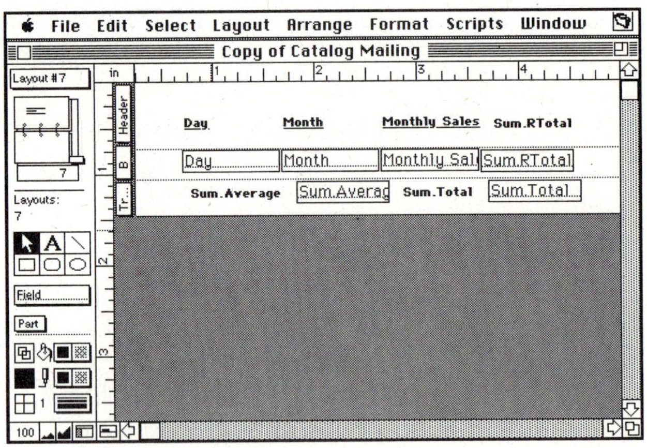

Fig. 14.1
The summary report layout.

Format the fields you have just created so that numbers are formatted with commas and dollar signs and are right-aligned. The fields look more professional that way.

To format your fields, follow these steps:

1. Click on the Arrow tool and select all the fields by dragging a marquee around them or press ⌘-A.
2. Align the fields right by pressing ⌘-Shift-R.
3. Deselect the Day and Month fields by holding down the Shift key and then clicking on their field boxes.
4. Select the Number Format command from the Format menu. In the dialog box, check the Format as Decimal Number radio button. Then click on the Use Thousands Separator and Notation check boxes. Finally, click the OK button.

Entering New Data

On the 28th day of every month, your chief financial officer calculates the sum of the previous month's sales, and the 1991 results are handed to you on a sheet of paper. You need to enter the results (shown in table 14.1) in the Day, Month, and Monthly Sales fields that you just defined.

Table 14.1
Sales Data for the Year 1991

Record	*Day*	*Month*	*Monthly Sales*
1	1/28/91	January	11000
2	2/28/91	February	22000
3	3/28/91	March	33000
4	4/28/91	April	44000
5	5/28/91	May	55000
6	6/28/91	June	66000
7	7/28/91	July	77000
8	8/28/91	August	88000
9	9/28/91	September	99000
10	10/28/91	October	100000
11	11/28/91	November	110000
12	12/28/91	December	120000

To enter the monthly sales figures, follow these steps:

1. Select the Browse command from the Select menu or press ⌘-B.
2. Drag the Slide Control Mechanism to the top to go to the first record.
3. Press the Tab key to activate the Day field; enter *1/28/91*.
4. Press the Tab key to advance to the Month field; enter *January*.
5. Press Tab to advance to the Monthly Sales field; enter *11000*.
6. Press Tab twice to advance to the Day field of the next record.
7. Repeat steps 3 through 6, inserting all the data shown in table 14.1.
8. Press the Enter key when you have finished entering the data. Your Browse window appears as shown in figure 14.2.

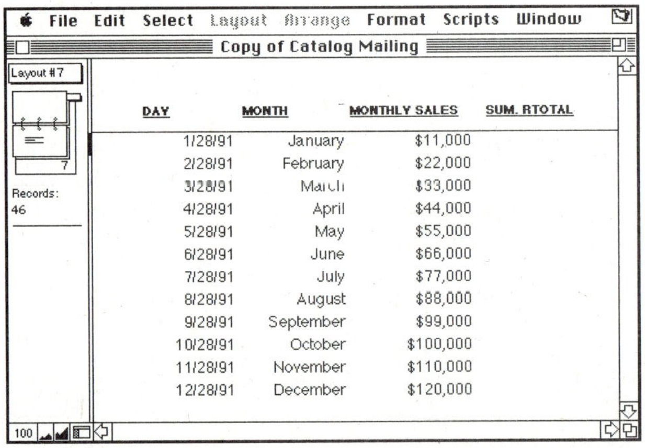

Fig. 14.2
Browsing the records.

The Sum.RTotal may be viewed in Preview; the Sum.Average and Sum.Total appear at the bottom of the Browse window (not shown).

The two summary fields in the grand summary part work fine in the Browse window. As you enter data for each record, the Sum.Average field shows the overall total average, and the Sum.Total field shows the overall total for all records. The Sum.RTotal field must be previewed to be seen. Check the Edit Paper Sizes option in the Page Setup dialog box from the File menu to make sure that US Letter size is selected. Select the Preview command from the Select menu or press ⌘-U. Figure 14.3 shows the results.

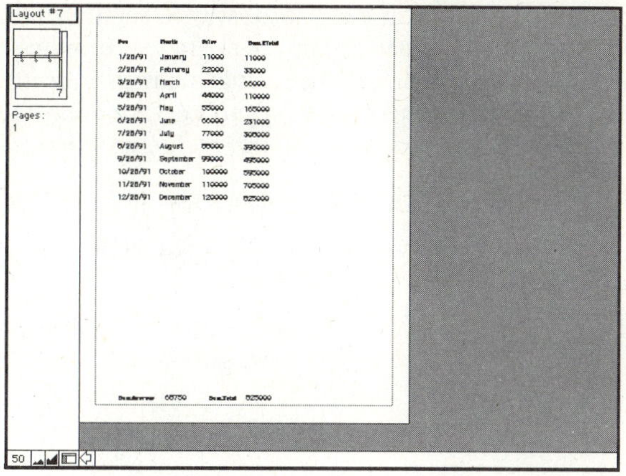

Fig. 14.3
The Preview window for the records with the three summary fields showing.

All the summary fields work properly. The Sum.RTotal field calculates the running total for the Monthly Sales field by adding every month to date from the beginning of the year until the month of December, when the running total is the same as the overall total. For more information about summary fields, refer to Chapters 5 and 9.

Press ⌘-B to return to the Browse window.

Finding and Sorting Records

You are interested only in the 12 records that contain the monthly sales data, not any other records you defined in earlier Quick Starts. To select the desired group of records, perform a find operation.

To find only the 12 monthly records, follow these steps:

1. Select the Find command from the Select menu or press ⌘-F.
2. Type = (the equal sign) only in the month field, or click on the = Exact button (the symbol for a blank field) in the Status Panel.
3. Click the Omit check box to exclude records with no month's data.
4. Click the Find button or press the Return key.

You can use any of these fields as the specified criterion field in your request.

Notice that you don't need to sort the records for summary fields placed in the body or trailing grand summary parts (see fig. 14.3). You can sort those records, and you will obtain different running totals.

You need some way to separate all 12 months into the four yearly quarters and define your running total by the Sum.RTotal field that adds each of those four quarters individually. To separate the 12 months into four quarters, you need to define a Quarter field that indexes the date so that you can sort by financial quarters.

To index the Day field, follow these steps:

1. Select the Define Fields command from the Select menu or press ⌘-Shift-D.
2. Enter the name *Quarter* into the Field Name text box, click the Number radio button, click the Create button to return to the Define Fields box, and click the Done button to return to the Layout window.
3. Select the Browse command from the Select menu to return to the Browse window or press ⌘-B.
4. Enter the following numbers into the Quarter field for each of the records:

    The number *1* for records 1 to 3 (January through March) for the first quarter

    The number *2* for records 4 to 6 (April through June) for the second quarter

    The number *3* for records 7 to 9 (July through September) for the third quarter

    The number *4* for records 10 to 12 (October through December) for the fourth quarter

Use the Tab key to advance through the fields and the ⌘-Tab key to advance through records. Or, click in the field to activate the field. You are now at the stage shown in figure 14.4.

You can define a Date calculation using nested If statements to achieve the same result as grouping months into quarters. If you plan to use a field in a calculation, however, you do not use a field name like “Day” or “Month” because that is the name of a calculation operator. Your Macintosh will behave strangely if you set up this kind of calculation. Refer to Chapter 5 for more information about operators and functions.

Create a sub-summary part below the body part on the layout and move the Sum.RTotal field into that part. Sub-summary parts are placed after or before a group of records, depending on whether they're placed below or above, respectively, the body part. Any summary field placed into a sub-summary part summarizes that group of records. The Sum.RTotal provides a running total of each financial quarter.

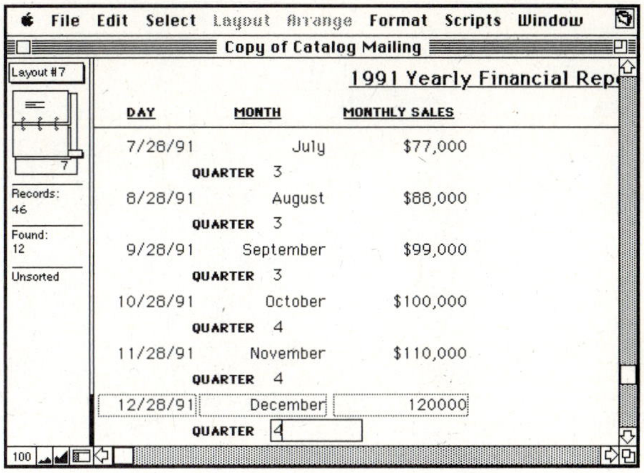

Fig. 14.4
The Browse window with the Quarter field data entered.

To summarize a subgroup of records, follow these steps:

1. Select the Layout command from the Select menu or press ⌘-L.
2. Click on the Part tool in the status area and drag the part outline above the trailing grand summary part (but below the body part).

   When you release the mouse button, the New Part dialog box appears, which offers you only the choice of a sub-summary part.
3. Double-click on the field name Quarter in the scroll box or click to highlight the name and then click on the OK button.
4. Drag the sub-summary part by its label or boundary line to make room for the Sum.Total field. Drag that field and the title of the field into the sub-summary part.

To add the title layout object, follow these steps:

1. Select the Text tool from the Tools Palette and then choose the following commands from the Format menu:

   Select 14 Point from the Size submenu.

   Select Bold from the Style submenu or press ⌘-Shift-B.

   Select the Underline command from the Style submenu or press ⌘-Shift-U.
2. Click an insertion point in the center of the header part and type the text object *1991 Yearly Financial Report*.
3. Click on the Arrow tool and drag the layout object to the desired location. You are now at the stage shown in figure 14.5.

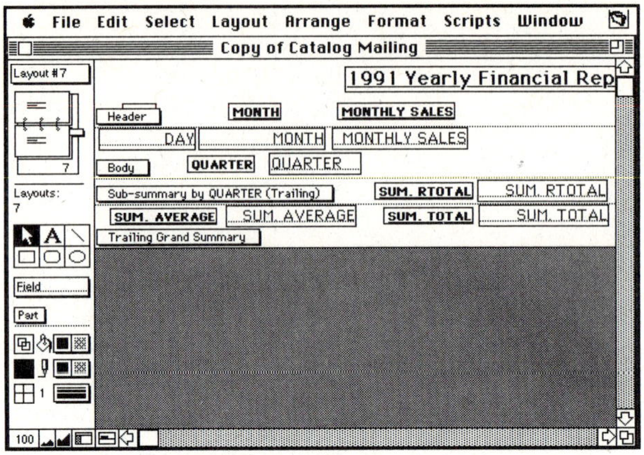

Fig. 14.5
The layout for the 1991 Yearly Financial Report.

If you viewed your browsed records at this point, you would not see the Sum.RTotal field displayed in either the Browse or Preview windows. A summary field in a sub-summary part requires that the records be sorted by the dependent field to display summations. Sort the 12 records by the Quarter field, which will be used as an index.

To sort your records, follow these steps:

1. Select the Sort command from the Select menu or press ⌘-S.
2. Double-click on the Quarter field name to move the field into the sort order or click on the field name and then click the move button.
3. Click the Sort button or press the Return key.
4. Select the Preview command from the Select menu. The Sum.RTotal and all other fields are operating properly (see fig. 14.6).
5. Click the Done button to return to the Browse window.

You can see summary fields in sub-summary parts only in the Preview window, not in the Browse window. Sub-summary parts are discussed in Chapter 9.

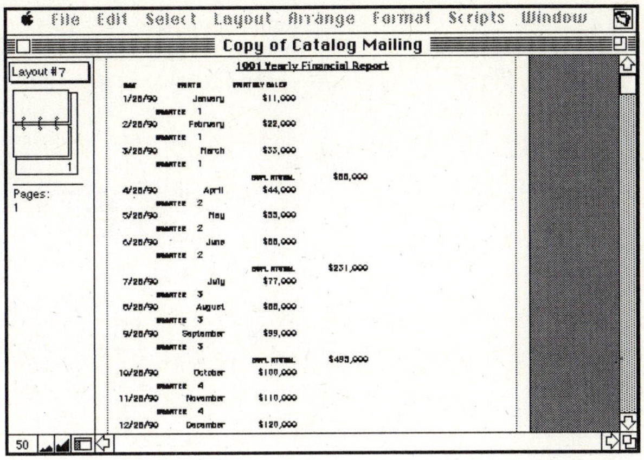

Fig. 14.6
The Preview window for the finished summary report.

Creating Scripts

Creating the summary report that was your 1991 Yearly Financial Report was a lot of work. You found a set of records, sorted them by a particular field, and selected a US Letter size page setup. When you change layouts, close the file, or continue working with your file, those settings are lost.

Losing your specified settings may not be important if you create this report once a year, but if this report were for daily sales, you could save a lot of time by freezing these settings inside a command.

Scripts are like macros. Scripts are small programs in which you tell FileMaker what to do. In a script, you embed your file's condition when you define the file. You are then free to execute that script later on. You can execute the script from wherever you are in the file and return to the condition you specify.

To create a script for the summary report, follow these steps:

1. Select the Define Scripts command from the Script menu.
2. In the Define Scripts dialog box, type *Summary Report* in the Script Name text box. The Create button is now enabled. Click Create.
3. The Definition for Script dialog box appears on the screen. Check the following options: Switch to Layout (Layout #7), Restore the Page Setup Options, Find (Restore Find Requests and Find), Sort (Restore Sort Order and Sort), Preview, and Include in Menu (see fig. 14.7).

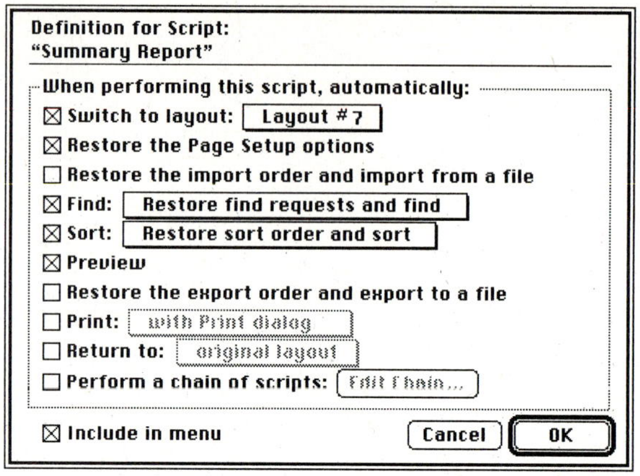

Fig. 14.7
The settings for the Summary Report script.

These settings bring back your file in its present condition. Previously in this Quick Start, you specified a find and sort operation; this script remembers the operations and performs them when the command is issued. Including the script in the Scripts menu is convenient; the first ten scripts are assigned the keystrokes ⌘-1 through ⌘-0 and are listed by their names.

4. Click the OK button to return to the Scripts dialog box and then click the Done button.

You can define and execute a script from within any FileMaker window. To see how the script you have created works, return to the third layout, which was the invoice form you created in Quick Start: Creating Mailing Labels. Select the Find All command from the Select menu to unsort your records and remove your find request. Change the paper size and page setup to something other than US Letter size.

To perform a script, follow these steps:

1. Select the Summary Report command from the Scripts menu or press ⌘-1 to perform the Summary Report script.

   Notice that the same Preview window you saw in figure 14.6 appears.

2. Press ⌘-B to return to the Browse layout.

3. If you want, examine the settings for Edit Paper Sizes in the Page Setup command from the File menu.

The power of scripts is obvious in this simple exercise. For more information about scripts, refer to Chapter 12. For practice, you may want to create a button on your layout that captures the script you just created. In Chapter 12, the section called "Adding Buttons To Execute a Script or Command," tells you how to create buttons.

CHAPTER 15

Importing and Exporting Data

Your data is not very useful if you cannot move it around. By using the Import and Export commands on the File menu, you can exchange the data contained in your files: from file-to-file inside FileMaker, or between FileMaker and other Macintosh applications. You can specify which records and what fields to transfer and in what order.

As you continue to work in FileMaker, you naturally will consolidate data into files in new, compact, or more powerful ways. You might want to create a master file from several other files by transferring data between FileMaker files. A master file is one that consolidates data from general files. When used for storage only, these files are more commonly called *archives*. Sometimes files need to shrink instead of grow. By creating an archive, you can remove data from files when it is no longer needed and make your files run faster with less confusion. Archives also offer a convenient means of safe storage.

If you have been using data in another application or on another computer, you might need to import that data into FileMaker. For example, you might import data if you use a power spreadsheet for extensive number crunching, and you want to use FileMaker for data storage or for its excellent forms-oriented graphics. This chapter provides detailed examples of importing data from Microsoft Works for those users trading up to FileMaker. Before you work with data imported from other applications, you may want to read those files with FileMaker.

Because FileMaker is so powerful and convenient, much of the data stored in database files may be useful to you if exported to another application, database, spreadsheet, word processor, or presentation-graphics program. To create a number of file formats that other programs can read, FileMaker creates output files without using the Clipboard for copy and paste. Examples of exporting are provided in this chapter for conducting mail merges in Microsoft Word and graphing data in Excel.

Copying Versus Importing or Exporting

The differences between copying a file, cloning it, and importing or exporting data between files all reflect FileMaker's distinctions between a file's structure and its data. File structure includes fields and their definitions, and all aspects of a layout, including scripts and other settings, such as page setup or paper sizes. Data, on the other hand, is any keyboard character you type and enter into a field.

When you copy a file with the Save a Copy As command (see Chapter 3), you are making a duplicate file with all its internal structure of a file without the data; you should use the Clone option with the Save a Copy As command (see Chapter 5). You can create a clone and import data into that file because it initially contains no records. Clones are helpful for creating a subset of a file, creating an archive, or for adding and removing information selectively.

If you want to copy aspects of one file structure to another FileMaker file, use the Clipboard instead of the Clone option. Any object from a layout can be copied across files—including fields—provided that the target file has the same field names and definitions (see Chapter 7).

To move only data to or from FileMaker, use the Import or Export commands. You can exchange all the records in your file or any subset of them. In any exchange of data involving a FileMaker file, you need to consider how to select and organize the records you transfer. Your browsed set of records in its current condition determines what may be exported or imported. When you modify records in some manner (by sorting them, for instance), their transfer is based on their current sorted order.

Creating an Archive

You should off-load your files from a floppy disk or hard drive when they are no longer needed. When you finish with data in database files, you can move the data to a special file and store it as an archive. By using archival storage, you choose and store meaningful data sets and help your active FileMaker files operate more quickly.

Creating an archive involves transferring data from one FileMaker file to another FileMaker file. The archive file can be a clone of the original file, containing all the layouts and layout objects in the original file and only the records you just added, or it can contain only the fields and data of interest. Usually, you can create a file to which you can continue to add records after you create it. You create a clone by using the Save a Copy As command from the File menu (see Chapter 3).

To create an archive of your current file, use the Save a Copy As command to create a copy of the file or, better yet, a compressed copy. Then input your archived records into the copied file.

A cloned file is useful for working with data viewed in its graphic display. If you have an invoice file, after the sale is completed and the invoice is paid you might want to retire the data to an archive. Viewing past invoices in invoice form might be more meaningful than viewing the raw data.

If all you want to do is store the data, you merely need to create a file that contains all the needed field names. Because you need to be sure that all the fields are in compatible data types, it is easier to clone the file than to create one. You can always delete layouts and objects as needed.

Moving Data between FileMaker Files

Exchanging data between FileMaker files is the easiest data transfer. You may want to exchange data for a number of reasons. You might want to create a file of your best customers by exchanging data from several sales files. If you have a file with repeating fields, you can split the repeating fields option to create undivided records. When the Fly-By-Night Travel Agency does mailings to previous customers, it splits the charter tour files into records for each individual client.

Start with the input file from which you want to copy data. Open the current file into which you want to input the data. FileMaker examines the field names in each of the two FileMaker files, and if their names match, their data is interchanged. You have no control over what fields are exchanged, because FileMaker exchanges all the fields. Make your record and data edits after the importation is complete.

When FileMaker searches the current file for matching field names, it considers every nonspace keyboard character to be significant, and it is not case-sensitive. For example, when the field name Field2 is encountered in an input file, data in that field is entered into any field named Field2, field2, or Field 2 in your current file. You cannot have the names Field 2 and Field2 in the same file. FileMaker ignores the space and considers them the same field. The fields Field2 and 2field, however, are considered different.

As long as names match, data is imported. Text, Number, Date, Time, Picture, or calculation fields in the input file can be copied into Text, Number, Date, Time, or Picture fields in the current file. Data cannot be copied into calculation or summary fields because they are calculated from data contained in records that are part of their field definition.

Although field types do not need to match, they at least must be compatible. For example, you can copy Text values into Number fields, but Picture fields can only be copied into other Picture fields. If a field cannot support the data to be input, that data is modified so that it is acceptable. For example, if the second field in your current file is a Number field and the second field in your input data file is a Text field, only numeric characters are imported. You lose all alphabetic characters.

Note

Before you exchange data, you may want to find, omit, or sort records from the input file. Save a copy of that file with the records of interest. When finished, delete the unnecessary file.

Transferring data between files is easier if the System, Finder, and all the files you are working with are in your disk drives—or in any combination of floppy drives and hard drives. If you do not have enough room for all these files, you will find yourself swapping disks frequently, and you likely will abort the operation due to frustration.

To import a FileMaker file, follow these steps:

1. Select the Browse command, if needed, to open the Browse window. Open the FileMaker file to which you want to add records.

   or

If you want to create a file that contains only the imported records, you can clone the input file and import the records into the clone. This can be done by cloning the file (see "Using Clone a Copy" in Chapter 3). You also can create a file using field names identical to those in the file to be imported.

2. Choose the Import command from the File menu. The Import dialog box appears (see fig. 15.1).

Fig. 15.1

The Import dialog box.

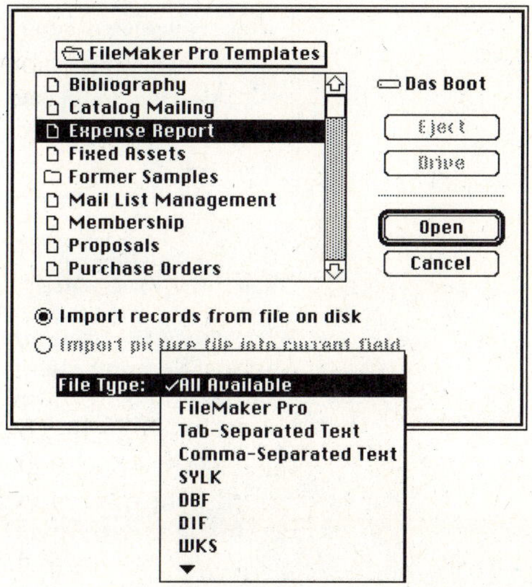

3. Navigate the file system in the Open File dialog box and click on the file name to highlight it.

4. Click the Open button or double-click on the file name.

FileMaker posts a dialog box similar to figure 15.2, which informs you of the name of the import file, the total number of its fields, and the number of fields that have compatible field types and will be imported. Calculation fields are not included in the field count of the current file because values cannot be imported into calculation fields.

When matching field names in the import file with those in the current file, FileMaker ignores capitalization and extra spaces between words. All other characters and punctuation must match.

Fig. 15.2

The Matching Fields dialog box.

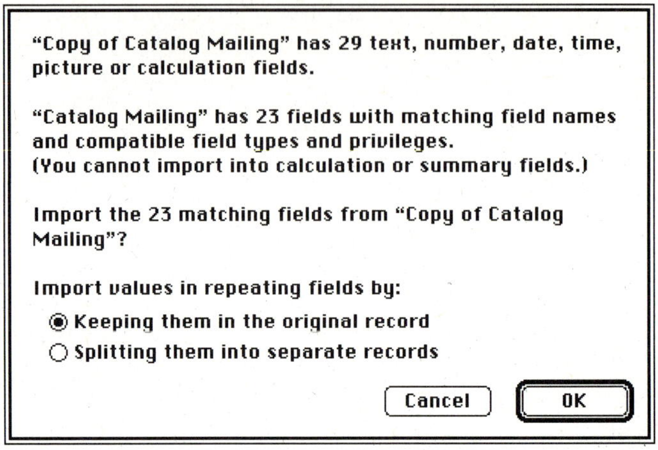

5. Click the option you desire for importing repeating fields.

   When you have repeating fields in the current layout, you have two options: Keeping Them in the Original Record (the default) and Splitting Them into Separate Records. When you choose the first option, the repeating fields are kept in the original record. With the second option, the repeating fields are split into separate records. The nonrepeating fields in the record are included once within each separate record.

   For instance, if you split an order with repeating sales fields, a new record is created for each sales field. The record, in addition to containing the individual sales field, contains the customer name, address, order number, and other nonrepeating fields. When you split up repeating fields into individual records, the field with the largest number of repetitions determines the number of records created; any nonrepeating field has its field value repeated in each record. In a situation with repeating fields of different repetition lengths, a blank value is carried over when there are not enough repetitions to fill all the created records.

6. Click the OK button to import the records.

If you change your mind, you can cancel the command by clicking the Cancel button. After you click OK, you cannot go back to the file's previous condition. FileMaker posts a message box that informs you of the progress of your data exchange (see fig. 15.3).

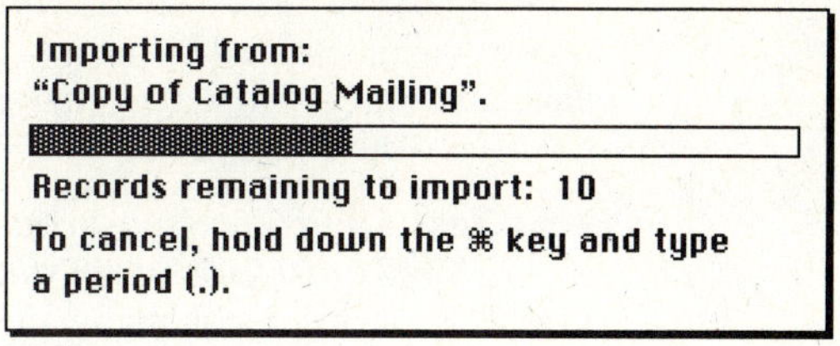

Fig. 15.3
The status message box for an internal file-to-file record transfer in progress.

If you have a large file, importing the records can take a long time. In addition to the message box shown in figure 15.3, FileMaker displays a ⌘-. (period) cursor on the screen during the operation. If you decide to abort the operation in progress, press ⌘-. (period). FileMaker completes the import of the record it is currently importing and then stops. You can delete the records that were imported by using the Delete Multiple command (see Chapter 4).

After you complete the data exchange, the imported records become the only records found. You then can browse those records, check their contents, and modify them if necessary.

Entry options specified in the current file are not executed during data exchange, so any serial number fields you defined are not disturbed. If you need to update these types of fields, do it at this point in the process. You may want to use the Relookup command (see Chapter 5) to have your new records updated to include lookup information.

Reviewing Supported File Formats

When you copy data from one FileMaker file to another, the transfer is direct. You do not have to use an intermediate file. When you want to transfer data from FileMaker to another application or from another application to FileMaker, you must use an intermediate file: a data file. This file can be set up in one of several file formats.

A *file format* is an organized set of data separated in some logically defined manner—like separating field values by a character, such as a tab or a comma—or separating each record by a return character. Defining what separators are used and other restrictions, such as the size of the data in each field and its allowed characters, also defines a file format.

FileMaker supports data exchange in the following formats:

Tab-Separated Text. With this format, fields are separated by tabs, and records are separated by return characters. If a field has a return character entered in it, that character is translated to a soft return or ASCII vertical tab character.

Text. Text is the format most commonly used by word processors (Microsoft Word, Claris, MacWrite, and Ashton-Tate FullWrite Professional) and is used with many other applications that can read Text, such as spreadsheets and databases. When in doubt about a format choice, use Text for Macintosh database applications. Text imposes the fewest restrictions on your data and gives you the most flexibility.

Comma-Separated Text. This format separates fields by commas and puts all text into ASCII characters. Returns within a field are ignored. Repeating fields become serial values. Only 256 characters per field are retained.

BASIC. BASIC format separates fields by commas and records by return characters. Return characters in fields are replaced by a space character. All field values are enclosed in quotation marks, except unformatted numbers, which are exported as they were typed and appeared. A field value with a double quotation mark (") is replaced by a single quotation mark ('). When a Number field includes nonnumeric characters, only the numeric characters are exported.

BASIC imposes some restrictions on the size of a field and on data-attribute formatting that you may find unacceptable. BASIC has a limit of 255 characters in a field. If you have more than that number of characters, FileMaker truncates from the 256th character on.

BASIC format gets its name from being the file format in which the BASIC programming language prints. BASIC uses commands like PRINT# or PRINT USING# statements. dBASE Mac and FoxBase+/Mac can use the BASIC format but more commonly use the DBF format. When using a file for transfer to another database, particularly one on the IBM PC, BASIC is the best format to use.

SYLK. The SYLK format separates fields into columns and records into rows. If a Number field contains nonnumeric characters, only numeric characters are exported. Each piece of text or number is recognized as a cell when imported into an application that reads SYLK. Date, Time, and formatted Number fields are output as Text fields with their field values enclosed in quotation marks. An unformatted Number field is output as that number without quotation marks. Because SYLK restricts output to no more than 245 characters for a field, additional characters are truncated.

SYLK is a link format promoted by Microsoft and is an acronym for *SYmbolic LinK*. It is most often used by spreadsheets and is the best choice for transfer to Microsoft Excel and Wingz by Informix.

DBF. DBF is dBASE format and was created for use with dBASE files. DBF file formats use a fixed field length. The length is determined when creating the field or modifying the field attributes. 4th Dimension also uses a fixed field length for certain types of fields. FileMaker Pro is compatible with dBASE III.

DIF. DIF stores data in rows and columns. This format is used by some spreadsheet programs, such as VisiCalc and AppleWorks software.

WKS. The WKS format also stores in rows and columns and is intended for use with Lotus 1-2-3 spreadsheets.

MERGE. The MERGE file is a format used by some Macintosh applications for doing data-merge operations. This file consists of a document in which fields are separated by commas and records are separated by return characters. The first record in a file is a header record, where field names are listed in sequence. When a field value contains a comma, the entire field is surrounded by quotation marks to indicate that everything within them is a character string and not more than one field. When a quotation mark occurs inside a field value, the MERGE format puts a second set of quotation marks around it, as in ""field value."" Return characters are output as ASCII vertical tab or soft return (Shift-Return in Microsoft Word) characters.

Microsoft Word uses the MERGE format to do mail merges: the equivalent of a data document in Word. Other Macintosh utilities and applications following Mac style also use the MERGE format. Silicon Beach's Silicon Press printing utility also uses MERGE.

When you split the values in repeating fields into separate records, the values output to Text, BASIC, and MERGE files are split by using an ASCII field separator character between values. This means that repeating fields result in records with more than the number of field values. SYLK cannot support more than one value per cell and only the first value is exported. To export all the values in a repeating field to a SYLK file, split them into separate records by using the Save a Copy As command followed by the Input From command, as described in the section "Creating an Archive."

WARNING

Pay particular attention to the truncation feature when you create data documents in BASIC and SYLK. You may lose data in the exchange, which might cause problems.

Most databases accept a variety of file formats, but Text and BASIC are the most common. Because MERGE is a variant of Text, you commonly can use MERGE for transfer where Text is applicable. In rare instances, the SYLK format is acceptable, mainly for Microsoft products.

Exporting Data to Other Applications

You may want to export data to another application for different reasons. For example, spreadsheets provide more sophisticated number-crunching tools, or you might want to export your sales to an accounting package.

When you export data, you need to do three things. First, specify the export order, which selects the fields to include. You can export Text, Number, Time, Date, and even calculation fields to your export file. Specifying the export order gives you some additional control regarding the field order. You can specify the order for placing fields and whether they are used with all the fields or any subset.

Second, specify the file format. To determine the file format appropriate to the application you're using, consult the discussion of formats earlier in this chapter or the documentation that came with that application.

Third, specify whether to include formatting. When FileMaker creates an output file, it does not copy character formats into the data, so all formatting, such as italic or bold, is lost. You can export data attributes, such as a number formatted to a certain decimal place or with a dollar sign or a Date in a certain style.

Your options are determined by the file format you choose. With Text and SYLK, Number, Time, and Date fields output the same values displayed on your Browse window. When these fields are output unformatted, only the characters you type are output. With SYLK, if Numbers, Time, and Date are not formatted or if you choose to output them without formats, the values appear as you entered them.

To create a data (or export) file, follow these steps:

1. Open the file containing the records you want to export and make it the current file.
2. Browse the records that you want to export by selecting them by using the Find or Omit command.
3. Organize the records by sorting them, if you want.

4. Choose the Browse command from the Select menu and open the Browse window.

5. Select the Export command from the File menu. FileMaker prompts you with the Export dialog box (see fig. 15.4).

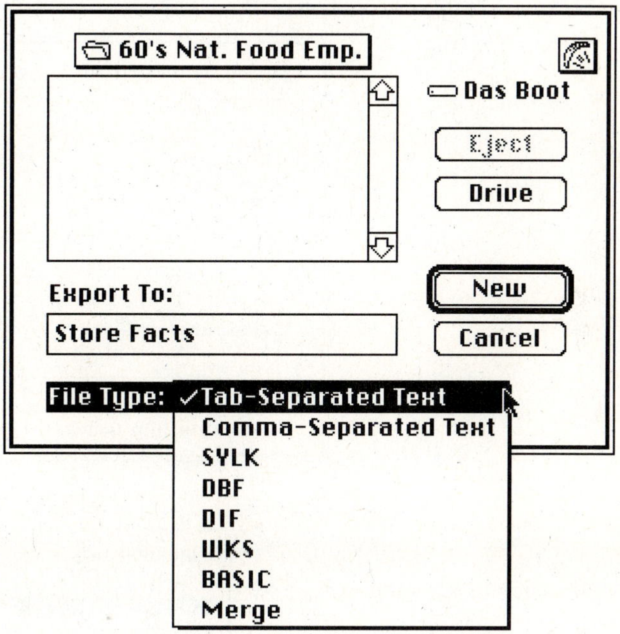

Fig. 15.4
The Export dialog box showing the loaded Claris file filters (translators).

6. Open the folder you want the file to be placed in, type a file name into the text box, and click the New button or press the Return key.

   FileMaker posts the Field Order dialog box shown in figure 15.5.

7. Make your selections in the Field Order dialog box. Choose the export file format you desire by clicking its radio button. Choose either Don't Format Output or Format Output Using Current Layout.

   To move a field, place the pointer over the field name. When the pointer changes to a double arrow, drag the field to the location you want.

8. Click the OK button or press the Return key to create the data or export file.

If you change your mind about exporting the data, you can press ⌘-. (period) to cancel the process. Writing a data file posts a status message similar to figure 15.6 and puts the ⌘-. (period) cursor on-screen. If you press ⌘-. (period), FileMaker completes writing the record it is currently on and then stops the data transfer.

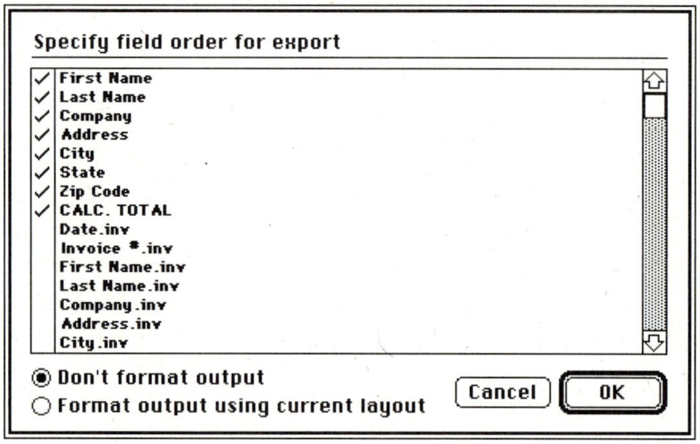

Fig. 15.5
The Field Order dialog box for exporting data.

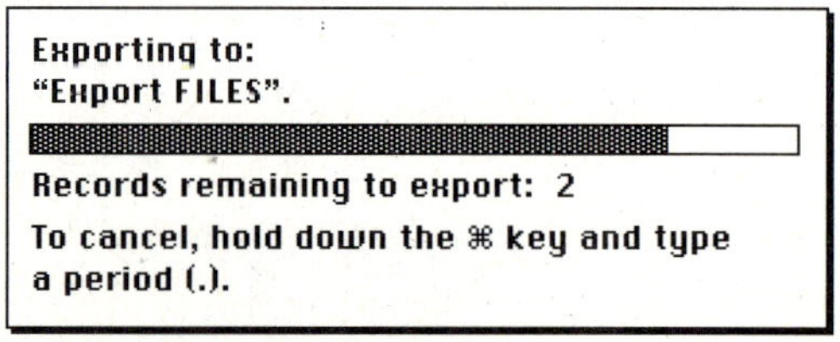

Fig. 15.6
The status message for data output in progress.

Doing Mail Merges in Microsoft Word

FileMaker makes doing mail merges in Microsoft Word a breeze. The MERGE document in FileMaker is the exact equivalent of the data document in Word. You therefore can use a MERGE file created by FileMaker to replace the data document in Word. This section shows you how.

To do a mail merge in Word, follow these steps:

1. Create your MERGE document in FileMaker, containing all the necessary fields and records you plan to use. You create the MERGE file by exporting records in the MERGE format.

Names of the fields in each file must match exactly. Unlike FileMaker, Word considers spacing when searching for field names. Your mail merge loads faster if you place the MERGE file in the same folder as your form letter. Each line in the MERGE file (past the header line) generates a form letter.

2. Open Microsoft Word and create your main document, which becomes the prototype of your form letter.

3. The first line of the main document contains the following:

   <<DATA File Name>>

   Type the << symbol by using the Option-\ keystroke, and the >> symbol by using the Shift-Option-\ keystroke.

4. On the next line and subsequent lines, type your letter.

5. At places where field information will be substituted, enclose the field name with the double arrow symbols:

   <<field name>>

   You can use field names as often as you like. Consult Word's documentation for additional options, such as formatting a field or using logic statements. Refer to figures 15.7 and 15.8 for an illustration of both the MERGE file and the main document. The MERGE format was discussed in the section called "Reviewing Supported File Formats" earlier in this chapter.

6. Select the Print Merge command in Word to initiate the printing, enter your print specifications, and sit back as your merged document prints.

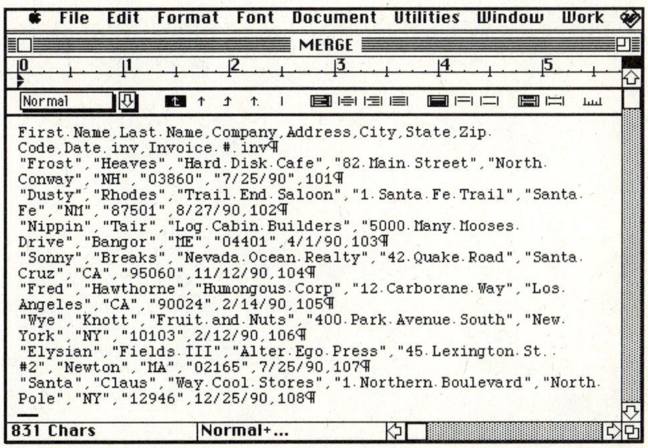

Fig. 15.7

The MERGE document in Microsoft Word for a mail merge.

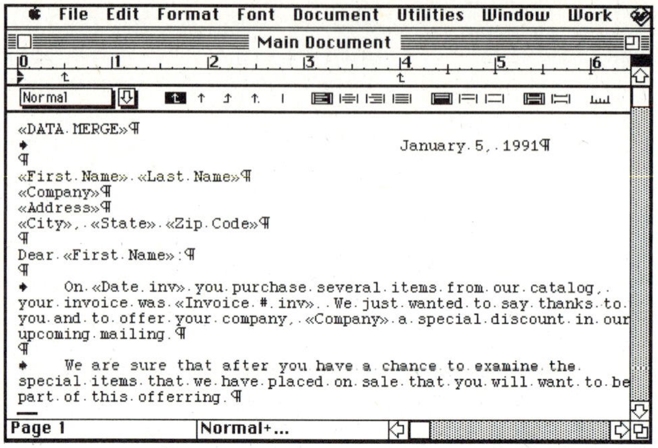

Fig. 15.8
The main document in Microsoft Word for a mail merge.

Graphing Data into Excel

To export data into Excel you need to use the SYLK format for your data document. Usually, you export only the Number fields of interest and maybe some Text fields that label the data. You do not need to have the SYLK document in FileMaker open to import it into Excel. You do not need to be overly concerned with perfect ordering of data or even specifying the right data set in FileMaker. Editing is easier inside Excel, where columns (fields) and rows (records) are easily deleted.

To export data to Excel, follow these steps:

1. Launch FileMaker and open the file with the data you want to export. Then find (select) and sort (organize) the records of interest.

2. Select the Export command in FileMaker, name the SYLK file, and specify the fields you want to export in the Field Order dialog box.

   You do not need to export Number, Date, Time, or calculation fields as formatted data types because Excel has a similar set of commands.

3. Select the SYLK format and then click the Export button.

4. Load Excel (quitting FileMaker, if necessary) and select the Open command from the File menu or press ⌘-O.

5. Navigate the file system and open your SYLK document by double-clicking on its name.

Your SYLK document is opened as an Excel worksheet, where you can cut, copy, and paste your data.

6. To graph your data in Excel, you first select it and then issue the New command from the File menu or press ⌘-N.
7. Click the Chart radio button, and Excel plots your selected data.
8. Using choices in the Galley and the Chart menus, modify your graph to suit your needs.

   Consult your Excel manual for further details and options.
9. Save your Excel chart and quit Excel.

   Excel Version 2.2 is not the strongest graphing product on the market. DeltaGraph is the current market leader for presentation graphics. KaleidaGraph is a good choice for a scientific/engineering graphing package. The Wingz spreadsheet offers a more complete graphing solution. All these applications can use the standard SYLK format.

Importing Data into FileMaker

At times, you will want to import data into your FileMaker database. For example, you might want to establish a lookup file with data in another program, or transfer data that has been manipulated by a spreadsheet back into FileMaker.

To import data, you begin with three choices. The first two decisions, about order and file format, have parallels in exporting data. Your third choice updates current records or creates records.

First, specify the import order of the data file. The import order controls which values and in what order those values are imported. FileMaker imports the data from each field in the data file in the order of occurrence in the data file. You are responsible for determining whether the fields that are being imported are in the right order and of compatible data types. Field names do not have to match; however, the field order must be compatible for the transfer to work correctly.

Second, choose the file format. You can use any of the standard file formats for your import operation—Text, BASIC, or SYLK—but you must specify a file type for FileMaker to import correctly.

If you used the MERGE format, which is similar to the Text format, specify Tab-Separated Text as its file format. You end up with a record that contains the header information, with field names as values in the first record. This header record can be useful in checking to be sure that the data exchange worked properly. You can delete this record when finished.

Most Macintosh applications allow data to be saved in several file formats, although one format is generally the default style. Word processors use Text; spreadsheets use SYLK; and databases use Text, BASIC, or, more rarely, SYLK. Databases built on dBASE or for DOS computers usually use DBF format.

Check the documentation that came with your application to see what style of data was created. If you cannot determine what file format was used, work with a copy of your current file and try a guess based on the choices just mentioned.

Third, add new records to your current file or update current records. When adding the data as new records, FileMaker imports the values and places the new records at the end of the file. Their natural record number in your file starts with the next number available. FileMaker also selects or finds only the records that you imported so that you may inspect, modify, and work with them. If you have additional fields in the import record and add the records, the fields are ignored. If you have fewer fields in the import record and add the records, FileMaker leaves blank the extra fields in your current file.

Updating records *replaces* the records you are browsing in the order they are browsed. If you have too few fields or records in the import (data) file, the values in the extra fields or records in your current file are not overwritten. If you have extra fields or records in the data file, FileMaker ignores the extra fields and updates only the number of records that you are browsing. FileMaker posts an alert message that warns you that additional data is in the data file but was not imported.

WARNING

If you use the Replace Records in Current Found Set option, you cannot undo that operation. You should work with a copy of your file because FileMaker permanently replaces the values in your file. This lack of an enabled Undo command is the result of the auto-save feature.

WARNING

When you update records, be sure that the field order is appropriate, in sequence, and compatible. Check your records carefully before you destroy your original copy.

Reading an Import File

Often you want to read data into FileMaker from an import file. An import file can be data saved by any Macintosh or non-Macintosh program in one of the standard file formats discussed previously.

To import data from a data file, follow these steps:

1. Check that the field order and definitions in the current FileMaker file and the data file are consistent. If the files are not consistent, rearrange the import file or the FileMaker file, or create a FileMaker file with appropriate fields, reorganize, and do a FileMaker-to-FileMaker exchange. Inconsistency between files results in lost or misplaced data. You can open a word processor and check your data file for content.

2. Open the current file and browse the records in the order that you want to update them. Use the Find, Omit, and Sort commands to order your records. Be sure to work on a copy of your file if you are updating records. See Chapter 3 for further instructions on creating a browsed set of records.

   or

   If you want to add records, browse any or all the records in your file.

3. Select the Browse command to open the Browse window, if needed. Then select the Import command from the File menu. FileMaker opens the Import dialog box.

4. From the pop-up menu, choose the file type you want to import.

   The choices are Tab-Separated Text, Comma-Separated Text, SYLK, DBF, DIF, WKS, BASIC, or MERGE. When you make your selection, the list displays only files in the chosen format.

5. Navigate the file directory and double-click on the file name of your data file. You also can click to highlight the name and then click the Open button or press the Return key. Click the Cancel button, ⌘-. (period), to abort the operation.

6. In the resulting Field Mapping dialog box (see fig. 15.9), make two selections.

   Click on either the Add New Records or Replace Data in Current Found Set radio button.

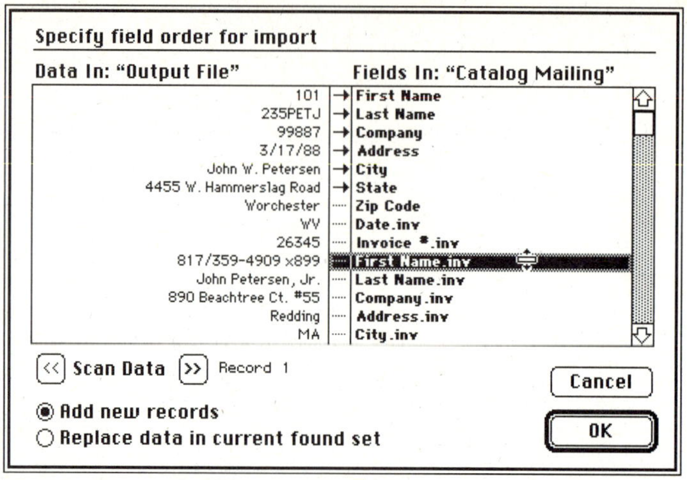

Fig. 15.9
The Field Mapping dialog box.

7. Indicate the relationship you want between fields in the external file and fields in the FileMaker Pro file.

   The first record in the external file is displayed on the left. You can move backward and forward through the records in the external file by clicking the Scan Data buttons. The available fields in your FileMaker file are displayed on the right. Fields that are not available, such as calculation and summary fields, are dimmed. The arrows indicate the mapping order: the data on the left will be put in the field named on the right.

   If the external file has data that you do not want to bring into the FileMaker file, click the arrow to deselect it. The arrow becomes dimmed to indicate no data will be brought into that field.

   To match a field in the FileMaker file with the correct field in the external file, move the pointer over the FileMaker field you want to move. When the pointer changes to a double arrow, drag the field name to the matching position.

   If the external file has more fields than the FileMaker file, the arrows for the extra fields are dimmed. You can exit Import, define new fields to receive the unmatched data and then return to Import. When you return to the Field Mapping dialog box, click the dimmed arrows to turn them on.

   At this point, no data has been transferred. To abort the operation, click the Cancel button or press ⌘-. (period).

8. Click the OK button to initiate the data exchange. FileMaker posts a message box displaying the status of the data exchange. A ⌘-. (period) cursor is on-screen while data is exchanged.

If there are additional records in the data file that is updating your records, FileMaker posts an alert box similar to the one shown in figure 15.10.

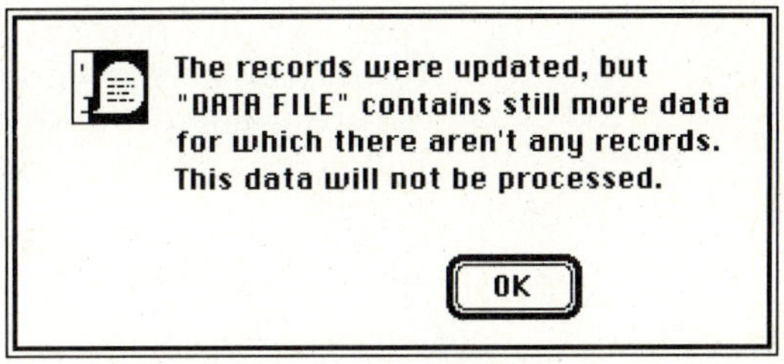

Fig. 15.10
The Extra Records Not Imported alert box.

If you decide to terminate the transfer while in progress, press ⌘-. (period). FileMaker finishes transferring the record and stops. If you are adding records to your file, you can use the Delete Multiple command to eliminate the additional records (see Chapter 4). If you are updating your records, make another copy of your original file and start the procedure again.

The Field Mapping dialog box (see fig. 15.9) functions the same as the Field Order dialog box. A detailed summary of the functions of the Export Order is given in "Reviewing Supported File Formats."

The import order updates your file from the first through last record entered into the imported file, corresponding to the order in your data file from left to right in a record.

Again, keep in mind that the SYLK and BASIC formats impose certain restrictions on the size of your field values and their formats. Be careful to check your imported data to see whether it is what you expected.

Importing Data from Microsoft Works

Microsoft Works contains a flat-file database based on the Microsoft program MultiPlan. Users who discover the power of FileMaker may want to transfer their Works files into FileMaker. Works creates export files based on the MERGE format: tabs between fields, returns separating records, and a header record, but without quotation marks around field values that contain commas.

To import data from Works into FileMaker, follow these steps:

1. Launch Microsoft Works and open the file that contains the data you want to export.

2. If you want to export *all records*, give the Save As command from the File menu in Works and continue to step 3. If you want to export selected records, select those records before proceeding to step 3.

   If you want export *selected fields*, use the Save As command to create a copy of your Works file. Delete each field that you do not want to include. Select any fields you want to include or use them all. Proceed to step 3.

3. In the Save As dialog box (see fig. 15.11), click on the Export radio button. Then click on the Save button or press the Return key.

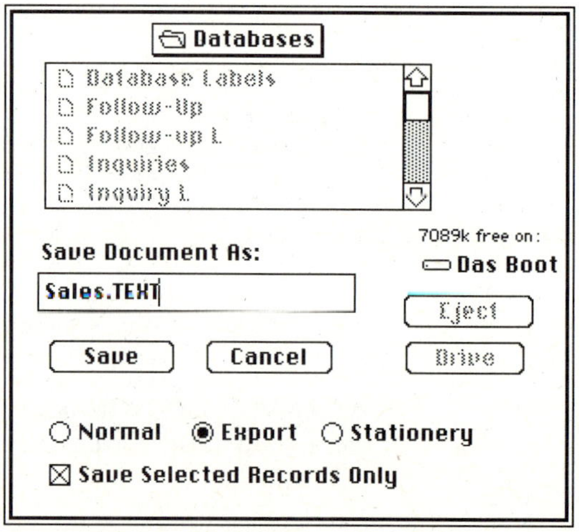

Fig. 15.11
The Microsoft Works Save As dialog box specifying an export file.

4. Quit Works and then launch FileMaker.

5. Open the file that is to receive the Works data file and give the Import command from the File menu.

6. Find and open the Works data file in the Open File dialog box by double-clicking on its name.

7. In the Import dialog box, specify that the data file is a Text file and then click the Open button.

8. Click an option to tell how you want to input values in repeating fields (keep in original record or split into separate records).

9. Click the OK button, and all the Works records are imported.

   Check to see that all of the records are what you expected. If you specified the Replace Data in Current Found Set option, by all means work with a copy of your FileMaker file. If you specified Add New Records, only the imported records are browsed after the records are intact. Check the first record with the header information to make sure that it has all the correct field names. Then delete that record if you no longer need it.

In Review

FileMaker uses the Import command on the File menu to transfer data between two FileMaker files. Browse the records that you want to export in the input file and then open the current file. Data exchange is automatic and occurs for any field that has the same field name. You do not need to specify an input or output field order. Only Text, Number, Time, Date, and Picture fields may be transferred. Calculation and summary fields cannot be exchanged because they are specific to records and groups of records, respectively, in a particular file.

When exchanging data between FileMaker and other applications, you must use an intermediate data file. FileMaker can create a data file in Text, BASIC, MERGE, and SYLK file formats, and, depending on the file format, can export Number, Time, and Date fields with their data format intact or as unformatted data.

Text is the most common Macintosh format for word processors. DBF is used by many databases (particularly dBASE-type programs). You may try BASIC as an alternative for databases if DBF doesn't work smoothly. SYLK is used by spreadsheets. MERGE is used for mail merges in word processors and some other Macintosh applications.

Use the Export command to export records to a data file that FileMaker creates. You can select the fields you want to export and the export order. Records are exported in the condition that they are being browsed. Only Text, Number, Date, Time, and calculation fields may be exported. Any subset of records, including all records in a file, may be output. If you sorted records, the sorted order is exported.

When importing data from a data file to your FileMaker file's fields, you must match the fields in the order of importation, or import order. Data in the data record is imported in the order in which it occurs in the file, going into the first field in the import order, then the second, and so on. As long as the data is compatible, the data is imported.

CHAPTER 16

Managing Files

In this chapter of *Using FileMaker Pro*, you find information that helps you manage your FileMaker files better. Some of these topics are basic; others are techniques most users want to know; and still others cover some advanced features and future developments that will affect FileMaker and Macintosh users.

System 6 offers you the choice of working with a single application in Finder or working with several applications simultaneously in Multi-Finder. In the first section of this chapter, "Comparing Finder and MultiFinder," the implications of using either mode are discussed. The Macintosh System software is in a state of flux with the introduction of the new System 7 operating system, due out in the spring of 1991. This operating system, available to all users with a Mac Plus or better and 2M of RAM, will offer changes and improvements in the way FileMaker interacts with your Macintosh and with all the other applications you use. In the section titled "Comparing System 6 and System 7," some of the developments that System 7 will offer are discussed. Some of these features will be helpful to you when you are considering equipment purchases and organizing your files.

Your database files probably are very valuable to you, and the data contained in them probably is sensitive. The section called "Backing Up Your Files" describes some of the backup routines that you may want to use to protect your files. Backups are like insurance: you only need a backup when you need it—but when you need a backup, you need it bad! Backups are the best way to protect your data. "Protecting Your Database" discusses a number of techniques that you can use to protect your files from unauthorized access or alteration. You can set passwords that limit the access of users and lock users out of certain layouts that contain confidential information. These techniques are useful to single users, but they are essential to FileMaker users operating in a work group environment. Whether you are on a "SneakerNet" (in which users run floppy disks around cooperatively) or on an AppleShare or TOPS network (in which computers move files around, mostly cooperatively), you learn to enhance the value of your files with these techniques.

"Protecting Your Data from Viruses" shows you how to keep your files intact while users all around you are reaching for aspirin.

FileMaker is robust. You very rarely will encounter problems that endanger your data. FileMaker's auto-save feature ensures that your data is written to disk at nearly the moment you enter the data into your computer. But hardware can misbehave (power failure during a disk write or a sector failure, for example), so FileMaker offers you a recovery procedure to help you retrieve your valuable work and get back up and running without much pain. "Recovering Data" contains a survival guide that takes you through some of the possibilities you may encounter. Recovery is easy to do and makes you appreciate the importance of backing up your data.

Comparing Finder and MultiFinder

The Finder is a program that runs above the Macintosh operating system and shields you from the complexities of the operating system. You don't need to know how to talk to your floppy disk drive because the Finder does the talking for you. When you want to delete a file, you drag the file to the Trash and select the Empty Trash command from the Special menu in the Finder. The Finder then interprets those commands into language that your Macintosh understands and performs the tasks. The net result is that your Macintosh finds the file on your disk's directory and deletes the file's entry, thereby releasing the space or blocks on the disk for other tasks so that the file can be overwritten. A set of *managers*, or software routines, are notified, and the task is accomplished. You are shielded from the real complexity of the computing tasks by this system.

It is important to note that you still can recover a file that is deleted if you use a utility program, such as Norton Utilities for the Macintosh, Symantec Utilities for the Macintosh (SUM), Disk 1st Aid's Complete

Undelete, and others. Norton Utilities is highly recommended. As long as the sectors containing the data have not been overwritten, you can retrieve the files completely. Files also can be restored partially in some cases.

Calling the Finder the Macintosh operating system is not wrong, but such a statement does not tell the complete story. More correctly, the System file defines most of the functions included in the Mac operating system. The Finder is a program that enables you to use those features. One of the implications of this arrangement is that the Finder can undergo evolution, resulting in improvement of the Finder. MultiFinder is one of the major improvements of the Finder that Apple has implemented.

System 5 was the beginning of Apple's efforts to build a multitasking operating system. With System 5, MultiFinder was introduced. In MultiFinder, you can have more than one application retained in memory and switch quickly between the applications. System 6 is an enhancement of System 5. System 6 contains many small changes. System 6 fixed many of the more clumsy aspects of System 5. In general, you should run the latest version of System software that your Macintosh allows. If you have a 1M RAM Macintosh, you can run System 6. You need 2M of RAM to run System 7.

Comparing System 6 and System 7

System 7 has recently been released. A slight digression in the exploration of FileMaker is needed to put that event in perspective. In System 7, Finder no longer will exist, and the System software will look much like MultiFinder. Numerous changes have been made to the Macintosh desktop. The changes include improved file handling, different DA and font handling, a new memory-management scheme called virtual memory (you need a 68030 or a 68020 Macintosh with a PMMU chip), a new print architecture, and improved sound and color. These features will change slightly how your FileMaker files look, but will not affect greatly how FileMaker runs. Some of the changes will affect future versions that FileMaker likely will offer, however, so the changes are worth a brief comment.

The Finder underwent considerable underlying changes in the manner in which it manages files. In Sysytem 6, the Finder keeps a table of contents of your disk inside an invisible file called the DeskTop file. If you have over 2,000 files on your hard drive, you may want to investigate the use of the Desktop Manager INIT from Apple (distributed as part of the AppleShare network software). Desktop Manager improves file access.

Searching the DeskTop file is what takes the time when you look for a file, so System 7 contains a new form of indexing. You still see standard Open and Save file boxes, but they operate more quickly. You also will discover new ways of organizing files in the Apple menus, and aliasing, which enables multiple icons to be defined that will open your files.

With System 6, if you want to find something in the hierarchical file system (HFS), you must navigate that file system, which can be awkward. This awkwardness has led to a number of utilities, such as Boomerang, Shortcut, and others, that remain inside your standard file boxes and aid you in searching the file system. Still others, like DiskTools II, DiskTop, and Find File, aid you from the desktop in the form of desk accessories. In System 7, Find File went through a major upgrade, but a utility such as Boomerang will still be helpful.

Networked databases are a current hot topic in the Macintosh world. Because so much important information resides in databases on large computers, many organizations use their Macintosh computers as smart terminals to increase the power of their network by accessing remote databases. Linking databases together currently is a major effort on the part of Apple and other developers. System 7 incorporates Apple's proprietary CL/1 language (now called DAL, for *Data Access Language*), which enables Macintosh databases to access large databases that use the Structured Query Language (SQL) used by large databases on mainframes. Several Macintosh databases now serve as front ends to SQL database-management systems. Perhaps some future upgrade of FileMaker by Claris also will serve as a front end to SQL database-management systems.

Also built into System 7 is a new type of *protocol* (or agreement) that enables applications to talk with one another. Called *Interapplication Communications* (IAC), the protocol holds the promise of enabling intelligent links to be created between applications. Consider a Microsoft Word merge file that you created in FileMaker (see Chapter 15) and imagine that you need to change a piece of data in the database. You change the piece of data, press the Enter key, and your Macintosh instantly updates both files.

Working with Memory

MultiFinder is not a true multitasking operating system. MultiFinder doesn't enable you to run multiple applications concurrently by artificially partitioning your microprocessor. MultiFinder does what's called *context switching*. Programs are saved in RAM, and you activate the programs by choosing them from the Apple menu and clicking on their windows on the desktop or clicking on the icons at the far right of the menu bar. When an icon is selected, the program is enabled, and the running of other programs is put on hold.

Although future versions of MultiFinder can be expected to contain more sophisticated memory-management routines, System 6 at least offers one important function: *cooperative multitasking-background processing*. In cooperative multitasking, a computer's memory manager partitions central processing unit (CPU—your computer) time in a round-robin fashion. Sometimes this process is referred to as *nonpreemptive* multitasking. The memory manager affords you at least one important advantage in MultiFinder background processing. This feature enables you to do lengthy finds, sorts, prints, and some other tasks while you work in another application, leaving FileMaker still open in MultiFinder. MultiFinder can accomplish these concurrent tasks because all devices (like printers and desk accessories) run in their own layer of memory and can be hosted by any Macintosh application.

System 6 does not have protected memory. The operating system does not do the real preemptive multitasking that more sophisticated operating systems do (like UNIX), so running out of application memory when using FileMaker is possible. Although the 1024K default memory allocation for the program usually is sufficient, you are advised to increase the memory allocation somewhat to run FileMaker for some memory-intensive operations. When your Macintosh gives you the message `FileMaker quit unexpectedly`, the message means that the memory (RAM) set aside for FileMaker has been used up and the application has closed to safeguard your file.

If you have the additional RAM available, you can set FileMaker's application memory higher. For FileMaker II, setting the memory partition to 1024K is particularly valuable. Not only does this alleviate the memory problem, but certain FileMaker operations (like finds, sorts, and prints) run faster.

To change FileMaker's memory allocation (or partition), do the following:

1. Open the folder containing the FileMaker program and click on the icon to highlight it.
2. Select the Get Info command on the File menu or press ⌘-I.

   The Get Info box shown in figure 16.1 appears.

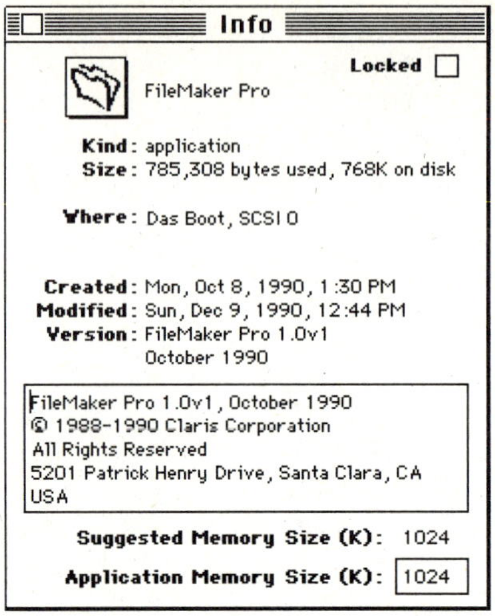

Fig. 16.1
Changing FileMaker's memory allocation in the Get Info box.

3. Double-click in the Application Memory Size text box or drag to highlight the number.
4. Enter the number *1024* (if needed) to raise FileMaker's memory allocation to that suggested level.
5. Close the Get Info box by clicking in the close box at the top left corner of the title bar, by selecting the Close command, or by pressing ⌘-W.

FileMaker Pro can run within a 512K memory partition but is not as fast or reliable as when given a full megabyte of RAM. Don't run with less than the recommended amount of memory allocation, if possible.

Database files tend to be large, and they often can outstrip the available RAM in your computer. The developers of FileMaker have created a form of virtual memory called *caching*. Blocks of files are swapped from disk in and out of memory, as needed. FileMaker is a disk-based system that reads and writes to disk the records it needs for a given operation. The caching helps read in more from disk than was requested and speeds up the process.

> **Note**
> You can prevent FileMaker and other applications from being modified and provide minimal virus protection by clicking the Locked check box in the Get Info box.

The program operates more quickly and with fewer difficulties if you turn off any system cache (in the Control Panel) that you may have set. To turn off the RAM cache, open the Control Panel and click on the General System file icon. Then click the RAM Cache Off radio button, as shown in figure 16.2.

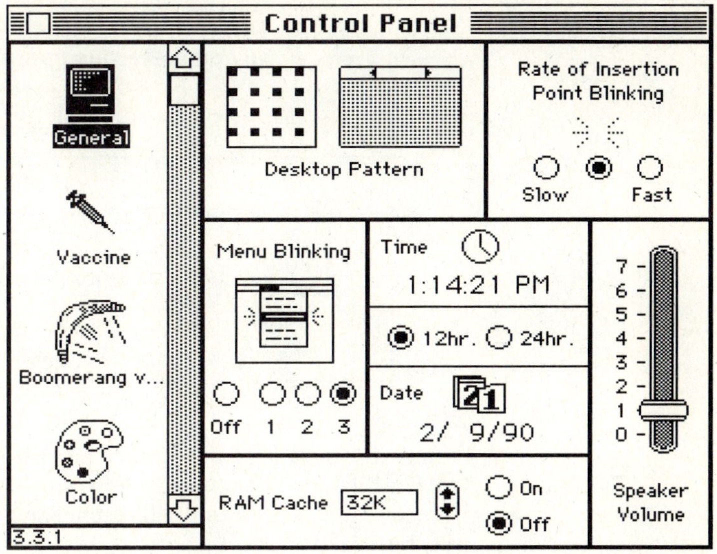

Fig. 16.2
The Control Panel with the RAM cache turned off.

When your Macintosh runs out of memory, FileMaker alerts you with several different, but similar, dialog boxes. This situation occurs most often when running in MultiFinder.

Finder generally doesn't suffer as much from memory problems because Finder is running only one application at a time and takes all available RAM. None of the following memory problems is a matter of serious concern. These memory problems don't indicate that any damage has been done to your data, only that you must reconfigure your current running set of applications.

When you run out of memory and the Clipboard contains something, FileMaker II places the flashing FileMaker icon in place of the Apple in the Apple menu to indicate an out-of-memory condition and displays a dialog box. Two out-of-memory dialog boxes from FileMaker II are shown in figure 16.3. These dialog boxes and the flashing icon can be found in whatever program you currently are using.

To release memory and eliminate memory problems, do the following:

1. Quit your current application and any other applications you are not using.
2. Close any open desk accessories.
3. Reopen FileMaker and attempt the operation that you were trying to complete when you received the out-of-memory condition.

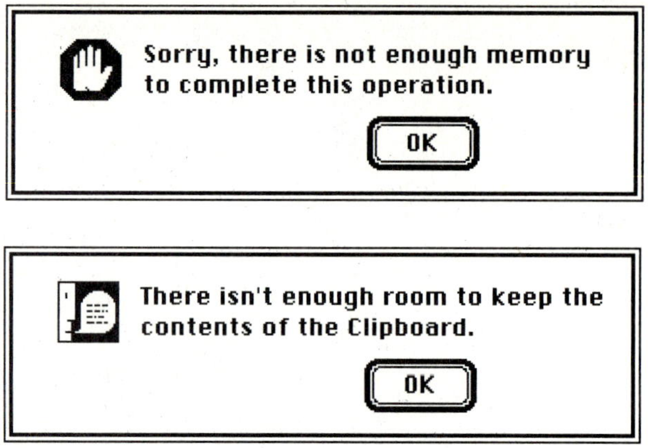

Fig. 16.3
Two out-of-memory indicators.

At times, the out-of-memory notices are posted even though you know RAM is available. When this happens, you have a fragmented memory problem; FileMaker doesn't think that enough contiguous memory is available in RAM.

To remedy the fragmented-memory problem, do the following:

1. Quit FileMaker and return to the Finder.
2. Select the Restart command from the Special menu and reboot your Macintosh.

   Using the Restart command instead of the mechanical hot restart switch on your Macintosh (if you have installed the switch) allows better shutdown.
3. Return to FileMaker and complete your operation.

The virtual memory in System 7 should delay memory problems like the ones just mentioned.

Backing Up Your Files

If you learn only one thing from this chapter, you should learn the importance of making regular backups. Because FileMaker does an auto-save every 45 seconds or so after any file changes, you possibly can do permanent damage to your files with some innocent operation that you haven't thought through. FileMaker has commands that enable you to delete layouts with a single keystroke. If you eliminate multiple records or delete a field and ignore the warning, all your field's or record's data is gone. After a while, as an experienced Macintosh user, you will find yourself hitting the Return key every time you see an alert box. In such cases, the only recovery is regular backups.

Just about anything bad that can happen to your database files can be minimized by keeping a good set of backups. The number and frequency of backups should be a function of the value of your data and the frequency with which your data changes. The ultimate question is, "How much work and time are you willing to lose?" At the very least, try to keep two sets of backups, one off-site. Rotate your backups so that you have one recent backup and one less recent backup. Three sets of backups to put into the rotation is even better.

If you are using FileMaker at home on an occasional basis, try to back up once a week. For a professional using FileMaker in a business capacity, back up your files once every day or two, and keep a set of backups from a week and two weeks back. In a business for which FileMaker files are the lifeblood, you should back up your files every morning and afternoon and keep additional sets of backups for one week, two weeks, and one month back. Use your judgment.

Before you back up, saving a compressed copy of your file is not a bad idea to save disk space and improve the speed of your backup. You can use several different methods to accomplish file backups. If your file is less than a floppy disk size (800K, or 1.44M for a SuperDrive [FDHD]), you can do a disk-to-disk copy in the Finder by dragging the file icon to your backup disk. Consult your Macintosh manual for details. If you have a removable SyQuest 45M drive or a hard drive that you back up to, you can still do a disk-to-disk copy for larger FileMaker files.

If you have to back up to a set of floppy disks, you need to use one of the standard commercial backup utilities on the market. Consider using Redux, Retrospect, Fastback II, DiskFit, or HFS Backup, recommended in roughly that order. If you are desperate, you can use the HD Backup that Apple provides in the Apple system software utilities set. Many of these utilities provide the option to do regular timed backups to various devices that you may have mounted. Additionally, if you have a unit for a backup (like a streaming tape drive), the units usually come with their own proprietary backup software or one of the previously mentioned utilities.

Protecting Your Database

The commands described in this section are for setting passwords, allotting access privileges, and defining confidential layouts. Passwords are access codes you define to enable you to open and manipulate files. The password levels you assign determine what users can do after they open a file, which are called *access privileges*. You can lock out users from an entire layout if you want by creating a password using the Access Privileges command on the File menu. These features were implemented to enable multiple users to work together on a network while maintaining file security. FileMaker's security features are useful in a single-user environment as well.

In a multiuser environment, such as a work group in which files are shared, you may want to protect your files for several obvious reasons. Regardless of whether the users are networked, the reasons for file protection still apply. Perhaps the files contain sensitive financial records or evaluations. You don't want everyone to view the information. If you still want other parts of your file available for use, alteration, and updating, you need to make the files accessible to others. These file-protection features offer you this capability.

To make sure that the right people see the right information, you can set up *groups*. Groups limit access to specific fields and layouts within a file. One password, for example, may enable the user to create, edit, or delete records. Another password, however, may allow only browsing records. Individuals within a group may have different passwords to limit their activities. The capability to define groups enables people to work together and share files without compromising security.

Password Protection

Passwords are character strings you type that permit access to your files. They can be words or, better yet, a random string of characters that you can remember. Words can be guessed, but gibberish isn't likely to be in a word dictionary. Passwords are like the keys to a lock; you cannot open the lock without the key. The difference is that passwords are defined and can be changed by you.

Passwords also are the key to assigning access privileges and denying access to a layout—that is, making the layout confidential. If you don't assign a password to a file, the file has no password condition. You still can assign a set of access privileges in this situation. If you manage a work group that uses FileMaker, you may want to limit the operations available but not concern users with a password. In that situation, access privileges come in handy. You keep full access privileges for yourself.

You can grant the following levels of access privileges:

- Access the entire file
- Browse records
- Print records
- Edit records
- Create records
- Delete records
- Override data-entry warnings
- Design layouts
- Edit scripts

At the lowest level, you only can view records; you cannot change them. The details of access privileges are covered in full in the next section.

As long as one of the passwords can access the entire file, FileMaker has no limit to the number of passwords that can be defined. You can create, delete, and modify passwords at any time. For more information about passwords and networks, refer to Chapter 17.

To create a password, follow these steps:

1. Select the Define Passwords command from the Access Privileges submenu on the File menu.
2. The Define Password dialog box appears. Enter a new password into the Password text box (see fig. 16.4).

   or

   Leave the Password text box blank for the group of users without a password.

   The password is not case-sensitive and can accept any string up to 31 characters long. Try not to use a word in the dictionary.
3. Click all the access privileges you want to give the user with this password. Refer to the next section, "Access Privileges," for a fuller explanation of your options.

4. Click the Create button or press the Return key to accept the password.

5. Continue to create passwords as you desire and then click the Done button.

   FileMaker posts the Full Access confirmation dialog box shown in figure 16.5 to make sure that you can access the entire file and change passwords; only full access can do that.

6. Enter the password that has full file access and then click the OK button or press the Return key.

Note

If you change your mind, click the Cancel button or press the Cancel command (⌘-.) to return to your file without making changes.

Selecting the Cancel button (⌘-.) returns you to the Password dialog box for further changes.

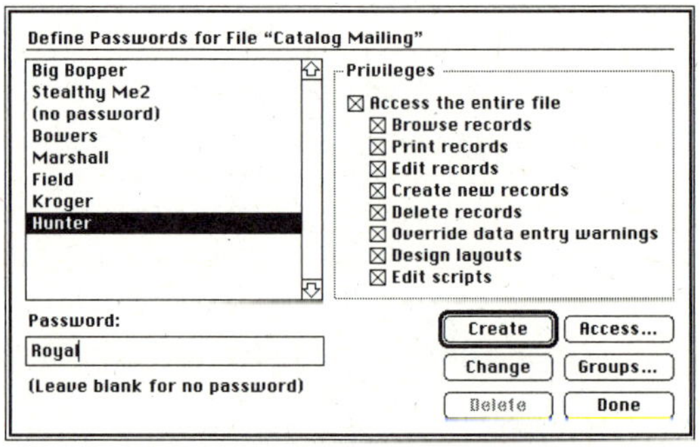

Fig. 16.4
The Define Password dialog box.

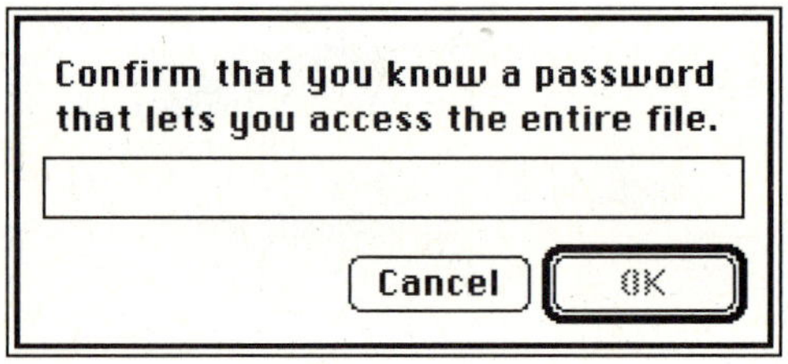

Fig. 16.5
The Full Access confirmation message box.

To open a file that is password-protected, follow these steps:

1. Select the Open command from the File menu or press ⌘-O.

2. Navigate the file system and double-click on the name of the file you want to open.

The Give Password dialog box appears, prompting you to enter your password (see fig. 16.6).

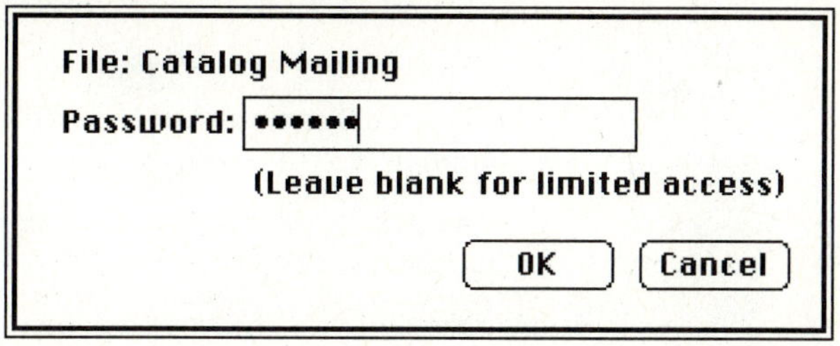

Fig. 16.6
The Give Password dialog box.

3. Enter your password into the Password text box. Click the OK button or press Return.

   If you change your mind, click the Cancel button (⌘-.) to return the file to its previous status in FileMaker. If you have set a No Password option (see "Access Privileges"), FileMaker places the text `Leave Blank for Limited Access` inside the Give Password dialog box. If that option is not set, this line is missing.

4. For the No Password access, do not enter any characters in the Password text box. Click the OK button or press the Return key to set the No Password access level.

   If you make a mistake, FileMaker posts the Incorrect Password alert box shown in figure 16.7.

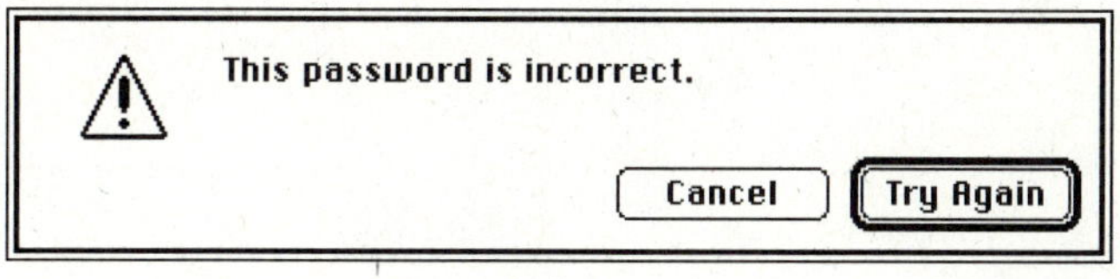

Fig. 16.7
The Incorrect Password alert box.

5. Click the Try Again button or press the Return key to reenter your password in the Give Password dialog box and then repeat step 3.

   or

   Click the Cancel button (⌘-.) to return the file to its previous condition in FileMaker.

To edit a password, you must have full access rights. Do the following to edit a password:

1. In the Define Password dialog box, click on the name of the password to highlight the password. Edit the password or make changes to the access privileges by clicking the check boxes on or off, as necessary. The Change button now is enabled.

2. Click the Change button.

3. Click the Done button. The Full Access confirmation message box appears.

4. Enter your password to confirm the change and click on the OK button.

If you have partial access privileges, you can change only the actual password. When you have limited access, the Change Password command replaces the Access Privileges command on the File menu (see fig. 16.8).

Fig. 16.8
The File menu showing the Change Password command.

To change the password if you have partial access privileges, do the following:

1. With the file open, select the Change Password command from the File menu.

2. Type your current password in the Old Password text box. Next, press the Tab key to advance to the New Password text box.

If you cannot remember your current password, another user with full access rights can go in and find your password. If you are the supervisor and you forget the password that accesses the entire file, you have a major problem.

WARNING

Do not forget your password or you will lose your entire file. Claris is unable to recover files with lost full access passwords.

3. Enter the new password in the New Password dialog box and then press the Tab key.

4. Enter the new password in the Confirm New Password text box to confirm your choice (see fig. 16.9).

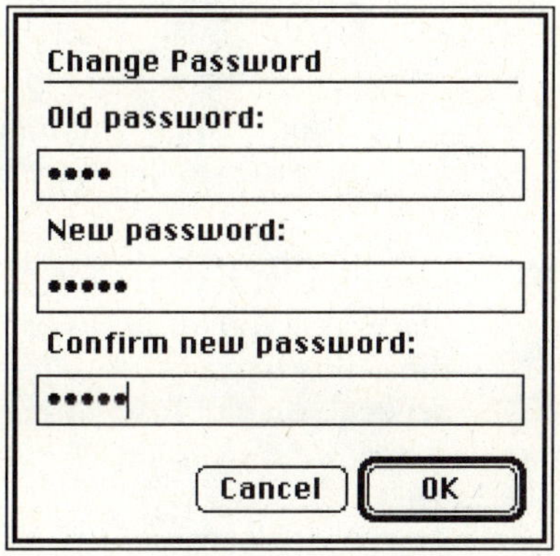

Fig. 16.9
The Confirm New Password dialog box.

5. Click the OK button or press the Return key to set the new password.

   or

   Click the Cancel button (or press ⌘-.) to retain your old password.

Only users with full access rights can delete a password and lock out a user who has a lower level of access. Remember, you must have at least one password with full access rights so that you can change privileges, if needed. You also can delete all passwords if you choose to grant every user full access rights.

To delete a password, follow these steps:

1. Choose the Define Passwords command from the Access Privileges submenu on the File menu.
2. Click on and highlight the password that you want to delete and then click the Delete button.

   FileMaker posts the Delete Password alert box (see fig. 16.10).

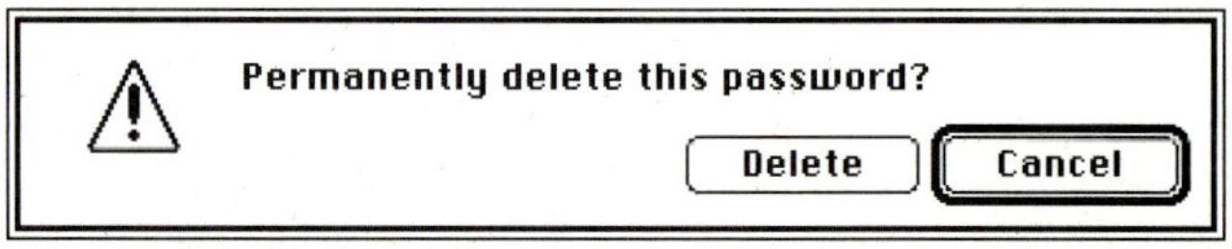

Fig. 16.10
The Delete Password alert box.

3. Click the Delete button to remove the password.

   or

   If you change your mind, click the Cancel button or press Return to return to the Password dialog box.

WARNING

It is critical that you remember your password, especially the password that grants you full access rights. If you forget your password, you lose the ability to access your file, and **if you forget the password with full access, you can lose your entire file**.

Access Privileges

Access privileges are your way of controlling who does what to your files. You can share your files with other people. By specifying what each password can accomplish, you essentially can lock out a user from sensitive or inappropriate information. Access privileges also are an excellent method for limiting the amount of damage that a beginning user can do to your file.

You can specify different levels of access. Only a user with full file access can set an access level. Access levels are defined within the New Password dialog box. You can specify various sets of access rights as desired.

The following is a summary of the access rights offered by the Define Passwords dialog box (refer to fig. 16.4):

Access the Entire File. The Access the Entire File level is the highest level of access, enabling a user with this password to browse and edit records; create and alter layouts of all types; and create, change, or delete passwords. No other user level can alter another user's password.

When you check the Access the Entire File option, FileMaker checks all the other option check boxes. This level of privilege affords the same capabilities as not setting passwords at all. Reserve this password for a system administrator with the responsibility of managing your database or for yourself as a single user.

Browse Records. Browse Records is the lowest form of access offered by password protection. The only privilege Browse Records affords is the ability to open a file and view the data contained in the records that can be accessed with nonconfidential layouts. A user at this level cannot enter data, find or sort records, or alter layouts. Use the Browse Records option for casual users who need to view data only for informational purposes.

Print Records. This option enables the user to print any record or found group of records.

Edit Records. Users with the Edit Records access level can enter information into a file. Records can be browsed, information can be added and edited, and records can be deleted. Users at this level cannot alter a layout or view confidential layouts. Edit Records is the default setting in the New Password dialog box. When you set this access level, FileMaker also chooses Browse Records. Use the Edit Records option for data-entry operators who need data access and entry but no other privileges.

Create New Records. The user can create and fill in a new record. When this privilege is selected, FileMaker selects Edit Records, which you may deselect if you want.

Delete Records. The user can delete one or more records. Be very careful about allowing this privilege.

Override Data Entry Warnings. The user can enter data that does not fit the criteria you set up when you defined the fields using entry options.

Design Layouts. The user with the Design Layouts level password protection can work in the layout mode, view confidential layouts, change a layout, and browse and edit records. When Design Layouts is chosen, FileMaker checks the Browse Records option. Give the Design Layouts level to an individual, such as the systems administrator or consultant, who can be trusted with the sensitive information that the file contains.

Edit Scripts. The user can create scripts or modify existing ones.

No Password option. By leaving the password text box blank, FileMaker enables you to offer an access level to users who do not enter a password. When a user opens a file, pressing the Return key or clicking the OK button in the Give Password dialog box grants this privilege. Use this option for a situation in which you want to allow most of your users certain privileges without them having to know a password for order entry, file access, and so on.

Defining Groups

FileMaker also enables you to define groups and set up passwords to establish access privileges. If you have several different groups, each with differing levels of access, you need to set up at least one password for each group that defines the type of work the group is allowed to do with the records, layouts, and scripts.

To define a group, you must be the host and the file must be exclusive. Only a host can be working with a file while these changes are being made. To link the group to a password and limit the group's access privileges, follow these steps:

1. Check that Exclusive on the File menu is selected (has a check mark next to it).
2. Choose the Define Groups command from Access Privileges on the File menu. The Define Groups dialog box appears.
3. Enter the group name and click on the Create button (see fig. 16.11).

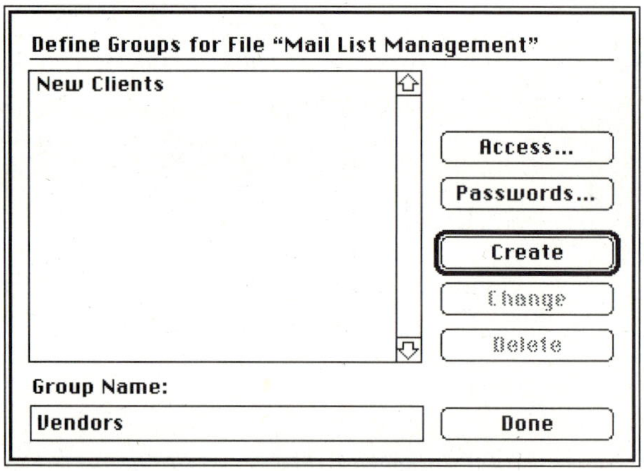

Fig. 16.11
The Define Groups dialog box.

4. Click on the Access button. The Access Privileges dialog box appears, which shows an overview of the passwords, groups, layouts, and fields (see fig. 16.12).

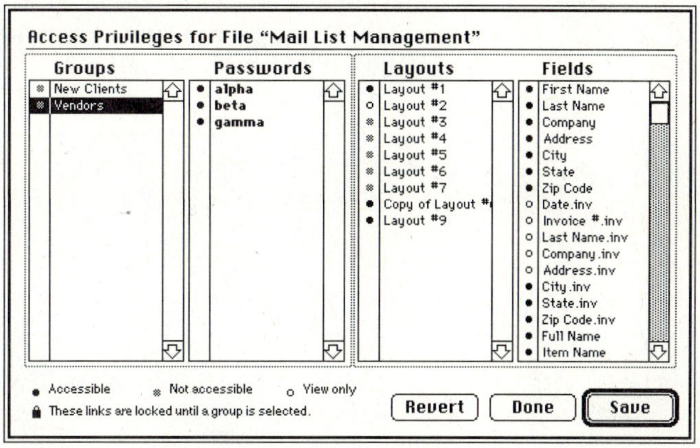

Fig. 16.12
The Access Privileges dialog box.

5. To make a field or layout accessible, click on the bullet to the left of the name.

   A solid bullet indicates that the field or layout is accessible to the selected group. A dimmed bullet means that the field or layout is inaccessible. An open bullet indicates that the field or layout can be viewed, but not edited.

6. Click on a bullet next to a password to associate the selected group with that password.
7. Click the Save button to save the current setup.
8. Click the Done button to return to the Define Groups dialog box.
9. Click the Done button in the Define Groups dialog box to return to your file.

Note

FileMaker has a large number of dialog and alert boxes to inform users when they are attempting an operation their password does not permit.

Protecting Fields or Layouts

Protected layouts enable you to lock out a user who doesn't have the password privilege to view that type of layout. You can protect sensitive information by placing the fields that contain this type of data on a protected layout. You can protect personal information, evaluations, financial information, and state secrets in this manner. Data in these layouts cannot be browsed, edited, or modified in any manner, nor can the layouts be changed by any user without the password privilege.

You always can tell when you're viewing a protected layout; all the fields and layout text objects on the layout are grayed out. Graying out layout text aids in hiding the purpose of the layout from nonprivileged users. Figure 16.13 shows an example of a protected layout.

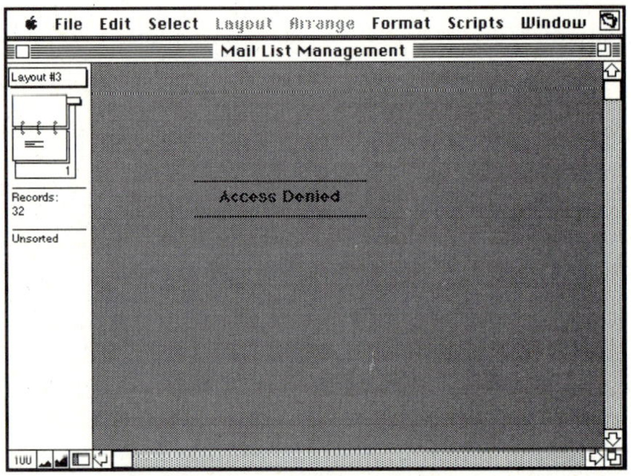

Fig. 16.13
A protected layout.

To make a layout protected, follow these steps:

1. Choose the Overview submenu from the Access Privileges command on the File menu. The Access Privileges dialog box appears (refer to fig. 16.12).

2. Select the group whose access you want to limit.

   Layouts and fields are listed in the two columns to the right. A layout or field marked with a solid bullet is accessible to the selected group. A dimmed bullet marks inaccessible fields and layouts. An open bullet indicates the field or layout can be viewed but not edited.

3. Click on the appropriate bullets to set the status for each field and layout. (The pointer changes to a check mark when it passes over the bullets.)

   The dimmed bullets mean that the fields or layouts cannot be accessed by the selected group. As defined by their password, the group has access privileges to the fields and layouts marked with solid bullets. The passwords shown with solid bullets are associated with the selected group and can access the fields and layouts indicated. Open bullets indicate the field or layout can be viewed but not edited.

4. Click the Save button to save the current settings.
5. Click the Done button to exit from the Access Privileges dialog box and return to your file.

Placing fields that contain confidential information only on protected layouts is important. If a viewer can view the field on any layout, the data the field contains can be browsed and possibly modified. If you place those sensitive fields on protected layouts only, the fields are not available to have data imported into them by using the Import command (see Chapter 15), and they cannot be modified in that manner, either.

Virus Protection

Computer viruses have been around for many years, but only recently have they come to the attention of the public because they have been written to attack personal computers. These programs are easier to write than most people would believe. About a year ago, a virus that destroys files on a Macintosh appeared. You can avoid these problems easily if you are a single user, and somewhat less easily if you are connected to a network. Avoiding viruses requires some special software and a little extra file maintenance on your part, but this protection is not particularly difficult.

The Macintosh community is highly connected through bulletin boards and communication networks. Word of new viruses travels quickly, and new ones are named and characterized very quickly. You can do very little if you are one of the very first people to get a new virus, but the odds of this happening are about the same as drawing four of a kind in straight poker. What you need to do is monitor for all the known viruses by using the best software available for the purpose. Numerous commercial products and some substantial shareware and freeware products are available that you can use to detect viruses. Some products actually monitor your disks and drives automatically, and others repair your files should you be unfortunate and contract a virus.

Rule Number 1 about virus protection is the following: *make regular backups*. A backup enables you to recover in case all else fails. You can replace the file if you need to delete the problem file. Don't panic; losing data to a virus is extremely rare.

The second thing to do is to pick one or two of the better virus detection and monitoring programs and run them on every disk and file you intend to copy to your hard drive or to your disks. Buying one of the commercial products is best. Consider a product such as SAM (Symantec AntiVirus For Macintosh), Virex, Anti-Virus Kit, and AntiToxin, in roughly that order. Versions of these programs change often because they are upgraded each time a new virus that defeats them is detected. Being a registered user puts you in the upgrade path and offers an additional level of protection not found in a static program. Most of these programs also offer monitoring and repair utilities.

Of the freeware and shareware programs (of which there are many), some of the better ones are Disinfectant, Virus Detective, Apple's Virus Rx, Interferon, and GateKeeper. You can obtain these shareware products from bulletin boards and local user groups. The Boston Computer Society Macintosh User's Group and the Berkeley Macintosh User's Group actively maintain a virus detection disk for sale. It is vitally important to make sure that you get the most recent versions of these programs.

One final word about viruses: your level of concern should be high if you are operating on a network. The more machines you're connected to, the greater your chances of getting a virus. The responsibility of your network administrator is to monitor the condition of a network, but your responsibility is to protect your own files by following the suggestions in this section. Your concern as a single user with an isolated Macintosh, although less than a connected user, still should be present. Some viruses, such as WDEF, travel when you insert a disk. Some recently discovered viruses, such as Mosaic, destroy your entire drive's files.

Recovering Damaged Files

In most cases, a system error, or "bomb," does not damage your FileMaker files significantly. FileMaker has an internal switch (like a light switch) that turns on when you open a file and turns off again when you give the Close or Quit command. If you reboot the computer when you next open the file, FileMaker detects that this switch was left open and starts to do file diagnostics, checking the internal index to see that all the data blocks are accounted for and in the right place. In this case, FileMaker posts the message box shown in figure 16.14. This message indicates a diagnostic test and should cause you no concern.

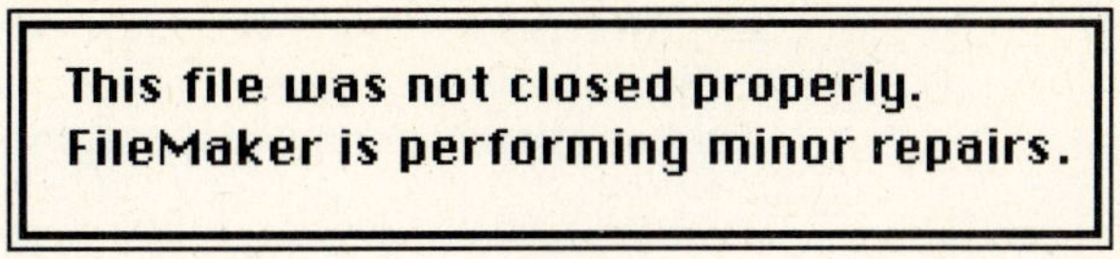

Fig. 16.14
The Minor Repairs message box.

In the rare cases of a power surge, disk malfunction (bad disk sectors), and other calamities that can cause file damage, FileMaker has a recover option that attempts to restore as much of your file as possible. Because FileMaker auto-saves your data, data loss is almost unheard of, although you can delete data accidentally if you are not careful.

Massive hardware malfunctions lead to the set of circumstances described in the rest of this section. The malfunctions can result in writing to a bad sector on your disk or, more likely, having a sector you wrote become bad, or having a disk head crash. Bad sectors occur because of disk fatigue, pieces of dust becoming embedded in the disk, and other, more mysterious reasons. Disk crashes are a matter of poor engineering, abusing your disk, or drive fatigue. Whatever the cause, when you have data on your disk that cannot be retrieved and that your FileMaker file index thinks should be there, FileMaker tells you that the file is damaged.

Depending on the degree of damage that occurs, FileMaker posts different levels of alerts, and you can use the Recover command to re-establish your file's integrity and restore your data. For severely damaged files, you see messages such as the one shown in figure 16.15. This level of damage requires direct manipulation of the damaged file by using the Recover command.

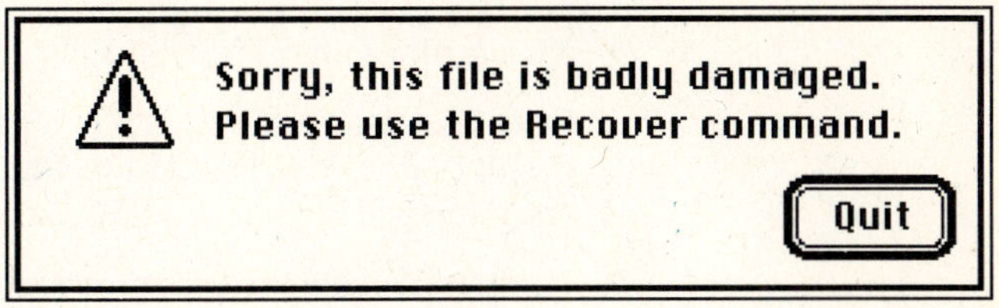

Fig. 16.15
The Badly Damaged File alert box.

When you get a message about severe file damage, stop what you are doing, close the file, and make a copy of the file by a direct file copy procedure from the Finder. Do not use the Save As command in FileMaker to create your copy. In the following instructions, use the original copy to attempt the recovery. Save the backup copy for later use, if needed. You are advised to proceed in this fashion because your likelihood of recovering information is greater.

To recover a damaged file, follow these steps:

1. If the damaged FileMaker file is open, close it.
2. Select the Recover command from the File menu. FileMaker prompts you to select the file from a standard Open File dialog box.
3. Double-click on the file name to specify the damaged file.

   or

   Click once to highlight the name and then click the Recover button.
4. In the Name New Recovered File (Save) dialog box, FileMaker prompts you for a file name for the recovered file and suggests as a default `Recovered Damaged File` (see fig. 16.16).

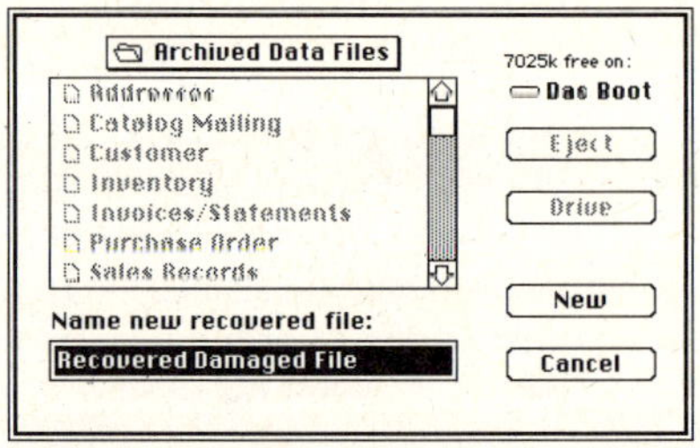

Fig. 16.16
The Name New Recovered File (Save) dialog box.

5. Type a new name, if desired.

   You must create a unique file name so that you can examine the results when you're finished. That file name must be different from the damaged file name or FileMaker alerts you.
6. Navigate the file system and open the volume and folder you want the recovered file to be saved in.

WARNING

Having enough free disk space to reproduce the entire file in the condition it was in before the file was damaged is very important. Failure to have enough disk space can result in a file that is unusable.

7. Click the New button to create the newly recovered file.

   FileMaker posts a status message that informs you of the action currently being undertaken. As each procedure is in progress, the procedure is highlighted (see fig. 16.17).

   If you change your mind, click the Cancel button to terminate the recovery without creating the file. While the recovery operation is in progress, you can press ⌘-. to abort the operation if you change your mind. FileMaker writes the record that it is recovering and then stops.

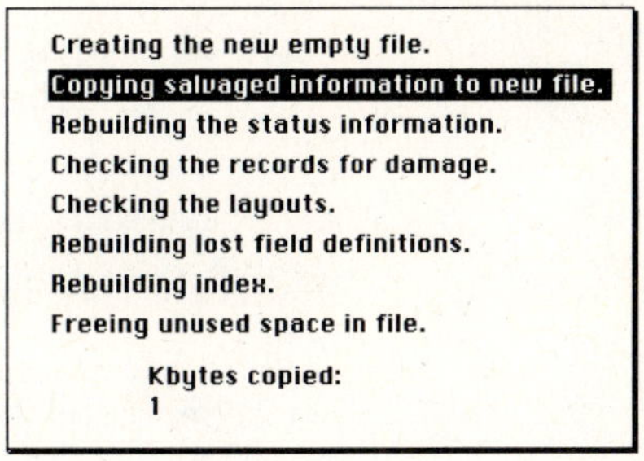

Fig. 16.17
The Recover operation status box.

8. When finished, FileMaker posts a second message similar to figure 16.18. The message informs you of the success of the recovery. Click OK to proceed.

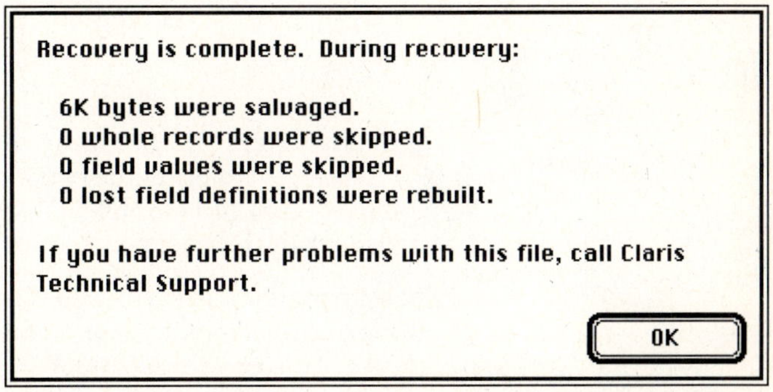

Fig. 16.18
The Recovery Completion dialog box.

9. Open your newly recovered file by using the Open command (⌘-O) from the File menu and examine your records and data to ascertain whether the recovery was successful. Look for things

such as fields with consecutive numbers, make sure that the file contains your most recent entry, and so on. If everything is in order, continue your work.

WARNING

Do not attempt to recover a file to a disk that does not have sufficient free space. Remember that the disk must have enough space to hold the file at its size before the file was damaged. If the file is not recovered fully, you do not get another chance, and the file can be damaged permanently and remain unusable if you don't have enough disk space.

Under extremely rare circumstances, FileMaker cannot recover information in your file. If this happens, try the following:

1. Create a file with all the same field names, data types, and field definitions that the damaged file had.

   If you have a previous backup copy of the file, clone that file to use here.

2. Select Import on the File menu, and in the Open File dialog box, select and open the damaged file. FileMaker posts a dialog box that tells you how many matching fields the files have.

3. Click OK to complete the data exchange, FileMaker file to FileMaker file.

4. Browse your records for accuracy.

In Review

System 6 offers you the choice of either Finder or MultiFinder, but System 7 merges the two into a version that looks and feels much like MultiFinder. FileMaker's operation is not likely to be affected much by this change.

The best insurance you can buy for FileMaker is backing up your files. The number of backups you maintain and the frequency with which you perform the backups are a matter of personal preference and should be based on the speed at which your files change. Keep one set of backups off-site.

You can protect data within your database by setting password protection. A password can authorize a user to perform only certain operations. The level of authorization is called an access privilege. Users are locked out of the operations that their access privileges do not entitle them to perform. You can have any number of passwords, including a No Password option, and you can change or delete passwords at any time. Only a user with full access privileges can modify passwords in a file. You are prompted for your password whenever you open a file that has passwords assigned.

Nine different kinds of access privileges can be authorized. A user can Access the Entire File, Browse Records, Print Records, Edit Records, Create New Records, Delete Records, Override Data Entry Warnings, Design Layouts, or Edit Scripts.

Users with full access privileges can specify that a layout may be protected. A protected layout has all fields and text objects grayed out for a user with a password that doesn't include the privilege of accessing protected layouts. Fields that occur only on protected layouts cannot be viewed, edited, or have data input or output by restricted users.

Groups can be defined to ensure that the right people see the right information. Groups limit access to specific fields and layouts within a file. Individuals within the groups may have different passwords to limit their activities.

You should install virus detection software to guard against contracting a virus. This precaution is particularly important when you operate FileMaker on a network.

In very rare instances, FileMaker files can be damaged. Most of these cases are due to hardware malfunctions. You can use the Recover command to retrieve as much of your data as possible from a file.

CHAPTER 17

Using FileMaker Pro on a Network

You can greatly improve the productivity of a work group by using FileMaker on a network. FileMaker Pro supports several different configurations of the program and runs on AppleTalk, AppleShare, and TOPS networks. You can use FileMaker Pro so that each user maintains a copy of the program and data files on his or her computer; this is called a *distributed network*. You also can create a *file server*, by placing FileMaker data onto a central device, usually a more powerful computer with a large hard drive and special software to process other users' requests. A file server is a computer that stores data (or files) and processes requests from two or more users for access to some or all of that data. Each approach has its advantages and disadvantages. Although network theory is beyond the scope of this book, this chapter shows you how to use FileMaker on a network.

FileMaker Pro is much more powerful to a company if a set of records is always available to every user. When the Fly-By-Night Travel Agency books luxury tours to the Caribbean, each travel agent can open the FileMaker database file, examine the available accommodations, and book a passenger without having to wait for another travel agent to close the file and job over with a disk.

USING FILEMAKER PRO

You may be unaware of this fact, buy you have a network built into your Macintosh. The AppleTalk serial port is a network that you use to connect a LaserWriter to your computer. AppleTalk is slow for a network, but you need only some cables and cable connectors to create your own network to include FileMaker. AppleTalk enables you to set up a distributed network, but AppleTalk is useful only for a small number of users.

AppleShare and TOPS permit file servers. Each computer on a TOPS network can be used as a file server, or a central computer can be used as a file server. AppleShare enables one designated computer to be the server. Either way, any user can access, modify, create, and store files across the network. AppleTalk networks also permit *hosting*, in which a user can control only files that reside on his or her own computer.

Control of who can do what to a database file is necessary when the file is opened by more than one user. FileMaker assigns another level of access rights to users on a network, depending on who opened the file first. The first person to open a file is called the *host*; subsequent users to open the file are called *guests*. This chapter describes what each type of user can do in the way of manipulating a file.

On an AppleTalk network, you can host only those files that are stored on your computer and drives. With a file server arrangement (AppleShare or TOPS), anyone can open and host any file residing on the file server. Moreover, TOPS permits access to any folder that is mounted on the network. If a user has a casual need for FileMaker, you can have that user download the program from a file server when the program is needed.

Imagine the resulting chaos if everyone could see every file, even files with sensitive information. Consider what would happen if two users tried to open the same record at the same time and modify the same information.

With passwords, access privileges, and protected layouts (see Chapter 16), you can control how you operate your files on a network. If you create a file, you can control who views your data and modifies your files. If you have full access privileges, you also have control over who has what password and what access privileges.

Claris requires a registered copy of FileMaker for each user on network. If you operate a network, you may want to inquire about site licenses for multiple copies.

Network File Management

When you open a file for the first time, you act as host. You can act as host only if the file you are opening is on your computer (for exclusive files) or if the file is nonexclusive. AppleTalk enables you to host only those files on your own Macintosh, but AppleShare and TOPS enable you to host a nonexclusive file anywhere on a network. Subsequent users of the same file are guests. Only nonexclusive files may be shared. (A nonexclusive file is one for which the host has removed the check mark on the Exclusive command on the File menu.)

To make a nonexclusive file available on the network, keep the file open. Other users can open the file at any time by using the Network button on the Open dialog box. You also can use a file sharing system, such as AppleShare or TOPS, so that users can open the file from their desktop.

Any changes made to a file by host or guests are processed across the network. When network processing of a file is in progress, the cursor on your screen becomes an animated double-headed arrow while it updates your window. Any changes made to a file—editing, deleting, or adding information—are auto-saved for each user. Sort orders, find requests, and page setups are specific to each user. If FileMaker is busy processing another user's request, the cursor turns into a steaming coffee cup.

To host a file, follow these steps:

1. Open the file by double-clicking the file icon in the Finder or by using the Open command from the File menu.

2. Select the file on your Macintosh and then click the Network button. Double-click the file name on the appropriate disk drive or volume (see fig. 17.1).

Fig. 17.1
The Open File dialog box.

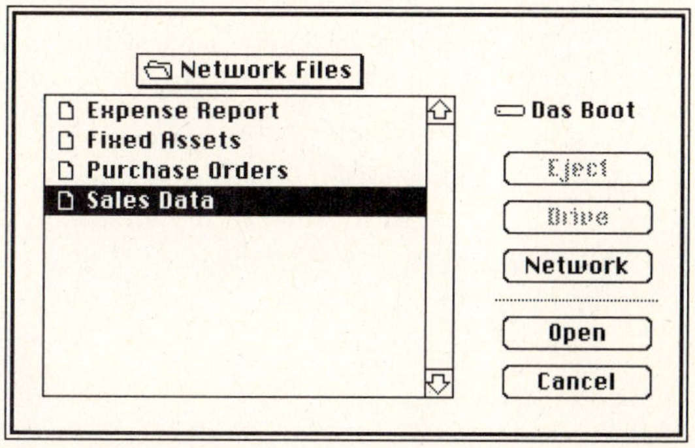

3. Leave the file open if you want to host the file. Other users on the network then can access open files on the network.

4. Place the file onto a file server by using AppleShare or publish the folder onto a TOPS network.

   Under this arrangement, another user can host the file (if you close the file first), and other guests can open the file in the normal manner.

5. Be sure to open any lookup files associated with the hosted file.

6. Close the file if you do not need it or if you do not want to host the file.

You cannot close the file as a host until all guests have closed the file on their computers. A host opens a file first and closes it last.

A host also affects the performance of the network, because the host computer is constantly being queried to retrieve information from the file. If you are using FileMaker as a host in MultiFinder, you should limit the use of other applications and avoid using applications that do not support background processing. This courtesy ensures smooth operation for other users.

Only one set of sorting orders, find requests, and page setups may be stored with a file. If, as host, you open a file that was previously hosted by another user, whatever settings are in place are with the file. You get the previous host's sorting order, find requests, page setup, and all the changes made to the file by both the previous host and guests. You can preserve your own settings by embedding them in a script or a button (see Chapter 12).

WARNING

When you use the Replace, View as List, Delete Multiple, Sort, Relookup, and Print commands in a file with a large number of records, you may hamper the operation of a network and freeze the file for other users. These operations are best accomplished as a single user.

If any lookup files are required for the file's proper operation, you as host must leave the lookup files open—or other users may create invalid data.

To lock a file from use by others, follow these steps:

1. As host, open the file and make the Exclusive command active.

   As a single user, making the Exclusive command active locks the file. If the file was opened and guests are using the file, FileMaker displays the dialog box shown in figure 17.2.

2. Click the Ask button.

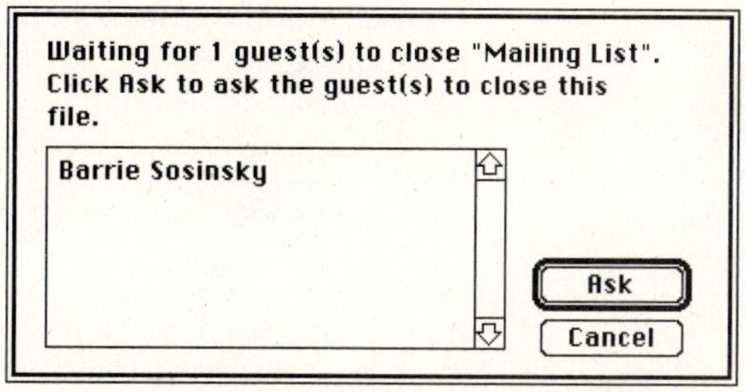

Fig. 17.2
The Request Guest to Close File dialog box.

FileMaker posts an alert box on each guest's computer, which requests that the guest close the file as soon as possible. When the last guest has closed the file, FileMaker automatically locks the file for the host. If you are a host and have the file open, select the Exclusive command from the File menu to remove the check mark to unlock a file. The file is now available for guests to use.

If you open a nonexclusive file as a second (or subsequent) user, you are a guest on that file. Occasionally, the host of the file may need to make changes, so you should close the file if the host requests that you do so. You should not keep unused files open on your desktop, because that slows down the network. As with any group of users on a networked file, you should not use the Replace, View as List, Delete Multiple, Relookup, or Print commands in a file with a large number of records, because these actions may slow the network to a crawl. These operations are best accomplished as a single user.

Guests can use open files in MultiFinder, but the same restrictions on using applications that support background processing apply to guests. Any other applications that you use slow down the network, although not as seriously as a host's actions do. To determine whether an application does background processing, consult your application's documentation. Communications normally support background processing. Constant graphic screen redraws called screen refreshes—such as arcade games, seriously slow down a network and should not be used.

To open a file as a guest, follow these steps:

1. Select the Open command from the File menu or press ⌘-O.

   FileMaker displays the standard Open File dialog box.

2. Click the Network button. FileMaker displays the Network dialog box (see fig. 17.3).

   Any nonexclusive file open on the network is listed along with the name of the host. When different users have the same name, FileMaker adds a random number to the name of each user to differentiate them.

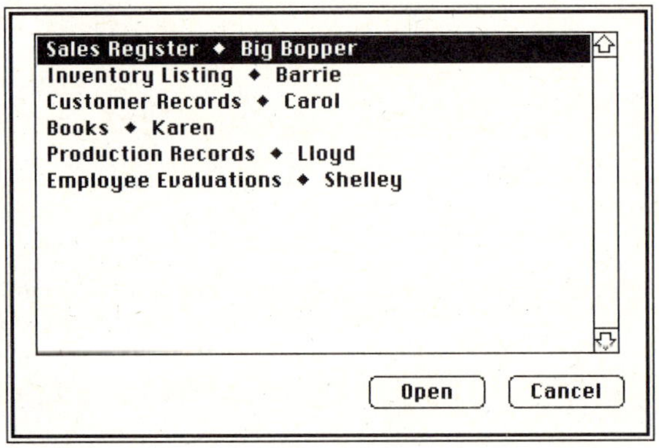

Fig. 17.3
The Non-Exclusive File List dialog box.

3. Click the file name you want and then click the Open button or double-click the file name.

   FileMaker displays a message telling you that you have opened the file as a guest.

Tip

If the file does not open, try opening the file by holding down the Option key and clicking the Network button. Continue to hold down the Option key until FileMaker indicates that you are opening the file as a guest.

Changes you make to a file are saved automatically to that file on the volume in which that file is stored. The Save a Copy As operation is restricted to the host or a single user, as discussed in the next section, "Network Privileges."

The preceding procedure works for an AppleTalk network. When you are working with a file server, such as AppleShare or TOPS, you have two additional methods for opening files as a guest. Use the Drive button in the Open dialog box to locate the volume your file is on. Or, if the file has been published or mounted, double-click the file's icon in the Finder.

Remember that a host's sort order, find requests, and page setup do not transfer with the file when you open the file as a guest. If you want to store these settings, you must create scripts to embed them.

To close a shared file, click the Close box in the title bar of the file window or select the Close command (⌘-W) from the File menu. As the host, you cannot close a file that guests are using. FileMaker displays a screen to the host. After the Ask button is clicked, FileMaker posts an alert box similar to the one shown in figure 17.4 on each guest's screen. Again, if the host requests that you close a file, you should do so as soon as you possibly can.

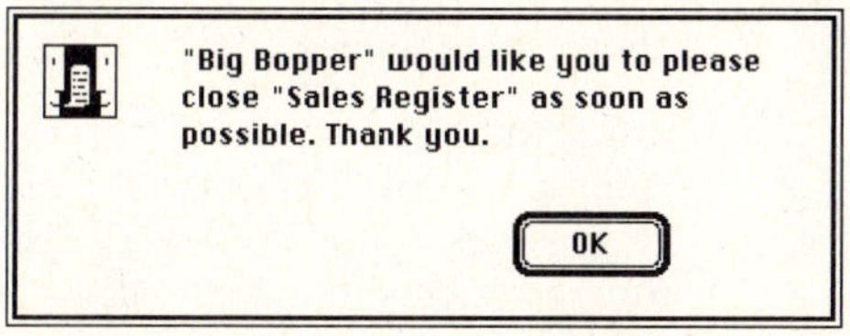

Fig. 17.4
The Guest Close File alert box.

WARNING

When you are using another application in the foreground in MultiFinder, you may not see the alert box shown in figure 17.4. Instead, you hear a beep. Switch back to FileMaker and close the file as soon as possible.

You quit FileMaker by issuing the Quit command from the File menu or by pressing ⌘-Q. If you are the host of a file, you cannot quit FileMaker until all guests have closed all the files you are hosting. FileMaker displays the dialog box shown in figure 17.2. Click the Ask button, and FileMaker displays the alert box shown in figure 17.4 to the other users. When your last guest closes the file, FileMaker automatically quits, returning you to the Finder.

Network Privileges

A shared file enables you to view and change layouts and data. Any change made to a file is saved to that file, and FileMaker updates the windows of any other user of that file. Remember that FileMaker offers record locking so that the record you are working with cannot be altered by another user while you are viewing it.

Depending on access privileges, hosts and guests may perform the following operations:

- Add, delete, or modify records
- Add, delete, or modify layouts
- Create, delete, or change scripts
- Create, delete, or change passwords
- Create or set paper sizes and page setups
- Input from a FileMaker file

If you have full access privileges, you can do all the operations listed above (see Chapter 16).

Any feature that works with groups of records, such as summary fields or summary parts, changes as the records they depend on change. FileMaker doesn't update those fields automatically, however; you must force a recalculation manually. To have FileMaker recalculate those fields, select the Browse, Preview, or Print command, and your data is updated. You can tell when another user is altering data in your file: the cursor on your screen becomes an animated series of double-headed arrows (only one shows at a time), as shown in figure 17.5.

Fig. 17.5
The Network cursor symbols.

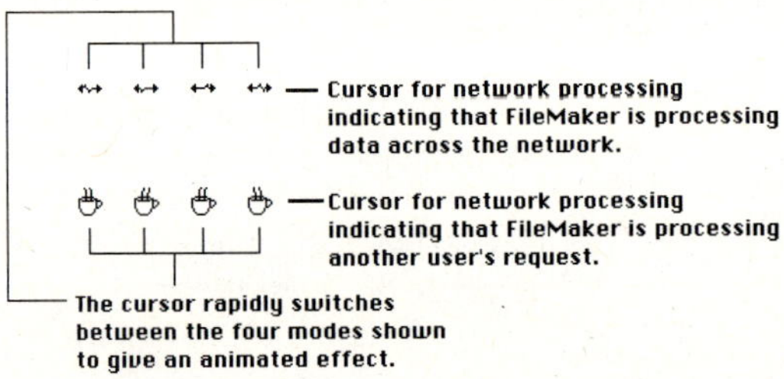

Although both guests and hosts can perform the preceding operations, some operations are specific to individual users: find requests, sort orders, and page setups. This feature enables users to work only with the set of records that they want when they manipulate a file. If multiple users had the same sorts, finds, and page setups, it would be impossible to browse individual sets of data, and networking FileMaker files would lose its utility.

Depending on access privileges, individual users can do the following:

- Sort records
- Find records
- Set page setups
- Hide windows
- Switch layouts
- Use scripts

Because only the host's finds, sorts, and page setups are stored with the file,you must store your requests in a script if you are a guest. The default setting for a label layout is an ImageWriter printer, so if you create a label layout and intend to use another printer, you must reset the page setup before you create the label layout.

Only a host can perform certain operations that affect all the guests. The following operations require that all guests close the shared file to allow the host to perform them. After you have completed the operation, guests can reopen the file, unless you checked Exclusive.

Only a host can perform the following operations:

- Define fields
- Define groups
- Change access privileges
- Import data
- Export data to another file
- Save copies (copy, clone, or compressed)
- Make the file exclusive

Operations on groups of records can hamper the network and should be attempted only by a single user. FileMaker requires a long time to complete some operations. Although finds are usually fast, finds in large data files can take time. Importing, exporting, or printing records is slow, as is any operation that requires your Macintosh to do internal calculations, screen refreshes, or graphics. Another slowdown problem is an operation that seeks information from a locked record.

To get the best performance from a network, perform the following operations as a single user:

- Delete multiple records
- Print records
- Sort a large number of records
- Relookup your records
- Recover files
- View as List records

The bigger the file, the more important it is to perform these operations as a single user.

WARNING

If you are using commands that depend on a group of records, some records on other users' screens may not be updated in time. If you are printing a report, for example, and another user modifies some of the records you are using, your records may not be current when FileMaker spools the data out to the printer. The only way to be absolutely certain that your data is current is to generate the report as a single user.

Use table 17.1 to determine what kind of network privileges are assigned to a host or to a guest

Table 17.1
Network Privileges

Operation	*Host*	*Guest*
Can be accomplished by a user:		
Open or close a file	X	X
Define fields	X	X
Input date from Text, BASIC, or SYLK files	X	
Save a Copy (copy, compressed, or cloned files)	X	
Output to a FileMaker file or data file	X	
Make a file exclusive	X	
Specific to each user:		
Find records	X	X
Sort records	X	X
Hide windows	X	X

Operation	*Host*	*Guest*
Change page setups	X	X
Use scripts	X	X
Switch layouts	X	X
Shared operations:		
Browse and edit data	X	X
Design and modify layouts	X	X
Create, modify, or use scripts	X	X
Use passwords	X	X
Create and set paper sizes	X	X
Input data from a FileMaker file	X	X

Troubleshooting a Network

Here are several common difficulties that people experience when using FileMaker files on a network.

- *FileMaker does not respond.* The cursor is a coffee-cup or a double-headed arrow. FileMaker is processing data and will be back in a moment. If you can, make the file exclusive to improve its speed.
- *Network button is dimmed.* Activate AppleTalk in the Chooser. If you have a Macintosh Plus, copy the AppleTalk System document from the FileMaker disk to your System folder. Carefully check the AppleTalk connectors; they are notorious for loosening.
- *File cannot be opened.* For a file on a file server, if you don't have FileMaker on your Macintosh, put the file into the folder with the FileMaker application on the server. The file may be exclusive and not open to guests. Consult the file's host for information.

  TOPS files that have been opened by another user can be password-protected to prohibit other users from accessing or writing to the file. Check the TOPS privileges for the file.

  If using the Network button and opening the file from the Open dialog box doesn't work, try holding down the Option key during the process.

- *New button is dimmed.* The folder or volume is write-protected.
- *The password-protection feature doesn't operate.* The No Password feature may be set and assigned full access rights.
- *Records or layouts are grayed.* The file is password-protected; the layouts are confidential; and you do not have the access privilege of viewing those layouts.
- *Summary fields are not accurate.* Other users may have altered data, used the Browse, Preview, or Print commands to update your records, and forced a recalculation.
- *Disk is full.* Delete unnecessary files.

APPENDIX A

Program Specifications

System Requirements

FileMaker Pro requires the following components to operate correctly:

- Minimum System: Macintosh Plus
- System 6 or 7
- 2M RAM recommended
- 1,024K of allocated RAM recommended when operating in MultiFinder
- Hard drive
- Macintosh-compatible printer: ImageWriter Series, LaserWriter Series, Apple Personal LaserWriter or Personal LaserWriter NT; or General Computer Personal Laser Printer. Any other Chooser-compatible printer, such as Hewlett-Packard DeskWriter, LaserJet, and PaintJet, Qume CrystalPrint, and many others, also is supported.

For network operation, you need *one* of the following:

- AppleTalk-compatible network
- AppleShare network
- TOPS network

Limits of the Program

Feature	*Specification*
Calculation formulas	Up to 250 characters each, counting all operators, text, numbers, field names, and so on for their characters
Calculation functions	Absolute value, integer value, if, round, average, count, sum, minimum, maximum, standard deviation, payment, present value, net present value, future value, day, month, year, date, DayOf Year, WeekOf Year, DayName, MonthName, today, extend, exact, position, proper, replace, trim, lower, middle, upper, length, left, right, DateToText, NumToText, TextToNum, TextToTime, TimeToText, modulo, sign, degrees, last, summary, log, random, sqrt, ln, pi, hour, time, minute, seconds, atan, radians, cos, sin, exp, tan
Calculation operators	+, –, *, /, ^ (exponent), =, ≠, >, <, ≥, ≤, and, or, not, +, " ", &
Dates	1/1/0001 to 12/31/3000 unformatted, 1/1/1904 to 12/31/2039 formatted
Field name length	Up to 63 characters
Field repetitions	Limited by layout size and free disk space
Field size displayed	Limited by layout size only
Field Types	Text, Number, Date, Time, Picture, calculation, and summary; calculation fields can be alphabetic, numeric, time, or date results.
Fields (indexed)	Text, Number, Date, Time, and calculation fields are indexed.

Feature	*Specification*
Fields, number per record	Limited by free disk space only
File formats for input	FileMaker, Text (tabs), Text (commas), BASIC (commas), SYLK, DBF, DIF, WKS, MERGE files
File formats for output	Text (tabs), Text (comma), BASIC (commas), SYLK, DBF, DIF, WKS, MERGE (Microsoft Word data document) files; cloned files can output layouts and field definitions only; no data is transferred
File size	Limited by free disk space, up to 32M on a hard drive
File, number open simultaneously	Up to 16 in Finder, 14 in MultiFinder within the limit of available RAM
Files, number per disk	Limited by free disk space only
Find criteria	Word prefix, exact (= value), empty (=), <, >, ≤, ≥, = (= value), range (...), duplicate (!), and, or, not (omit)
Find requests	Limited by free disk space only
Labels, number across page	Up to 99
Layout parts	Title header, header, body (record), sub-summary parts, grand summary parts, footer, and title footer; summary parts may be placed above or below the records to which they pertain
Layout parts size	Limited by layout size only
Layout size	Up to 36" by 36"; minimum of 1" by 1"
Layouts, number per file	Limited by free disk space only
Number of scripts	Limited by free disk space only
Number of sort levels	Limited by free disk space only
Numeric formats	Commas, dollar sign, specified number of decimal digits, yes/no, percent, or as typed

Feature	*Specification*
Numeric precision	15 floating decimal point digits
Record size	Limited by free disk space only
Summary types	Total, fraction of total, subtotaled when sorted by, running total, average, weighted by, count, running count, minimum, maximum, standard deviation
Text field	Number of characters limited to 32,000K

APPENDIX B

Installing FileMaker Pro

You can install FileMaker onto a hard drive or onto two 800K floppy disk drives. Before you begin, you should make working copies of your original disks and use those for the installation procedures.

To format disks to use for the working copies, follow these steps:

1. Insert your blank disks into your disk drive.
2. Format the disks.

Your Macintosh prompts you for the capacity of the disk you desire (single- or double-sided) and its name. Use the greatest capacity of your disk and drive: 800K for a double-sided, double-density disk (2DD) and an 800K disk drive or 1.44M for a double-sided, high-density disk (2HD) and a floppy disk high-density (FDHD) disk drive (a 1.44M disk drive). The difference between the disks is easy to spot: 2DD disks have one small notch, 2HD disks have two small notches.

After formatting the disks, use one of the following procedures, depending on the number of disk drives you have, to finish making the working copies.

For a two-disk drive system, follow these steps to finish making copies of the disk:

1. Insert the FileMaker disk into your second disk drive.

2. Drag the icon for the FileMaker disk onto the icon for the copy and release.

   Your Macintosh asks you to confirm the disk-to-disk copy.

3. Click the OK button or press the Return key.

4. After the copy process is finished, drag each disk icon in turn to the Trash to eject the disk and remove the icon from the DeskTop.

For a single-disk drive system, follow these steps to make copies of the FileMaker disk:

1. With the blank disk inserted, select the Eject command from the File menu or press ⌘-E.

2. Insert the FileMaker disk and drag its icon into the dimmed icon of the copy disk.

   Your Macintosh asks you to confirm the disk-to-disk copy.

3. Click the OK button or press the Return key.

   As the copy progresses, you are prompted to switch disks.

4. When you are finished, drag each disk icon to the Trash to eject the disk and remove the icon from the DeskTop.

   You are prompted to insert the dimmed disk when it is needed.

Working with copies of the FileMaker disks ensures protection of your originals. In case of a virus or an accident, you still have the original disks.

Using FileMaker on a hard drive is the recommended configuration. Hard drives increase the speed of the program and greatly enhance flexibility. Because of the size of database files, you rapidly encounter restrictions when storing files onto floppy disks.

To install FileMaker on your hard drive, follow the procedures listed in the rest of this section.

To copy the application, do the following:

1. Open the folder where you want to place your FileMaker program files.

2. Select the New Folder command from the File menu or press ⌘-N.

3. While the folder is still named Empty Folder, type the name of the folder—*FileMaker Pro*, or whatever you want.

4. Insert the disk labeled FileMaker Pro and double-click its disk icon to open its disk window.
5. Drag the icon of the FileMaker Pro application into the new folder icon on your hard drive.
6. When FileMaker indicates that you are finished, drag the FileMaker disk to the Trash to eject the disk.

To set up the support files, follow these steps:

1. Insert the disk labeled FileMaker Pro Utilities into the disk drive.
2. Double-click to view the contents of the disk: a folder named Claris Translators and icons for the Main Dictionary, User Dictionary, Claris Help System, and AppleTalk.
3. If you do not already have a Claris folder on your hard drive, select the New Folder command under the File menu or press ⌘-N. Name the new folder Claris, not Claris Folder. Place the Claris folder inside your System folder by dragging its icon to the System folder. (When the System folder is highlighted, release the mouse button.)

Note

If you use other Claris products, you may already have a Claris folder containing support files, such as Help stacks and dictionaries.

WARNING

If you already are using a dictionary from another Claris product, do not place the User Dictionary anywhere on your hard drive. By installing the User Dictionary, you unintentionally may replace the existing dictionary. FileMaker is able to use the User Dictionary from other Claris products.

4. If you do not already have them installed from other Claris products, select the Main Dictionary and the User Dictionary and drag them into the Claris folder.
5. Select the Claris Help System icon and drag it to the Claris folder.
6. Select the Claris Translators folder and drag it to the Claris folder.
7. If you are using a Macintosh Plus, drag the AppleTalk icon into your System folder.

   AppleTalk is needed to use FileMaker Pro on a network with a Macintosh Plus. If you install AppleTalk, you must reboot the machine before FileMaker can access the network.

   If you do not have a Macintosh Plus, do not copy AppleTalk into your System folder.
8. Drag FileMaker Pro Utilities to the Trash to eject the disk.

To copy the templates and tutorial files, follow this procedure:

1. Insert the FileMaker Pro Templates disk into your disk drive.
2. Select both the Templates Folder and the Tutorial Folder by dragging a selection marquee around them or by choosing Select All from the File menu. Drag them into the FileMaker Pro folder on your hard drive.
3. When the copy is complete, drag the FileMaker Pro Templates disk to the Trash to eject it.

You always may choose to run the Filemaker Pro HyperTour from the floppy instead of using space on your hard drive. If you do want to place it on your hard drive, follow these steps:

1. Insert the FileMaker Pro HyperTour disk into your disk drive.
2. Select the FileMaker Pro HyperTour icon and drag it into the FileMaker Pro folder on your hard drive.
3. When the copy is complete, drag the FileMaker Pro HyperTour disk to the Trash to eject it.

Upgrading from FileMaker II

FileMaker Pro can recognize and open FileMaker II files in the Open File dialog box. The process is straightforward but requires caution: after you open a FileMaker II file within FileMaker Pro, you cannot reopen that file in the FileMaker II program.

To upgrade from FileMaker II, follow these steps:

1. Put the System, Finder, and printing resources on an 800K disk. (Using a 1.44M disk and drive gives you additional resources and places the FileMaker program on that disk.)
2. Copy the FileMaker Pro application from the FileMaker master disk onto a second 800K disk.
3. If you want to use the FileMaker Help file, copy the FileMaker Help file into the folder that contains the application on the second disk.

FileMaker Pro requires that the FileMaker Help file be in the same folder to operate correctly.

Use the remaining space on your second disk to store your data files. If you have room on your system disk, move the Help file there to create more space on your second disk. FileMaker prompts you to use the Open command to find the Help file when you request it.

If you are using FileMaker on a network, your system administrator probably installed FileMaker for you. FileMaker's speed is greatly enhanced when each computer on the network contains its own copy of the FileMaker application; only data flows across the network, not parts of the program itself. This setup is referred to as a *multiuser configuration* of the program. If your system administrator hasn't installed FileMaker Pro, you should install FileMaker on either your hard disk or on two 800K disk drives, as described in the preceding sections.

You also can install FileMaker centrally on a server, a computer that enables users to request FileMaker over the network. This method is referred to as the *multilaunch configuration*. A TOPS network allows this type of installation.

For more information about installing FileMaker on a network, refer to Chapter 17 and your network documentation.

Using FileMaker on a network may require that you purchase additional copies of FileMaker to comply with the Claris licensing agreement. Site licenses also are available.

APPENDIX C

Menu Summary

The following menu description proceeds from left to right across the menu bar. Each menu contains a short description of its purpose, and each command in that menu also is briefly explained. Keystroke equivalents of commands are noted. For example, to use the Open command, you can use the ⌘-O keystroke. Hold down the Command key (the one with the ⌘ on it) and then press O to invoke that command. Although letters in a keystroke are written in uppercase, you only need to press the letters themselves. Certain commands contain submenus. A menu command followed by an ellipsis (...) indicates that a dialog box comes up on-screen. A menu command with a right-facing small triangle indicates that the command opens a submenu of additional commands to choose from. Check marks are used with commands that have an on or off state, such as T-squares. A check indicates that the command is on. Select the command again to turn it off.

FileMaker contains nine menus: Apple, File, Edit, Select, Layout, Arrange, Format, Scripts, and Window. Not all menus are available to you in each window. What you see depends on where you are in the program. In the Browse window, you are not able to change the layout, therefore FileMaker disables and dims the Layout and Arrange menus. Other commands and menus are disabled only if the user has a password that restricts file access privileges (see Chapter 16).

Apple Menu

The Apple menu is available from all windows in the program. Figure C.1 shows the Apple menu in Finder; figure C.2 shows the Apple menu in MultiFinder.

Fig. C.1
The Apple menu in Finder.

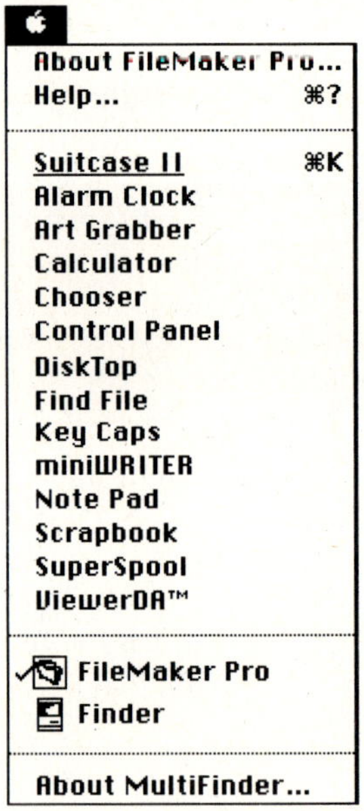

Fig. C.2
The Apple menu in MultiFinder.

About FileMaker Pro...

Choosing this option brings up a dialog box with a Show Info button that provides program information, including FileMaker version number, copyright data, the size of the current disk, the number of kilobytes used, and the amount of free space available. The Credits button provides information about the authors.

Help...

Keyboard equivalent: ⌘-?

Choosing this option opens the FileMaker Help file, which is based on a HyperCard system. Use the list of contents or the buttons to move around the Help file. The Help window can stay open while you work. Help is available in all windows (see Chapter 3).

Desk Accessories

All entries below the Help command and above the second set of dashed lines are desk accessories, which are available to you anywhere inside FileMaker (see Chapter 3).

Program Listings

In MultiFinder, you see open applications listed at the bottom of the Apple menu. To switch to another program, select the program of your choice. This action is equivalent to clicking a program window on your desktop.

File Menu

The File menu is available to you at all times (see fig. C.3).

New...

The New command creates a file. When New is chosen, FileMaker opens a standard file Save dialog box that asks you to place and name the new file (see Chapter 3).

Fig. C.3
The File menu.

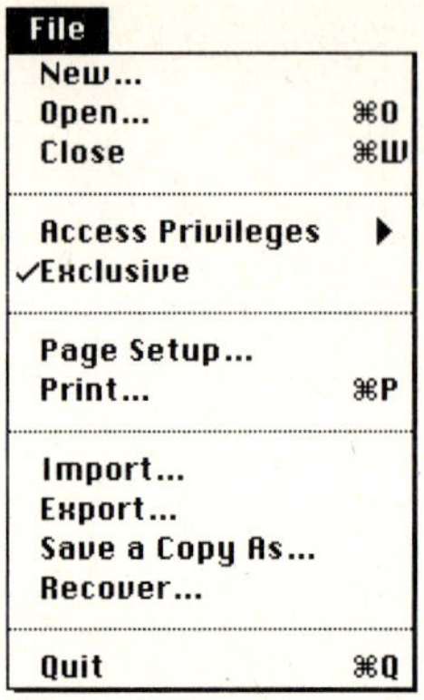

Open...

Keyboard equivalent: ⌘-O

The Open command shows a standard Open File dialog box that asks you to choose a file to open. You can open up to 16 files on your desktop in Finder and up to 14 in MultiFinder, depending on memory size. Any open files are listed in the Window menu.

Close

Keyboard equivalent: ⌘-W.

Using this option closes the current file or active window. This action is equivalent to clicking the close box in the title bar.

Access Privileges

This option opens a submenu that enables you to define or change groups and the password security code that allows access to a file. Different passwords can be assigned different levels of access, and passwords can be changed or deleted. Depending on the access privileges that you have assigned, FileMaker may disable additional menus or commands (see Chapter 16).

Define Groups. This command lets you add, change, delete, or rename access groups.

Define Passwords. Using this command creates new passwords, establishes the access privileges you want for each password, and deletes or changes access privileges.

Overview. The Overview command defines the relationship between groups and passwords and specifies which fields and layouts are available to specific groups.

Exclusive

When enabled, the Exclusive command restricts the use of the current file to one user on a network. On is the default setting. No guests can use the file (see Chapter 17).

Page Setup...

If you use the Page Setup option, you can specify options for printing: orientation, paper size or style, reduction, smoothing, and so on. The choices you see are determined by the output device you selected in the Chooser desk accessory. The Edit Page Sizes section enables you to specify a nonstandard paper size for output (see Chapter 10).

Print...

Keyboard equivalents: ⌘-P

⌘-Option-P (bypasses the dialog box)

This option presents you with the choices you need to specify a print job. The choices include quality of printing, number of copies, range of pages to print, which records to print, and so on (see Chapter 10).

Import...

The Import command copies the data from a file into your current file. The data file can be a FileMaker file, or it can be a file in the Tab-Separated Text or Comma-Separated Text, BASIC, DBF, DIF, WKS, MERGE, or SYLK format. The transfer between FileMaker files is automatic. For input from a data file, you can choose what data is imported in a certain order by setting up an import order (see Chapter 15).

Export...

Using Export To exports the data in your current file to a new data file that you create. You have control over the fields and the order in which they are output by setting up an export order. File formats selected are Tab-Separated Text or Comma-Separated Text, BASIC, DBF, DIF, WKS, SYLK, or the file format of Microsoft Word (see Chapter 15).

Save a Copy As...

This choice saves a copy of the current file as an exact copy, a compressed copy, or a clone of the file. Exact and compressed copies have all features of your file, including records and layouts. Clones have all fields, field definitions, and layouts, but lack the records.

Note

FileMaker has no Save command because FileMaker auto-saves your changes as you enter them (see Chapter 3).

Recover...

Using the Recover command creates a file and salvages as much of the information from a damaged file into the new file as possible (see Chapter 15).

Quit

Keyboard equivalent: ⌘-Q

Quit closes all files, exits the FileMaker program, and returns you to the Finder (see Chapter 3).

Edit Menu

The Edit menu is available to you regardless of your location in FileMaker (see fig. C.4). Choices on this menu are dimmed when inappropriate to the situation or if the user has browse-only privileges.

Undo

Keyboard equivalent: ⌘-Z

Use the Undo command to reverse your preceding action. Most typing, editing, graphic, and formatting changes can be undone. When Undo is unavailable, the phrase `Can't Undo` appears on the menu.

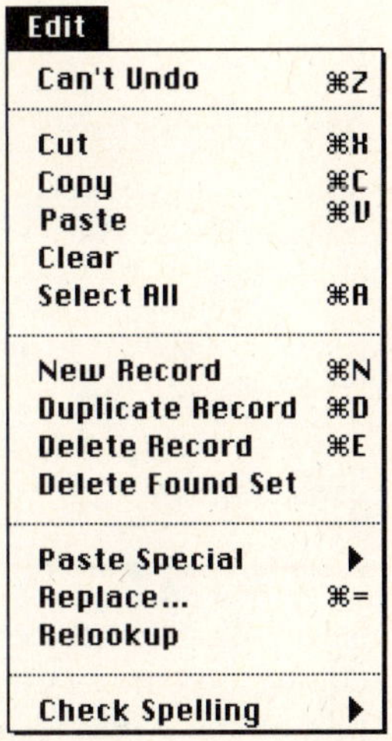

Fig. C.4
The Edit menu.

Cut

Keyboard equivalent: ⌘-X

Choose Cut to remove selected items from your FileMaker window and to place them onto the Clipboard. You can cut objects or text, move them to the Clipboard, and paste them into other locations (see Chapters 1 and 7).

Copy

Keyboard equivalent: ⌘-C

Using the Copy command copies selected items from your FileMaker window and places a copy onto the Clipboard. You then can paste them into another location (see Chapters 1 and 7).

Paste

Keyboard equivalent: ⌘-V

Paste copies the contents of the Clipboard into a new location you specify. The contents of the Clipboard are left unchanged for additional pastes (see Chapters 1 and 7).

Clear

Keyboard equivalents: Clear on the numeric keypad or Delete

Shift-Clear clears a field's contents and advances to the next field.

Clear removes selected data or layout objects without placing them onto the Clipboard (see Chapters 4 and 7).

Select All

Keyboard equivalent: ⌘-A

Select All selects the entire contents of the current field when you are editing a record in the Browse window. In the Layout window, the Select All command selects all objects on the layout. Selected objects or data can be cut, copied, or pasted (see Chapters 4 and 7).

New Record / New Layout / New Request

Keyboard equivalent: ⌘-N

In the Browse window, this command is the New Record command, which creates a new record at the end of your file; in the Layout window, this command is the New Layout command, which creates a new layout at the end of your layouts; in the Find window, this command is the New Request command, which creates a new request in your find operation. The New Record command is discussed in Chapter 3; the New Layout command is discussed in Chapter 6; and the New Request command is discussed in Chapter 4.

Duplicate Record / Duplicate Layout / Duplicate Request

Keyboard equivalent: ⌘-D

This option duplicates the current record, layout, or request that you are viewing while in the Browse, Layout, or Find windows, respectively. The Duplicate Record command is discussed in Chapter 3, the Duplicate Layout command is discussed in Chapter 6, and the Duplicate Request command is discussed in Chapter 4.

Delete Record / Delete Layout / Delete Request

Keyboard equivalents: ⌘-E

⌘- Option-E eliminates the feature without showing the dialog box if one is to be shown.

This option deletes the current record, layout, or request. See Chapters 4 and 6.

Delete Found Set

The Delete Found Set command deletes all the records in your browsed set.

Paste Special

Paste Special opens a submenu that contains commands used to paste information onto a layout at the insertion point or into records or requests (see Chapter 3).

From Index (⌘-I). This choice opens a scrollable window that contains all the different values entered into a field. Text, Number, Date, and calculation fields are indexed, and each word is a separate entry in the index. You can paste entries into the field at the insertion point.

From Last Record (⌘-'). This option pastes all the data from the field in the last record you modified into the same field in the current record or request.

Current Date (⌘-). The current date is pasted into any Date, Text, or Number field on the layout. The Macintosh internal calendar determines the date.

Current Time (⌘-;). The current time is pasted into any Time, Text, or Number field on the layout. The Macintosh internal calendar determines the time.

Date Symbol. This option pastes two slashes (//) on the layout. When you browse, print, or preview records, the two slashes are automatically replaced by the current date.

Time Symbol. This option pastes two colons (::) on the layout. When you browse, print, or preview records, the two colons are automatically replaced by the current time.

Page Number. This option pastes two number symbols (##) on the layout. When you print or preview the records, the two number symbols are automatically replaced by consecutive page numbers. When you use the Print command, you can specify the starting number you want to use.

Record Number. This option pastes two "at" symbols (@@) on the layout. When you print or preview records, the two "at" symbols are replaced by record numbers.

Replace...

Keyboard equivalent: ⌘-=

The Replace command puts the contents of the current field into the same field in all the records of your browsed set (see Chapter 4).

Relookup

Relookup reestablishes your lookup values, based on the values in the current file. The new values are then copied from the lookup files into the lookup field.

Check Spelling

The Check Spelling command searches for spelling errors. The Main Dictionary and the User Dictionary must be accessible to FileMaker Pro. Be certain that they are in your Claris folder. Choosing the Check Spelling command brings up a submenu of commands. Select one of the options and the results appear in the Spelling dialog box.

Check Selection. The current selection is checked for spelling.

Check Record/Check Layout. In the browse mode, this option checks the spelling of all Text and Number fields on the current layout but does not check layout text. In the layout mode, this option checks the spelling of all the layout text but does not check the Text and Number fields.

Check Found Set. This option checks the spelling of all Text and Number fields on the current layout that are in the current found set.

Spell Word (⌘-Shift-Y). The questionable word appears in the Spelling dialog box, along with the best guesses as to the word you meant. This command is available only when you have used the Spelling Options command to tell FileMaker to check your spelling as you type.

Spelling Options. Selecting this option opens a dialog box that enables you to control the "spell as you type" option and the position of the Spelling dialog box on your screen.

Install Dictionaries. This choice enables you to specify what dictionaries you want to use. If your dictionaries are in the Claris folder or the same folder as the FileMaker Pro application, you do not need to use this command unless you want to switch to another Main or User Dictionary.

User Dictionary. Using this option opens a dialog box that lets you add words to or remove words from a User Dictionary.

Select Menu

The Select menu is key to changing modes within the program (see fig. C.5). The mode currently in use is check marked on the menu. The Select menu is available in all windows within FileMaker, but certain commands on the Select menu may be disabled if inappropriate (like Sort in the Layout window) or if a password access privilege limits access.

Browse

Keyboard equivalent: ⌘-B

This choice opens the Browse window that shows data. You can select records for browsing by using the Find, Refind, Find All, Omit, Omit Multiple, Find Omitted, and Import commands. Browsed records may be edited, sorted, printed, and exported. The appearance of your Browse window is determined by the current layout (see Chapters 3 and 4).

Fig. C.5
The Select menu.

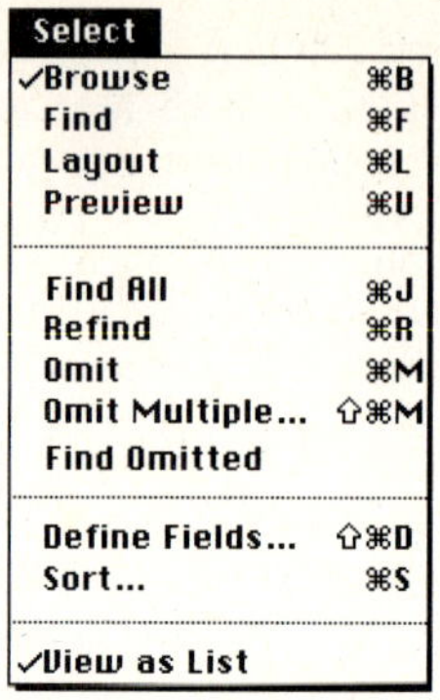

Find

Keyboard equivalent: ⌘-F

Find opens the Find window, where you can create a find request to select records. You enter criteria in that window, and you can string requests together to further specify the records you desire. Click the Find button to return to the Browse window with your records selected (see Chapter 4).

Layout

Keyboard equivalent: ⌘-L

This option opens the Layout window, where you can modify the appearance of objects on-screen. The current layout controls what you see on the Browse window and what you can edit and output. You can have as many layouts as your free disk space allows (see Chapter 6).

Preview

Keyboard equivalent: ⌘-U

Choosing this option shows, within a window, exactly what your printed output will look like. Preview is preset to a 50 percent reduced view. The zoom controls can change the viewing size (see Chapter 10).

Find All

Keyboard equivalent: ⌘-J

This option selects all the records in your current file for browsing.

Refind

Keyboard equivalent: ⌘-R

Using Refind opens the Find window, with your last request or group of requests displayed. You can modify the old find operation or leave it the same (see Chapter 4).

Omit

Keyboard equivalents: ⌘-M

⌘-Option-M bypasses the dialog box and deletes the current record.

Use this command to remove records from your browsed set of records.

Omit Multiple...

Keyboard equivalent: ⌘-Shift-M

This option opens a dialog box that enables you to specify the number of records, starting from the current one, that are to be temporarily left out of the set of records you are browsing.

Find Omitted

The Find Omitted command switches the found set and the omitted set.

Define Fields...

Keyboard equivalent: ⌘-Shift-D

Using the Define Fields command enables you to create fields and change field definitions. Use this command to specify auto-entry options, calculations, summaries, lookups, and other field properties (see Chapters 3, 4, and 5).

Sort...

Keyboard equivalent: ⌘-S

Sort orders the records by the values contained in their fields. You specify what fields are sorted and in what order. FileMaker uses ASCII code to sort values. FileMaker Pro includes a world icon that enables you to sort records based on the requirements of a different country (see Chapter 4).

View as List

The View as List command displays records in the Browse window as a list that you can scroll through. Only one set of headers, footers, and grand summary parts are displayed; sub-summary parts appear where they summarize a group of records. When the View as List command is not active, each record is displayed individually and each window can have headers, footers, sub-summary, and grand summary parts, as appropriate.

Layout Menu

The Layout menu contains a set of commands that enables you to work with your layouts (see fig. C.6). The Layout menu is only enabled when the Layout window is on-screen.

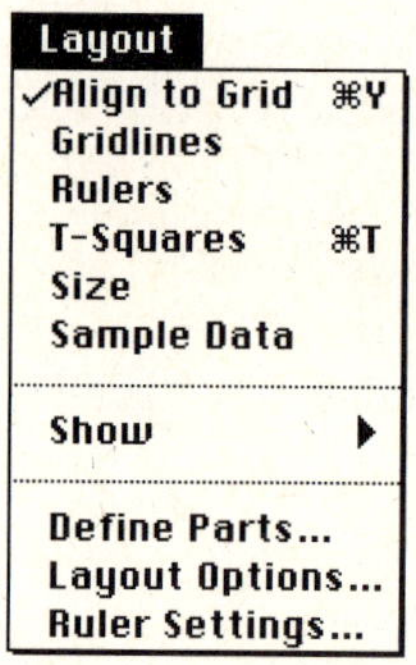

Fig. C.6
The Layout menu.

Align to Grid

Keyboard equivalents: ⌘-Y (a toggle)

⌘-drag temporarily disables the grid.

Align to Grid places an invisible "magnetized" grid on your Layout window, which enables you to align objects easily. You can temporarily disable the grid by holding down the Command key; release the key to reactivate the grid.

Gridlines

This command displays or hides the gridlines (a network of dotted horizontal and vertical lines). The gridlines correspond to the current ruler settings.

Rulers

Choosing the Rulers command displays or hides horizontal and vertical rulers. To change the units of measurement, click on the origin square, or use the Ruler Settings command on the Layout menu.

T-Squares

Keyboard equivalent: ⌘-T (a toggle)

This option displays horizontal and vertical position lines called T-squares, which enable you to position objects on your Layout window. Objects align to the T-square with their edges or centers; text objects align with their baselines. The T-squares are "magnetic" (see Chapter 7).

Size

The Size command opens the size box, which is a floating window that shows the position and size of a selected object, the T-square, or part. The units of measure correspond to those used by the rulers. When an object is selected, the upper four measurements in the size box indicate the object's position relative to the edge of the page or to the page margin. What you see depends on what you chose as the printable area in the submenu. The lower two measurements are the object's width and height. To reposition or resize a selected object automatically, type directly in the size box.

Sample Data

The Sample Data command fills all the fields on a layout with arbitrary data in the correct format and shows field types and format.

Show

The Show command offers a submenu of commands that enables you to specify how objects are displayed in the Layout menu.

Buttons. Choosing this option places gray borders around every button you created in the Define Button dialog box.

Text Boundaries. When checked, the boundaries around each text object are visible. Boundaries aid you in lining up layout text with other objects. Text boundaries do not appear in browse, preview, or print modes.

Field Boundaries. When checked, lines marking the boundaries and the baselines for values entered in the field are visible. Boundaries aid you in lining up fields with each other and with other objects. Text boundaries do not appear in browse, preview, or print modes.

Sliding Objects. When this option is selected, sliding objects are marked with arrows showing the direction.

Non-Printing Objects. This option marks the nonprinting objects with a gray border.

Non-Printable Area. When this option is selected, the page margins (the area where the printer cannot print) are visually distinguished from the rest of the page.

Define Parts...

This command creates, defines, deletes, and reorders parts. Page breaks and numbering options also can be selected by using Define Parts. Parts are used to control where information appears on the screen and the printed page.

Layout Options...

By using the Layout Options command, you can specify the number of records (columns) you want printed across the page and whether you want the records to print across first or down first.

Ruler Settings...

The Ruler Settings option presents a dialog box that enables you to set the measurement units for both the rulers and the grid. The options are in inches, centimeters, or pixels. The default for grid spacing is 6 pixels. The chosen units for the rulers also affect the gridlines and the size box.

Arrange Menu

The Arrange Menu contains many features useful for designing layouts (see fig. C.7). Some commands were available on the Gadgets menu in previous versions of FileMaker. The Arrange menu is only available in the layout mode (see Chapter 7).

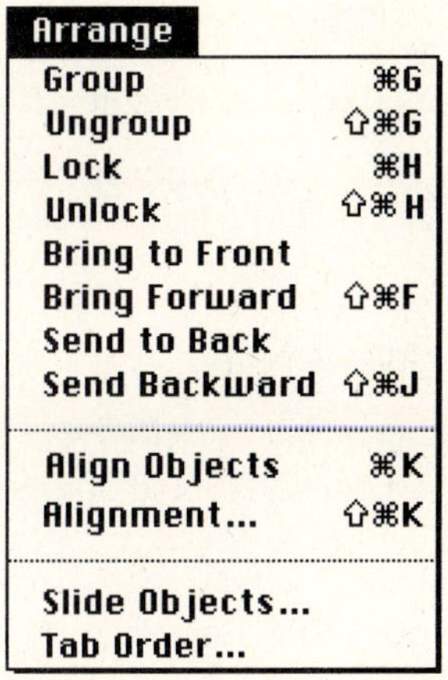

Fig. C.7
The Arrange menu.

Group

Keyboard equivalent: ⌘-G

The Group command makes it easy to manipulate several objects as a single object. By grouping objects, you then can resize, position, or format them as one unit. Grouping is a handy feature for combining address fields. Groups can be locked to prevent them from being changed. You can ungroup objects at any time.

Ungroup

Keyboard equivalent: ⌘-Shift-G

Ungrouping reverses the Group command. A grouped object must be ungrouped in order to edit any of the individual objects within it.

Lock

Keyboard equivalent: ⌘-H

Locking a selected object prevents it from being moved or changed. A locked object's handles change from black to gray. An entire layout can be protected by choosing Select All and then using the Lock command.

Unlock

Keyboard equivalent: ⌘-Shift-H

The Unlock command reverses the Lock command. When Unlock is selected, the handles change back from gray to black.

Bring to Front

The Bring to Front command moves any selected objects in front of all other overlapping objects in a stack of objects.

Bring Forward

Keyboard equivalent: ⌘-Shift-F

Bring Forward moves any selected object (or objects) one layer closer to the top in the stacking order of overlapping objects. The selected object actually changes place with the object in front of it.

Send to Back

Send to Back moves any selected objects to the bottom of the stack of overlapping objects.

Send Backward

Keyboard equivalent: ⌘-Shift-J

Send Backward moves any selected object (or objects) one layer closer to the bottom in the stacking order of overlapping objects. The selected object actually changes place with the object behind it.

Align Objects

Keyboard equivalent: ⌘-K

The Align Objects command is useful for aligning and distributing sets of objects repeatedly. The Alignment dialog box enables you to choose settings for aligning and distributing selected layout text, graphic objects, and fields.

Alignment...

Keyboard equivalent: ⌘-Shift-K

Choosing Alignment presents the Alignment dialog box in which you can specify how the selected objects are to be aligned relative to each other.

Slide Objects...

The Slide Objects command removes the blank space at the end of a field's data. If the field is blank, this command removes the field itself. Sliding can be up or to the left. You also can specify that blank parts not be shown or slide up. The Slide Objects Up option should not be used on labels or forms because they will be out of alignment when printed. When the Slide Objects feature is on, fields have small arrows on their borders indicating the direction of the slide.

Tab Order...

Use the Tab Order command to change the manner in which you can tab through fields to enter data (see Chapter 5). Unless you change the tab order, FileMaker moves through fields left to right, top to bottom.

Format Menu

The Format menu (see fig. C.8) is active only when you are in the Layout window. Depending on the password-protected access privilege you have, you may not be able to view this menu and work with it. You must have at least the right to design layouts to have this right assigned; otherwise, the entire menu may be inactive. The commands for formatting text are also available to you in the Browse window.

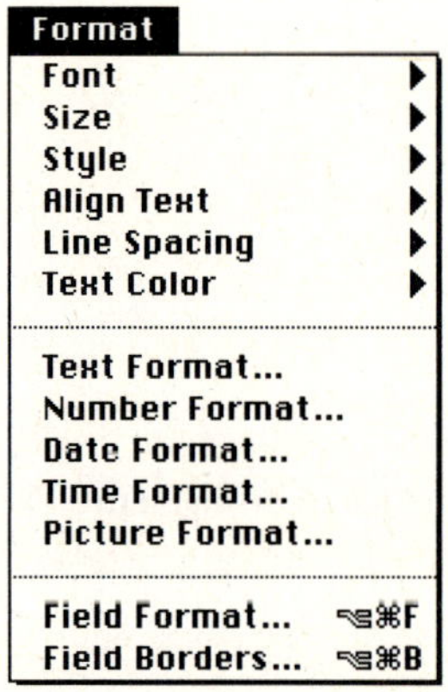

Fig. C.8
The Format menu.

Font

Use the Font command to specify the font for data. You also can specify a font for text objects. The fonts available are those in your System file or those that are available to you through a font manager, such as Suitcase II or Master Juggler.

Size

Choose the Size command to select a size (in points) for your text or text objects in the Layout window. In the Browse window, you can use Size to change text inside fields only. An outlined point size indicates the installed font sizes available to you. Selecting the Custom choice displays a Custom Font Size dialog box that enables you to format text in a nonstandard font size. You can type in any size between 1 and 127.

Style

Keyboard equivalents: ⌘-Shift-P for Plain

⌘-Shift-B for Bold

⌘-Shift-I for Italic

⌘-Shift-U for Underline

⌘-Shift-O for Outline

⌘-Shift-S for Shadow

This option enables you to set the style for your text in a field or for text objects (when in the Layout window). You can set multiple styles. Select Plain style to remove all styles.

Align Text

Keyboard equivalents: ⌘-Shift-L for Left Align

⌘-Shift-C for Center Align

⌘-Shift-R for Right Align

Text objects and values in fields may be aligned left, center, or right.

Line Spacing

Selecting Line Spacing produces a submenu that enables you to choose the line spacing for layout text and fields. Options include single-spacing, double-spacing, or custom spacing. The Custom Line Spacing choice lets you enter any number from 1 to 128. The spacing you set appears last on the Line Spacing submenu.

Text Color

The Text Color command lets you change the color of text. In layout mode, the layout text and fields are affected. In the browse mode, the text color affects selected text in a text field. The type of pop-up color chart you see depends on the setting for your monitor: black-and-white, gray scale, or color.

Text Format...

Keyboard equivalent: Double-click layout text or a text field in layout mode.

A combination of text attributes can be assigned all at once for layout text and fields. The Text Format dialog box includes pop-up menus for Font, Size, Alignment, Line Spacing, and Color.

Number Format...

Keyboard equivalent: Double-click a Number field in layout mode.

This command enables you to change the display and output of the data in a Number field or in a calculation field with a numeric result. Choices available are Leave Data Formatted as Entered, so that numbers appear as entered; Format as Decimal Number, using currency, percentage, and thousands separators; and Boolean Yes or No (see Chapters 3 and 7).

Date Format...

Keyboard equivalent: Double-click a Date field in layout mode.

This option enables you to change the display and output of the data in a Date field or in a calculation field with a date result. Unformatted dates appear as you enter them; you also have the option of using dates in several styles. (Date Format is discussed in Chapters 3 and 7.) You can use this command to format the date that appears on a layout as the layout object (see Chapter 9).

Time Format...

Keyboard equivalent: Double-click a Time field in layout mode.

Use this command to format a time field, a calculation field with a time result, or the time symbol (::). Options include 12- or 24-hour formats and a pop-up menu with choices for hours, minutes, and seconds.

Picture Format...

Keyboard equivalent: Double-click a Picture field in layout mode.

This command enables you to alter the display of your picture to data in a Picture field or to a picture in the form of an object on your layout. The choices available to you are Resize Picture Proportionately to Fit Frame, Resize Picture to Exactly Fill Frame, and Crop Picture within Frame. You also can align pictures of Picture fields by using the Alignment pop-up menu (see Chapters 3 and 7).

Field Format...

Keyboard equivalent: ⌘-Option-F

The Field Format command enables you to specify how to display a field's value list (created during field definition) or to set up repeating fields.

Field Borders...

Keyboard equivalent: ⌘-Option-B

Using the Field Borders command enables you to create field borders and baselines for fields on the layout. Field borders can be seen in browse, preview, or print modes.

Scripts Menu

The Scripts menu contains the Scripts command and any scripts that you might have defined (see fig. C.9). This menu is enabled wherever you are in the FileMaker program and with whatever access privileges you have available.

Fig. C.9
The Scripts menu.

Define Scripts...

Keyboard equivalent: ⌘-1 to ⌘- 0 (optional for the first ten scripts)

A script is a small program that alters the state of your file or orders a command (see Chapter 12). Defined scripts return your file to the specified state when executed. You can specify that a page setup, find, sort, import/export order, and other features be remembered. The first ten scripts can have the ⌘-1 through ⌘-0 keystrokes assigned to them.

Define Button...

The Define Button command enables you to create buttons on your layout to perform frequently used scripts or commands or to switch between layouts (see Chapter 12).

Window Menu

The Window menu contains the Hide Window command and a listing of all FileMaker files open on your desktop (see fig. C.10). The Window menu is always available.

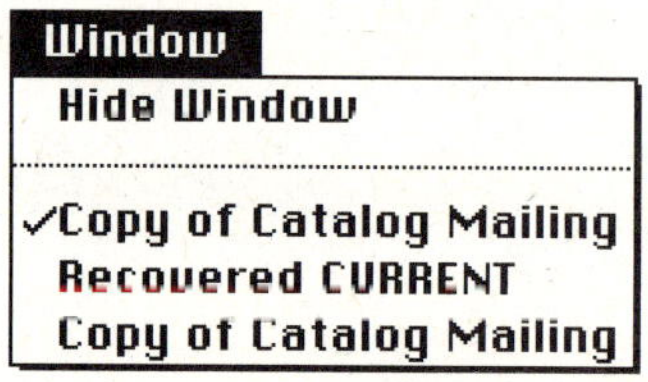

Fig. C.10
The Window menu.

Hide Window

The Hide Window command removes your current file from view but not from memory. The hidden file is placed inside parentheses in the Window menu. Lookup files are referenced, and they are opened as hidden windows when you open a file that depends on them.

File Name

Choose the file you want to make the current file. Choosing a hidden file displays that file and removes the parentheses from view.

APPENDIX D

Product Index

Software Sources

This section contains a list of products available for the Macintosh. The list is not exhaustive.

4th Dimension, Version 2.0, $795. Acius, Inc., 10351 Bubb Road, Cupertino, CA 95014, (408)252-4444.

Address Book Plus, $89.95 ($129.95 with leather binding). Power Up Software Corp., 2929 Campus Drive, San Mateo, CA 94403, (800) 851-2917 or (800)223-1479 (CA).

Adobe Type Manager, $99. Adobe Microsystems, Inc., 1585 Charleston Road, P.O. Box 7900, Mountain View, CA 94039, (415)961-4400.

Aldus FreeHand, Version 2.0, $495. Aldus Corporation, 411 First Avenue South, Suite 200, Seattle, WA 98104, (206)622-5500.

Aldus Persuasion, $495. Aldus Corporation, 411 First Avenue South, Suite 200, Seattle, WA 98104, (206)622-5500.

Anti-Virus Kit, $79.95. 1st Aid Software, 42 Radnor Road, Boston, MA 02135, (617)783-7118.

USING FILEMAKER PRO

AntiToxin, $99.95. Mainstay, 5311-B Derry Avenue, Agora Hills, CA 91301, (818)991-6540.

AutoMac III, Version 2.0, $79.95. Genesis Micro Software, 17124 NE 8th Pl., Bellevue, WA 98008, (206)747-8512.

Berkeley Macintosh User's Group, BMUG Inc., 1442A Walnut Street, #62, Berkeley, CA 94709-1496, (415)549-BMUG (2684).

Boomerang, shareware. Zeta Soft, 2425B Channing Way, Suite 492, Berkeley, CA 94704. Available from many on-line services and bulletin boards and on distribution disks from the Boston Computer Society Macintosh User's Group and the Berkeley Macintosh User's Group.

Boston Computer Society Macintosh User's Group Virus Disk. BCS-Mac, 48 Grove Street, Somerville, MA 02144, (617)625-7080. From the group's disk library.

CA-Cricket Presents, $495. Computer Associates International, Inc., 10505 Sorrento Valley Road, San Diego, CA 92121, (408)432- 1727, (800)531-5236.

Canvas, Version 2.1, $299.95. Deneba Software, 3305 NW 74th Street, Miami, FL 33122, (305)594-6995 or (800)622-6827.

Carta. Adobe Microsystems, Inc., 1585 Charleston Road, P.O. Box 7900, Mountain View, CA 94039, (415)961-4400.

CrystalPrint, Series II, $1,999. Qume Corporation, 500 Yosemite Drive, Milpitas, CA 95035, (408)942-4000.

dBASE Mac, $495. Ashton-Tate, 20101 Hamilton Avenue, Torrance, CA 90502, (213)329-8000.

DeltaGraph, $195. DeltaPoint, Inc., 200 Heritage Harbor, Suite G, Monterey, CA 93940, (408)648-4000.

DeskWriter, $895. Hewlett-Packard Co., 19310 Pruneridge Avenue, Cupertino, CA 95014, (800)752-0900.

Disinfectant, Version 2.1, freeware. John Norstad, Academic Computing and Network Services, Northwestern University, 2129 Sheridan Road, Evanston, Illinois 60208. Available from many on-line services and bulletin boards and from BCS-Mac and BMUG.

DiskFit, $99.95. SuperMac Technology, 485 Potrero Avenue, Sunnyvale, CA 94086, (408)245-2202.

DiskTools II, $49.95. Electronic Arts, 1820 Gateway Drive, San Mateo, CA 94404, (415)571-7171 or (800)245-4525.

DiskTop, Version 4.0, $49.95. CE Software, Inc., 1854 Fuller Road, West Des Moines, IA 50265, (515)224-1995.

Double Helix, Version 3.0, $495. Odesta Corp., 4084 Commercial Avenue, Northbrook, IL 60062, (312)498-5615 or (800)323-5423.

Fastback II, $189. Fifth Generation Systems, Inc., 11200 Industriplex Blvd., Baton Rouge, LA 70809, (504)291-7221 or (800)873-4384.

FastForms, $149.95. Power Up Software Corporation, 2929 Campus Drive, San Mateo, CA 94403, (800)851-2917 or (800)223-1479 (CA).

FileMaker Course for Business Users, $399. Claris Corporation, 5201 Patrick Henry Drive, P.O. Box 58168, Santa Clara, CA 95052, (408) 727-8227 (customer relations), (800)544-8554 (U.S. upgrades) or (800)334-3535 (U.S. dealers).

FileMaker Pro, Version 1.0, $299. Claris Corporation, 5201 Patrick Henry Drive, P.O. Box 58168, Santa Clara, CA 95052, (408)727-8227 (customer relations), (800)544-8554 (U.S. upgrades), or (800)334-3535 (U.S. dealers).

FileMaker Report and the Elk Horn Library. Elk Horn Publishing, P.O. Box 126, Aromas, CA 95004, (408)726-3148. Joe Kroger, publisher. Back orders are available only to subscribers.

Find File, System software. Apple Computer, Inc., 20525 Mariani Avenue, Cupertino, CA 95014, (408)996-1010.

FindsWell, Version 2.0, $59.95. Working Software, Inc., P.O. Box 1844, Santa Cruz, CA 95061, (408)423-5696.

Focal Point II, $199.95. TenPoint, 3885 Bohannon Drive, Menlo Park, CA 94025, (415)329-7630.

FoxBase+/Mac, Version 2.0, $495. Fox Software, Inc., 134 W. South Boundary, Perrysburg, OH 43551, (419)874-0162.

Freedom of the Press, $495. Custom Applications, Inc., 900 Technology Park Drive, Bldg. 8, Billerica, MA 01821, (508)667- 8585.

Full Impact 2.0, $395. Ashton-Tate, 20101 Hamilton Avenue, Torrance, CA 90502, (213)329-8000.

GateKeeper 1.1.1, by Chris Johnson. Available from many on-line services, bulletin boards, and from the BCS-Mac and BMUG disk libraries.

Gradient Resources, 369 Massachusetts Avenue, Suite 233, Arlington, MA 02174, (617)646-8799. A library of FileMaker business templates and related developer services. Contact Bill Dodson, developer.

Heizer Software Catalog, Excellent Exchange, and Works Exchange. 1941 Oak Park Blvd., Suite 30, P.O. Box 232019, Pleasant Hill, CA 94523, (800)888-7667.

HFS Backup 3.0, $99. Personal Computer Peripherals Corporation, 4710 Eisenhower Blvd., Tampa, FL 33634, (813)884-3092 or (800)622-2888.

Illustrator 88, Version 3.0, $495. Adobe Microsystems, Inc., 1585 Charleston Road, P.O. Box 7900, Mountain View, CA 94039, (415)961-4400.

ImageWriter II, $595 (LQ—$1399). Apple Computer, Inc., 20525 Mariani Avenue, Cupertino, CA 95014, (408)996-1010.

InFormed, $295. Shana Corporation, #105, 9650 20th Avenue, Edmonton, Alberta, Canada, T6N 1G1, (403)463-3330.

Innovative Synthesis, 1425 Beacon Street, Newton, MA 02168, (617)244-9078. Contact Barrie Sosinsky, developer.

Interferon 3.0, shareware. Send as much money as you want to The Vision Fund, c/o Robert Woodhead, Inc., 10 Spruce Lane, Ithaca, NY 14850. Available from many on-line services, bulletin boards, and from the BCS-Mac and BMUG disk libraries.

KaleidaGraph, Version 2.0, $249. Synergy Software (PCS, Inc.), 2457 Perkiomen Avenue, Reading, PA 19606, (215)779-0522.

Laser Labels Technologies, 1333 South Jefferson St., Chicago, IL 60607, (800)882-4050. Distributes Avery labels and others.

LaserWriter SC, NT, and NTX, $2,799 (IISC), $4999 (IINT), $6,999 (NTX). Apple Computer, Inc., 20525 Mariani Avenue, Cupertino, CA 95014, (408)996-1010.

Lightning Scan, $495. Thunderware, Inc., 21 Orinda Way, Orinda, CA 94563, (415)254-6581.

MacAcademy Video Training Series, FileMaker Tape 1 and 2. Florida Marketing International, Inc., 477 Nova Road, Ormand Beach, FL 32074, (904)677-1918. Contact Keith Kiel.

MacDraw II, Version 1.1, $399. Claris Corporation, 5201 Patrick Henry Drive, P.O. Box 58168, Santa Clara, CA 95052, (408)727-8227 (customer relations), (800)544-8554 (U.S. upgrades) or (800)334-3535 (U.S. dealers).

MacInker, $42. Computer Friends, Inc., 14250 NW Science Park Dr., Portland, OR 97229, (503)626-2291.

Macintosh Computers (Plus—$1,799, SE—$3,169, II—no longer manufactured, SE/30—$4,369, IIx—$5,269, IIcx—$4,669, IIci—$6,269, Portable—$5,799). Apple Computer, Inc., 20525 Mariani Avenue, Cupertino, CA 95014, (408)996-1010.

MacPaint, Version 2.0, $125. Claris Corporation, 5201 Patrick Henry Drive, P.O. Box 58168, Santa Clara, CA 95052, (408)727-8227 (customer relations), (800)544-8554 (U.S. upgrades) or (800)334-3535 (U.S. dealers).

MacPsych, $225. BHC Publishing, 619 Aspen Drive, Plainsboro, NJ 08536, (609)799-2061.

MacroMaker, System software. Apple Computer, Inc., 20525 Mariani Avenue, Cupertino, CA 95014, (408)996-1010.

MacWrite II, $249. Claris Corporation, 5201 Patrick Henry Drive, P.O. Box 58168, Santa Clara, CA 95052, (408)727-8227 (customer relations), (800)544-8554 (U.S. upgrades), or (800)334-3535 (U.S. dealers).

Mailing Lists. American List Council, 88 Orchard Road CN-5219, Princeton, NJ 08543, (201)874-4300.

Master Juggler. AlSoft, Inc., P.O. Box 927, Spring, TX 77383, (602)290-9790.

Microsoft Excel, Version 2.2, $395. Microsoft Corporation, One Microsoft Way, Redmond, WA 98052, (206)882-8080.

Microsoft File, Version 2.0, $195. Microsoft Corporation, One Microsoft Way, Redmond, WA 98052, (206)882-8080.

Microsoft Word, $395. Microsoft Corporation, One Microsoft Way, Redmond, WA 98052, (206)882-8080.

Microsoft Works, $295. Microsoft Corporation, One Microsoft Way, Redmond, WA 98052, (206)882-8080.

MyTimeManager 2.0. MacShack Enterprises, 19 Harrington Road, Cambridge, MA 02140, (617)876-6343.

Norton Utilities for the Macintosh, V. 1.0. Norton Computing, Inc., 100 Wilshire Blvd., 9th Fl., Santa Monica, CA 90401.

Of Counsel Software, Church St. P.O. Box 335, Arkville, NY 12455, (914)586-3129, fax (914)586-2797, Ralph Barile, developer.

Omnis 5, $695. Blyth Software, Inc., 2929 Campus Drive, Suite 425, San Mateo, CA 94403, (415)571-0222.

On Cue, $59.95. Icom Simulations, Inc., 648 S. Wheeling Road, Wheeling, IL 60090, (708)520-4440.

OrderTrak. Database Associates (Div. of Network New England Associates), 612 Highland Avenue, Needham, MA 02194, (617)449- 8387, fax (617)449-8386, Bill Taube and Bruce Yogel, developers.

PageMaker, $595. Aldus Corporation, 411 First Avenue South, Suite 200, Seattle, WA 98104, (206)622-5500.

Personal Laser Printer II (PLP)—$1,399, Fonts Plus—$239. GCC Technologies, Inc., 580 Winter Street, Waltham, MA 02154, (800)422-7777.

Personal Laser Writer SC—$1,999, NT—$3,299, SCTV NT upgrade—$1,300. Apple Computer, Inc., 20525 Mariani Ave., Cupertino, CA 95014, (408)996-1010.

PowerPoint, Version 2.01, $395. Microsoft Corporation, One Microsoft Way, Redmond, WA 98052, (206)882-8080.

QuickDex, Version 1.4a, $165. Casady & Greene, Inc., P.O. Box, 223779, Carmel, CA 93922, (408)624-8716.

QuicKeys, Version 1.2, $99. CE Software, Inc., 1854 Fuller Road, West Des Moines, IA 50265, (515)224-1995.

Redux, Version 1.5, $99. Microseeds Publishing, 7030-B W. Hillsborough Avenue, Tampa, FL 33143, (813)882-8635.

Retrospect 1.1, $349. Dantz Development Corporation, 1510 Walnut Street, Berkeley, CA 94709, (415)849-0293.

SAM (Symantec AntiVirus for Macintosh). Symantec Corporation, 10201 Torre Avenue, Cupertino, CA 95014, (800)441-7234 or (800)626-8847 (CA).

ScanMan for Macintosh, $499. Logitech, Inc., 6505 Kaiser Drive, Fremont, CA 94555, (415)795-8500.

Shortcut, $79.95. Aladdin Systems, Inc., 217 E. 86th Street, Suite 153, New York, NY 10028, (212)410-3080.

SideKick: The Desktop Organizer, $99.95. Borland International, 1800 Green Hills Road, Scotts Valley, CA 95066, (408)483-8400.

Small Business Retailer, $295. Packer Software, 12 Roosevelt Avenue, Mystic, CT 06355, (203)572-8955.

SmartForms Designer 1.1, $399 (SmartForms Assistant 1.1—$49). Claris Corporation, 5201 Patrick Henry Drive, P.O. Box 58168, Santa Clara, CA 95052, (408)727-8227 (customer relations), (800)544-8554 (U.S. upgrades), or (800)334-3535 (U.S. dealers).

SmartScrap and The Clipper, $89.95. Solutions, Inc., P.O. Box 783, Williston, VT 05495, (802)865-9220.

Suitcase II, $79, Fifth Generations Systems, Inc., 11200 Industriplex Blvd., Baton Rouge, LA 70809, (504)291-7221 or (800)865-9220.

SuperGlue II, $119.95. Solutions, Inc., P.O. Box 783, Williston, VT 05495, (802)865-9220.

SuperLaserSpool, $149.95 (SuperSpool—$99.95). SuperMac Technology, 485 Potrero Avenue, Sunnyvale, CA 94086, (408)245- 2202.

SuperPaint II, Version 2.0, $199. Silicon Beach Software, P.O. Box 261430, San Diego, CA 92126, (619)695-6956.

Tempo II, Version 1.2, $99. Affinity Microsystems, Ltd., 1050 Walnut Street, Suite 425, Boulder, CO 80302, (303)442-4840.

TOPS/Macintosh 2.1, $249. Sun Microsystems, TOPS Division, 950 Marina Village Parkway, Alameda, CA 94501, (415)769-8700.

TrueForms, $395. Adobe Microsytems, Inc., 1585 Charleston Road, P.O. Box 7900, Mountain View, CA 94039, (415)961-4400.

Virex, $99.95. HJC Software, Inc., P.O. Box 51816, Durham, NC 27717, (919)490-1277.

Virus Detective, shareware ($35 requested). Jeffrey S. Shulman, P.O. Box 521, Ridgefield, CT 06877-0521, (203)792-1521. Available evenings and weekends. Available from many on-line services, bulletin boards, and the BCS-Mac and BMUG disk libraries.

Virus Rx, Version 1.6, freeware. Apple Computer, Inc., 20525 Mariani Avenue, Cupertino, CA 95014, (408)996-1010. Available from many on-line services, bulletin boards, and the BCS-Mac and BMUG disk libraries.

Wingz, $399. Informix Software, 16011 College Blvd., Lenexa, KS 66219, (913)599-7100.

WorksPlus Command, $149.95. Lundeen & Associates, P.O. Box 30038, Oakland, CA 94604, (415)769-7701 or (800)233-6851.

WorksPlus Spell, $99.95. Lundeen & Associates, P.O. Box 30038, Oakland, CA 94604, (415)769-7701 or (800)233-6851.

Books

This section lists some of the books you can refer to if you want to learn more about computers and databases.

Computers

Beyond the Desktop by Barrie Sosinsky (New York, NY: Bantam Books, 1991). ISBN 0-553-35244-X.

The First Book of Personal Computing by R. K. Swadley (Carmel, IN: Howard W. Sams & Company, 1990). ISBN 0-672-27313-6.

Introduction to Personal Computers, 2nd Edition, by Katherine Murray (Carmel, IN: Que Corporation, 1991). ISBN 0-88022-758-3.

Que's Computer User's Dictionary, 2nd Edition, by Bryan Pfaffenberger (Carmel, IN: Que Corporation, 1991). ISBN 0-88022-697-8.

Using Computers in Business by Joel Shore (Carmel, IN: Que Corporation, 1989). ISBN 0-88022-470-3.

Understanding Computers (Richmond, VA: Time-Life Books, Inc.). Contains general information.

Database Theory

Database: A Primer by C. J. Date (Reading, MA: Addison-Wesley, 1984). ISBN 0-201-11358-9. An introduction by Mr. Database himself.

An Introduction to Database System by C. J. Date (Reading, MA: Addison-Wesley). 4th Edition, Vol. I, 1983, ISBN 0-201-14201-5; Vol. II, 1983, ISBN 0-201-14474-3. Database theory and design.

Computer Data-Base Organization, 2nd Ed., by James Martin (Englewood Cliffs, NJ: Prentice-Hall, 1977). ISBN 0-13-165423. An introductory college text.

Database Systems Management and Use by Alice Y. H. Tsai (Scarborough, Ontario: Prentice-Hall Canada, Inc., 1988). ISBN 0-13-196833-5. An introductory college text.

Computer-Based Information Systems: A Management Approach, 2nd Ed., by Donald W. Kroeber and Hugh J. Watson (New York: Macmillan, 1984). ISBN 0-02-366870-9. A broad introductory college text.

Database System Concepts by Henry F. Korth and Abraham Silberschatz (New York: McGraw-Hill, 1986). ISBN 0-07-044752-7. The logic and relational calculus theory of databases.

Macintosh

The Big Mac Book, 2nd Ed., by Neil Salkind (Carmel, IN: Que Corporation, 1991). ISBN 0-88022-648- X . Winner of the Computer Press Association's "Best Product-Specific Book (Hardware) of 1989" award. Nuts to bolts; a veritable smorgasbord of the Macintosh.

The Apple Macintosh Book, 3rd Ed., by Cary Lu (Redmond, WA: Microsoft Press, 1988). A technically well-written introductory book.

The Macintosh Bible, 3rd Ed., ed. by Arthur Naiman (Berkeley, CA: Goldstein & Blair, 1988). Tips and tricks from the wizards for use with the Macintosh.

The Human Interface Guidelines: The Apple Desktop Interface by Apple Computer, Inc. (Reading, MA: Addison-Wesley, 1987). ISBN 0-201-17753-6.

Macintosh, Vol. I, by Apple Computer, Inc. (Reading, MA: Addison-Wesley, 1988). ISBN 0-201-17731-5.

Macintosh Printer Secrets by Larry Pina (Carmel, IN: Hayden Books, 1990). ISBN 0-672-48463-3.

Macintosh Repair & Upgrade Secrets by Larry Pina (Carmel, IN: Hayden Books, 1990). ISBN 0-672-48452-8.

Networking

Networking Personal Computers, 3rd Ed., by Michael Durr and Mark Gibbs (Carmel, IN: Que Corporation, 1989). ISBN 0-88022-417-7.

Using Novell NetWare by Bill Lawrence (Carmel, IN: Que Corporation, 1990). ISBN 0-88022-466-5.

Understanding Computer Networks by Apple Computer, Inc. (Reading, MA: Addison-Wesley, 1988). ISBN 0-201-19773-1. Good introductory-level text.

Microsoft Word

Using Microsoft Word 4: Macintosh Version by Bryan Pfaffenberger (Carmel, IN: Que Corporation, 1989). ISBN 0-88022-451-7.

Working With Word, 2nd Ed., by Charles Kinata and Gordon McComb (Redmond, WA: Microsoft Press, 1989). ISBN 1-5561-5218-3.

Other Macintosh Software Books

Using Microsoft Works: Macintosh Version, 2nd Ed., by Ron Mansfield (Carmel, IN: Que Corporation, 1989). ISBN 0-88022-461-4.

Using Microsoft Excel: Macintosh Version by Christopher Van Buren (Carmel, IN: Que Corporation, 1990). ISBN 0-88022-494-0.

Using MacWrite by Mark Bilbo (Carmel, IN: Que Corporation, 1990). ISBN 0-88022-547-5.

Index

Symbols

A

B

C

D

E

F

G

M

N

O

P

Q

R

S

U

V

W

Y

Z

Que Gives You The Latest Macintosh Information!

The Big Mac Book, 2nd Edition
Neil J. Salkind
Covers All Aspects Of The Mac Environment
$29.95 USA
0-88022-648-X, 1,000 pp., 7 3/8 x 9 1/4

The Little Mac Book
Neil J. Salkind
For All Mac Users
$12.95 USA
0-88022-651-X, 320 pp., 4 3/4 x 8

Que's Macintosh Multimedia Handbook
Tony Bove & Cheryl Rhodes
Macintosh Multimedia Hardware & Software
$24.95 USA
0-88022-577-7, 400 pp., 7 3/8 x 9 1/4

Using Excel 3 for the Macintosh
Chris Van Buren
Macintosh Excel 3
$24.95 USA
0-88022-715-X, 750 pp., 7 3/8 x 9 1/4

Using MacDraw
Marvin Bryan
MacDraw II Version 1.1 V2
$24.95 USA
0-88022-600-5, 450 pp., 7 3/8 x 9 1/4

Using MacroMind Director
Tony Bove & Cheryl Rhodes
Through Version 2.0
$29.95 USA
0-88022-578-5, 400 pp., 7 3/8 x 9 1/4

Using MacWrite
Mark Bilbo
MacWrite & MacWrite II
$24.95 USA
0-88022-547-5, 400 pp., 7 3/8 x 9 1/4

Using Microsoft Works: Macintosh Version, 2nd Edition
Version 2
$24.95 USA
0-88022-461-4, 464 pp., 7 3/8 x 9 1/4

Using PageMaker: Macintosh Version , 2nd Edition
C.J. Weigand
Through Version 4.0
$24.95 USA
0-88022-607-2, 450 pp., 7 3/8 x 9 1/4

Using Microsoft Word 4: Macintosh Version
Bryan Pfaffenberger
Through Version 4
$24.95 USA
0-88022-451-7, 436 pp., 7 3/8 x 9 1/4

To Order, Call:
(800) 428-5331 OR (317) 573-2500